Many talk and write about fees but often forget the other parts of the equation—value provided in return and professional standards. John De Goey hits the nail squarely on the head. The candour and passion with which he presents and discusses these issues is refreshing.

—Dan Hallett, CFA, CFP, President, Dan Hallett & Associates Inc.

A protracted bear market coupled with accounting scandals and questionable investment analysis have all led to a more thorough examination of the value offered by advisors. With this thoughtful book, John De Goey weighs into the debate about just what should define the professional advisor and how that individual should be paid.

—Darin Diehl, Editor, *Advisor's Edge*

The financial services industry and the role of the financial advisor along with it, are in a hyper state of evolution. To be candid, advisors who do not make the shift from 'salesperson' to 'professional' in regard to the scope of their services and the role they play in their clients' lives will find themselves on the outside looking in. *The Professinal Financial Advisor* is an excellent resource, worthy of shelf space in advisors' offices across North America.

—Dennis Moseley-Williams, Consultant, Pareto Systems

A growing number of Canadians is concerned about the sorry state of investment counselling in this country, but it has taken a rare breed of bird—an insider with a conscience—to both identify the problems and propose solutions. John De Goey's book may not win him too many friends among advisors, for the core of his argument questions the grounds for calling them "professional" in the first place. But it will earn him thanks from small investors who, for too long, were convinced that somebody was picking their pockets. De Goey not only names the pickpockets; he identifies the best methods of eliminating them.

—John Lawrence Reynolds, Author and Winner of the 2002 National Business Book Award for *Free Rider: How a Bay Street Whiz Kid Stole and Spent $20 Million*

Each generation of advisors learns the wrong lessons from a bull market. When it collapses, they learn another set of wrong lessons. John De Goey has provided a valuable description of these wrong lessons, and the sounder principles that should replace them. The advisor who wants to build a lasting practice must have a correct understanding of the issues dealt with in this book: earning trust by dealing with conflicts of interest, recognizing the nature of asset classes, judging the suitability of investments by their effect on the portfolio rather than in isolation, knowing how the benefits of diversification are realized. They will enable the professional advisor to deliver value to the investor, not the pipe-dream of forecasting stock prices.

—Bill Hutchison, President, MoneyWare Inc.

Whether you are an investor who is assessing the benefits of the relationship you have with your current financial advisor, a financial advisor reflecting on the value proposition you are offering to your clients or a member of the regulatory community seeking to define a new standard and vision, John De Goey's thought-provoking and controversial thesis will challenge you to participate in the redefinition of professionalism in the financial services industry.

—Evelyn Jacks, President, The Knowledge Bureau and bestselling author of over 30 books on personal income taxation

Increasingly, consumers are seeking real value from their financial advisors. Consumers want a transparent partnership founded on trust and full disclosure. Separating financial advice from financial products provides benefits to both parties. John De Goey repeatedly illustrates how the "professionalization of financial advice" is a winning position for everyone. He demonstrates how prudent and knowledgeable advisors can save consumers time and money through this common-sense strategy. Consumers and advisors imperil their success if they avoid this profitable trend.

—Dale Ennis, Publisher, *Canadian MoneySaver*

The ongoing health of any industry or organization is enhanced by periodic self-assessment, even when the results of that review are not always kind. John De Goey has presented a probing critical assessment of the world of financial planning, along with his passionate prescriptions for what ails it.

—George Hartman, author of *Risk Is Still a Four Letter Word*

This book offers a thoughtful and long-overdue diagnosis of what's wrong with the financial planning industry. I'm impressed by De Goey's intelligence and honesty, and I hope his recommendations for reform are widely adopted.

—Ian McGugan, Editor, *MoneySense magazine*

Whether fee-based or commission-based, all financial advisors can benefit from reading *The Professional Financial Advisor* because John De Goey's desire is to hold financial advice to a higher standard like accounting, legal or medical advice. All investors should read this book, too. It is not a "how to invest" book and it is not written for "dummies" or "idiots." Use this book as your companion to maximize the relationship with your advisor. You don't have to agree with De Goey on every point, but you must address every point.

—Steve Kangas, Managing Editor and Fund Analyst, www.fundlibrary.com

The
PROFESSIONAL
Financial Advisor

The

PROFESSIONAL
Financial Advisor

Ethics, Unbundling and Other Things
to Ask Your Financial Advisor About

John J. De Goey
MPA, CIM, FCSI, CFP

INSOMNIAC PRESS

National Library of Canada Cataloguing in Publication Data

De Goey, John J., 1963-
    The professional financial advisor: ethics, unbundling and other things to ask your financial advisor about / John J. De Goey.

Includes bibliographical references and index.
ISBN 1-894663-48-9

1. Investment advisors—Fees. 2. Financial planners—Fees. 3. Investment advisors—Professional ethics. 4. Financial planners—Professional ethics. I. Title.

HG179.5.D44 2003   332.6'2   C2003-904474-2

The publisher gratefully acknowledges the support of the Canada Council, the Ontario Arts Council and the Department of Canadian Heritage through the Book Publishing Industry Development Program. We acknowledge the support of the Government of Ontario through the Ontario Media Development Corporation's Ontario Book Initiative.

Printed and bound in Canada

Insomniac Press
192 Spadina Avenue, Suite 403
Toronto, Ontario, Canada, M5T 2C2
www.insomniacpress.com

DISCLAIMER

This material is provided for general information and is subject to change without notice. Every effort has been made to compile this material from reliable sources however no warranty can be made as to its accuracy or completeness. This material is not intended to provide, and should not be construed as providing individual financial, investment, tax, legal or accounting advice.

The opinions expressed are those of the author and not necessarily those of Assante Corp. or its subsidiaries. *(Dec. '06 – Andy Watson's new associates)*

Using borrowed money to finance the purchase of securities involves greater risk than using cash resources only. If you borrow money to purchase securities, your responsibility to repay the loan and pay interest as required by its terms remains the same even if the value of the securities purchased declines.

Tax laws change frequently and often without prior notice. Every effort has been made to use current information as of the date of publication.

Commissions, trailing commissions, management fees, and expenses may all be associated with mutual fund investments. The indicated rates of return are the historical annual compounded total returns including changes in unit/share value and reinvestment of all distributions/dividends. They do not take into account sales, redemption, distribution or optional charges or income taxes payable by any security holder that would have reduced returns. Mutual funds are not guaranteed, their values change frequently and past performance may not be repeated. Please read the prospectus and consult a professional advisor before investing.

For Logan

TABLE OF CONTENTS

N.B.

N.B.

INTRODUCTION

Over the past generation, sweeping changes have hit the financial services industry around the world. There has been considerable consolidation on both the manufacturing and distribution levels. Competition is becoming increasingly fierce and new products and concepts are being introduced at a breakneck pace. The lines are also blurring between manufacturers (mutual fund companies) and distributors (financial planning and brokerage firms). Distributors are trying to protect and enhance their margins by manufacturing proprietary products, and it seems all companies are morphing to become one-stop shopping centres for an increasingly wide variety of related financial products and services. This "all things considered" approach is called convergence.

The once-separate silos of investments, insurance, savings, loans and associated advice are coming together—even as compensation structures for these products and services are coming apart and being charged separately. It is now possible to buy a wide array of investment products that feature no payment to the advisor within the pricing of the product. This idea of charging for financial advice after removing product compensation is called unbundling.

It seems everyone is involved in everyone else's business as companies and advice providers compete to become the repository of choice for time-starved consumers who want meaningful and simplified reporting and advice from a single qualified and trusted source. Do-It-Yourself (DIY) consumers of financial products continue to work under the premise that they can cut out the advice-giver, who usually adds cost. They do this because they are doubtful that advisors are adding sufficient value to justify their fees, so they choose to pocket the difference. This is called disintermediation.

The three trends of convergence, unbundling and disintermediation are evolving quickly as the industry works to distinguish between those who merely sell products and those who add value through the application of professional advice. This distinction will become important to consumers, who will come to seek financial advice based on who can meet their needs. It is in this context that people offering financial advice to the general public must work. For the purposes of this book, we'll lump all advisors and planners together with traditional brokers and salaried employees and call them all Financial Service Providers or FSPs.

Until now, those who had a licence to sell one or two types of financial products have positioned themselves as professionals. Most haven't needed to differentiate themselves further. Going forward, however, consumers will come to understand that selling products and offering comprehensive advice are very different things. One can only marvel at why the distinction wasn't made sooner. Whether they go by the title stockbroker, financial advisor, financial planner or any similar moniker, FSPs are under huge pressure to be all things to all people by providing meaningful, integrated and professional advice in a trustworthy manner. Most earn commissions, but want to be perceived as professionals.

The real value added will be in the field of integrated financial planning and advice, where individuals trained in the emerging multidisciplinary concepts of wealth management will be more necessary than ever before. But what are the attributes that consumers should seek out and reasonably expect from a professional financial advice-giver? That's where intelligent and fair-minded people have differed in the past. The true creation of a profession will involve a variety of factors that are only now becoming clear. Until now, there has been some uncertainty about what the salient attributes of professional advice should be.

Unfortunately, many of the steps taken to date to ensure both meaningful standards and practical quality controls have been met with cynicism. This is changing as a consensus emerges. Traditional elements of professionalism, like required academic training, continuing education, standardized procedures and mandatory errors and omissions insurance are gaining prominence. The business model employed by most FSPs will need to change if they want to receive the same degree of respect that is accorded to other professionals. The focus will be on justifying the cost of advice. Account aggregation and online access are now decidedly mainstream and consumers routinely go online and view all elements of their personal finances at one simple, integrated and secure website.

These trends will put pressure on FSPs to demonstrate that they are genuinely adding value. Until recently, FSPs were the focal point of decision-making by virtue of their exclusive access to the product information necessary to make informed choices. Will the democratization of financial product information lead to the marginalization of FSPs? Perhaps—if one equates access to information with meaningful personal advice. The most important industry trend is the switch from giving away the advice and charging for the transaction to giving away the transaction and charging for the advice. Many of the concepts found in *The Professional Financial Advisor* stem from taking these undeniable current trends to their logical conclusion.

Going forward, the question of genuine independence will be seen as the critical "missing link" in completing the transition from a culture of sales to a culture of professionalism. The notion of FSP independence has not been a meaningful part of the debate in the past, but the industry's compensation models clearly undermine the principle of independence. The biggest change that has to occur is the total eradication of embedded compensation. People who offer financial advice want desperately to be seen as independent, even though most know in their hearts that they aren't.

The Professional Financial Advisor is a summary of current trends filtered through the thinking of one person who has spent a decade in the industry. There are a number of logical inconsistencies that the industry has never addressed in a compelling manner and that need to be openly considered. This consideration ultimately led to the financial planning equivalent of the fairy tale "The Emperor's New Clothes." Everyone in the business knows that the fundamental premise of the book is true, but no one wants to be the person who steps forward and articulates the concept because it might lead to being ostracized from the industry.

The fundamental premise is this: real professionals charge separate, transparent fees for rendering services, rather than earning commissions for placing products. Furthermore, real professionals don't recommend what is most profitable for them personally, but what is right for their clients. As long as some products pay more than others, the predominant culture of financial services will be one of sales, and if the culture is ever to change, embedded compensation simply has to go. There's nothing wrong with sales as a calling in life, it's just that the term "professional salesman" is a practical oxymoron. A recent survey showed that 75% of FSPs agreed that payments from manufacturers affect advisors.

Furthermore, as long as there's embedded compensation, the consumers who seek qualified professional advice will remain justifiably skeptical about motive. In the professions, the impartiality and appropriateness of what is being recommended must never be called into question and the interests of the consumer must always be paramount. A careful sequence of events will have to be followed to ensure that embedded compensation can be eliminated while neither consumers of financial advice, nor the FSPs who offer it, are appreciably hurt in the process. Many stakeholders have been talking a good game for a decade about "raising the bar" while doing relatively little to effect truly meaningful reforms.

For instance, advisory firms often talk about corporate standards, but would never dream of sacking a productive FSP who refuses to get a Certified Financial Planner (CFP) or similar designation, especially if that person is a big producer. When rhetoric meets reality, the bottom line always wins out. Since moral suasion doesn't really work and meaningful professional corporate standards have a negative impact on the bottom line, the only way to move these contentious elements of the industry forward is to legislate those reforms into effect. That way, FSPs and their firms have nowhere to hide and bad apples can be disposed of.

Demographics and the increasingly busy and complex nature of today's lifestyle suggest that the need for holistic advice will actually grow substantially in the future. At present, much financial advice is based on personal opinions and often wildly divergent assumptions. This has to change if FSPs are serious about being professionals.

Ultimately, the wisdom and knowledge offered by FSPs who are comprehensive wealth managers will likely be the only sustainable competitive advantage in a crowded marketplace. Genuine professional FSPs (those who add value through the concerted implementation of principles, concepts, wisdom, discipline and associated services) will flourish. Those who earn commissions by selling products will be in trouble, since financial products and details about their attributes are easily attainable. Many of the opinions written in the popular media focus on getting consumers to fire their FSPs in order to save money. The rationale is that it often costs more to work with an FSP and these additional costs are a drag on performance.

On top of that, consumers are becoming more knowledgeable, demanding and fickle, especially in light of poor market performance in the recent past. This is a case of the media being penny-wise and pound foolish, not to mention self-serving. While the personal finance media suggests consumers can do as well or better by themselves, independent research indicates just the opposite, especially for larger accounts and more complex situations. When accounts grow, the need for qualified, holistic advice is almost certain. Many FSPs add considerable value in ways that are not obvious and often difficult to quantify, but still very real. Many of these activities are behavioural. Getting people to buy low and sell high, to take a longer-term view and to generally do things that are mostly right and that might not have been done otherwise, simply don't show up on a quarterly report. Furthermore, the media tend to focus exclusively on portfolio management, while other critical issues like integrated tax, estate, insurance and business succession planning issues often go unnoticed.

By the same token, if a consumer's situation is exceedingly simple and/or the FSP is not genuinely adding value, firing the FSP and pocketing the difference may well be the best thing to do. The popular media has got it half right. The utility of financial advice is not dependent on price, but value. Price is merely the conspicuous half of the equation. What are consumers getting in return? Unfortunately, this other half is far more difficult to measure in a meaningful way. Therefore, the advice industry really only has it half right too. Good advice adds value, but cost is certainly a real factor. Think of accounting; no one suggests that everyone should or shouldn't use an accountant's services or that anyone is particularly shrewd or foolish based on the decision taken. The decision is a personal one and depends on a number of personal factors. So it is with financial advice.

Part of the problem, of course, is that most people don't even know how or how much their FSP is being paid. Conceptually, if consumers believe the value of the advice meets or exceeds the price they pay, they should probably continue to pay for it. In essence, there are two ways to add value in any service industry: provide identical services for a lower price or provide superior services at a price that is less than the value of those services. Those products and services that cannot demonstrably justify the fees they charge may well have to be sacrificed. Examples might include a mutual fund with a long-term track record that lags its benchmark or an FSP who does nothing more than pick funds.

Unfortunately, much advice is predicated on the use of certain products. Mutual funds in particular—once the investment vehicles of choice—have come to be viewed with increasing skepticism. They're still decent products, but people want improvements. More comprehensive, all in one customized wrap accounts, sometimes called the next generation of investing, are generally more expensive than the products they are replacing and less flexible too, although they also have a number of useful features and benefits. The "open wrap" platform that promises greater flexibility is just in its infancy and requires further development. Once complete, it will allow FSPs to construct "best of breed" portfolios that can be highly customized, yet cost effective.

When I was in graduate school, a professor of mine suggested that the term change agent was really a sanitized corporate euphemism for shit disturber. I fancy myself a change agent in the best sense of the term. If we're not purposeful, the industry might fall short of transforming itself in ways that are in everyone's best interest. I hope this book can be a constructive touchstone for what needs to happen as part of this change.

We have a fabulous opportunity to transform the financial advice channel into an integrated, holistic and bona fide profession, complete with all the trappings of other professions. *The Professional Financial Advisor* won't try to be predictive and talk about what will likely happen. Instead, it will examine the trends that are already under way and look forward by trying to forge a consensus about what ought to happen once the financial services industry reaches maturity. Only when the concerns raised in the pages that follow are addressed can the industry be recognized as a profession.

There are a number of implicit questions that will need to be resolved. What might the financial services landscape look like in the future? More to the point, what *should* the industry look like? Perhaps most of all, readers should consider what they believe the hallmarks of a qualified *professional* Financial Service Provider ought to be.

The recent unbundling of products and services is the harbinger for an emerging profession. Paying for genuine professional financial advice will require everyone to rethink both the role and the value of that advice. The transition will be challenging, but it has to come. We need a more formalized societal recognition that rendering comprehensive financial advice can and should be transformed into a professional activity in every sense. Perhaps we can call it the "youngest profession," even if many people think its credibility today is at par with the world's "oldest profession."

To many, the concepts considered within these pages will involve seemingly radical ideas regarding products, standards, disclosures and services. In the end, politicians, regulators, FSPs, consumers, the media, member companies and industry associations will all need to voice their concerns in a dialogue on the creation of a new profession.

Until now, many of the discussions have not involved apples-to-apples comparisons of business models and their underlying logic. It will be a delicious debate! Many hurdles need to be cleared before the associated respect and confidence accorded to any true profession can be won, but the time to begin earnest, forward-looking and substantive industry-wide reform is clearly upon us.

John J. De Goey, Toronto, August, 2003

FINANCIAL ADVICE
Past, Present and Future

The past gives us experience and memories; the present gives us challenges and opportunities; the future gives us vision and hope.
— William Arthur Ward

It is not the strongest of the species that survive, nor the most intelligent, but the one most responsive to change.
— Charles Darwin

It is often noted that the Chinese word for change is comprised of symbols for risk and opportunity. Many people also like to cite the famous Chinese curse "may you live in interesting times." One can safely surmise that there is indeed a great deal of change going on in the financial services industry and that we most certainly live in "interesting times." The question this begs is "How will we deal with it?" especially since the framework of financial advice rests on rapidly shifting sands. Financial advice—and the somewhat more prestigious term "financial planning"—is now being offered by virtually everyone, or so we are led to believe.

In spite of this, there are many in the financial services industry who are equally fond of the phrases "the more things change, the more they stay the same" and "when all is said and done, more will be said than done." Although there has been an undeniably large amount of change in the industry over the past decade, it is almost certain that even greater changes lie ahead. In the past, most people in the financial services industry had titles that described their compartmentalized roles: bank teller, insurance agent, mutual fund representative and stockbroker are all narrow titles for narrow roles. As the distinctions blurred and everyone became involved in everyone else's business, those titles seemed increasingly inappropriate. The current trend is toward holistic advice.

These various "stakeholders of the past" can now be lumped together under the generic term Financial Service Providers or FSPs. This is simply a term designed to capture all of the monikers mentioned above (and others like them), accepting that strengths, weaknesses and biases are still present, but becoming less conspicuous and less relevant. All of these stakeholders have a core competency and training which has likely been augmented by some additional training in other financial fields. The one thing that virtually everyone agrees on is that FSPs provide financial services of one kind or another, but the breadth and depth of those services, and the training required to offer them, is all over the map. In time, the compartmentalized titles of the past will fade from the lexicon of ordinary usage as FSPs become genuinely proficient in all areas of finance assisting individual consumers. That's happening because of change—something most people naturally resist. It forces people and companies out of their comfort zones. As a matter of fact, companies, regulators, the media, consumers and FSPs are all dealing differently with the changes going on in financial services.

What kind of changes are we talking about? On the front lines, where individual consumers of financial products and advice meet face to face with their FSPs, new factors are coming to the surface—many that never even registered in the consciousness of consumers a few years ago. Issues of disclosure, conflict of interest, compensation, cost, standards, regulation, branding, liability (both corporate and personal) and even ideology are under scrutiny. Most FSPs are overwhelmed, frightened and stressed as a result. A select few are focusing on the "opportunity" aspect of the Chinese proverb and are moving to aggressively redesign their business models as a result of these changes. The majority of FSPs are simply scrambling to keep pace in a difficult environment that has been made even more difficult by turbulent markets.

In spite of what needs to be done, it is doubtful that any industry has changed as much over the past decade as the financial services industry. It has seen explosive growth worldwide and the breadth and depth of new product and service offerings remain unparalleled. Merger and acquisition activity has drastically reconfigured industry players as the march toward globalization and the need for comprehensive product lines backed by national and international brand identities has accelerated. Many consumers and FSPs have been made to feel like pawns in a giant high-stakes chess game. Printing companies have been doing brisk business printing up new business cards and letterhead as a result.

Where Did We Come From?
Financial services have certainly come a long way. Until the late 1980s, the dominant paradigm for retail investor portfolio design was one of working with a stockbroker or insurance agent who earned commissions while constructing a portfolio of individual securities or sold insurance products. Financial advice was free, but clients paid handsome commissions for the buying and selling that transpired as a result of that advice. On the investment side, people really had no choice but to work through full-service brokers because discount brokerages were just coming into existence.

The problem with a transaction-oriented business model was that it rewarded all transactions—good, bad or otherwise. As a result, the brokers of the 1980s who were the most successful were often those who could get their clients to trade frequently. More trades meant more commissions for the broker (and usually more taxes for the client). The problem, of course, is that transaction costs and portfolio turnover both correlate negatively to investor performance. The cardinal rule of the industry is that advice should be offered with the best interests of the client in mind, so there was a problem.

The paradigm of the 1980s effectively pitted the client against the broker. High trading volumes favoured the broker; low volumes favoured the client. With the passage of time, the moniker "broker" gave way to terms like "financial advisor" or "financial planner," but the inherent conflict remained. The largest retail institutions, the banks, got into the act too, by rebranding their tellers as "mortgage specialists," personal relationship managers and "mutual fund specialists" among other things.

These employees were generally paid a salary plus a bonus based on their ability to encourage clients to take on debt through mortgages, loans and credit cards. Prudent planning initiatives, like encouraging clients to pay down non-deductible debt, were not rewarded because they compromised corporate profitability. In spite of these prevailing practices, all the industry players sanctimoniously insisted that they were acting in the best interests of their valued clients.

Those were relatively simple times. Most people didn't talk about capital markets at social gatherings, since relatively few of us could afford to work with a stockbroker. It was a sort of status symbol to have a broker you could call on as you "played the market." Simply put, relatively few people had the means to participate in the stock market by building portfolios made up of individual securities.

Furthermore, many found the market to be complicated and intimidating, a sentiment that continues to this day. Most stayed away and viewed it from afar or ignored it altogether while focusing on other, "more important" things. Looking back, GIC rates were reaching all-time highs in the 1980s, so there was money to be made on a risk-free basis by just parking it in a term deposit. Personal wealth was starting to grow exponentially and personal tax rates were going up exponentially too. In time, people would have to start looking at other investment instruments.

Three things happened in 1987 that began to change the way people thought. In October of that year, stock markets around the world took a major tumble. My parents woke up on the morning of October 20th—their twenty-fifth wedding anniversary—to headlines of global chaos and unprecedented carnage, in dollar terms, on capital markets. Reading of how much money people were losing overnight gave a lot of ordinary people a huge dose of reality. Wealthy people had been investing in stocks and were "getting their comeuppance," but how much money had they made before the meltdown? They seemed to collectively think to themselves: "Wouldn't it be great if we could somehow get in on it too?" So it was that a stream of consciousness gained a foothold.

John J. De Goey

The second major development was the deregulation of the financial services industry. From 1987 onward, the "four pillars" of the industry: banks, trust companies, insurance companies and brokerage houses were allowed to compete against one another and were no longer mandated to operate as separate, stand-alone silos of products and services. Until then, each had its own regulatory framework.

Ironically, the third development was seen as the least important at the time, but may well be the most notable. Throughout the 1980s, mutual funds were eking out an existence as a sideshow that many "serious" investors ignored. After all, they may have offered professional management and instant diversification, but who would want to give up 9% of their initial investment on the day of their purchase just to get in on the action? Better to work with a broker. Ordinary people (who could not afford to work with a broker) soon came to realize that they would like to participate in the long-term wealth-creating aspects of capital markets. Since they didn't have the means to buy diversified baskets of securities directly, they were inherently more receptive to funds—if only they could be made (or at least seem) painless.

It just so happens that 1987 was also the year that Canada's first traditional Deferred Sales Charge (DSC) or "back end load" mutual fund, the Industrial Horizon Fund from Mackenzie, was launched. The concept of a back end load was a salesperson's dream. Instead of having only $9,100 of $10,000 working for clients, the full $10,000 would go to work for them. This went a long way toward breaking down the barriers inhibiting the completion of a sale. Sales representatives (and that's frankly what virtually everyone in the business was in those days) received a 5% commission and a 0.5% "trailer fee" on equity-based funds, in exchange for completing the sale and offering ongoing support and "advice." Investors would only be "charged" on a sliding scale if they redeemed their units in the first seven years or so (it was usually about nine years when DSCs were first introduced).

Even this wrinkle had a positive angle to it. As a result of the charges, FSPs constantly told clients to stay invested for the long run. Those clients who chose to redeem prior to the DSC schedule expiration would be faced with a charge—a charge that could be avoided if the client simply stayed the course—or switched to other funds in the same family. As a result, even the negative attributes of mutual funds had a positive spin to them. Back end load charges could be depicted as legitimate penalties applied only to those consumers who didn't use mutual funds for their intended purpose—long-term participation in equity markets featuring diversification, professional management and reasonable costs. What could be better? Mutual fund sales exploded and the concept of democratized capitalism was off and running.

Meanwhile, the cost of running the fund and paying the commission was buried in the Management Expense Ratio (or MER) of the fund. Fund returns were reported net of MERs, so there were no real reminders of these costs. Brilliant! In effect, the new DSC format was merely allowing major mutual fund companies to amortize their payments to FSPs in a structured, commercially acceptable manner. Note in particular that this was seen not only as acceptable, but also *reasonable* to both the consumer and the FSP.

Across the country, FSPs loved getting paid handsomely on fund sales and ordinary consumers loved their newfound capacity to "play the markets" like the big boys. Central banks had found religion and were acting as though they were serious about fighting inflation and ensuring price stability. The primary offshoot of this (once the punitive economic effects of artificially high interest rates in the early 1990s wore off) was that inflation had indeed been curtailed. Mortgage rates were lower. Loan rates were lower. Most importantly, GIC rates were much, much lower. The phrase "GIC refugee" was coined to describe the resulting stampede into mutual funds.

On top of that, the bull market of the 1990s was among the strongest and longest in history. A whole army of novice investors ended up not asking about what they were paying and simultaneously delighted in the fact that their accounts were going up far more rapidly than they would have had they stayed in GICs. Few consumers understood mutual fund pricing. A typical equity fund MER of 2.75% might be comprised of 1.15% going to the mutual fund company, 1% ultimately going to the FSP and 0.6% in trading, administrative, reporting and accounting expenses, as well as GST. If the mutual fund company was effectively making just over 1% a year from clients, but paying FSPs 5% at the time of the sale and 0.5% annually for as long as the client held the fund, it would lose money if the client redeemed early.

The deferred sales charge (DSC or "load," as it is often called) allowed fund companies to recover their sunk FSP compensation costs if the client pulled out early. Mutual fund companies simply needed a way to ensure they would not lose money if a client redeemed early, so they shifted the onus. Clients could forego an upfront commission, but would still be handed a bill if they invested for anything less than the long term.

Hundreds of thousands of people bought mutual funds in the early 1990s and in so doing, locked themselves into redemption schedules that would prove costly to undo. Furthermore, each additional purchase typically brought a new seven-year redemption schedule with it, so people would have to go a long time without investing in additional DSC funds before they could be rid of all their DSC charges. Unfortunately, most people are not particularly wealthy. A recent study showed that only 11.8% of the total population held investment assets in excess of $100, 000. Throughout the 1990s, it was these ordinary citizens who were most likely to flock to mutual funds.

Because the marketing involved for the new DSC structure of these vehicles was so clever, because disclosure was poor and because capital markets were performing so well, mutual fund sales mushroomed—even if consumers didn't always understand what they were buying. For instance, most consumers never really cared too much about Management Expense Ratios, which are the embedded annual costs of running the funds. People were getting double-digit returns on their mutual funds while those who chose the safety of GICs looked silly in comparison.

Traditional stockbrokers had dismissed mutual funds as a passing fad. By the time they realized the staying power of these novel products, financial planners (who to this day are largely not even licenced to sell individual securities) had scooped up billions of dollars in assets. Banks, in a desperate attempt to stem the tide of massive asset outflows, also had little choice but to come out with mutual funds of their own. Although partially successful, the strategy was detrimental too, as it gave both mutual fund companies and the FSPs who recommended them the legitimacy they could have never attained otherwise. Ordinary consumers thought that if the banks were selling mutual funds, they must be worthwhile.

Note that by this time, the banks had already bought virtually all the major national brokerage firms. Curiously, the banks treated their brokerage houses like stand-alone silos and tried to stave off redemptions by offering GICs with additional bells and whistles and relying on old relationships for far too long. They could have simply referred their GIC clients who wanted mutual funds to their brokerage arms, but were too busy waging internal battles for corporate development dollars. Traditional brokers were unduly fixated on the paradigm of individual stocks and bonds anyway, so they missed the boat too. A proverb that banks and brokerages learned the hard way is that "the enemy of my enemy is my friend."

A whole series of small to medium-sized financial planning firms cropped up across the continent. Throughout the second half of the 1990s and up to the present, these firms have been joining forces, developing their size and scope to compete with banks head-on. Banks, of course, still oversee the large preponderance of assets, but there are now a few national and increasingly well-financed planning firms that are competing aggressively for investor assets and financial services. The advent of new technologies has allowed them to operate as "virtual banks," with a full suite of traditional bank offerings such as mortgages, loans, credit cards and GICs. We live in interesting times.

Many people still do not know exactly how mutual funds work, what they cost or how FSPs are compensated, yet there is presently over $410 billion invested in mutual funds in Canada.[1] The system has worked phenomenally well over the past number of years, but there are now rumblings that the time has come to start working on a wholesale overhaul.

The next generation of investment products is past due since the current system, while undeniably popular and successful in the 1990s, has fallen on tough times. Most observers believe investment products and processes can be improved in a number of useful ways, since most mutual fund companies were experiencing net redemptions throughout 2002 and 2003.

Prevailing Business Models

There are four primary ways that FSPs are compensated at present: hourly fees, fees based on assets being managed, salary and commission. Of the four, only the last one is inconsistent with the generally accepted principles of professional compensation.

A very small minority of FSPs charge hourly fees. These are generally boutique firms that do high-end planning for professionals, corporate executives and high net worth individuals and families. It should be stated that the FSPs who work at these firms do important work, but that it is generally beyond the purview of the main body of the Canadian financial services industry.

Charging an ongoing fee based on assets being managed is quickly gaining market share as a viable business model that more closely aligns the interests of the FSP with those of the retail client. In some instances, the fee is embedded in the cost of the product. This is the case with "no load" mutual funds and with so-called "wrap" accounts, where a number of services are wrapped together in one all-inclusive package for the client. In other instances, the fee is charged externally, making it more visible, but not compromising portfolio returns.

Banks and trust companies use the salary model almost exclusively—their FSPs are employees. Of the four business models, banks and trust companies have by far the least skilled FSPs offering financial advice. There are virtually no CFPs at bank or trust company branches at present, although that too is beginning to change. This could have important implications regarding the pricing of products and services, since the price of bank and trust company products, which includes an embedded price for advice, is essentially identical to the price for other more highly trained distribution channels. Banks and trust companies effectively charge a premium for the convenience they offer. Pricing is also a function of competition. In rural areas, banks and trust companies may be the only game in town. Perhaps the problem with many banks is employee turnover. The banks' "financial services managers" who assist customers are often highly transitory individuals, making the establishment of meaningful relationships particularly difficult.

Within the independent advisory channel, the business model of choice continues to be commissions. It has been estimated that approximately 75% of all assets being invested in this channel at present, involve the placement of a commission. Advice is essentially given away as an offshoot. Remember that FSPs are essentially self-employed entrepreneurs and, as such, generally want to make as much money as quickly as possible—all else being equal. Commissions can offer substantially higher compensation than either fees or salary when new money is rolling in, so that is the model most FSPs prefer. However, now that the salad days of investment management are over, many are being forced to rethink their business model.

There are many who make reference to consumers' preferences for buying investment products through the "advice channel." This is a somewhat disingenuous form of characterizing the process. It might be more accurate to say that consumers prefer to buy products through the "embedded compensation FSP channel," where FSPs earn commissions and trailing commissions based on their ability to encourage clients to buy products. All stakeholders purport to offer advice. The salient difference is that the FSPs who earn commissions and trailing commissions are gaining market share.

Various FSPs have struggled with the need to make the transition to a fee-based business model. They want to become fee-based, but given their past history, don't know how to actually make the leap. Many lack the courage and conviction to make it. The truth is that it is never easy to do the right thing when competitors are making more money by picking low-hanging fruit (earning commissions). This is especially true since clients are not generally demanding fee-based arrangements and often don't understand the important differences between the models.

More forward-looking FSPs have chosen to throw caution to the wind and to change before they have to. That's perhaps the most telling aspect of the industry today. The delivery of comprehensive financial advice is at a crossroads as we speak. Many in the industry have come to believe that we are now at the point where all forms of embedded compensation need to be systematically and purposefully eliminated in order to make way for a new breed of financial service providers. There is no conspicuously right or wrong model. There are also pros and cons associated with each, but both advisory fees and total client costs should be clearly explained in writing either way and the decision surrounding appropriate compensation structure should rest with the client.

If an FSP wants to move to a fee-based arrangement, what needs to happen? On the consumer side, the most compelling reason to move to a fee-based arrangement is that it more closely aligns consumer interests with the interests of the FSP. Because consumers are paying fees based on the size of their portfolio, FSPs have a clear incentive to make portfolios grow and to mitigate portfolio declines. This is in contrast with a large commission payment up front, nominal trailer fees over time and a potentially punitive DSC schedule that consumers have to endure if they want to change course. It might also allow for fee deductibility for non-registered accounts that otherwise would not be possible.

On the FSP side, a fee-based system should mean more product flexibility and independence. Even if FSPs firmly believe it is in their clients' best interest to do so, clients cannot be forced to share that view. Any FSPs considering the switch should know that it generally takes about three years to accomplish. Because costs and compensation are generally buried in so-called "A Class" mutual fund MERs, many consumers are deluded into thinking that mutual fund investments are "free." As a result, some consumers might instinctively resist what is likely a better arrangement for them. Understanding the merits of a more client-centred business model usually has nothing to do with it. The biggest obstacle to making the switch is the notion that there will still be some DSC penalties. This is unavoidable.

What's Been Going on Lately?

More recently, financial advice has been continuing its metamorphosis from an industry founded largely by product placers and sales agents to something nobler—a profession. Banks and brokerages have finally come to view themselves as mutually supportive specialists within larger financial service complexes by offering a wide range of complementary products and services to their clients. They have learned to cross-refer clients, recognizing that if they do not do their utmost to serve their client, that client might well leave.

Over the past number of years, growing through mergers and acquisitions has been the business strategy of choice for firms that want the size, scope, synergies and the shelf space that come with a recognized national brand. Nowhere was this truer than in the financial services industry. Banks bought other banks. Mutual fund companies bought other mutual fund companies. Brokerage and advisory firms bought one another at a breakneck and breathtaking pace and the trend is continuing. We're now seeing mergers between insurance companies, banks and investment planning companies.

The concerns and potential liabilities associated with an industry predicated on protecting and managing other people's life savings, all cost money. Smaller firms have had little choice but to get in bed with bigger players with deeper pockets and a greater capacity to meet the terms imposed by regulators. As with so many other elements of society, there is a "go big or go home" attitude that is being felt across the industry for all but the most focused and determined niche players. The buzzwords of the financial services industry are size, scope, brand, integrated offerings, holistic planning, simplification of decision-making and comprehensive wealth management. *Andy?*

Local mom-and-pop financial advisory firms have been effectively regulated and merged into extinction, as a series of competing and increasingly urgent imperatives have also been beating down on financial planning firms in general and their FSPs in particular. Only a handful have survived and even their days are likely numbered. They are finding themselves stuck in an environment of dwindling revenues, increased costs, reduced client returns (and return expectations) and an increasingly strict and expensive regulatory environment, spurred on by litigious consumers. Where there were once dozens of local and regional planning firms, there are now a handful of regional firms and national firms. All of the banks own brokerage houses too. In fact, two indications lead to the conclusion that we are now in the mature stage of the mutual fund product life cycle. The first is that the industry's revenues are stagnant and the second is the consolidation trend that is well under way.

There seems to be a consensus that there will be a greater degree of homogeneity in the financial services industry going forward, although cultural differences that are part and parcel of merger and acquisition activity may take many more years to disappear. The challenge for the entire financial services industry is to deliver a consistently superior customer experience. Due to the intangible and information-based products and services being offered, the achievement of this goal requires a shift of focus from products to clients. According to Cap Gemini Ernst and Young, there are three basic steps to perform this change: build an understanding of the customer, design the organization accordingly and invest in delivery capability.

Becoming a Profession

The act of offering comprehensive financial advice *is becoming* a profession. Some people reading this might be thinking that giving financial advice already is a profession. In fact, that's what people in the industry would have us believe. They refer to Financial Service Providers as "trusted advisors" since offering trusted advice seems like an entirely professional thing to do. After all, lawyers are called "counsellors" and they're professionals.

But this approach merely exposes the presumptiveness in the industry. Many FSPs seem to think that if they refer to themselves and their peers as professionals often enough, that over time, the public will come to view them as precisely that. To some extent, this approach has worked. There's only one problem: actions speak louder than words. While progress has certainly been made, we haven't established a true profession yet. In fact, we're not even close.

Since the financial services industry is rooted in a background of product sales, the predominant cultural mindset in financial services remains one of selling. Most FSPs routinely refer to their "book of business" as opposed to their "professional practice," which is what other professionals do. Old habits die hard. In order to complete the transition, FSPs need to shed the last vestiges of their heritage and that means extricating themselves once and for all from sales-related paradigms. Here are the primary challenges the industry faces in the years ahead.

1. Regulation

As with any industry that begins with low barriers to entry and then grows exponentially for the better part of a generation, there have been opportunities for phenomenal success for FSPs. In some instances, individual FSPs who were particularly resourceful, competent, client-centred and/or adept at marketing, were able to gain a massive amount of assets and make massive amounts of money in the process. Part of the reason for this success was the relative lack of regulation. To this day, regulators have been more reactive than proactive regarding consumer protection. It seems that systemic changes that would better protect consumers have been slow to come because of resistance from well-financed industry participants who seem to think transgressions must be conspicuous and rampant before anything needs to be done.

Right now, regulatory challenges present the mother of all problems in the financial services industry. That's especially true because in times like these, when investor confidence has been badly shaken, clear leadership and consumer protection are conspicuously necessary. Effective regulation becomes absolutely imperative in this kind of environment and corporate governance has become a major issue. The problem with having a holistic industry growing out of a number of disparate specialties that overlap is standardization. Whatever the specialization of the FSP was when he got into the industry, that subset of the new, more holistic industry believes it ought to be regulating the entire field. The problem is that until now, no group has been prepared to cede control of their piece of turf in order to move toward the higher purpose of harmonized regulation.

In the past, brokers had their own regulators, as did banks and insurance agents. Recently, the mutual fund industry got into the act by creating a new body to regulate mutual funds. Each stakeholder group thinks its perspective (based on the products they regulate) is the correct one, so each regulator is skeptical of the other. To make matters worse, the regulation of financial institutions is a provincial jurisdiction, so each financial services "entry point" has ten provincial and three territorial regulators, all of them now encroaching on one another's turf. Canada's FSPs need to have clear and consistent ground rules, given the amounts of money and implicit levels of trust that are at stake, but until now, very little has been done to actually get on with the job.

The regulatory framework has two main groups of participants: provincial government regulators, who actually legislate the regulatory framework and industry and trade associations that work as Self-Regulatory Organizations (SROs) by setting and monitoring internal standards. Much like the associations for doctors, dentists, lawyers and teachers, SROs have a mandate to police themselves and to protect the generally good reputation their members enjoy. On the brokerage side, the most conspicuous example of the former is the Ontario Securities Commission (OSC), while the most conspicuous example of the latter is the Investment Dealers' Association (IDA). Similar parallels exist in insurance.

It was only in 2002 that the Mutual Fund Dealers' Association was created with a similar SRO mandate for the mutual fund industry. Already, commentators are suggesting that this is needless duplication and that there should only be one self-regulatory organization for the entire investment industry. Joe Oliver, the IDA President, has shot down any talk of merging the two along with the recently created Market Regulation Services to create a national "Super SRO."

Earlier in 2003, an effort to harmonize practice standards was put forward by the Joint Forum of Financial Market Regulators, the co-ordinating body for securities, insurance and pension regulators. The committee that offered a report consisted of representatives from the Canadian Securities Administrators, the Investment Dealers' Association, the Mutual Fund Dealers' Association and the Canadian Council of Insurance Regulators.

The industry liaison group offering input included the Financial Advisors' Association of Canada (Advocis), the Investment Funds Institute of Canada

(IFIC), the Canadian Bankers Association and the Canadian Securities Institute. Four initiatives were covered in the report: common minimum entry standards, the co-ordination of licencing of intermediaries in more than one category of service/advice, establishing industry-wide best practices and a common code of conduct and requirements for continuing education.

The Joint Forum proposed a number of uniform standards to cover a number of subsections, including client interest, professionalism, confidentiality, conflicts of interest, disclosure, client redress and compliance. These proposed standards were based on high-level principles rather than detailed rules, and the lack of detail was seen as necessary in order to facilitate harmonization. Final recommendations are expected shortly, along with an implementation plan.

Even as all the stakeholders try to grapple with regulating the sum total of the financial services industry, certain sectors are trying to come to terms with the notion of standardizing their own little corner of the world. In March 2003, Finance Minister John Manley announced that prominent industrialist Michael Phelps would chair a seven member "wise persons" committee with a mandate to examine the creation of a national system of securities regulation. The committee is slated to table its report in November 2003. It seems the political will to force harmonization, that has been so conspicuously absent in the past, might actually be present this time.

Brokerage firms have always been subject to reasonably good levels of scrutiny and compliance regarding investment suitability. Where suitability was concerned, there are now branch managers in place who ensure procedures are in place and followed. The major national securities regulator, the IDA, has long performed regular branch audits for its member firms. Meaningful sanctions have been brought to bear on those brokers who engage in various forms of unsavoury conduct, however, there are some very real concerns about the even-handedness of the IDA, given its dual role as both an SRO and a trade association for investment dealers.

In a recent edition of *Advisor's Edge* magazine, editor Darin Diehl pointed out that this potential for conflict required immediate action. He noted that a draft report by the Review Committee stated that the "conflict, including the appearance of conflict, must be contained and that the most appropriate way to do this is to separate the IDA's functions as an SRO from its role as a trade association." In other words, even if concerns about legal regulation are addressed, there are practical self-regulation issues that need to be addressed too.

Nonetheless, the Investment Counsel Association of Canada (representing seventy-one companies) recently released a position paper advocating a "Super SRO" as a solution to dealing with the "significant irritant" of having to deal with disparate rules across the country. Political efforts toward harmonization are continuing, spurred on by the raised public consciousness stemming from the corporate malfeasance fiascos of 2002.

The need for regulatory reform, as one might expect, is not an affliction confined to Canada, nor is it confined to financial products. All over the world, people are trying to come to terms with the burgeoning industry of financial advice. Irrespective of what Canada does, there are international standards being put into place, although these are embarrassingly low by Canadian standards. The International Standards Organization has released a draft international standard: TC 222. Everywhere around the world, there is a consensus that standardization is vital and that minimum accreditations, skills and best practices need to be instituted and monitored.

This is somewhat curious and potentially dangerous, because two different standards are developing: the relatively low international standard as set out in TC 222 and the de facto North American standard of the Certified Financial Planner (CFP) designation. Until the end of 2002, Canada and the U.S. were taking divergent paths on the topic of international planning standardization. The U.S. (traditionally an isolationist nation) was embracing the TC 222 standard *concurrently with* the CFP designation, while Canada (traditionally an internationalist nation) was not involved in meetings to set an international standard. It wasn't until November 2002 that Canada struck a committee to offer a Canadian perspective on what the international standards ought to be.

There are problems at the FSP level too. Until recently, virtually anyone could call herself a financial planner. There are literally dozens of financial advisory credentials available today, all with the intention of "raising the bar" and offering consumers some certitude and confidence in those people who hold one or more of these designations. The pettiness about "my designation is better than your designation" only creates confusion in the general public.

It has even been suggested that certain designations were created by some groups simply because they knew intuitively that the people they represented would not be able to meet the standards set out by other organizations. They set new (lower) standards so that their titleholders would be able to put some letters after their names and reap the rewards of consumer legitimacy.

To date, only the province of Quebec has chosen to regulate financial planning. The English-speaking provinces attempt to regulate advice by conferring licences (as though salesmanship and professionalism were somehow synonymous). Quebec clearly has the most complete and comprehensive supervision in Canada. Planners there need to acquire certificates in two of four disciplines (actuarial studies, economics, law or administration) and then need to complete a certificate in financial planning *offered by a university.* Only then can they take a forty-five-hour summary course and write a uniform exam that entitles them to practice as financial planners if successfully completed. Practitioners must also complete sixty hours of compulsory professional development every two years.

The question of how any industry or profession can practically regulate itself raises many questions. For instance, the IDA has a policy on its books that calls for a member to report wrongdoing—"whistle-blowing." This was in place well in advance of the spate of corporate malfeasance news in 2002. While the intent is laudable, there aren't many people who think it would be prudent to let any industry group "mark its own papers" regarding conduct and the sanctions that are ultimately brought forward.

To make matters worse, the insurance side of the advice-giving industry is regulated separately and has its own disparate objectives and structures. The federal government is stepping in to bring together divergent provincial insurance commissions. In the world of insurance, a more piecemeal harmonization seems to be preferred. Still, "The odds of getting one securities law are higher than they are of getting one single regulator," says Brian Davies, CEO and superintendent of financial services at the Financial Services Commission of Ontario (FCSO), which regulates insurance. Davies thinks insurance regulators are going to start "picking off issues and getting them harmonized one at a time." For instance, although it took four years from inception to consultation to implementation, the Life Licence Qualification program (LLQP) was set as the standard licencing program across all provinces except Quebec on January 1, 2003, specifying a one-step licencing system based on a mandatory pre-licencing course and a qualifying exam.

2. OSC Fair Dealing vs. BCSC Deregulation Project

Even as the industry works to regulate itself, the next practical question is to determine what form that regulation should ultimately take. The issue at hand is whether regulation is best accomplished by harmonizing provincial laws and improving co-ordination among provincial regulators or by creating some sort of national regulator. Regardless of the solution, everyone agrees that the biggest problem right now is the hodgepodge regulatory framework that comes from a decentralized system based on provincial jurisdiction. The major shortcoming of the current system is the excessive volume, detail and complexity of the rulebook, which undermines the achievement of regulatory objectives. On the securities side, the twin logistical demons of regulatory reform are whether the new regulator should be centralized or decentralized and whether it should espouse a rules-based philosophy or a principles-based philosophy. The debate is heating up.

The Ontario Securities Commission (OSC) recently released its vision of regulatory reform in a concept paper called the "Fair Dealing Model." It includes an interactive website (www.fairdealingmodel.ca) to solicit input on how to reform the FSP/client relationship, specifically, how to regulate the provision of financial advice. Julia Dublin, senior legal counsel to the OSC, noted that both the quality and quantity of input was strong. The paper proposes three basic relationship models: "managed for you," "advisory" and "self-managed." The former is a full fiduciary relationship as expressed through discretionary trading; the middle is the traditional consultative approach; and the latter is essentially self-managed or Do-It-Yourself (DIY), where the onus lies almost entirely with the client and where compensation is transactional. Issues like suitability, conflict and disclosure were brought to the forefront. One wonders why a provincial securities commission is left to bring these sorts of suggestions forward in the first place. Shouldn't it be the mandate of the SROs?

The Fair Dealing Model is particularly interesting since the "self-managed" stream of recommendations deals with the major trend going on today: disintermediation. In this model, people who choose to forego the services of an FSP will be on their own in terms of ensuring suitability. Discount brokers quite properly want no blood on their hands if a DIY investor blows up his own account. It is expected that such a reform would represent a major upheaval to the industry, since brokerage firms and planning firms would all have to reset their compensation systems within the model's parameters. They would have to overhaul their disclosure practices to improve point-of-sale product and compensation disclosure. In spite of the natural resistance this entails, many observers believe this kind of reform is long overdue.

The regulatory focus is finally shifting from placing products to offering holistic advice. Regulators are simply trying to keep up with market realities, and they finally see that policing products while ignoring advice is outdated. Qualified FSPs have long wanted to compete on the basis of value-added advice rather than the mere ability to execute trades. Similarly, astute investors want to see a connection between what they are paying and the value added by the FSP or institution they are working with.

Until recently securities regulation has assumed that advice was offered only in the furtherance of a trade. In fact, trades have always been executed in the furtherance of financial advice. Talk about putting the cart before the horse!

At the micro level, individual FSPs have long known that the systems of compensation, and advancement in particular, tend to reward "top producers," as opposed to ethical and competent professionals. This is just another example of how things are set up to be rational using a sales paradigm, but end up becoming systemically dysfunctional in a true "client comes first" professional paradigm.

It seems everyone has an opinion and position surrounding regulatory reform. Christopher Nicholls, a prominent lawyer who penned a paper on the prospects of regulatory reform, favours a slow but sure approach, saying, "there are sound reasons favouring regulatory patience." David Brown is the Chair of the OSC. He believes the solution needs to balance the interests of investor protection with the added cost and burden of increased regulation, given the regulatory role of fostering fair and efficient markets. In other words, Fair Dealing is just the tip of the iceberg. Doug Hyndman, Chair of the British Columbia Securities Commission (BCSC) offers yet another concern. He thinks Canada's SROs are becoming monopolies, leaving dealers with no choice as to what organization they work with. He wants to inject the system with some competition and challenges the notion that the world would be a better place if all SROs were merged into one. Hyndman's view is that smaller, more localized SROs would do a better job of tackling the volume and complexity of Canada's regulatory requirements and that most regulation is already uniform through the use of National Instruments.

The BCSC has floated a proposal for regulatory reform focused on guidelines and principles as the regulatory framework, effectively shifting the perspective to make it more conceptual. The rule making and policing onus would fall to the industry participants themselves. The proposal has met with early approval and a recent poll showed that 92% of all Investment Funds Institute of Canada (IFIC) participants are in favour of it. However, the DIY principles-based regulatory approach of the BCSC lacks clarity. Then again, given the red tape involved with the prevailing view, that may be a good thing.

Those advocating a move away from a prescriptive, rules-based system to a more principles-based system cite the current complex regulatory framework as something that could be more effectively dealt with by focusing on principles. Their aim is to focus more on corporate governance through continuous disclosure in the belief that harmonization alone will not reduce the regulatory burden in a meaningful way. They believe their approach would also streamline registration processes for FSPs registered in multiple jurisdictions.

More importantly, the people at the BCSC believe that a principles-based approach would attack the real threats to market integrity with tools that fit the job. Their thinking is that the goal of harmonization can best be achieved by simplifying the rules; applying compliance, enforcement and education tools to enforce basic principles of fairness and honesty; and by deterring and removing from the market those who cheat investors. The BC model aims to make regulation more effective and to make markets more efficient and competitive in the process.

Canada currently functions with thirteen separate provincial and territorial regulators, each with its own set of rules and regulations. Of course, this multiplies as you add different disciplines. For instance, each province has its own regulator for insurance too. If we're going to regulate securities nationally, why not the various forms of insurance? Furthermore, since these are all various types of financial services and we're all moving headlong into a converged world of "one-stop shopping," why not regulate absolutely everything under one roof?

For years now, David Brown has been arguing vehemently for the need for a national regulator much like the Securities Exchange Commission (SEC) in the U.S. The other provinces—notably Quebec—simply don't want to be seen to be giving in to central Canada. One thing that unites Canadians above all else is disdain for anything that seems like corporate patrimony rooted in Toronto.

Brown's push has not only been to standardize regulations, but also to increase them considerably. This second element has just as many people up in arms as the first. An initiative of the federal government entitled "Fostering

Confidence in Canada's Capital Markets," aims to expunge all unsavoury activity through even more regulatory constraints. Since the whole idea here is to make things simpler and more cost-effective, the OSC approach has not been getting very far. Proposals for reform have traditionally involved an ever-expanding rule book.

Many observers believe that if Canada were to enact highly stringent regulatory hurdles such as those enacted in the U.S. through the Sarbanes-Oxley Act, it would do more harm than good in allowing FSPs to function properly. There is a clear need to give investors confidence that the system offers meaningful regulation in protecting against failures in corporate governance and disclosure that might lead to serious investor losses. But are draconian measures the best route for consumer protection? *Not likely*

Ordinary consumers are seldom approached for input on these matters because they are too disparate and unable to clearly articulate a coherent consensus about an industry that can be highly complex and intimidating. Still, Finance Minister John Manley announced in early 2003 that Ottawa plans to strengthen the corporate governance standards in the Canada Business Corporations Act (CBCA), sending a strong signal that it intends to play a more active role going forward.

Many observers have noted the alarming reality that the BCSC's Regulation Project and the OSC's Fair Dealing Model are bold initiatives that are proceeding independently. To date, no one has talked of a compromise. Ironically, both the BCSC and the OSC models focus on disclosure as a means of mitigating potential abuses.

Given that abuses often occur because FSP compensation is effectively "hidden" in the MERs of mutual funds and segregated funds, wouldn't it make the most sense to remove all embedded compensation from the products so that consumers could see for themselves just how and how much they were paying FSPs? Disclosing embedded compensation is nice, ~~but surely to goodness,~~ putting compensation front and centre is better.

3. Industry Associations and Professional Standards

Every profession has its own association for individual practitioners. Not about to be outdone by the ongoing regulatory turf war, five separate industry trade associations have sprung up claiming to speak for the interests of consumers in vetting the professional standards and competencies of individual FSPs. This is surely the clearest evidence of a nascent profession. There exists a broad consensus on the general attributes of what constitutes a professional FSP, but a whole lot of backbiting about who will monitor those attributes and protect consumers along the way. To make matters worse, FSPs needn't join any of these organizations if they don't want to. What good are standards if a person can simply opt out of being governed by them?

All five organizations purport to be the true source of professional standards enforcement. Their attitude is "Would the others please get in line to reduce consumer confusion?" Consumers, not surprisingly, are more confused than ever. Fortunately, one is considerably more credible as the association of choice. The most credible of the five is Advocis (pronounced ADD-vo-kis), the new brand name for the merged association that was formerly the Canadian Association of Insurance and Financial Advisors (CAIFA) and the Canadian Association of Financial Planners (CAFP). These two well-established industry trade associations voted to merge in 2002 in order to do what regulators have not yet been able to do—come together in the interest of common goals. Credibility is highest for Advocis because it has over ten million Canadians who are clients of its members in one way or another. No other professional association comes close to that number.

The goals of Advocis, whose formal name is the Financial Advisors' Association of Canada, include high standards of advice, consumer advocacy and FSP education. It believes it can become the single voice for the needs of the financial services industry simply because consumers, regulators, FSPs and companies all crave this kind of leadership. Advocis has long understood the difference between a trade organization and a professional organization and has always strived to be the latter. That said, most fair-minded people don't believe any of the five groups will ever achieve true professional association status. Advocis is predicated on championing the concept of the "Four Es:" Ethics, Education, Experience and Expertise.

Launched with an ambitious branding campaign in January of 2003, Advocis is aiming to blend the traditions of both financial planning and insurance into one comprehensive organization. With a broad membership base and long combined history, Advocis stands the best chance of emerging as the trade association of choice and is already the de facto voice for FSPs. With the tag line of "listening first," Advocis will aim to fairly represent not only qualified FSPs, but also their clients.

The next most prominent upstart in the industry is the Canadian Institute of Financial Planners (CIFPs), which already has over 1,000 members and is open exclusively to holders of the CFP designation. Its tag line is "Building a strong profession today, for tomorrow." Although the CIFPs presently lacks the critical mass to be sustainable as a national force in the long term, its commitment to a high and consistent standard is laudable. In this respect it is more like a professional association than Advocis. Now if only the two could merge and incorporate each other's strong suits.

The issue of standards is dicey. That's because North America is so far ahead of virtually all of the rest of the world that international standards are essentially worse than useless—they are dangerously misleading. In North America, there are thousands of people who are trying desperately to become true professionals by obtaining the designation of choice for qualified financial advice; the CFP. There is also room for recognized FSP specialization within the context of a CFP designation. For instance, The Canadian Securities Institute might still want the Fellow of the Canadian Securities Institute (FCSI) to be the designation of choice for advanced competency in securities advice. Similarly, Advocis might want to continue to promote the Chartered Life Underwriter (CLU) as a symbol of demonstrated advanced competency in the field of insurance. Finally, the Association for Investment Management Research (AIMR) might want the Chartered Financial Analyst (CFA) designation to become the standard for portfolio management.

The problem is this: most other nations have virtually no CFPs at all. In fact, most of the rest of the world is just getting around to setting the most rudimentary standards possible. Agreeing on common standards first and then "raising the bar" once everyone is on the same page is all fine and well for nations where there's little training to begin with, but in North America, low international standards effectively mean no meaningful domestic standards.

Because of the disparity between de facto North American standards and those likely to be adopted for the rest of the world, we will soon find ourselves in a very tricky situation. We'll have thousands of FSPs in North America holding themselves out as being "ISO Certified" (i.e., meeting international financial planning standards), even though those standards will be laughable. Consumers will naturally be inclined to radiate toward FSPs who hold themselves out as meeting this seemingly credible benchmark, while unwittingly putting their life savings in the hands of someone whose training might be on par with a bank teller from El Salvador.

Laws need to be enacted now to ensure that consumers are protected. This can only be accomplished by allowing them to clearly differentiate between basic providers and true experts. In spite of whatever change financial services has witnessed in the past, there is clearly a need for more. In fact, North Americans need to lift their gaze immediately to recognize the magnitude of this situation. Would you willingly seek professional services using an accountant from Uganda, a physician from Mongolia or a lawyer from Colombia? With no disrespect to these countries, they have different standards than we do.

By and large, a professional in those parts of the world is not on par with a professional from North America. Consumers recognize this intuitively, but because financial advice is such a new field and not yet a true profession, these same consumers could easily be duped into believing that the international standard and the North American standard are one and the same. The bottom line is that there could be thousands of FSPs calling themselves "professionals" and "ISO Certified" in a couple of years, even though most of them will not measure up to the standards set internally by their own professional associations in Canada.

4. Best Practices Consistency

Sadly, no one in the industry is bound by a set of consistent assumptions when doing planning. One FSP could illustrate a portfolio return at 8% and another FSP could illustrate *an identical portfolio* (in terms of underlying investments) with a return expectation of 10%. If the portfolios are identical, shouldn't their expected returns also be identical?

The need for consistency of assumptions is huge, given what's at stake. Let's assume we start with $100,000 and let it compound for the next twenty years. Let's also keep everything else about our assumptions the same. How would the portfolio earning 8% fare as compared to the portfolio earning 10%? At 8%, the twenty-year total is $466,095.56. At 10%, it's $672,749.88. That's a difference of over $200,000! The discrepancy is even more pronounced if the consumer is adding money to the account annually, as is usually the case. People with a background in insurance will know that the vanishing premium fiascos of the past are all predicated on impossibly optimistic assumptions. In the field of financial advice, your assumptions can be whatever you want them to be as long as they are seen as "reasonable." There are plenty of observers who would say either a 10% or 8% assumption is reasonable for an aggressively weighted, but balanced, portfolio.

Which planner (and which plan) is better? Since no one has a crystal ball, the case could be made for either. Observers might have a stronger opinion if they could see the portfolio's strategic asset allocation (that is, if it actually had a strategic asset allocation), but even then, it would only be an opinion. The problem here is that consumers might think 10% is more reasonable, potentially leading them to miss their financial independence targets if they fall short. Conversely, consumers might feel the 8% assumption is correct, only to become bitter when they exceed their target and conclude that their FSP encouraged them to set aside more than was necessary in order to maximize personal profitability. Liability cuts both ways.

Remember that at the end of the day, it's the same portfolio we're talking about, just different assumptions about what that portfolio might return in the long run. Consumers, being human, generally choose the path of least resistance and therefore are more likely to sign on with an FSP who illustrates at 10%, as opposed to one who illustrates at 8%. Note that no one is saying which number is right or wrong, only that *consumer decisions are being made based entirely on arbitrary assumptions used by the FSP.* How's that for a competitive advantage? If FSPs want to land that big, but unsophisticated account they've been trying to land for years, all they have to do is run an illustration that shows the client making pots of money. If it turns out to be pie in the sky, who cares? After all, it's *only an illustration*. What about costs? Do the illustrations take into account the cost of the FSP's advice? Again, an argument could be made either way, but surely there should be some standardization so that consumers can make basic apples-to-apples comparisons when interviewing FSPs. Accountants have generally accepted accounting principles; why don't financial advisors have a similar set of guidelines?

Perhaps even more disconcerting is who will oversee the planning recommendations being made. Currently, branch managers oversee activity to ensure investment suitability, not sound planning. As a result, as long as the FSP can justify the contents of a portfolio as being suitable for the client, the "plan" can be almost anything at all—including nothing at all. Worse still, a portfolio that is 60% stocks and 40% bonds illustrated at 11% would never have a peer review regarding the reasonableness of that assumption. Regulation continues to focus on products, not process, even though the process is where most of the real value is added.

5. Proficiency

How are consumers going to determine what credentials are most appropriate if the financial services industry can't even agree within itself which are most appropriate? Consumers intuitively understand that if they go to see a physician, they should expect to see a diploma displayed prominently in the office, attesting to the fact that the person they are seeing is an MD.

If they go to see a lawyer, they would look for a law degree hanging on the wall. The same goes for dentistry, accounting, engineering and architecture. Professions hold themselves to a consistent standard as set by consistent and rigorous training, suitable experience, peer review and ethical conduct. This in turn gives consumers a degree of confidence about a minimum level of competence. There is no such standard regarding financial advice in English Canada.

Because of the recent coming together of various financial disciplines under the umbrella of holistic wealth management, different trade associations have each come to espouse their training as the best, most comprehensive and most suitable. There should be no surprise here, since we're really talking about survival. Any organization that has a primary responsibility to train and licence practitioners would be thrown on the trash heap if it ever got out that the training was inferior to what was offered elsewhere. Besides, each organization believes its product solutions are most appropriate.

For instance, insurance educators and licensors believe more emphasis should be put on insurance products and solutions than securities educators and licensors, who take a diametrically opposed view. There's no consensus on what constitutes appropriate advice because there's no consensus regarding what constitutes appropriate training. Designations flow from these perspectives and consumers end up getting advice based on product-oriented solutions as opposed to client-centred, problem-solving solutions.

At the turn of the twenty-first century, there were over twenty designations available to FSPs who wanted to demonstrate competency in some field of financial advice. Many FSPs had more than one, leading to an "alphabet soup" following the names of those FSPs who were trying diligently to cover all their bases in a bid to become professionals. Aside from boosting the egos of those FSPs who held them, many people in the industry, including myself, felt the situation was outright embarrassing. What self-respecting profession can't even agree on what it takes to join?

The industry is coalescing around the Certified Financial Planner (CFP) designation conferred in Canada by the Financial Planning Standards Council of Canada (FPSCC) as the designation that most accurately denotes an FSP who can offer qualified holistic advice to the public. This doesn't mean the other designations are poor, only that they often convey competence in a more specialized area.

The FPSCC mandate is to "benefit the public and the financial planning *profession* (emphasis mine) by establishing and enforcing uniform professional standards for financial planners."

There are presently over 80,000 CFPs worldwide. Canada, at about 16,000, has more CFPs per capita than any nation on earth. In spite of this, there are some who insist that the CFP is not the appropriate standard that FSPs should be held to. These groups often do not want the CFP to be adopted because they are fearful that their existing registrants will be unable to handle the rigours of becoming a CFP. Without saying so explicitly, they want a lower standard.

An initiative was undertaken to harmonize titles. This was necessary because anyone licenced to sell a financial product could call herself a "financial planner" *without having attained any of those designations*. To this day, there are no restrictions on a person who wants to call herself anything at all regarding financial advice, provided she has a licence to sell a financial product!

The OSC initiative, called Multilateral Instrument 33-107, was established in the hope of creating a national proficiency standard for anyone "registered to trade or advise in securities, and who uses business titles that convey to consumers the impression that they are providing financial advice or services." This proficiency standard was to be measured by the institution of a manda-tory Financial Planning Proficiency Exam (FPPE). On top of having to pass this test, FSPs would need to have two years' experience anywhere in Canada over the five previous years and would have to commit to a satisfactory ongoing education program.

People at the FPSCC were predictably unhappy with MI 33-107, because it was viewed as yet another level of red tape that would only serve to confuse consumers. "Why not just insist that qualified planners get the CFP designa-tion?" they asked. They also pointed out that over 50,000 FSPs might have to be grandfathered into receiving an FPPE exemption. Most of the FSPs who would have been exempted from demonstrating proficiency through the FPPE were members of associations that left the FPSCC. This, to the FPSCC, was proof that certain stakeholder groups were intimidated by high professional standards. Although there is no uniform proficiency standard that must be met in order for an FSP to call himself a "financial planner," the FPPE is essentially ready to go, but has not been legislatively approved. The FPSCC remains skeptical of both the motives and actual practices of the Securities Administrators, noting that the exam has been created by the people who want their own members to pass it, making for a conspicuous per-ceived conflict of interest.

Ultimately, the two factions should come to some resolution on one exam. Julia Dublin, senior legal counsel at the OSC, suggests that there be a two-year period following the implementation of MI 33-107, in which anyone who passes the CFP would not need to write the FPPE. The opposite wouldn't work, however, and people who pass the FPPE would still need to attain their CFP designation independently. Once an FSP passes the FPPE, he or she would be able to choose from a restrictive list of job titles. Anyone who does not pass the FPPE will be precluded from using those same titles.

All this is underscored by the recent case surrounding the conduct of Brian Costello. Mr. Costello held dozens of seminars across the greater Toronto area in the 1990s, without holding a licence to sell products, and was ultimately fined and reprimanded for offering financial advice in his appearances.[2] What regulators failed to acknowledge is their assumption that being licenced to sell a product is tantamount to offering advice. In fact, relatively few people anywhere in Canada have a demonstrated competency in offering advice. Most merely have licences to sell products—something Mr. Costello lacked. He could have had a CFP, but no licence, and regulators would presumably still be upset at this lack of qualification to offer advice. This, even though the CFP is the pre-eminent designation for financial advice in Canada.

Trends in Financial Services

Having examined the challenges, let's turn to trends. The distinction is simple. The challenges are things that need to be ironed out before the industry can truly hold itself out as a profession. The trends are changes that are already underway, but the ultimate outcome is less than certain. If you think the changes of the past are remarkable, you haven't seen anything yet. The transformation that will hit the financial services industry in the next few years will be nothing short of breathtaking. No matter what comes of the aforementioned challenges, there are a number of near-term developments on the horizon that will have a major impact on how we think about financial services.

1. Probabilistic Forecasting

Until now, most planning has revolved around the use of relatively static assumptions, something called "deterministic forecasting." Most FSPs give clients plans that involve setting aside X dollars for Y years at a Z rate of return in order to arrive at some magical dollar figure that would hopefully represent financial independence as defined by the client. The problem is, life happens. Just like the old story of cars being worth 25% less the moment you drive them off the lot, financial plans are essentially worthless the day they are presented. In order to be truly meaningful, they need to be updated constantly. That's because so many things happen between the day the plan is presented and the day the person in question actually retires. But what could be more reasonable than a "best guess" of how things are likely to turn out?

The way to break the impasse is to offer people planning tools that are more "robust," resulting in plans that display a greater sensitivity to the permutations of possible outcomes we all face as we go through life. The best guess approach represents a kind of "over/under" line where people are about equally likely to reach or exceed their target as they are likely to fall short. In other words, if your plan says you're going to have $972,204 in your account when you retire at age 65 in 2027, it really means there's a 50/50 chance you'll hit that target.

The good news is it's entirely possible you'll exceed that target. In fact, the odds are that about 50% of all people planning in this manner are likely to exceed their target, provided reasonable assumptions are used. The problem is that fully half the people who have gone to the trouble of developing a financial plan with an FSP are still *likely to fall short of the target they've set as their requirement to be financially independent.* That's a staggering deficiency in the system as it is presently structured. What if half of all open-heart surgeries fell short of their objectives? Think of the lawsuits brought against the negligent professionals once the word got out.

Life is about trade-offs and, with the possible exception of politics, nowhere is that more true than in financial planning. If it seems you're going to fall short of your (single) independence target, there are really only four remedies: save more, earn a higher rate of return, work longer or accept a lower standard of living once you retire. Most people never truly come to terms with those trade-offs. It drives FSPs crazy when they have to convince people that saving $200 a month for the next twenty-five years is not enough to make them into millionaires—unless the expected return is astronomical (i.e., because the necessary return implied is unattainable).

Considering client needs and expectations, it is better to develop investment portfolios and financial plans that dovetail with one another by taking into account what we know about behavioural finance. The concept that does this is called "probabilistic forecasting." In essence, this is when probability and statistics are used to forecast future portfolio values based on a *range of probable outcomes.* The shift then moves from a single expected rate of return to a series of potential returns.

These sorts of depictions will go a long way in both educating clients and in managing the anxiety that goes hand in hand with short-term market fluctuation. Depicted below is a bell chart or "normal distribution" of possible outcomes for an event. Consumers need new and better ways to visualize the risk associated with the portfolios and strategies and this one might be useful. In all cases, the midpoint in the graph is the expected return—say 9%. Let's say a one-year (i.e., for any given year) standard deviation is 13%. That means there's a two-thirds chance of the portfolio returning between –4% and +22% and a 95% probability it will return between –17% and +35% that year. Risk in this case is what is known to statisticians as standard deviation, which explains both the likelihood of missing a target and the degree by which the target might be missed.

As the saying goes, in the short run returns are all but unknowable, but in the long run, they are all but inevitable. This is because short-term outcomes 'regress to the mean' or tend toward the long-term average. In the very long run (i.e. 20 or more years), a standard deviation might drop from 13% to 1%, meaning there would be a two-thirds probability of the portfolio returning between 8% and 10% and a nineteen-twentieth probability of it returning between 7% and 11%. Very few portfolio alternatives are presently depicted in this manner.

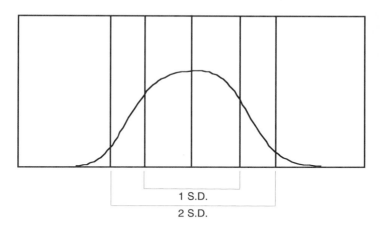

1 S.D.

2 S.D.

2. Account Aggregation

As the financial services industry continues its inexorable march toward some final destination that no one can reliably predict, the newest catch-phrase of the industry is Account Aggregation. The concept is predicated on simplifying and enhancing consumers' lives by allowing for all relevant financial information to be available through one easily accessed source with comprehensive advice offered through a single, trusted and qualified financial service provider.

In essence, account aggregation involves the ability to see all accounts—brokerage accounts, mortgages, RRSPs, lines of credit, chequing, etc.—on one single website. The idea is that it "aggregates" the data from various sources in order to provide a single one-stop shopping experience, that allows consumers to make decisions with current information readily available to them. Account aggregation is already being touted as the next great "killer application" in the provision of integrated financial advice and a superb way for FSPs and their firms to gather additional assets to boot.

3. Your Money and Your Life

Perhaps the most interesting trend in the industry is the shift toward "life management." Some FSPs are reinventing themselves not only as experts on money matters, but also as qualified points of contact on a whole host of financial planning issues. Life management has an almost zen-like quality to it. It represents a coming paradigm shift that many believe will be necessary for financial advice to remain relevant. As society ages, it becomes more "right brained." Right-brained people are more in tune with their emotional side and often more interested in redefining the next phase of life. Whereas early adulthood is often identified with defining, quantifying, analyzing, articulating and documenting life goals, our later years often involve experimenting, visualizing, innovating and integrating these and other ideas that have been learned over a lifetime.

The best FSPs will talk to their clients in terms of how their money relates to their lives. Life goals are important, and the concept is beginning to catch on. The early adopters are FSPs who work with high net worth individuals. This makes complete sense, since senior corporate executives, athletes, entertainers and the like, have some very unique and specialized needs. Furthermore, these people often need additional specialized services like contract negotiation, endorsement representation and high-end financial planning solutions, all of which could make their lives more rewarding if done properly. Such people generally have lots of money, but very little time, expertise or inclination to deal with the details of things like buying and selling homes, being sure the lawn has been mowed and so forth. FSPs co-ordinate those services, in the hope that it will simplify and enhance their clients' lives.

There will ultimately be applications for ordinary people too. For instance, people need to think about their lifestyle both while working and when in retirement. What will it be like? What will it cost? The focus here is on quality of life. More than anything else, people will need to have their lives simplified so there's an opportunity to do the things that are important to them. To what extent can one's life be "planned" the way finances can be planned? Do people do things on purpose? Do they have a "top ten" list of things to do while they're on the earth? Qualified FSPs are natural "life coaches" for helping people get the most out of life. The philosophical question, "What is your purpose in life?" is one that FSPs might help in answering in the not-too-distant future.

As a matter of fact, the whole notion of retirement as we know it today is outdated. The concept of retirement came from Germany in the 1800s. The state promised to offer full benefits for all its citizens over the age of seventy, at a time when the average life expectancy was forty-six! Later on, America advanced the concept when President Taft suggested the retirement age be lowered to sixty-five when life expectancy was fifty! This paradigm of retirement hasn't changed in half a century. Look at it this way: the goal that many well-to-do people have clung to in our generation is to retire at age fifty-five. Actuarially speaking, people may well live another thirty years after retirement. That's 10,950 days and a huge shift in reality from the old paradigm. How will these days be filled? To many, the new paradigm represents the triumph of meaning over rest and personal fulfillment over relaxation. People are more vigourous than ever as they head into retirement, and FSPs have to be able to help their clients focus on "what money does" rather than "what money is."

4. Comprehensive Wealth Management

This concept lies at the heart of all financial service objectives. It is unlikely that a single company in the industry today does not purport to offer comprehensive wealth management. Simply put, this is the coming together of investment management, financial planning, tax planning, estate and insurance objectives, business succession planning and a variety of other specialized, but related, financial imperatives. Charitable giving is a major concern for high net worth individuals, for instance.

The business model of the future for virtually the entire industry is one of one-stop shopping where all elements of one's financial life can be met. Now that FSPs can offer a multiplicity of products, there is a move toward becoming diagnostic, relationship-driven generalists who can offer routine advice on virtually all financial matters, but with access to trained specialists to provide more comprehensive knowledge and solutions when called upon to do so.

The best professional analogy is the family physician, also known as a general practitioner or "GP" for short. A truly professional FSP would be skilled at diagnostics and entirely capable of delivering basic to mid-level procedures as they might arise in her practice, just like a GP. However, since no physician can be reasonably expected to know everything about all things physiological and psychological, she might need to refer some patients to specialists from time to time as the circumstances present themselves. In spite of the rhetoric, it is simply unreasonable to expect an FSP to be expert in the fields of tax planning, corporate structure, estate planning, insurance usage and concepts, offshore planning, pensions, asset allocation and family law all at once. Like any other real profession, specialists will be required.

5. Wrap Accounts

There is some confusion over what constitutes fee-based advice. Some people believe fee-based refers to "unbundled" products that pay FSPs nothing, allowing the FSP to charge a direct fee on top. More on this later. Others believe "fee-based" refers to FSPs who use so-called "wrap" accounts where customized portfolios are designed based on responses given to a purposeful questionnaire.

A "wrap account" is one in which all the elements of portfolio construction, design and monitoring are combined (wrapped) into a single package in order to simplify decision-making and ensure consistency of purpose. Contrast this with the term "fee-based," which means the client pays an FSP based on the amount of money invested in the portfolio, irrespective of the products or methodologies employed. A handful of fee-based FSPs bill hourly.

Wrap account programs are generally also fee-based programs, although some still involve discreet payments for pools of different asset classes. This is in contrast to the more traditional commission-based model where the manufacturers of investment products pay FSPs a commission and/or trailing commission out of the expenses of the product. The choice of which method to use, in turn, should be clearly discussed and agreed to by both the client and the FSP.

That being said, many people in the financial services industry are dangerously liberal in their use of terminology. There are wrap accounts that are not fee-based and fee-based programs that are not wrap accounts. There is a substantial subset of FSPs who use the terms "fee-based" and "wrap account" interchangeably. This is incorrect; the terms are far from synonymous. Wrap accounts are basically a model for portfolio design. The term fee-based is a description of a business model. Although most wrap accounts are fee-based, this is not always the case. In fact, the terms are often mutually exclusive.

What are the general attributes of wrap accounts? There are a number of benefits and some drawbacks too. On the positive side of the ledger, wrap accounts generally offer a more scientific portfolio design through customization that comes from the applied principles of both Modern Portfolio Theory and (sometimes) Behavioural Finance.

The second major attribute is rebalancing. Although this is usually part of the package, it is not necessarily included. There is considerable weight to the notion that regularly selling a small portion of your portfolio that has gone up and using the proceeds to buy asset classes that are temporarily out of favour will improve the risk/return trade-off. Returns generally suffer slightly, but risk can be reduced considerably.

Third, most wrap accounts offer "pure" pools where managers generally have a mandate to be fully invested using a particular style. Again, a note of caution, since the concept of "purity" is open to interpretation. Many managers are fully invested and employ a distinct and rigorously followed style, but do not keep all the money in one asset class. This can compromise the strategic asset allocation of the overall portfolio. It is wise to verify the true nature of the "purity" of asset classes before buying.

Fourth, wrap accounts almost always produce an Investment Policy Statement (IPS) that is used to benchmark performance and manage expectations regarding risk, reward, liquidity, asset allocation and other important considerations. Again, it should be noted that one can get an IPS without using a wrap account, but this is still relatively rare in the Canadian financial services industry. According to the 2002 Dollars and Sense survey done by *Advisor's Edge*, only 15% of all FSPs use IPSs today.

Fifth, most good wrap accounts offer consolidated reporting, with client-specific and time-weighted rates of return over relevant time frames and since inception. Clients know how well they are doing.

On the negative side, wrap accounts generally cost more than other approaches. This is only natural since clients get more in return. Still, cost is a legitimate consideration when designing a portfolio and should not be ignored.

The other problem that many perceive in wrap accounts is their lack of flexibility. This is about to change as the "open wrap" or "open architecture" concept begins to take hold. Today, if a client wants a specific manager who is not involved in the wrap program of choice, that client will simply have to do without and use whatever managers are available through their chosen program. Perhaps even more limiting is the choice of asset classes and sectors. Even if a wrap account uses a wide range of asset classes and management styles, there are viable investment options that may be left off the table. For instance, few wrap accounts allow for the specific inclusion of individual sectors, or alternative assets like emerging markets, high yield debt, venture capital and hedge funds.

The open wrap concept will allow for the best of both worlds: use of superior products that are chosen independently to perform a specific portfolio role, yet linked together in a systematic way in order to improve risk-adjusted returns, tax efficiency, reporting and the like. If a manager within the program is not pulling his weight, you can replace the manager without having to replace the whole program.

In time, managers may not even need to be replaced. The ETFolios program from Guardian Capital allows consumers to build completely customized portfolios out of Exchange Traded Funds. Furthermore, the Logix Program, launched in Canada in early 2003, is a wrap program that uses strategic asset allocation and regular rebalancing *without simultaneously using primarily actively managed pools*. It stands to reason that more will follow. There are at least three other programs in Canada that offer some index components, but they are relatively inflexible regarding customization and still cost about as much as the programs using active management exclusively, thereby defeating the purpose of using indexes in the first place.

We are only now coming to see products that are logical in both their design and pricing in the marketplace. Why? Because manufacturers and distributors are effectively forced to accept thinner margins on index-based products. As a result, they resist introducing them, since clients might actually use them and cannibalize their higher-margin actively managed wrap products in the process. As it now stands, hefty fees are charged for services that explain almost none of the relative variance on average (i.e., security selection), yet fees are not charged (beyond modest cost recovery) on services that explain almost all of the relative variance (i.e., strategic asset mix).

If you're a believer in active management, it makes sense to use well-managed pools that are cheaper than most conventional portfolio building blocks. That way, you can have the benefits of reasonable cost combined with professional money management and all the other attributes of wrap accounts, too. The leader in this approach is Standard Life, which offers both the Eclipse and Legend products.

Wrap accounts are a solid option for those people who understand the rationale behind simplifying and consolidating portfolios and are willing to pay a premium for these attributes. They have been gaining market share because both FSPs and their companies are increasingly concerned about the liability associated with portfolio suitability and monitoring.

6. Unbundling

This is a concept that has only caught on with a handful of FSPs at present, but is already successful in the U.S. Simply put, through unbundling, investment products are made available without any embedded compensation for the FSP. That way, there can be no second guessing the FSP's motive. Clients no longer have to think, "Is this guy recommending the product because it's best for me or because it will pay him more than others?"

Until late in 2000, most mutual funds recommended by FSPs were available only in a format that paid the FSP in some way. At the end of that year, industry leader and pioneer Mackenzie Financial was the first third-party mutual fund company to offer funds with no embedded compensation (and correspondingly lower MERs) to the public. The idea was that FSPs could charge a separate fee for the advice being offered, but that the compensation that had previously been embedded in the product would no longer be allowed to cloud the issue of appropriateness. Acceptance from FSPs has been disappointing to say the least. Most investment products today are still sold with embedded compensation going to the FSP for completing the sale.

Bundling is closely related to tied selling, the idea that access to a given product or service is predicated on doing something else that you may not want to do. For instance, banks used to make acceptance for a loan predicated on the use of their products, while some planning firms to this day offer more comprehensive wealth solutions, provided that you use their investment products along the way.

The financial services industry needs unbundling because *unbundling creates trust*. This has been slow to occur, because FSPs generally don't want to have full and frank conversations with their clients about how and how much they are being paid. The majority of FSPs want "shelf space" in the minds of consumers as bona fide professionals. In fact, they position themselves as professional advisors who can wisely discern suitable options in a sea of complicated financial choices. Without unbundling, however, that positioning rings hollow.

The best FSPs know all about the importance of trust. They know that without trust, they can say whatever they want and their clients still likely won't believe them, even if what they say is measured, appropriate and fundamentally true. There is a clear need to suspend self-interest when offering financial advice, and unbundling does that. There's a certain kind of unimpeachable integrity that comes from being able to say, "There are three options here; the pros and cons of each are as described and no matter which you choose, I'll be paid the same. The best option is the one that works best for you."

Without trust, advice might not be followed. It has been said that the fundamental job of the FSP is to create a space where the truth can be spoken, heard and believed. Unbundling does that. Without unbundling, much of the advice that is offered, no matter how fundamentally sound it may be, may well fall on deaf ears. People will remain reticent about taking action.

The transparency that stems from unbundling has obvious benefits. The lessons of corporate malfeasance, through a lack of transparency, are being felt throughout the world. In fact, most people had probably never heard the term "corporate malfeasance" until recently. It has been said that those who ignore the lessons of the past are condemned to repeat them, so there will almost certainly be a premium placed on good governance and transparent accounting.

People have come to demand a forthright clarity that was absent from the lexicon of responsible management in the past. This trend will almost certainly filter down to the relationship between FSPs and their clients. Consumers demand more these days. They want to know what they're paying for and what services should reasonably be expected in return. In order to make informed decisions, consumers know that apples-to-apples comparisons will have to be made and that the facts will need to be placed before them in terms they can understand. Most people understand that everyone needs to earn a living and simply request that the value of the services rendered be equal to or greater than the fee being charged.

Until now, the financial services industry has been fraught with convoluted disclosures made on a rather ad hoc basis, allowing a number of FSPs to work without ever having to explain how (or how much) they get paid. Most consumers can check records to determine how much they paid their dentist or lawyer or accountant over the past year. The same level of transparency and disclosure will soon come to be required of all financial service providers.

7. *Planning Linkages*

All of the above trends lead to financial independence planning being linked to actual portfolio holdings. As it currently stands, a client might have a portfolio that is 60% stocks and 40% bonds, which is widely viewed as a balanced portfolio with moderate objectives that trade off risk and reward. Imagine if that person opened an account with that allocation and used an IPS that depicted that allocation and established a New Client Application Form (NCAF) that articulated that allocation. As long as the objectives remained consistent and the portfolio was regularly rebalanced to the target, there would be no appreciable risk to the FSP or the firm, right?

What if this same client had a financial plan that suggested this portfolio was expected to realize a 14% annualized rate of return? Today, any litigation between a client and the FSP and his firm would generally be tried by testing client suitability in accordance with the stated guidelines as set out in the NCAF as compared to the actual contents of the portfolio. No one is regulating the contents of financial plans. Neither is anyone supervising the contents of financial plans. In fact, with a handful of exceptions, no one is even writing true, comprehensive financial plans.

Companies are only now coming out with software that will allow FSPs to make clear linkages between the financial plan, IPS and NCAF. Consistent planning assumptions will populate all relevant documents in a consistent manner. As a result, the days of planning based on wild-eyed assumptions are drawing to a close and a balanced portfolio might allow for a planning assumption of somewhere between 3% and 5% above inflation. Cynics would say that a 14% return assumption is therefore still attainable—all you would need is for inflation to go into double digits.

8. Principal and Agent Status

In 2003, the IDA and provincial securities commissions backed off in the enforcement of employee status for FSPs at IDA-member firms. Those FSPs working with mutual fund licences and/or insurance licences have long had this status. Finally, IDA member firms will be allowed to structure themselves using a principal and agent business model, with the FSP acting as an agent for his or her firm. Some people refer to this a "independent contractor" status.

The IDA had previously insisted that FSPs be employees even though the rules as set out by Canada Customs and Revenue Agency (CCRA) suggested otherwise. Now that FSPs are considered self-employed for tax purposes, they will be allowed to claim deductions that are not ordinarily available to employees. The CCRA document in question is a checklist known as RC4110, entitled Employee or Self-Employed? It spells out conditions under which these sorts of determinations are made, including control of working conditions, ownership of tools and risk or expectations of profit. Clearly, FSP status has been settled as a tax issue, not a securities issue.

As a result of this ruling, securities-licenced FSPs are now allowed to stop paying into Canada Pension Plan and Employment Insurance on the grounds that they will not be allowed to collect if they lose their position. It also means FSPs will now be allowed to incorporate. This allows for a greater degree of independence for a large number of FSPs, since more entrepreneurial FSPs will have more freedom in the structuring of their personal affairs. Now that the issue has been settled, there's one less reason for FSPs with only a mutual fund licence to upgrade to a full securities licence. Although there is no impact on clients, it seems as though the industry is working through the inconsistencies associated with having multiple entry points coalescing into one homogeneous industry.

The FSP of Tomorrow

To understand what the FSP of tomorrow will look like and do, we'll first have to consider the FSP of today. Most FSPs have a background in sales. I started in the business more than a decade ago and when I look back at my early training material, I marvel at how much of it is rooted in selling techniques: what to do to increase appointments, how to improve "closing rates" and how to deal with objections. The general tenor of this training was manipulative: just demonstrate to your prospects that you care about them and are like them; once you can fake that, you've got it made.

Whatever might have been said about the FSP-client relationship, there really was never much of a true relationship at all. The FSP earned a commission if you bought something and never thought that charging an ongoing fee for ongoing advice was an option. The old paradigm is captured in phrases like "eat what you kill" and ABC, for "Always Be Closing." Mercifully, that paradigm is giving way to a more contemporary kind of thinking; ABC now stands for "Always Be Consulting" and *enlightened* FSPs are now making a *genuine* effort to overcome their early career training.

It should come as no surprise that the psychological aspects of offering financial advice are coming to the fore. Today, it's all about the client; what the client wants on the client's terms and using terminology the client can comprehend. In fact, Advocis has adopted the tag line "Listening First."

Fans of the television program *Frasier* will recall that he always begins his conversations with incoming callers using the phrase "I'm listening." The idea is that to both build trust and respond to someone else's deepest, most heartfelt needs, any reputable FSP has to listen. Prescription before diagnosis is malpractice. Therefore, if an FSP has a Master's degree in psychology, that's probably a very good thing.

Since commissions are becoming increasingly less common as a means of investing new assets, FSPs will have to learn to get by without earning commissions. Either that, or the stragglers will be forced out of business by those FSPs who turn out to be early adopters. Given the choice, with all else being equal, consumers will always prefer to be free of the handcuffs of a back-end load. Commission-based FSPs have only lasted this long because most consumers don't know enough to ask for—nay, demand—products that are available without redemption penalties.

The Toronto-based research firm Investor Economics has verified that FSPs have been quietly shifting assets from a DSC format to front-end load (typically in a 0% front-end or "no load" basis) format since the mid-1990s. Although back-end load funds still comprise about 75% of all sales, assets in funds with a front-end charge have more than tripled since 1996, from $27 billion to $77 billion. Meanwhile, the assets in DSC funds have only doubled as the DSC market share has slipped from 78% to 72%. Furthermore, as competition accelerates, it will be logical for that trend to accelerate, too. Investor Economics has gone on to suggest that in a slowing sales environment, selling front-end funds at "zero load" is a powerful value proposition. Are commission-based FSPs getting the message?

As a result of this trend, it stands to reason that FSPs will need to be managing more assets than present in order to remain viable. Without a big "eat what you kill" kind of payday associated with new DSC money invested, critical mass will be crucial for mere survival. Virtually all FSPs managing less than $20 million will be unable to survive, while those managing over $50 million will likely "make it." The fate of the ones in between will depend primarily on perseverance, foresight and luck. For years now, talk within the industry has been that commissions are being eradicated. Virtually everyone agrees it will happen. The disagreement is over how soon it will happen and under what terms and conditions.

If a decision is reached that sales commissions and trailer fees will no longer be tolerated, the necessary change will come about swiftly. Still, the system is beginning to crumble under its own weight as consumers are coming to demand more transparent service offerings from their FSPs and some FSPs are making the shift away from commissions in an attempt to gain an early mover advantage relative to their peers. Competitors (and in this environment, that's an apt description for FSPs) who are less adaptive to the changing environment may well be left behind and forced into other lines of work.

The consensus about the industry's compensation direction is perhaps the only thing that all participants agree on. The debate now revolves around how to do it most practically and how long it should take. Few clients understand that any FSP who makes this transition has to endure temporary poverty in the name of doing what is believed to be best for clients. Many FSPs, in turn, think the transition can be made quickly, which is not the case if ethics are considered simultaneously. The transition will be difficult for all concerned. Nonetheless, if everyone agrees on where things are going, we should roll up our sleeves and work on getting there. It is time to accelerate our future.

Both FSPs and their clients will need to adjust to the emerging world order. Since virtually everyone agrees commissions and trailer fees have to go, there's no sense in continuing to fret about the necessary transformation that lies ahead. Neither FSPs nor their clients particularly want to go through it, but it seems to be an unavoidable rite of passage that needs to be confronted directly and considered fully.

Here's where a number of the aforementioned concepts come together. If the decision is made by the consumer to use a fee-based arrangement, a further decision needs to be made about which way the concept can be implemented. We can use a managed money (or "wrap") product, which offers scientific portfolio customization, superior performance reporting and simplified paperwork, or we can use an unbundled approach that features a combination of F Class mutual funds (the kind that offer no embedded FSP compensation) and Exchange Traded Funds (ETFs) with fees charged on top. Both have merit.

With all requisite disclosures and explanations having been made, the decision should be up to the client. People generally make buying decisions based on value and price, and financial services are no different. Those who see value in the managed money features generally choose that option, while those who are most sensitive to price choose the latter. In time, the predominance of "open architecture" reporting and tracking platforms will allow firms and their FSPs to offer the best of both worlds—scientific customization at a more reasonable price.

Where Consumers Fit In

There is obviously a wide range of consumer demand in the marketplace for financial services. One-stop shopping can be a nebulous objective in a world of "different strokes for different folks." Simply put, it's difficult for FSPs and their firms to deliver a consistent "brand experience" when consumer wants and needs are all over the map. Some consumers want excruciating detail on statements, while others would be quite content to get fewer statements altogether since they often don't open them anyway and generally see reporting as a nuisance. No one is saying this is an appropriate attitude, only that it is representative of a large segment of the population.

When considering retail financial planning advice and services, a continuum can be drawn that clearly demonstrates the dilemma. On the one extreme, we have people who want to do everything themselves and find any contact with the financial services industry a nuisance. On the other end of the continuum, we have people who do virtually nothing for themselves, choosing instead to virtually abdicate their responsibilities to someone else. Both extremes can be dangerous. Here's a quick glance at that continuum:

Do-It-Yourselfers (DIY)   Collaborators   Delegators   Abdicators

While most people would agree that it is reckless to totally abdicate responsibility for their own financial well-being, there are certainly those who do it. These are people who find the whole business of money, investing, taxes and estate planning too overwhelming and distasteful to merit serious consideration.

Most consumers find themselves somewhere in the middle of the continuum and are generally inclined to some degree of collaboration, with an increasing likelihood of working with an FSP as they move to the right. The challenge for FSPs is that many are trying to be all things to all people, working with whoever comes through the door. They would likely be better off if they focused on one psychographic subset of the population—the delegators.

Note that abdicators are even more likely to do as they are advised, but the best FSPs want their clients to feel a sense of ownership; abdicators don't make for fulfilling client relationships. If FSPs are offering stewardship to clients who appreciate it, everyone feels more fulfilled. Just as physicians would rather have their patients quit smoking of their own volition than by prescribing a patch, rendering advice is more cathartic when there's a sense that the person being advised really wants to take destiny in his own hands rather than be prescribed a band-aid solution.

Think ahead. Imagine an FSP saying, "Don't just do something, stand there," and ultimately being paid to coach a client to keep his mitts off his own money! This is part of the paradigm of the future rooted in the emerging science of behavioural finance. Other professions would never be so audacious, but then again, assisting people in managing their life's savings and arranging their life's affairs is a calling like no other.

ARE FSPs TRUE PROFESSIONALS?

The nice thing about standards is that there are so many of them to choose from.
—Andrew S. Tanenbaum

Hold yourself responsible for a higher standard than anyone else expects of you.
—Henry Ward Beecher

There can be little doubt that we are in the final stages of the creation of a new profession focused on the rendering of financial advice. People have been giving financial advice for years without it being a bona fide profession, just as people built structures before there were engineers. Over time, the need to formally train workers and standardize the building work being done moved from being a good idea to being entrenched as a mandatory precondition of doing business. What about financial advice? Here's how the dictionary defines the term "profession": "A calling requiring specialized knowledge and often long and intensive preparation, including instruction in skills and methods as well as in the scientific, historical and scholarly principles underlying such skills and methods, maintaining by force of organization or concerted opinion high standards of achievement and conduct, and commiting its members to continued study and to a kind of work which has for its prime purpose the rendering of public service."

On the surface, it might seem that today's FSPs meet the definition set out above. Then again, maybe they don't. There are thousands of people selling mutual funds today who have taken a week off work to study for, and successfully complete, the mutual fund licencing exam. Just how rigorous does professional training have to be?

After many years of bickering and squabbling, the financial advice stakeholder groups are coalescing around one designation: the Certified Financial Planners (CFP) mark. Any consumer who is working with an FSP who does not have a CFP designation (or, in the interim, at least some kind of formal designation) might be working with someone who is not committed to genuine professionalism. No one is suggesting that FSPs who do not hold the CFP or other designations are not intelligent, diligent or otherwise responsible people, only that the discrepancy between the total number of FSPs and the number of FSPs with formal and related designations is quite large. The fact that there are so many people holding themselves out as true professionals without having met a demonstrable and relevant proficiency requirement underscores the fairly obvious notion that all serious professionals need to have a recognized designation.

This is potentially quite enlightening considering how many FSPs there are in Canada. Research done in 2002 by *Advisor's Edge* magazine found it nearly impossible to reliably quantify the number of FSPs in Canada because of fuzzy titles, nebulous job descriptions, multiple licencing arrangements and bureaucratic red tape. Estimates put the total somewhere between 100,000 and 300,000 FSPs. How's that for certitude? In contrast, it was easily verified that there were 81,237 lawyers in Canada (only 50,920 of whom were practicing) and 58,659 doctors.

Even if one were to accept the low end of the bandwidth, it seems intuitively obvious that we have more FSPs than are needed, assuming the numbers used for other professions can serve as a reasonable guideline. If a large number of FSPs were to leave the industry, they would not be terribly missed. Those remaining would be more than capable of picking up the slack. That's a not-too-subtle sign for marginally useful FSPs to consider jumping out of the business now, before reforms push them out of business later.

Practitioners of all true professions have an accepted degree of formal training in their field of endeavour to back up their assertion that they are indeed professionals. If you were sick, you'd want to visit a doctor. If you needed legal advice, you'd want to see a lawyer. In any other instance where a professional was required, there would be a degree of comfort that stems from seeing the diploma on the wall and knowing that the person offering professional services has demonstrated a minimum level of competency.

Colleges and universities are now offering courses that lead to the CFP designation, just as they provide training for would-be accountants, doctors, lawyers, engineers and other professionals. The objectives of the academic programming remain all over the map. Wilfrid Laurier University in Waterloo and Laval University in Quebec both have programs leading to the CFP designation. Other schools, like the University of Calgary, offer insurance-based degrees in actuarial studies and risk management.

Sheridan College in Oakville, Ontario offers a unique program in which students are put through an intense one-year full-time curriculum that prepares them to work as financial professionals. George Brown College and Seneca College target high-school students and teach them to work in the industry as entry-level FSPs.

In the Sheridan model, graduates will have passed all the necessary licencing examinations required to offer advice. Remember that the industry still regulates itself by determining who is licenced to sell things, rather than who is intellectually qualified and properly trained to offer holistic advice. Much like an MBA, Sheridan students need to have an undergraduate degree or diploma before being considered for the program in financial planning. In fact, some of the students have MBAs already. Graduates will have completed the Canadian Securities Course, Conduct and Practices Handbook and Canadian Insurance Course now known as the Life Licensing Qualifying Program (LLQP). Upon graduation, they are qualified to take the CFP proficiency exam, allowing them to hit the ground running as qualified players in the field. Passing the CFP would offer demonstrable evidence of holistic training. Of course, other professions require up to two years of apprenticeship or internship training. Doctors serve internships and it seems the financial industry is moving in a similar direction.

In the future, formal academic programs will have to be revamped and expanded so that the coursework represents broad exposure to a number of related disciplines. Self-study licencing courses would never be permitted for law, accounting or medicine. The depth and breadth of knowledge simply requires formal classroom training. Besides, the stakes are much too high to consider offering anything less to the public. Licencing people to sell products without arming them with the wisdom that comes from proper context and a well-rounded education is tenuous at best. Real progress is being made in laying an academic foundation, but much remains to be done.

At present, there is no mandatory equivalent second hurdle that one needs to clear by demonstrating an applied competency in the field of financial advice. Things like medical or accounting internships, bar ads or Professional Engineer exams, do not exist for graduating CFPs. They don't exist for people entering the industry with less than a CFP designation either.

Make no mistake, professional standards are being set and will be quite rigorous once they are fully operational. On January 1, 2003, a new professional organization was formed to integrate what had previously been the two most prominent financial advice associations in Canada. Advocis members are *required* to "walk the talk" of professionalism. In other words, FSPs who are members of Advocis cannot call themselves "financial planners" unless they are actively engaged in providing financial planning services to clients. Sadly, it is not currently mandatory for FSPs to join such an organization, so those who wish to forego an adherence to these standards can knowingly and deliberately do so.

It is important to distinguish between industry trade associations and professional organizations. Advocis is the former, but aspires to become the latter. The goal is quite similar to what engineers do in policing themselves and maintaining their standards.

The bottom line is that professionals get respect. People listen to what they have to say because they are experts in their fields. They studied long and hard to gain the knowledge required to perform their roles and other people look to them to tell them what to do. The phrase "Trust me, I'm a doctor" reeks of assurance and the presumption of knowing what's best for the situation at hand. When your accountant hands you a bill for services rendered and you scoff at the price, she might very well simply shrug at your scoff, as if to say, "What do you expect? That's what professional services cost." No further justification is required.

There can be little doubt that FSPs aren't there yet. Most are still seen as salespeople with in-depth product knowledge and little else. Although that's a bit oversimplified, it's probably not too far off the mark, and there's a good reason for this. As a career choice, "going into sales" is entirely honourable and certainly challenging. The nature of the work is competitive, often unfair and generally difficult. The highs can be exhilarating and the lows can test your faith. Public opinion of salespeople, however, is generally low all the time.

There are many industries in which commission-based compensation is almost certainly the most appropriate way to pay people. Take real estate for example. Most people buy one to three homes over the course of their adult lifetime, meaning they might move two or three times over a half-century. There are special skills and knowledge required in appraising and legally transferring the title of a property, so it's not the sort of thing that you would generally want to do yourself. Furthermore, the sporadic nature of moving means there is no need for an ongoing relationship with a real estate agent. Instead, people call on one only when required, so it's quite fitting that society has devised a way to compensate people honourably for performing a valuable service that most people would be unwilling or unable to do on their own.

But real estate sales is not perceived by the general public as a profession. By definition, peole who use the services of a real estate agent are customers; they buy something once and then move on. There's no real relationship in place. In contrast, professionals have clients, people who come back again and again to use the services (not the products, necessarily) offered by that professional. In other words, FSPs want to be seen as professionals even though most are compensated like salespeople.

Compensation Reconsideration

Now that we know how most FSPs are being paid, let's consider what an appropriate compensation structure for a *professional* FSP of the future might look like. Would it involve commissions? Certainly not. Doctor's don't earn commissions. Would you respect a doctor's opinion if one treatment paid him 20% more than another? Whatever the compensation format is, it should leave the FSP beyond reproach regarding potential ulterior motives. As soon as the client can call the FSP's rationale into question, professionalism is compromised and credibility is lost.

There are two ways the problem can be solved. The first is to do what lawyers, accountants and other professionals do: charge a transparent hourly fee. The good news for an FSP who charges $200/hour is that anyone who pays that fee is highly likely to pay attention to what is proposed or written. Furthermore, the likelihood of acting on the advice is also high. Who in their right mind would pay that kind of money for recommendations that were merely interesting? The meter is running and time is precious, so there's very little bantering about taking the beagle to the vet or getting new shingles put on the roof. At $200 an hour, it's all business and it's likely that whatever advice is rendered will be followed. Ultimately, this is where the financial services industry is heading.

The second, more common way that qualified FSPs charge for their services, is through an annual fee linked to the client's account size. It has been said that the financial advisor of the past gave away the advice and charged a commission for implementation. In today's environment, where anyone can open a discount brokerage account and trade online for next to nothing, the situation is exactly the opposite. Advisors now do the implementation for next to nothing and charge separately for advice.

The logic is unassailable. An FSP should have no interest in recommending anything other than what is best for his client. If the client is unhappy for any reason whatsoever, he can simply pick up his marbles and go home. In simple terms, the more the account rises, the more money the FSP makes; the more it declines, the less the FSP makes. This represents a clear performance linkage that more closely aligns the interests of the client with those of the FSP. The FSP, in turn, can go to the client and honestly say, "I succeed when you succeed"—a hallmark of true professionalism.

It needs to be said that FSPs are generally not paid nearly as well as other professionals. That shouldn't be surprising, since the concept of an FSP includes bank tellers and other front-line workers who tend to have little more than basic training in order to respond to basic financial questions. People working in the financial services industry have a wide variety of career paths, these include, but are not limited to:

- regional sales representatives
- supervisors of inside sales for mutual fund organizations
- account managers for personal financial services in banking
- financial advisors for personal services in banking
- mutual fund advisors in planning companies
- stockbrokers at brokerage companies
- personal financial planning practictioners
- credit counsellors
- risk management advisors, including insurance agents
- estate planning advisors

Obviously, the term financial service provider casts an extremely wide net. But what about those people who hold themselves out as bona fide financial professionals, the ones with credentials offering holistic financial advice? If the designation of choice for that career path is the Certified Financial Planner designation, what do CFPs make, on average? The Financial Planners Standards Council (FPSCC) annual report for 2000-2001 showed that the top 31% of all CFPs earn over $150,000 annually. Another 21% earn between $100,000 and $150,000. Therefore, almost half of all people in the industry *with the highest designation* earn less than $100,000 a year. There's a strong correlation between compensation and experience, since most CFPs have a client roster that grows over time and their compensation grows accordingly. Still, although the pay isn't spectacular, it isn't bad either.

Furthermore, there is a broad societal consensus that offering financial advice is a great career choice. The *Jobs Rated Almanac* recently listed financial planning as the most desirable career on earth, based on job satisfaction and quality of life. The same study showed that 56% of planners take three to six weeks of vacation annually and 19% take more than six weeks. No wonder so many people are clamouring to work as advice-givers.

In spite of these desirable benefits, there are a number of related compensation concerns that will have to be addressed in the future. These include co-op marketing expenses, written disclosure regarding proprietary products and various incentive programs.

Some companies offer to subsidize the marketing efforts of those FSPs who recommend their products in their ads and letters, others do not. Is it truly professional to gain access to money from "partners" while other companies with comparable products offer no such assistance? What does that say about independence? What about in-house products? Are consumers being told *in writing* that the product they are buying is proprietary, with the potential ancillary impact on profitability and share price? Finally, what about trips, trinkets and trash that FSPs get from companies if they sell a certain number of products or a certain amount of a certain type of products? Is that the sort of incentive you might reasonably expect from a genuine professional who is dispassionate about products and focused on client-based solutions?

For now, it might be best to suggest that the professional FSP of the future will have little choice but to make use of a fee-based model. It might also be instructive to examine the additional attributes one might associate with a professional advice-giver.

Deductibility of Planning Fees

Various professional services are tax deductible. Investment Counselling Fees are tax deductible for non-registered accounts under Section 20 (1) (bb) of the Income Tax Act. I'll go into more detail about investment counselling deductibility later on, but for now, let's focus on the deductibility of financial planning fees. You wouldn't believe the confusion over this issue. In the Spring 2002 newsletter to members of the Canadian Association of Financial Planners, there was an article entitled "Can Your Clients Deduct Your Fees from Their Taxes?" The cheeky answer was "yes, no and maybe." The yes and no portions were discussed a moment ago; if the fees are for investment counselling, they are deductible for non-registered plans and are not deductible for registered plans (RRSPs, RRIFs, etc.).

The prevailing view is that the Income Tax Act does allow for the deduction of fees incurred while earning income. This has generally meant that any portion of the fee that relates to advising on investment strategy for open money, is tax deductible. However, although some people have made allowable claims for deductions based on this rationale, the general position of CCRA is that financial planning fees are not deductible. This is really putting the cart before the horse, since investment decisions flow from planning decisions. In spite of this, the present view is that fees associated with implementing investment choices can be deductible, but professional advice that focuses on first principles (general situation, tax bracket, asset allocation) are not. Many believe that if only one of these two activities could be deductible, it should be the planning, not the investment counselling.

For instance, it follows that one would not be allowed to deduct fees for estate advice, cash flow advice, or any other financial planning advice that does not relate specifically to investment counselling. The problem is that there is ample scope for our friends at CCRA to interpret the relevant sec-*always* tions of the Act differently. As a result, fees charged by a financial advisor for analysis that creates the foundation to determine the client's capacity to assume investment risk, might be allowed as a deduction. If that linkage cannot be made, the deduction will likely be denied. Actual results seem to depend on the strength of the argument the taxpayer makes when the deduction is questioned and the facts of the situation, which itself is unlikely to occur.

Each individual taxpayer is responsible for the veracity of his or her own return. This is partially due to the notion that FSPs are still not getting the respect they should be accorded as true professionals. One of the things that FSP lobbyists should press for is the clarity and certitude that comes with legislation that says plainly that financial planning fees are always and entirely tax deductible. The most contentious aspects of deductibility surround the use of fees charged when using 'F Class' mutual funds for portfolio construction. Since it is the fund manager who is technically making the buy and sell decisions and since it is the fund that owns the underlying securities, there is some uncertainty whether or not fees for these accounts are deductible. Although they are generally not disallowed when claimed, CCRA has not offered a definitive position on the question. The industry has decided not to press for clarity. Sometimes it's easier to ask for forgiveness than it is to ask for permission.

The fact that investment counselling fees are deductible while financial planning fees are not can lead to some interesting business models. Just as some grocery stores advertise a special on a basic item and put that item at the back of the store as a loss leader, some financial services companies offer to do free (i.e., non-deductible, loss-leading) financial planning *provided that* they are allowed to offer investment counselling services for portfolios of a certain minimum size. If the client wants the financial planning as a stand-alone service from this same company, it would not be available to that client *at any price.*

As long as financial services companies can make their profits, there's no real concern for where the money comes from or how it is depicted on the invoice. Clients love this, because they gain a legitimate deduction where one may not have existed otherwise. *This is a perfectly legal practice,* but likely not the sort of conduct one might expect from a true professional services company. Everyone knows that individuals are allowed to arrange their affairs in order to minimize their tax bill and that it is dangerous to neglect such activity. Still, the Income Tax Act could be made more clear and consistent regarding deductibility for financial planning and investment counselling fees, even though certain segments of the industry actually seem to prefer the latitude offered by the uncertainty.

Continuing Education

If you accept the premise that the world is becoming more complex and inter-connected all the time, then the people who are offering advice in light of those changes should also be keeping abreast of them. Membership organizations have made it mandatory for their members to complete a minimum of contin-uing education activity. Thirty hours of continuing education work is the annual benchmark. This continuing education usually includes course work on ethics and is verified with questionnaires that are signed off by members and audited throughout the year. Since the FPSCC has an identical education condition, this makes the professional association hurdle a little redundant. Still, FSPs who are members of these sorts of associations while not holding the CFP designation will be held to a reasonable standard of continuing education.

The problem is that even though membership organizations are promoting continuing education and making it mandatory, joining these membership organizations is entirely optional. The net effect at present is that FSPs who want to be properly seen as professionals self-select into these groups. Those who may not be up to snuff are allowed to look in from the outside and, in the process, save both their annual membership dues and the trouble of being held to a higher standard that comes with membership. They flout the same principles that the organizations they are avoiding are trying to uphold. Most consumers are none the wiser.

When looking for an FSP, be sure to ask if she is a member of an industry trade organization committed to the promotion and enhancement of profes-sional financial advice-giving.

Every profession needs standards. My wife is an engineer. After graduating with a BASc., she went to work for a couple of years. After years of supervised work and passing a separate ethics and case study exam, she was allowed to use the P. Eng. designation. Engineers are now moving toward the implemen-tation of meaningful continuing education standards.

After Enron and Worldcom, people are skeptical of accountants. Doctors, engineers, professors, surgeons—every profession comes with some baggage. If being a qualified professional FSP is going to gain any credence, we have to learn from the established professions about how to gain the confidence of consumers out of the gate.

Offering Financial Advice: A Profession of Our Times

The world has become more complex and it seems everything spills over into everything else. Life is as much about maintaining a balanced schedule, lifestyle and diet as it is about a balanced chequebook and a balanced portfolio. It all interrelates. If you don't eat right, you might have health problems, which can lead to time off work, which may lead to a reduction in income.

As this complexity takes hold, people need someone they can trust to co-ordinate all the relevant aspects of their life, a "quarterback" or "go-to guy." This person will either need to know answers or know where to find them. Financial decisions are more complex than ever because of the explosion of products, services and concepts that have come out of the woodwork. In the 1970s, financial planning and advice was about stocks and bonds. In the 1980s, it was about real estate and tax shelters. In the 1990s, it was about mutual funds and professional money management. Going forward, it will likely be about all of these things and many, many more.

The need for qualified financial advice is especially acute for professionals, corporate executives and business owners. These people often lead busy lives and need to consider a wide range of options that take into account a wide variety of variables and possible outcomes. There may be multiple objectives where trade-offs between income, security, lifestyle, creditor protection, financial independence, estate planning, tax planning and other matters need to be taken into account. Quite apart from the growth of Canada's population of professionals, there's the unparalleled growth in the number of Canada's seniors. According to Statistics Canada, there were 3.9 million Canadians over sixty-five in 2001 (13.6% of the population). By 2031, that number is expected to mushroom to 7.1 million (about 24%). Qualified financial professionals can strike the motherlode if they can add value and otherwise capitalize on being uniquely situated to address the growing concerns of seniors.

If the financial advice-giver of the future is a professional who addresses the holistic needs of stressed-out, time-deprived people, what attributes should such a person possess? There is much to learn from the more established professions. For instance, some professions (engineering, medicine, law) require that the new practitioner spend at least two years working in the field before being allowed to practice. Articling and bar ads are well-established fundamentals in the legal profession, whereas engineers have to pass an applied case study and ethics exam before being allowed to hold themselves out as professions to the general public.

Let's see if we can borrow some best practices from these professions in order to get a sense of how a professional in the field of financial services might operate. A little bit of levity has been added to the beginning of each to show that no profession should ever take itself too seriously.

63

Doctors

Q. What do you call someone who finishes last in his graduating class in Medical School?
A. Doctor.

Physicians and surgeons, including those who finish last in their class, are among the most revered professionals on the planet. It's like a club; once you meet the minimum standard and agree to abide by it on an ongoing basis, you're in, no matter how narrowly you made it. People trust and respect medical professionals implicitly, especially surgeons. Although these medical specialists perform a number of delicate procedures routinely, they usually insist on written disclosure and consent before proceeding.

It is standard procedure to sit down with the patient and explain, *in terms the patient can understand*, the risks and limitations of the procedure they are considering. What is the likely outcome to the patient if they do nothing? What is the probability of success? How long is the recovery likely to take if the operation is successful? More nebulously, what is the probability or frequency of failure? What is the worst that can happen? Has the patient consented to the procedure of his own free will?

This is all documented in writing and the patient signs a consent form waiver acknowledging these discussions and disclosures before heading to the operating room. The chips fall where they fall, but at least the decision about what to do was made with a clear and purposeful understanding of what the problem was and what the risks, rewards and limitations were before getting started. It should be obvious that this process also protects the professional.

There are many who feel "professionals" who offer financial advice should be obligated to make similar disclosures before products can be purchased. Virtually everyone in the industry preaches the mantra of taking a long-term view, yet virtually no FSP discloses how well funds in a particular asset class have performed *against their benchmarks* in the long run, generally accepted as *at least* five years.

A clear example of where this might come in handy is with regard to actively managed mutual funds and the effect of costs on performance. For instance, prior to purchasing a mutual fund, clients could be asked to initial total return disclosures like the one illustrated below:

Investment/Benchmark	5 Year Return	10 Year Return	Initial
TSX 300 Total Return	1.3%	9.1%	_____
Ave. Canadian Equity Fund	1.8%	8.1%	_____
Ivy Canadian Fund	5.1%	9.8%	_____

In this instance, the recommended product illustration is Mackenzie's Ivy Canadian Fund. The return number shown is for the "A Class" version of the fund (the most common version, which includes 1.07% in embedded trailer fees and GST). The FSP could say that the Manager, Jerry Javasky, was recently voted mutual fund manager of the year and that Javasky has a long and impressive track record that precedes his affiliation with Mackenzie. When applicable, the FSP may need to note that when the fund does not have a ten-year track record, there still may not be sufficient data to feel assured that the manager is genuinely talented as opposed to merely lucky.

Although individual funds may well be outperforming their benchmarks over any given timeframe, it will become obvious that the average fund is almost always below the appropriate benchmark. Humble managers (even those with track records north of their index) might be well advised to utter the mantra "there but for the grace of God go I." This is especially so because it is a near mathematical certainty that even the most conclusive outperformers will turn out to be underperformers in the fullness of time. Real professionals should freely acknowledge the likelihood of active managers lagging their benchmarks. They should do so because performance history represents relevant information that would assist clients in making informed decisions about their financial future, not because FSPs are in some way biased regarding the product alternatives.

Disclosure documents such as these could be updated and distributed semi-annually on a national basis for all asset classes. Alternatively, tear sheets could be included in prospectuses to allow for easy access to current information regarding any fund under consideration. This would allow for the mass customization of portfolio recommendations that could be clearly and neatly summarized in order to assist consumers in making informed and meaningful decisions about the products being recommended to them based on current, consistent data.

There would still be a "sales pitch" element to many recommendations, but at least the consumer would see some uniformity of disclosure regarding pertinent facts relating to their choices. Other salient points that could be included in the point of sale disclosure might be: product cost (MER), FSP Fee, Sharpe Ratio (historical return per unit of risk), portfolio turnover (tax efficiency) and correlation coefficients compared to one or more complimentary investment products.

There are some who believe a clear depiction of actual returns compared to a relevant index is the simplest, clearest and fairest way to make a disclosure prior to making a sale. Active managers are hired specifically to beat a benchmark (i.e., to add value after fees). If these managers can demonstrate having done so over the longest possible time horizon, that would be a compelling reason to engage that manager's services and buy the fund. Otherwise, it's caveat emptor for the consumer. Improved disclosure might hurt sales a little in the short run, but it would also add some humility to an otherwise macho line of work.

This also raises the sticky question of new products managed by hot new managers. The manager's pedigree may be impressive, but without a track record, there's always a chance the product may be a "pig in a poke." No one is suggesting that a lack of track record is a pre-emptive reason to stay away, only that disclosure ought to be made before purchasing that there is no meaningful track record that can be used to judge what the investor might reasonably expect.

Most FSPs recommend products based on superior short-term performance, even though there is resounding evidence that in the long run, most actively managed investments lag their benchmarks and that the few that do outperform cannot be reliably identified before the fact. As time expands, the universe of funds that beat the benchmark decreases. This is a crucial point that very few FSPs disclose and few consumers ask about.

Another problem is benchmark appropriateness. Many Canadian equity funds, for instance, have only a bare majority of the fund invested in Canadian equities, so a blended benchmark might be more appropriate.

Perhaps most tellingly, research done almost twenty years ago shows that a portfolio's strategic asset allocation accounts for over 90% of the relative variance in risk and return.[3] It also showed that security selection accounts for only 4% to 5%. This leads one to conclude that security selection (whether through stock picking or fund picking) is almost entirely meaningless. As a result, anyone working as an FSP who focuses primarily on identifying superior investments is clearly missing the point and not acting as a professional. Professionals focus on things they can quantify and control: things like taxes, portfolio turnover, costs, type and amount of insurance and strategic asset allocation.

The lack of future return predictability is clearly disclaimed on every mutual fund prospectus, yet many consumers do not fully comprehend the risks they are taking. If the disclosure of suboptimal actively managed benchmark-related performance was made more clearly, it is likely that many more consumers would be inclined to simply purchase the benchmark. Many would remain convinced that superior managers exist and add value. Since the ultimate choice rests with the client, they should be free to use active managers if it is their wish. At the very least, consumers should be made to understand that security or fund selection—whether brilliant, horrible or anywhere in between—has little impact on their overall portfolio variability.

Apart from fairly and dispassionately explaining the implications, pros and cons of various options to the client in terms that the client can understand, there should be no perceived preference for one product or procedure over another. Once these considerations are clarified, the FSP should act in accordance with the client's wishes. The most crucial point here is that professional advice should be predicated on scientific facts and the best information available, not a sales pitch. The FSP should have no conflicts when offering opinions or advice and should obtain verifiable consent to proceed, knowing that all material disclosures and explanations were made. Commissions pose precisely the kind of potential conflict that could skew the content of the advice rendered. Without proper sign-off, what happens if something goes wrong?

If a surgeon explains every reasonable facet of a procedure to a patient, but does not receive written consent to proceed and then something goes wrong, there may be a substantial liability. Why should the standard be different for your fiscal health than your physical health?

Provincial "colleges" regulate medical professionals. For instance, Ontario has the College of Physicians and Surgeons of Ontario (CPSO) regulating professional medical practitioners in that province. The CPSO issues certificates of registration to qualified members, allowing them to practice medicine. It also monitors and maintains standards of practice through peer assessment and remediation, investigates complaints made by the public and disciplines those guilty of misconduct or incompetence. All Ontario doctors *must* be member so the CPSO, which has its role set out in the Regulated Health Professions Act, the Health Professions Procedural Code and the Medicine Act. Governance is structured so that there are approximately equal numbers of practitioners and non-practicing "public" members, with practicing members having the majority. Initiatives include developing a plan to increase the number of physicians, including a streamlined registration and assessment system for foreign-trained professionals currently practicing in other jurisdictions.

Dentists

A woman phones her dental office and asks to speak to the dentist. "How much is it to have a wisdom tooth extracted?" she asks.

The dentist replies that it will be $200 to have the wisdom tooth taken out and that owing to the use of the latest techniques, there is a guarantee that there will be no pain or swelling.

The woman responds saying that would be too expensive.

The dentist then suggests that he can extract the tooth for $100, but there will be some pain and a fair amount of swelling afterwards.

The woman again complains that that is still too expensive.

The dentist grudgingly replies that if price is the primary concern, he can always extract the wisdom tooth the old fashioned way for $50, but that there would be considerable pain and swelling as a result.

"Well, that sounds fine" says the woman, "can you book an appointment for my husband tomorrow?"

Professional services are like that. People don't want to pay for them, no matter how much they are needed, and, they'll do incredible things to avoid paying them, even if the "pain" of payment pales in comparison to foregoing those services. If the cost can be made less painful (by hiding it), people are more inclined to use the service. Dentistry is perhaps the best example of a professional service that is dreaded by the average consumer, primarily because of the associated trauma.

The thing about dentists, however, is that they are predictable, reliable and systematized. My dentist has a hygienist whom I call the "floss Nazi." I can always count on her to make my mouth throb before my dentist comes in to do the dirty work. Say what you will about the operation they have going, but it is a model of consistency where appointments are concerned. First the hygienist does the relatively general spadework, then the dental surgeon comes in to do whatever specialized procedures are required.

At the end of each session, I book my next session for about twenty-seven weeks later and head out. About twenty-six weeks later, I get a postcard from my dentist's office reminding me of my forthcoming appointment. Two days before the appointment, I get a phone call reminding me again of my obligation. How many FSPs do this? Meetings with your FSP are just not the sorts of things that are scheduled. Many clients only need to come in once a year, but there are those who may need or wish to come in two, three or even four times a year. There should always be a system in place to ensure meetings are happening in a consistent, predictable and purposeful manner. Anything less would be unprofessional.

Lawyers

Q. What's the difference between a lawyer and a catfish?
A. One of them is a scum-sucking bottom feeder and the other one's a fish.

Cracks about lawyers are a dime a dozen. Unlike other professionals, lawyers seem to get a lot less respect from the general public. There are three things that lawyers do, however, that are extremely professional: they use letters of engagement, have a set fee schedule and carry liability insurance. All three are critical hallmarks of a true professional. Let's take a look at each and explore how the use of a similar series of documents would raise the bar substantially for those FSPs who wish to hold themselves out as professionals.

The Law Society of Upper Canada recently took the unusual step of defining professionalism for legal practitioners in Ontario. The Law Society states that: "as a personal characteristic, professionalism is revealed in an individual's attitude and approach to his or her occupation, and is commonly characterized by intelligence, integrity, maturity, and thoughtfulness. There is an expectation among lawyers, whose occupation is defined as a profession, and in the public who receive legal services, that professionalism will inform a lawyer's work and conduct." The LSUC goes on to itemize the various components of professionalism. The "building blocks" listed are: scholarship, integrity, honour, leadership, independence, pride, spirit, collegiality, service and balanced commercialism.

The widely accepted concept of professional practice standards is gaining credence everywhere. One of the most important aspects of such standards is the letter of engagement. Here, both the nature and the scope of the engagement between the client and the professional is mutually defined and agreed upon before services are rendered. There are many aspects to this concept, including:
- identifying services to be provided
- disclosing both the nature and amount of remuneration involved
- identifying the responsibilities of both parties
- establishing the duration of the agreement

• disclosing any related ties or potential conflicts of interest (both real and perceived)
• confirming confidentiality

FSPs need to be absolutely clear about how much they charge by using a compensation disclosure document. Many clients are told to "read the prospectus" when buying a mutual fund, but in fact most do not and the small, but intrepid few who do, generally have no idea what they just read when they're finished. A separate disclosure document at the point of sale would go a long way toward clarifying how and how much FSPs are paid.

All professionals carry liability insurance to cover errors and omissions. Lawyers deserve some credit because they are perhaps the most keenly aware of the liabilities they assume when offering their services to the public. Clients should have some assurance that they will be covered in the unlikely event there should be a major oversight or error on the part of their advice-giver. After all, their personal fortune is usually at stake.

Lawyers are self-regulating through the use of law societies. Ontario legislation, primarily the Law Society Act, authorizes the LSUC to educate and license lawyers and to regulate their conduct and competence. The society's bylaws set out the professional and ethical obligations of all members of the profession. Those who fail to meet these obligations are subject to the society's complaints and disciplinary process. The society is governed by a Board of forty-eight directors (known as benchers), forty of whom are lawyers and eight of whom are ordinary citizens known as "lay benchers."

Lawyers are also inclined to use a letter of engagement when being put on a retainer to do their job. That way, there are no surprises as to what will be required and what the services might ultimately cost. On pages 70 and 71 is an example of a letter of engagement for the financial services industry.

Disclosure and Client Choice

After defining the scope of the engagement, what other disclosures might a professional make? It is important for clients to have some choice regarding FSP compensation and vital that proper disclosure is made before transacting business. Any FSP who is committed to delivering outstanding advice and service should also accept that clients deserve to be told how he is paid in a clear, written format that can be easily understood. Clients have the right to both understand the differences in various compensation models and to choose which one best meets their needs.

There are three primary compensation models available to independent, non-salaried, FSPs. The first is fee for service, in which the client pays the FSP an hourly fee for planning deliverables that typically involve no product sale or implementation. Next comes commission-based sales, in which FSPs receive compensation from product suppliers when their products are used. Finally, fee-based planning in which clients pay FSPs directly, based on the amount of assets being managed.

Letter of Engagement
Made Between Joe Brilliant, FSP and Jane Doe, Client

The FSP can prepare either a *comprehensive or modular* personal financial plan for you, analyzing your current financial situation and making written recommendations to assist you in achieving your financial goals. All factual information will be provided by you through the Personal Financial Review previously provided. It will *not* be verified for accuracy. Assumptions will be in keeping with both your Information Statement and your Investment Policy Statement, unless you indicate otherwise. In order to fully agree on the scope of the work to be done, please check all boxes that apply.

The FSP should focus on risks and opportunities in the following areas:
- ☐ Goal setting and financial independence projections
- ☐ Investment portfolio design, including return enhancement and risk reduction
- ☐ Estate planning
- ☐ Retirement income planning
- ☐ Savings for more immediate objectives
- ☐ Tax planning strategies and products
- ☐ Cash flow and debt management
- ☐ Education savings
- ☐ Insurance (both life and disability)
- ☐ Net worth statement

The FSP should specifically address the following life transition situations:
- ☐ Marriage
- ☐ Birth or adoption
- ☐ Inheritance
- ☐ Divorce
- ☐ Retirement
- ☐ Death
- ☐ Job transfer/relocation
- ☐ Job loss with or without severance
- ☐ Serious illness
- ☐ Cashing stock options
- ☐ Major expense or anticipated purchase of _____
- ☐ Selling your business
- ☐ Other _____

Limitations of the Financial Plan
The financial plan will be based on commonly accepted financial planning principles and the detailed financial and personnel information provided by you or your other advisors. This data will be treated as confidential information and I will not disclose it, except to your advisors to assist in the engagement. Once again, this information will not be reviewed or audited for accuracy.

The illustrations and calculations in the financial plan will be based on assumptions about the future. There is no guarantee that these assumptions accurately reflect the future and there may be material differences between the anticipated and the actual results.

The plan does not include accounting services, preparation of any legal document, or any other services not specifically outlined in this letter.

Implementation

You are not required to follow any of the recommendations in the written plan, nor do you need to implement any of them with me. You are free to take the plan, or portions of it, to any person or firm you wish. I will be available to assist you or your other advisors with any recommendations in the plan and will bill you for these additional services for the time spent, based on my standard hourly rate of $200. Alternatively, fees may be charged based on the quantum of assets being managed. These are disclosed in a separate document entitled Compensation Disclosure, which also required your written consent.

Limitation of Scope of Service

These services should not be considered a substitute for your own judgement. The financial plan is designed to supplement your own personal planning and analysis and to assist you in fulfilling your financial objectives. These services are not designed to discover fraud, irregularities or misrepresentation made in the materials provided for use concerning existing or potential investments.

Review

It is recommended that the financial plan be reviewed every three years or when there is material change in your circumstances, tax and other legislation, or in economic conditions. The review would access your progress and recommend any adjustments needed to stay on track.

Unfortunately, since most FSPs are not members of any professional or trade organization, the vast majority of FSPs in Canada do not make renumeration disclosures, largely because they do not have to. Compensation disclosure is a difficult thing when consumers don't want to come to grips with what the best FSPs are trying to tell them: qualified financial advice is not free.

In the meantime, many FSPs resist making this type of disclosure, insisting that they are fundamentally entrepreneurial and that this type of disclosure would be "bad for business." If the term "professional salesman" is oxymoronic, then surely "professional entrepreneur" cannot be far behind.

Disclosure and Choice Supercede Compensation Models—For Now
Since totally unbundled compensation is not yet upon us, the best we can reasonably expect from FSPs in the interim is not only client disclosure, but also client *choice* regarding FSP compensation. There are some people who genuinely prefer to work in an arrangement where the FSP's compensation is buried in the MER. Some people just resent being reminded that financial advice costs money, just as some people resented being reminded about taxes when the GST was introduced. Most people vaguely understood that there were already taxes embedded in the products they were buying, but were just plain annoyed when it was put out in the open and billed on virtually every transaction they made.

Until commissions and trailer fees are abolished, it is impractical to have any meaningful philosophical or moral opposition to FSPs earning them. It is absolutely their prerogative to do so if they wish. In fact, there are a number of products that are presently only available on commission basis, like life insurance and labour-sponsored funds.

More to the point, FSPs need to set their compensation levels fairly and plainly and then ask their clients to make a decision based on personal preference and full and plain disclosure. They also need to offer the same level of professionalism regardless of the approach chosen.

People Don't Care What You Know...
Professionals are expected to exercise a standard of care that is consistent and reputable. It is generally accepted that this standard of care be delivered in a professional manner, with conduct befitting the profession in question. Perhaps most tellingly, consumers of professional services have been known to choose their professionals on the basis of relationships and the "gut feel" they get once they come into contact with them. We're all human and no one wants to feel like a "number" or "an account" or the living embodiment of a certain number of "billable hours." The saying that every FSP comes to learn within weeks of starting on the job is that *people don't care what you know until they know that you care.* Aside from being a little trite, this is generally good advice.

Financial Service Providers are often reminded that they work in a "relationship business" in which connecting with the client is more than half the battle. Unfortunately, most consumers don't have the wherewithal to make a meaningful judgement in assessing the services provided (or about to be provided) by the professional. They look at the décor of the office, gauge for a suitable firmness of handshake and hope that the person who referred them did not have a uniquely positive experience prior to recommending the services of the person in question. All the while, the prospective client is thinking: "I sure hope I can trust this guy."

The client has to presume that the FSP has a certain level of competency and a reasonable degree of personal integrity. Conversations are held, goals are explored and written recommendations are made before most clients embark on a business "relationship." As a general rule, the more empathic the FSP seems, the more likely he is to get the business. This represents the triumph of compassion over competency.

The day will come when some FSPs will be asked (indeed forced) to leave the industry because of their lack of competence. That will be the day when the industry has fully reinvented itself as a true profession. That day is coming sooner than many people (including FSPs) think. Every so often, one comes across a story of a small-town doctor who flunked out of medical school, but somehow managed to maintain the charade of a practicing professional in good standing in spite of incomplete training. When this happens, the imposter doctor is generally viewed with pity by his former patients, who had really come to like the guy, as he is made to endure public humiliation for having been a fraud throughout his career. Statements like "He's looked after my family for twenty-four years and it's a damn shame that he's being forced out of medicine" are not uncommon. That's because of the triumph of compassion over competency.

What if financial services were a real profession like all the others? Imagine if laws were passed that said "You've got five years to get a CFP or we'll disallow you from offering holistic financial advice" to FSPs. Think of the uproar. There would be FSPs managing over $100-million in assets saying, "Do you know who I am? I'm managing oodles of money and have been doing so for twenty-four years with hundreds of happy client relationships to show for it (my company *loves me*)." The FSP's former clients would do media interviews to solicit support: "It's a damn shame Bruce has been forced out of offering financial advice. We had really come to like the guy." Standards of competency, if they are worth anything, have to be enforced uniformly and rigorously across the board. That's the way it works in professions.

The point is that competency is paramount. There can be no doubt that competency combined with compassion is preferred, but given the choice, society has clearly chosen competency over compassion. In the professions, it is better to be a brilliant technician with horrible people skills than a horrible technician with brilliant people skills. Imagine a "nice gal" in medical school whom everyone liked immensely and who had the most pleasant bedside manner in the class. Should her professors pass her, even if her grades indicate otherwise, just so that prospective patients could have access to her wonderful demeanor?

Many of the most valuable benefits that accrue to those who work with effective FSPs are emotional rather than logical or intellectual, as we will see in the chapter about behavioural finance. It's too bad that exams for would-be FSPs can't incorporate a reasonable weighting for "soft" issues involving compassion, understanding and listening with empathy. How can anyone solve human problems if consideration is only given to non-human questions of dollars, tax rates, income levels and pension plans?

People who offer financial advice for a living will also need to offer tangible evidence of some base level of intellectual ability. That base level will need to be much higher than the base levels offered today. There's so much that FSPs don't know, largely because they haven't been taught. After all, so much of what FSPs convey to those they work with is predicated on what they were taught in the first place. This brings us to the question, what are FSPs taught in the first place?

BACK TO SCHOOL
Economics, Marketing and Logic 101

Men are men before they are lawyers, or physicians, or merchants, or manufacturers; and if you make them capable and sensible men, they will make themselves capable and sensible lawyers or physicians.

—John Stuart Mill

We know what a person thinks not when he tells us what he thinks, but by his actions.

—Isaac Bashevis Singer

Any kind of meaningful reform needs to begin by considering the state of affairs of the thing being reformed. If it wasn't broke, it wouldn't need to be fixed. I can't even begin to count the number of FSPs I've met who think a rise in interest rates is good for fixed income investments. This lack of instruction about certain basic economic concepts demonstrates how narrow some product licencing training is.

Worse still, there are a number of inconsistencies and flaws in logic associated with the financial services industry that underscore an obvious need for reform. Many of the perceived flaws are systemic, meaning they are part of the system of how things are done. There are problems with mutual fund rating books and the "value proposition" FSPs bring to the table as a result, problems with the independence of recommendations being made and problems with the lack of consistency throughout the industry. In short, the system is broken and needs to be fixed. When the very basis of doing business is flawed, the option of using band-aid solutions and tinkering should be passed over in favour of wholesale revisions.

Let's start with first principles. How do things work presently? How would fair-minded people want things to work in the future if they could redesign financial services to be more logical and consistent? How do we go about making the necessary changes once they are agreed to so that no one is hurt? The ultimate question is "How would the financial services industry be structured if FSPs were *real* professionals?"

Virtually all FSPs call themselves professionals, but actions speak louder than words. Consumers are now saying, "Don't just tell me why I should look at you as a professional, show me." Some FSPs are attempting to do precisely that. Sadly, the majority are continuing along with the sales regime that they have been using since they started in the business. The trappings of that mindset are everywhere and if FSPs are ever going to be taken seriously as professionals, they had better do away with the sales-oriented logic that underpins so much of the industry today.

Who Teaches FSPs?

To get a handle on the kinds of recommendations many FSPs make, we first need to examine the kind of training they receive in order to be considered qualified to offer financial advice in the first place. Right away, we have a problem. Until now, the financial services industry has regulated the ability to sell products, while looking at advice as an ancillary function. Only recently has the industry started to come to grips with its own flawed logic.

As a result of the notion of giving advice as an adjunct to selling a product, virtually all FSP educational training has been done by the organizations that grant licences. They are predisposed to portray their products in a favourable light, yet are not regimented like a university. Training courses that grant licences to sell financial products are predictably focused on the narrow attributes of the products themselves. As a result, graduates might know a lot about stocks, mutual funds or life and disability insurance, but little about the broader context in which these products can be applied, disciplines like economics, law, public policy and ethics.

Virtually all FSPs working in the industry are effectively self-taught; meaning they bought textbooks and studied them for a while and then wrote exams that allowed them to sell financial products if they passed. Unless FSPs take special preparatory courses, there is no formal classroom learning going on at all.

Now imagine if your doctor or lawyer was allowed to practice without the benefit of a formal post-secondary education. Many FSPs have a post-secondary education and many even have graduate degrees, but the only education *required* for offering financial advice in Canada is the education *associated with the licencing of product sales*. This simple lack of standardization underscores the fact that there are no meaningful requirements for offering integrated *advice*.

Regulators have tried to regulate financial advice in the past. The problem with these initiatives, which ultimately and mercifully failed, was that FSPs *had to have a licence to be regulated*. If you had a licence to sell stocks, you could refer to yourself as a broker, investment advisor, financial advisor or use any of a number of similar monikers. If you had no licence to sell stocks, you could call yourself anything you wanted.

It was preposterous. People with training in product sales would have been able to call themselves anything from a long list of possible financial service titles, even though they might not have had formal training in economics, accounting, tax, real estate, law or corporate governance. Regulators are set up solely to oversee product sales. They have no mechanism to monitor advice.

Regulators apparently thought that FSPs with no licence to sell products could say just about anything and not hurt consumers in the process, because people only get hurt when they buy things. Imagine someone with no training at all charging $300 an hour as a *High Net Worth Investment Specialist* (I made that up; you could literally use any title you want) to offer financial advice. No training, no licence and no regulation, but consumers are supposed to feel protected since the person across the table can't sell them anything. Get a licence and your titles are limited; avoid licences and your opportunities are almost endless. Any client receiving advice from this kind of charlatan would have no meaningful legal recourse. There would be no licence to revoke, because the person offering the advice would not have one in the first place.

What are FSPs Taught?

Our society respects teachers because they are seen to have expertise. They also have a massive responsibility, since they collectively shape the opinions, attitudes and competency of future generations. Students tend to believe much of what they've been taught simply because they trust their teachers. As a result of teachers' presumed expertise, there's an implied credibility associated with many established teachings, allowing for a certain degree of intellectual imperialism.

When broadly based teaching gives way to more concentrated sales-based training, the perspective that comes from the more formal (and often more rigorous) approach may be lost. The healthy skepticism that normally comes from a well-rounded university education might well be lacking in the more focused "curriculum" associated with the Canadian Securities Course, Life Licencing Proficiency Exam or the Investment Funds Institute Course. In these instances, teaching people about an industry can be tantamount to presumptive indoctrination regarding product sales.

Such indoctrination might arise through what is *implied* precisely because it is *not taught*. For instance, where are the references in licencing textbooks that the vast majority of money managers fail to beat their benchmarks over long time frames? The evidence to that effect is everywhere for those prepared to be inquisitive and dispassionate, but newly minted securities and mutual fund salespeople are essentially never taught about how rare it is for their kind to actually succeed at beating the market. Nor are they taught about how few of the people they often delegate this responsibility to (mutual fund managers) manage to do it. In short, training for FSPs is presumptive since it teaches FSPs to presume that active management is sensible management.

This lack of balanced training (regulators might also cite a lack of disclosure) creates the false impression that active management is virtually always superior to passive management. Empirical evidence offered by Nobel Prize winning economists demonstrates exactly the opposite.

To clarify, active management is a manager buying and selling securities on behalf of a number of similarly minded unit holders for some stated objective, which almost invariably includes some element of superior performance.

Passive management, when done correctly, is an attempt to replicate the market being tracked as accurately and cheaply as possible, with no attempt to outperform whatsoever. Virtually all FSPs exclusively recommend active management to their clients.

True professionals would never stoop so low as to withhold relevant information simply in order to perpetuate their own existence. Can you imagine a physician going through medical school oblivious to the principles of basic good health? What if this physician were allowed to practice without ever being told that many ailments can be addressed simply by eating a balanced diet, getting regular sleep and maintaining an active lifestyle? As a result of this fantastic hole in the training provided, the physician would be doing a massive disservice to his patients. Obviously, this could never happen because our society is too knowledgeable about health matters. *o h ?*

But what if people didn't know about basic health dictums and relied implicitly on their physicians to guide their decision-making? Imagine if medical schools around the world came to the collective realization that much of a physician's work could be eliminated if people simply took better care of themselves? Imagine professors commiserating in the common room, conspiring to cover up facts in order to preserve tenure and their paycheques? *don't the*

The added costs of mutual funds (their Management Expense Ratios, or MERs) are like that. The industry wants people to presume they are sensible, justified and add value. In most instances, however, MERs can't be justified since fund performance lags the appropriate benchmark performance. *N·B·*

Centuries ago, the Catholic Church did some very nasty things to Galileo when he came up with hard visual evidence that Copernicus was mathematically right in suggesting that the Earth did indeed circle the Sun. Telling the truth can involve risks to one's professional reputation and personal welfare when that information threatens the power, integrity and authority of the people and institutions that rule the roost. In the financial services industry, much of that authority is rooted in the books used to train the FSPs on the front lines.

Similarly, until Magellan's circumnavigation of the globe, the prevailing view of the world was that it was flat. In fact, for many years after Magellan's voyage, people continued to cling to a position that had been thoroughly discredited, because it took a long time for the rest of the world to "get it" and digest the irrefutable evidence that changed history. Well intentioned people who were "educators at heart" had spent generations blithely spreading misinformation to impressionable young students.

Magellan didn't want to "stir the pot" so much as he wanted the truth to be known as an end in itself. Ideas that challenge authority are considered "radical" and their proponents are considered "heretics." As a result, scientific trailblazers say things that are considered inappropriate in their day, only to be proven right in the fullness of time. Unfortunately, some ideas take longer to make their way into textbooks than others. This often occurs not because these ideas lack merit or proof, but because people in positions of authority actively suppress the ideas themselves. They often do this while insisting they are fighting for what is right and protecting or advancing the industry in question. Mutual fund marketing departments are uniformly dismissive of index options—why is that?

There's an old saying that if you think education is expensive, try ignorance. This is certainly true when it comes to the formal training we offer to financial advice-givers in Canada. There are two primary investment licencing requirements in Canada. Essentially everyone who is selling investment products in Canada needs to have passed either the Canadian Mutual Funds Course offered by the Investment Funds Institute of Canada (IFIC) or the Canadian Securities Course (CSC) and Conduct and Practices Handbook (CPH) Exam offered through the Canadian Securities Institute. On the insurance side, the industry has now coalesced around the Life Insurance Qualifying Program (LLQP) offered through Advocis.

The emphasis in licencing courses is on the strategies employed by professional money managers on both the macro and micro level; government fiscal and monetary policy, security valuation techniques and the effects on security prices if they are trading ex-dividend or cum-dividend. There's a little bit about some related planning activities like having retail investors average down their cost base or do some tax-loss selling, but it's a very minor part of the training.

Excellent courses as far as they go, both IFIC and the CSC teach our advice-givers little about how capital markets perform from an academic perspective. In short, they do not go nearly far enough. Instead, the perspective is essentially sales-oriented and rooted in the old-school world view that money managers can consistently add value. Selling investment products and offering holistic counsel on financial matters are far from synonymous activities. That's half the problem. The other half is that there has been no mandatory disclosure of the most likely ramifications associated with the actual advice given. As a result, consumers could end up "being sold" when they think they are being advised.

University Education Leading to a Professional Degree in Financial Planning

In order for society to be truly competent in financial matters, our FSPs need to be competently taught. Otherwise, misinformation, no matter how good the intention, can take hold and lead to poor planning decisions down the road. Most people giving financial advice today were not formally (i.e., academically) trained to do so. In fact, many FSPs do not even have a university degre.

This is not to suggest that most FSPs have anything less than the best of intentions. Rather, many FSPs simply wish to convey what they have been taught to their clients as best they can. But if what the FSPs know comes largely from *licencing courses* that will allow them to *sell products* rather than *offer competent, professional and holistic advice*, there are bound to be biases and blind spots in the advice given.

Ironically, many of the most important theories about capital markets that are taught in first year MBA finance texts are mentioned only as passing footnotes in Canada's licencing texts. On top of that, there are a number of academically sound concepts that are never really explored in licencing textbooks at all.

This gap in the preparation of FSPs could be highly instructive when considering their predisposition against basic concepts like indexing. It might even be said that a major reason why most FSPs don't recommend index-based products for at least part of their clients' portfolios, is that they are blissfully unaware of the evidence in favour of an index-based money management approach. They honestly believe active management is *always* better because that is *the only approach they have ever been taught*. The mutual fund industry does a great job of teaching people how well they would do if they invested in mutual funds. It is silent about the fact that clients would likely do better still if they just owned the indexes those funds were benchmarked against. The people granting licences to sell products are looking out for their own interests and perpetuating their own existence. The people who educate FSPs do not look out for the interests of the consumers they purport to be protecting.

Even the most steadfast Catholic school boards allow for the teaching of evolution. Whether you're a creationist or an evolutionist, people ought to be told fairly and frankly about both approaches and then allowed to decide for themselves. By remaining silent on the merits of alternative approaches, licencing bodies make a misleading inference that those approaches are somehow inferior.

The inconsistencies of the FSPs who are products of this "education" are quite amusing. For instance, some point out that in the bear market of 2000-2002, the majority of active managers outpaced their indexes. When I hear that comment, I demurely agree and ask them what their point is. Not recognizing their own bias, they reply with words to the effect of "Why, that active management beats passive management, of course!" I ask if they counsel their clients to take a long-term or short-term view. The rote response is that their perspective is a long one. I next ask why only two years of data is relevant to their thinking. They usually say something to the effect that long run returns are just a series of short run returns laid end to end. Again, I calmly agree and ask why they don't use the last twenty years of data instead of two. I am generally met with puzzled looks and silence. The unspoken answer, of course, is that no one wants to use a more relevant time horizon if it disproves his or her basic hypothesis. In a twenty-year time horizon, the index almost always comes out on top.

Unwittingly then, most FSPs have become co-opted as de facto sales agents for active management rather than true professionals who are dispassionate protectors of their clients' collective welfare. This is in addition to the concerns mentioned earlier about embedded compensation for FSPs and the obvious financial interests of actively managed mutual funds. The compensation structure of the industry effectively ensures that most FSPs will recommend active management, even if they know that it is usually inferior.

When giving testimony in a court of law, witnesses are obligated to tell the truth, *the whole truth* and nothing but the truth. Two out of three ain't bad. There are some who believe that by not telling the whole truth to FSPs when training them to offer advice to retail clients, we hurt ourselves. More to the point, we do a major disservice to the same clients we aim to protect. The primary obligation of all FSPs is to put the interests of their clients first, yet there's virtually no one in the industry today who makes meaningful disclosure about how unlikely it is for an active security selection strategy to beat an index in the long run after fees. If rational, self-interested clients were made aware of this reality, many would want a substantially different approach to portfolio monitoring and design.

Of course, it would also mean a lot of securities firms' research departments would end up on the scrap heap. Imagine the repercussions when it gets out that most companies generally do research that does more to add cost than add value.

Basic Academic Concepts

Three academic concepts that help to explain how the obligation of putting clients first is not always being met, are the Efficient Market Hypothesis (EMH), the Capital Asset Pricing Model (CAPM) and Modern Portfolio Theory (MPT). If these three concepts could be internalized and applied with the same vigour as many of the other concepts in licencing texts, FSPs would have no choice but to alter the nature of their product recommendations. In applying these concepts, the basic objective of any investor should be to *maximize long-term, investor-specific, risk-adjusted returns on an after tax and after fees basis.*

The Efficient Market Hypothesis

The EMH suggests that it is exceedingly difficult for active managers to add value in the long run, after fees are taken into account. The view here is that a mature stock market is "efficient" and that it is highly unlikely one could make abnormal profits by using all available information regarding buy and sell decisions. That's because everyone has the same information at the same time and it is impossible for any one manager to consistently act on the information before everyone else does. Some managers will beat their index some of the time, most managers will be able to act on inefficient information about half of the time, but all managers will incur costs in excess of indexing all of the time. Put another way, it's impossible for any one manager to *consistently* beat the market in digesting financial information and acting on it.

It follows that most pension fund managers, mutual fund managers and discretionary brokers do not add value through security selection in their well-intentioned work. Ironically, their hyper-competitiveness against one another only ensures the efficiency of the market in general and the futility of their efforts in particular. In efficient markets, active managers generate returns that are in excess of a benchmark only by taking on a similarly high level of risk relative to that benchmark.

The Capital Asset Pricing Model

Risk and return are related and the CAPM shows that the expected return of an asset will be related to the measure of risk associated with it. This is true both at the micro level (individual securities) and at the macro level (entire asset classes). Historically, high return asset classes, like stocks, have had higher associated risks, while low return asset classes, like cash, have had lower associated risks.

In this instance, "risk" is often defined as the likelihood and degree to which one might lose money due to volatility. Other equally real risks, like outliving your capital, are not part of the model. The model is predicated on a series of assumptions about rational investor behaviour and perfect securities markets. These assumptions generally suggest that investors are rational, self-interested people who want increased return and decreased risk, all else being equal.

More recently, Rex Sinquefield and his team of researchers at Dimensional Fund Advisors, a research-based money management firm in California, have added two additional variables to make the model more robust. These include style (value/growth) and market capitalization (large cap/small cap). The general theory still holds: if you want greater than market returns, you need to take on greater than market risk.

Modern Portfolio Theory

Nearly half a century ago, a radical breakthrough occurred when Harry Markowitz demonstrated that portfolios could be created that combine different asset classes in a way that would increase return and/or lower risk when compared to portfolios of individual asset classes. This approach, now known as Modern Portfolio Theory (MPT), was radical at the time since it took a total portfolio approach to investing. Incidentally, regulators still look at portfolios as being the sum of the parts rather than as one deliberate and diversified single entity. It has now been forty-four years since Markowitz released his research and thirteen years since he won the Nobel Prize in Economics for it, yet regulators continue to insist they've been "changing quickly to keep up with the times."

Harry Markowitz's big breakthrough was the "efficient frontier," a mathematically derived continuum of risk/return trade-offs that prescribed a certain mix of asset classes in order to maximize returns for any given amount of risk.

Of course, quantifying risk tolerance is an exceedingly difficult thing to do. It is also fraught with innumerable personal opinions and biases. Still, the mathematical theory became widely accepted. It quantifies the personal tolerance for risk and then maximizes returns within that constraint. One would expect any nuances to be captured and reflected in writing and implemented through an Investment Policy Statement (IPS).

You'll Need a University Education

Corey Wentzell is the Vice President, Learning and Research, at the Canadian Securities Institute. Not only does he think FSPs need more training, he thinks it's dangerous that newly minted FSPs can begin offering advice the day they get their licence to sell products. Other professions have various types of internship programs in which new practitioners can make the transition from learning the mechanics, to gaining context through sitting in on meetings, to ultimately gaining experience by offering advice in a controlled environment of mentorship. All established professions have entry-level positions in which new people can learn the ropes in a non-threatening way.

Financial services is a major industry and there is a widely acknowledged demographic need for qualified financial advice as people age, estates grow and lives become more complex. Furthermore, there's a crying need to ensure that FSPs can dovetail their generally excellent technical product knowledge with less clearly defined, but equally important and personal, client considerations. Our universities, with their multidisciplinary academic resources, are far better equipped than Advocis, the CSI and IFIC to deliver these courses. Specifically, since advice is so circumstantial, new FSPs could be taught using a case study approach, with a number of activities that simulate the real world of financial advice. Consumers need to be assured that they are indeed receiving independent advice that is of the highest quality.

The transition will take time, perhaps five or more years. Anyone who has not attained a CFP designation by 2009, for instance, could be politely asked to leave the business of offering comprehensive financial advice. The grounds would be that the industry will have transformed itself into a bona fide profession by that time and the CFP will be the certification of choice. No professional accreditation means no professional status.

Of course, anyone who is licenced to sell products could still do so. That person would simply be precluded from calling himself a "professional" and would be expected to forego the rights and privileges associated with that status. Such a person would simply be called what he is: a salesman.

With only a few post-secondary institutions in Canada offering a post-secondary (much less post-graduate) degree in financial planning, there's room for significant expansion. Students should be encouraged to pursue a CFP, much the way they might pursue an MBA, as a degree leading to a rewarding career in the financial services industry in advising retail clients. Many of the core professional financial planning courses would be identical to those offered in MBA programs, so schools with MBA programs would be first on the list of where CFP programs could be established.

Presently, most of the FSPs offering advice to retail clients never went to university to get direct training as financial advice-givers. They simply decided at some point that they wanted to sell investment products or insurance and then got licenced to do so. The responsible ones continued to get more formal training regarding holistic advice. Today's Certified Financial Planners (CFPs) are the effective founders of the world's newest profession.

Practical Professional Challenges

There's a lot that goes into creating a profession. Many of the biggest challenges discussed earlier are quite distinct form the academic requirements that might present themselves. Still, there are a number of technical questions that need to be consistently addressed in the academic training provided before financial advice becomes a truly professional calling. Here are some of the most notable:

1. Integrating Suitable Investments with Actual Goals

The cardinal rule of the investment industry is the need for suitability as expressed through the New Client Application Form, also called a Know Your Client Form, or "KYC" for short. These forms are mandatory when opening new accounts and they must be refreshed every two years or whenever there is a material change in the client's circumstances (career change, physical move, change in marital status, etc.).

Aside from a handful of superficial questions about risk tolerance and liquidity, there's very little about personal tastes and objectives. In the context of contemporary financial advice, there has never been one iota of mandatory documentation of specific goals. In other words, KYCs don't ask clients to document their life goals.

The objective "to retire at age sixty-five in 2017 with no debts and a retirement income that is equivalent to at least two-thirds of what I averaged in my last five years on the job and lasting for as along as I live," is seldom found anywhere on a KYC. This is in spite of the fact that such a sentence would demonstrate that the client had succinctly defined financial independence in personal, measurable and practical terms. It seems logical to hold FSPs responsible to offer advice within that kind of context. We're simply dealing with an industry that is defined and regulated by product choices, not the lifestyle choices that are made as a result of those product choices.

If financial services is to redefine itself as a profession of our times, it had better be able to respond to the wants and needs of the people it hopes to serve. To that end, there needs to be a clearer integration of superficial numeric objectives with more meaningful lifestyle objectives. There might even be a continuum for trade-offs if the entire list of client objectives becomes unattainable. What could be more professional than to ask a client to prioritize her personal objectives in working toward them, especially if there is professional liability associated with falling short?

2. Fee Impact on Calculations

What rate(s) of return should be used in doing financial independence calculations? Popular choices include:

- a "best guess" of how that asset class might perform over time
- historical return data for the asset classes used—if so, what time period?
- historical average return data for mutual funds in the asset classes used
- top quartile average return data for mutual funds in the asset classes used

As a simple illustration, let's say someone has a portfolio invested 100% in Canadian stocks. What rate of return should that person expect? Would it help to plan based on different assumptions for one asset class? Also, is it reasonable to use an expected rate of return that is higher if fees are charged outside the account rather than against the portfolio's return (i.e., through the mutual fund's MER)? If the expected return for the asset class is 5% above inflation and the FSP charges a 1% fee on top, should the sensitivity to the fee be used in the illustration and assumptions? Many people believe that true professionals need to not only justify their fees, but also to account for them when called upon to do so.

Financial commentator Nick Murray is wildly popular among FSPs, largely because he tells them they do important work and that theirs is the greatest, most rewarding industry out there. In fact, he frequently refers to the industry as a "profession" when he speaks to FSPs across the continent. He is widely revered because he simply refuses to let FSPs throw him off his fundamental message, which is that everyone should be invested 100% in actively managed equities and take a long-term (three generation) point of view.

Let's consider the professionalism of this approach. If we assume that a generation is twenty-five to thirty years, we're talking about counting our chips only after a minimum fifty years have passed, when the grandchildren are as old as their grandparents are today. Is there any evidence anywhere that a portfolio made up of a number of actively managed mutual funds is likely to outperform a similarly allocated portfolio of indexed products over a half-century? Is it still possible on an after-tax basis, even with FSP fees tacked on top? If evidence exists, no one has produced it. Still, thousands of FSPs buy Murray's books and are compelled by the simplicity and power of his "logic."

3. Return Expectations

In the 1990s, there were some unscrupulous FSPs who were telling their clients they should plan to get long-term returns in the neighbourhood of 15% annually. After all, they figured, that's what people had been getting for the past three to five years. Why not extrapolate that return out further? Some people were getting returns in the high teens, so why not use 18% as an expected long-term return?

The trouble is the presumption that the long-term future will resemble the short-term past. In fact, uncommonly good periods for capital markets are frequently followed by uncommonly bad periods. Over any long-term time horizon, the expected outcome for any given asset class is actually quite narrow and nowhere near as high as has been projected by charlatan FSPs. One element of time diversification is that long-term returns tend to "regress to the mean," meaning they trend toward their historical long-term average.

Many of the most highly respected students of capital markets, including Dr. Jeremy Siegel of the Wharton School at the University of Pennsylvania, expect long-term equity returns to come in at the 5% to 6% range for the foreseeable future. That's a far cry from 12% or more that many FSPs have been known to assume when doing financial independence modelling for clients. In truth, everyone should plan for retirement based on the notion of real return, the return above inflation. After all, you'll be living your retirement (and paying for it) in inflation-adjusted dollars, not today's dollars.

Nobel laureate in Economics William F. Sharpe is one of those people who believe long-term returns will be considerably more modest for the foreseeable future. He believes it would be dangerous to take time series data and extrapolate that rate of return. Sharpe's reasoning is simple; he believes the world has changed fundamentally. The return that one might expect for any given investment is tied to the expected risk. More risk means more return. In spite of whatever real or imagined crises may loom in the future, the prevailing view is that the world is almost certainly more stable now than it was prior to, say, the Great Depression. Lower risk in stocks means lower expected returns for stocks. That will mean cost will matter like never before.

Sharpe also believes that whatever risk does exist is now being more effectively shared. Since global markets and financial instruments make sharing risk more plausible, the ultimate risk in the markets themselves is reduced. Finally, Sharpe believes that since people are richer today they are more risk averse, accepting less risk in exchange for less reward in a world where capital preservation holds greater sway than ever before.

As a result of these factors, Sharpe has recently gone on record to suggest that people might be wise to expect a risk-premium (return above inflation) in the 5.5% to 6.5% range for stocks. How many Investment Policy Statements (IPSs) and financial independence calculations take this line of thinking into account? Indeed, if 6.5% above inflation (and before FSP fees) is the best an all equity investor can do, what should an investor with a balanced portfolio come to expect—4.5%? Many other respected market watchers, including Warren Buffett, have offered similar views.

Historically, equity markets have returned 6% to 9% above inflation throughout the twentieth century. The question all this begs is, "Which is best?" Should long-term planning assumptions be based on wild assumptions about returns (15% absolute returns), historical data (8% above inflation) or intelligent projections about the future (5% above inflation)? Which is the most professional? Which holds the most liability?

"buy low, sell high!"

4. Time Diversification

There's a well-known attribute of capital markets that demonstrates how time and risk are related. Specifically, there are charts that are available demonstrating that returns for higher-returning asset classes are more volatile than returns for lower-returning asset classes. What's instructive is that all asset classes have higher highs and lower lows in the short run. Extend the time horizon and there's less variability in return outcomes. Extend the time horizon and the percentage variability becomes quite modest.

That's why Nick Murray tells people that in the short run, returns are unknowable, but in the long run they are inevitable. This is just another way of saying that asset class returns regress to the mean. The professional thing for an FSP to do is not only to use reasonable assumptions regarding long-term returns, but also to make meaningful disclosures regarding the risks associated with the variability of those returns as they pertain to certain asset classes over different time horizons.

5. Variability of Returns

The first cousin of time diversification is variability of returns. When writing investment policy statements and doing planning projections, there is a debate that rages between two competing risk measurement models. The essence of the question is, "How do you define risk?" There are two parts to this question. The first involves the debate between probabilistic versus unvarying rate illustrations and the second concerns the use of either mean variance or semi-variance models.

At present, virtually all illustrations done by FSPs involve assumptions that include a single unvarying rate of return based on some assumed average. In actual fact, markets are highly volatile, so the results generated may deviate substantially from actual experience. As a result, the "Monte Carlo Simulations" offered through stochastic modelling offer far more meaningful data for financial decision-making.

William F. Sharpe, who along with Merton Miller and Harry Markowitz won the Nobel Prize in economics for work in the field of modern portfolio theory, calls unvarying illustrations "financial planning in fantasyland." In spite of this, unvarying rate illustrations are still the predominant model for financial planning and decision-making. One can only imagine the raft of lawsuits that might lie ahead for those financial "professionals" who do not adopt the more robust methodology of probabilistic modelling.

Assuming probabilistic modelling is ultimately adopted, this leads us to the second conundrum: do we use a mean-variance or semi-variance definition of "risk?" Proponents of the mean variance (two-tiered) model, suggest that risk is defined by standard deviation and is the likelihood by which the expected outcome deviates from the actual outcome. Proponents of the semi-variance (downside risk) model, suggest that doing a whole lot better than you expect isn't really "risk" so much as it is "uncertainty" and focus entirely on reducing the risk of loss. For instance, let's say you run a financial independence

"involving a variant at each moment of time" 87

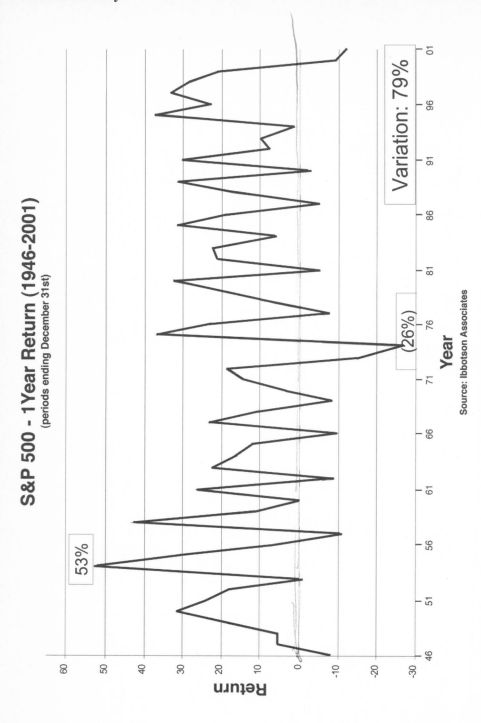

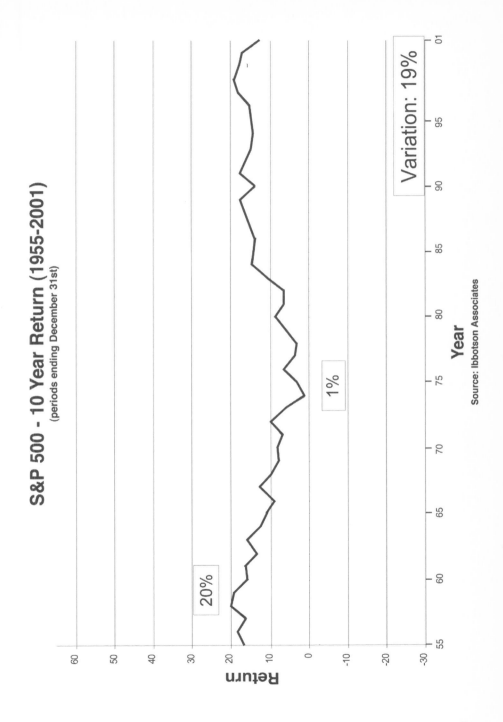

S&P 500 - 10 Year Return (1955-2001)
(periods ending December 31st)

Return

Year

Source: Ibbotson Associates

Variation: 19%

20%

1%

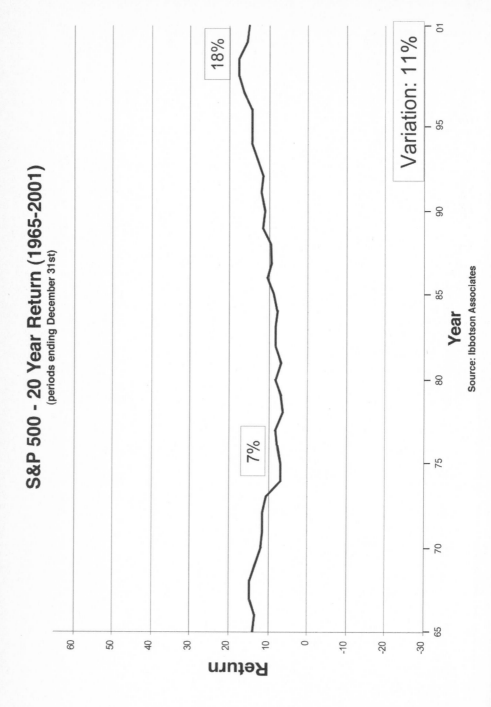

S&P 500 - 20 Year Return (1965-2001)
(periods ending December 31st)

Return

Year

Source: Ibbotson Associates

18%

7%

Variation: 11%

calculation that presupposes a long-term portfolio return of 6% above inflation. Over that time frame, the odds are extremely high (let's say 95%) that
your actual return will be between 3% above inflation (a poor market) and 9%
above inflation (a good market).

The question is: would you consider it "risky" to get 9% above inflation
over that time frame? Although there's really only a 2.5% chance you'll actually
experience the return of more than 9% above inflation, is that really something that you believe should be depicted as a risk? After all, you'll have far
more money than you planned for as a result. Most people would agree that it
is logical to use a downside risk model, since the risk of substantially outperforming expectations isn't really a risk at all, just a benign form of uncertainty.
Would people ever buy lottery tickets if winning the lottery was considered a
"risk" of doing substantially better monetarily than you would otherwise?
When planning, there also needs to be a reasonable amount of thought given
to just how certain the consumer needs to be that her financial independence
objectives will be met.

Consistency Challenges

Even as the profession of offering financial advice finds its feet, there will be
a number of additional challenges associated with its formative years, moving
beyond financial product sales. These will also need to be considered in the
creation of a new profession.

1. Compensation Logic

Have you ever met an accountant who sends himself an invoice after preparing
his own tax return? It would be a bit silly, wouldn't it? In fact, the concept is
entrenched in law. For instance, you can hire a maid or a gardener to do work
around the house, but you can't legally pay yourself (or your spouse) for doing
the same work.

Accountants bill their clients for services rendered, but it is equally true
that there are millions of Canadians who file their own returns and forego
paying professional fees in the process. Whether it is wise to use a tax professional or not depends on the complexity of the person's situation and the
ability of that person to implement appropriate tax strategies. Nonetheless, it
is a personal decision that is made on a household by household basis. People
generally do what they believe is in their own best interest.

No one in their right mind would bill themselves and then add the bill
payment to their personal income. If an accountant was making $100,000
a year, would he bill himself an additional $1,000 to prepare his own
return? He would have to pay nearly $500 in tax that would otherwise not
be due if he did! Does that sound like someone who has a solid grasp on
finding ways to legitimately reduce his own (and by extension, his clients') tax
liabilities?

In spite of the sheer stupidity of sending yourself a bill for professional
services rendered, that is what virtually every FSP is doing today. That's

because most FSPs buy mutual funds with embedded compensation (A Class) for their own accounts, even though the fund companies would allow them to buy funds without embedded compensation for their own accounts if they wanted. These "unbundled" funds are called F Class mutual funds.

Remember that A Class mutual funds include commissions and/or trailer fees included in the fund's MER. The FSP pays the full MER, then has the embedded compensation added to his taxable income. For instance, a $100,000 mutual fund portfolio invested entirely in equities, means the FSP is effectively paying himself $1,000 a year for his services due to a 1% trailer fee paid to him by the fund companies. This payment is added to his taxable income and taxes are due on it. The firm gets its pound of flesh, then the FSP pays other personal costs associated with his or her own practice (things like rent and salary for staff) and then gets to keep what's left over after the taxman takes his cut too.

Many people fail to consider that FSPs don't get to keep 100% of their commissions and fees. That's because some of that income is paid to the firm to cover the costs of staff, administration, compliance, licencing, marketing and the like. For those FSPs who work at a traditional brokerage firm, they might be allowed to keep 40% of their gross earnings as revenue. For those FSPs who recommend primarily mutual funds to their clients, the payout rate is usually much higher; they might be allowed to keep 70% of their income, paying the remainder to their firm in overhead costs. The difference is because brokers have a lot more services provided to them by their firm, which pays for these services by charging them more to work there. In reality, both types of companies pay their FSPs on an increasing scale, based on their revenues to the company. *(like realtors)*

Let's also assume that FSPs in both environments are in the top marginal tax bracket. In using an A Class mutual fund instead of an F Class fund, the FSP is adding 1.07% to his annual MER; 1% in an embedded trailer fee and 7% GST on that trailer fee. For example, a fund that has a combined MER of 2.65% in an A Class format, should cost about 1.58% in an F Class format. Let's say the FSP invests $100,000 in an A class equity fund that pays him a 1% annual trailer fee. If the top marginal rate is assumed to be 46%, just look at the *annual* leakage involved. Remember that planners are paid at a 70% payout rate and brokers at a 40% payout rate:

FSP Environment	Cost	- GST	- Payout Loss	- Tax Loss	=Total Loss
Planner	$1,070	7% ($70)	30% ($300)	46% ($322)	$622
Broker	$1,070	7% ($70)	60% ($600)	46% ($184)	$784

The planner only gets to keep $378 of the $1,000 he is effectively charging himself. He is $622 worse off (every year!) as a result of his using A Class funds...and that's not as bad as our broker friend. He only gets to keep $216 of his additional $1,000 cost to himself, a massive leakage of nearly 80%!

Would you entrust your life savings to someone who acts in such a dysfunctional manner? What credibility do FSPs have when they seem more interested in boosting their gross income through increased sales volume than in making sensible financial decisions with *their own money*? The culture and predisposition toward sales, to the point where damage might be done to the financial well-being of FSPs themselves, needs to change. Would you expect your accountant, doctor or lawyer to act in such an illogical manner? Would you have faith in that person's "professional" services if she did?

This bit of flawed reasoning is not entirely the fault of narrow-minded FSPs, however. Embedded compensation mutual fund companies have had F Class mutual funds available to Canadians for almost three years now and they insist that brokerage and planning firms have agreements and systems in place with all clients where F Class funds are being purchased. The stated rationale is that they wouldn't want clients getting advice without paying for it. Of course, paying for advice and then not getting it (A Class funds offered through discount brokerages) is perfectly fine.

Obviously, no FSP in his right mind would offer F Class funds to his clients without charging a separate fee, because personal bankruptcy would surely follow. Mutual fund companies acknowledge that FSPs should not be made to charge for effectively advising themselves, so the requirement to charge is waived for FSPs. Curiously, the vast majority of FSPs who recommend mutual funds to their clients use A Class funds for their own accounts too.

In spite of this circumstance, discount brokerages offer only A Class funds to their clients when F Class funds could just as easily be used. Obviously, there are some funds that are only available in an F Class format, however, if both classes are available, the discounters only make the A Class version available to clients. Lobbying efforts to force them to use F Class funds have proven fruitless. It seems that in the mutual fund world, "discount brokerage" can be just as much an oxymoron as "commission-based professional." The industry recognizes that it is unfair for FSPs to have to bill themselves for doing their own research and planning (even though most FSPs continue to do so), but does not recognize that an embedded fee for "advice," where no advice is given, is a rip-off for consumers.

If you're getting professional advice, you should expect to pay for it. It follows that if you're not getting advice, you shouldn't *have to* pay for it. If we were talking about tax preparation, people could either hire an accountant and pay for the service or do it themselves and forego the professional fee. Imagine if people were forced to actually pay a "tax preparation charge" even if they did their own taxes? That's what DIY investors are faced with in today's investment planning environment.

As for FSPs, there's nothing stopping them from using F Class funds right now. The fact that so few take advantage of this option demonstrates that the mentality of FSPs is predominantly rooted in sales rather than advice. Eliminating embedded compensation will force FSPs to act in a more consistent, client-centred, advice-oriented manner. Sometimes, the only way to get people to act appropriately is to force them to do it. As the saying goes, you can lead a horse to water, but you can't make him drink. Lawmakers have a way of "making people drink."

2. Picking Funds

Why do so many FSPs hold themselves out as being superior fund pickers? "Fund picking" is a thoroughly discredited value proposition in today's financial services industry. Unfortunately, the majority of consumers fail to see it that way, having been bamboozled by a plethora of self-serving books, magazines, newsletters and websites dedicated to identifying top performers to assist people with their investment decisions. These "resources" are really just perpetuating the myth of fund picking as a science.

In sales parlance, this is called a "presumptive close." For example, a salesperson might say, "Which would you prefer, a meeting next Tuesday morning or Tuesday afternoon?" Asking this question presumes that a meeting is both desired and required and that Tuesday is also available. Of course, this isn't necessarily so. The presumptiveness of mutual fund sales is more like this: "We have looked at both your circumstances and the funds available to meet your objectives. Which would you prefer, this Mackenzie Fund or that AGF Fund?" This kind of proposition, while seemingly innocuous, is full of presumptions. These include:

- that investing is the logical next step
- that the client needs a mutual fund as opposed to another product
- that the funds noted are the best alternatives in the universe of available funds
- that the decision at hand is primarily one of fund picking rather than asset allocation, tax minimization or some other objective
- that superior funds can be reliably identified
- that the FSP is uniquely qualified to identify superior funds

Perhaps the client response to many of these presuppositions is that the presumptions are, in fact, correct. Perhaps most of the presumptions were entirely correct. But what if one or two were, well, presumptuous? For instance, what if the two funds noted are in an asset class that already represents over half of the client's portfolio? At that point, wouldn't it be more appropriate to talk about strategic asset allocation before jumping ahead to fund picking?

Most conspicuously, the sheer volume of information rating funds infers that there must be something to it. After all, why else would so much energy be put into analyzing, compiling and ultimately comparing performance? The reason these sources exist as ubiquitous reference points, is that people use them. Tautologically, people use them because they believe they are useful. People believe the reference sources are useful because the reference sources say they're useful. But are they really? Unfortunately, behavioural finance shows us that most people use these services in exactly the wrong way. They end up buying high (based on relatively recent performance) and selling as soon as there's a sign of weakness. It seems rating services are only useful in exacerbating self-destructive behaviour. Ironically, FSPs can often temper this behaviour through a more sanguine outlook and improved perspective.

At the peak of the mutual fund craze in the 1990s, there were seven mutual fund rating books available to Canadian consumers. Why so many books if, as the books themselves imply, top performing funds can be reliably identified before the fact? Wouldn't one book suffice? Wouldn't they all be identifying the same funds? Why was there so little consensus on which funds were likely to be top performers? Which sources should consumers believe?

Given the massive divergence in mutual fund rating books on which funds were best (read: likely to outperform in the future), there can only be two possible explanations: one of them is essentially right and the others are wrong or they are all wrong. Guess which explanation industry watchers have coalesced around. The lack of credibility of fund picking, combined with the conspicuous saturation of the marketplace, has led to the reduction of annual mutual fund guide manuals. There are only three available in 2003. There will be no more than two in 2004. Here's to getting the number down to zero. Those who have stopped publishing at least had the decency to implicitly acknowledge that their research wasn't doing what it set out to do. Those "gurus" who continue to publish do so largely because consumers continue to buy their books in spite of the lack of credible evidence contained therein.

These fund-ranking manuals can't even agree with themselves (as opposed to amongst themselves) regarding which mutual funds are best. I took a look at a 1999 edition of one of these books and then looked at the 2002 edition compiled by the same author. Of the one hundred funds recommended in 1999, only twenty-three appeared in the 2002 edition. Not all of those twenty-three funds were recommended in each of the years in between, either. Isn't that an implicit message to trade mutual funds, like stocks, rather than to buy and hold? If quality products can indeed be identified before the fact and are to be held for the long term, why is the recommended list so malleable? One obvious reason is built-in obsolescence. If this year's edition was nearly identical to last year's, even the most naïve dupes on the market might resist buying it.

Fund ranking books, magazines, newsletters and websites are what industry consultant John Bowen of CEG Worldwide calls "investment pornography"— it gets people all excited, but in the end it doesn't amount to much. More to the point, the kind of flavour-du-jour information so readily accessible on the Internet surely doesn't pass as wisdom or advice. Research shows that consumers generally do the opposite of what they are constantly and tritely admonished to do: buy low and sell high. Instead, consumers, especially when left to their own devices, tend to buy whatever fund or asset class has the highest rating, which is based primarily on short-term performance, which is just another way of saying they "buy high."

The rationale of fund picking can be quite amusing. Imagine if a consumer bought a mutual fund book in 1999 and used it to make purchases of $100,000 into a balanced portfolio of eight funds. That same consumer could then pick up a 2002 edition of the same book and could, based on its contents, be inclined to sell six of those original eight funds in order to be sure he only had current highly recommended funds in his portfolio. Does this pass as "long-term investing?"

Furthermore, these books don't tell you what to do with previously purchased funds once they fall out of favour. Rather, the authors simply put out new editions every year in the hope that consumers will "get their fix" by forking over another $20 or more to see who made this year's not-so-short list.

Just how reliable should mutual fund ranking books be anyway? For instance, if one were to throw darts at a business section to identify funds, one would expect to find a randomly distributed cross-section of the industry. For instance, one hundred funds might feature approximately twenty-five funds in each of the first, second, third, and fourth quartiles. Obviously, it would be unreasonable to expect all funds identified by ranking services to be top performers all the time. The mutual fund industry features disclaimers that stress variability of returns, the fact that previous returns may not be repeated and the highly unpredictable nature of the industry. Even as all this "research" is painstakingly set out, it is just as painstakingly disclaimed.

What's the difference between a card-carrying member of the Flat Earth Society and a fund picker? One of them clings to a world view that has been thoroughly discredited by empirical research. The other thinks the Earth is flat.

Perhaps we could take a page from the cigarette industry. Legislators ultimately became so fed up with the societal costs associated with smoking, that they took what seemed like radical action. They couldn't stop people from smoking (remember that everyone has a right to be wrong), but they could put a bold disclaimer on every package attesting to the harmful effects of smoking to any would-be purchasers. The tobacco industry had been silent on many of these matters, in the hope that no one would notice, just as the financial services industry has been silent on matters of security selection. A parallel solution would be to put a vivid disclaimer on all mutual fund prospectuses. Much like cigarette package disclaimers, these could state certain relevant points in bold, unmistakable messages:

- most active managers lag their benchmark in the long run
- the few who beat their benchmark cannot be reliably identified beforehand
- security selection explains very little in terms of relative variance on average
- passive strategies are generally purer and more tax efficient than active ones

You get the picture. Of course, critics would say this is a "radical and wholly unnecessary approach." That's debatable. Professional FSPs wouldn't want to be lumped in with small-town hoodlums who peddle cigarettes to high-school students on the side. Professional physicians are certainly thankful for the cigarette disclaimers. They don't want any of the liability associated with cigarette smoking to trickle down to them, in case there's some smoker under a rock somewhere who hasn't heard that smoking can be hazardous to your health. By doing it this way, anyone who wanted to buy an actively managed fund would still be entirely free to do so. One would think compliance departments would be delighted, marketing departments a little less so. At least this way, the possibility of a class action suit from investors who lagged their benchmark index for a fund that has an objective of "superior performance relative to its index in the long run" would be covered.

Speaking of which, have you ever wondered why most mutual funds compare their performance to other mutual funds rather than to the index they are benchmarked against? It shouldn't be too surprising, given that the majority *again!* of funds lag their benchmark in the long run. Better to compare yourself against your peers than against the yardstick you ought to use if your peers are easier to beat. By way of illustration, I spoke with Morningstar Canada and asked them to look into mutual fund returns for Canadian and U.S. equity funds offered in Canada over the last ten years.

There are 146 actively managed Canadian equity funds that have a ten-year track record. Of these, fifty-eight beat the ten-year annualized S&P/TSX composite return of 9.07% through to December 31, 2002. That's just under 40%. The American funds did far worse. There are forty-five actively managed US equity funds that have a ten-year track record in Canada. Only three of these funds beat the ten-year annualized S&P return (in Canadian dollars) of 11.7% for the ten years ended December 31, 2002. That's less than 7%. Study after study has shown that as the time horizon extends further, the likelihood of active management beating the index becomes increasingly unlikely. In *11* light of this, how professional is it for FSPs to exclusively recommend active management to their clients? Does anyone really believe "good FSPs" would have reliably identified the three that outperformed? If so, why is there so much money invested in the other 42 funds?

3. *Managing the Relationship*

In spite of all the shortcomings associated with how many FSPs work, their advice remains invaluable to millions of Canadians. So often, consumers who work with FSPs are inclined to fire their FSPs when the funds recommended lag their peer group. They do this in spite of the virtual impossibility of picking consistently top performers. In fairness, many FSPs have no one but themselves to blame if their "value proposition" is picking funds. It often doesn't matter if a fund has done well for three or four consecutive years. Sometimes consumers fire their FSPs because one or more of the recommended funds lagged their peer group and/or benchmark over a certain period. Many FSPs continue to try their hand at fund picking in spite of the overwhelming evidence that it cannot be reliably accomplished. *k?*

Why then do so few FSPs recommend index-based products? In a world where FSPs should only take the credit or endure the wrath from clients where they can be reasonably expected to control outcomes, surely they should not have to endure being fired due to funds that underperform, either temporarily or over a longer time frame. Fund managers will do what they do and there is no way FSPs can alter their behaviour. Yet often that's exactly what happens: a manager performs poorly for whatever reason and consumers take it out on the FSP who recommended the use of that manager's fund.

If FSPs want the credit for "good" fund picking, then they have to take the heat that comes with "bad" fund picking. Knowing that to be the case and that the entire undertaking is hopelessly unreliable, why would any self-respecting, *professional* FSP ever hold herself out as a fund picker in the first place? It's a murky value proposition at the outset and even if most of the funds recommended beat their peers, as soon as one doesn't, the client will justifiably say, "Why did you recommend this load of hooey?"

If FSPs are truly sincere about working with clients in a way that focuses strictly on the things that are controllable and measurable, they should be prepared to embrace the notion of using index-based investments for at least part of their recommended portfolios. If a client agrees on the strategy of indexing, she has no basis for firing an FSP based on manager performance. The index investment, if properly constructed, will perform as the index it tracks performs, minus a small cost, plus or minus a modest tracking error. As long as this is understood at the outset, it will allow both the FSP and the client to focus on the things that are truly important in the relationship: asset allocation and rebalancing decisions, tax strategies and estate planning considerations. That said, if the client wants a traditional portfolio of 100% active investment options, that should be fine, too, provided suitable disclosures are made. The point is that no FSP should be unduly enamoured with, or opposed to, active or passive products. Professionals should simply tell the whole truth and then let the client decide what works best.

The FSP's job is to get clients retired and keep them retired in the lifestyle they have come to expect by making smart financial decisions over the course of the relationship. In other words, the FSP's job, if contemplated honestly, is *not* to beat any index or mix of indexes. It never was. Unfortunately, the sales element of the industry grabbed hold of the agenda in the go-go days of the 1990s. Today, we all have to step back and reconsider what elements of advice really add value.

4. Marketing Expenses

The true no-load companies do not spend nearly as much money on marketing as do those companies that have embedded compensation. Many spend nothing at all. One of the reasons why management expense ratios (MERs) are higher for mutual funds with embedded compensation is that they charge more than other funds so they can market their funds. As a result, although FSPs are allowed to approach fund companies for "co-op" marketing expenses, it is only those companies with embedded compensation who are willing and able to provide co-op marketing support. Where permitted, marketing expenses are split fifty-fifty between the FSP and the mutual fund company.

It used to be worse. In the 1990s, some mutual fund companies were offering 100% co-op marketing support for "top producers," prompting some FSPs to run seminars and the like as profit centres. The first dime of new business was pure profit for them.

Wouldn't it be reasonable to outlaw co-op marketing entirely, since it allows FSPs to gain access to fifty-cent dollars to "build their business" from some companies, while others (those who try to control costs for consumers through lower MERs) do not offer subsidized marketing? As with embedded compensation, as soon as there is money to be made (in this case, a penny reimbursed is a penny earned) by recommending one product over another, there is an opportunity for bias and bias compromises true professionalism. The existing practice effectively punishes those companies that are making a meaningful effort to control costs. By refusing to offer subsidized marketing support, conscientious companies are not finding their way onto FSPs' recommended lists.

5. Lessons in Economics

If clients are indifferent about how their FSP is paid, yet FSPs have a definite preference for one model over another, what are we missing? The difference is in something economists and financial analysts call the "Time Preference of Money." If earnings are about the same amount over time, people generally prefer the option that pays the most in the early years. Most people (and most rational, self-interested FSPs) prefer to get more money sooner. This leads to an interesting question: By how much would the recurring FSP compensation have to increase in order to bring the ratio of fee-based and commission-based sales to fifty-fifty (i.e., for FSPs to be indifferent as to the compensation model used)?

Stated differently, by what amount does one need to increase recurring annual fee compensation so that the FSP has no expressed preference between being paid for working on a commission-based model as opposed to a fee-based model? The notion here is something economists call an indifference curve. Wouldn't there be a sensitivity involved where recurring revenue would be proportionately higher for smaller accounts and relatively lower for large ones in recognition of economies of scale and practice economics? Important questions, yet no one has ever polled FSPs to ask them.

An economist who has a lesson for us is Vilfredo Pareto, who suggested that economic decisions should be made, to the greatest extent possible, where one or more parties are better off and no one is worse off. In applying his thinking, we'll need to find ways to transform the industry of selling financial products into the profession of offering financial advice. Because there are risks and limitations associated for both clients and FSPs, each needs to be made aware of the obligations and sacrifices of the other. Controls need to be put in place to ensure FSPs do not abuse their positions of trust in transforming themselves from salespeople into professionals. That's because there are particular abuses that might manifest themselves in dangerous ways if creative and self-interested FSPs are allowed to unilaterally dictate the terms by which they will transform themselves.

Some FSPs are forging ahead quickly in the hope of gaining an "early mover advantage" over the competition (other FSPs).

Remember that inertia is a natural part of the human condition; clients will have to be educated regarding the benefits of new business models and the advice being offered through them. The FSPs who are the "early adopters" therefore have a number of things working against them:

• Reduced income as they move from a commission-based sales paradigm to a fee-based professional paradigm, since commission income needs to be foregone in the short-term.

• The derision of commission-based peers who want them to fail out of personal self-interest.

• A large number of clients who take an "if it ain't broke, don't fix it" attitude to their working relationship.

Unfortunately, these clients often don't understand the industry well enough to pass a meaningful judgement on what the industry needs.

What Next?

As the consensus emerges on how the financial services industry will evolve over time, the next questions revolve around what needs to be done to ensure an honourable and responsible transition to the end game that is fairly clear. In essence, everyone in the industry agrees that fees are here to stay and that commissions are on the way out. The only things left to be decided are how and when this change is going to occur. Obviously, if everyone understands where we are and everyone agrees on where we're going, then the next question must surely be to determine how to get there from here. Having come this far, it seems pointless to delay further. The most important attribute that has to be ensured now, is that everyone fully understands the rationale and benefits associated with abolishing embedded compensation and in moving to direct and transparent fees. Everything else flows logically from that one change in the landscape.

EXPLANATORY VARIABLES AND BEHAVIOURAL FINANCE

The principal reason for articulating long-term investment policy explicitly and in writing is to enable the client and portfolio manager to protect the portfolio from ad hoc revisions of sound long-term policy, and to help them hold to long-term policy when short-term exigencies are most distressing and the policy is most in doubt.

—Charles Ellis

I can calculate the motion of heavenly bodies, but not the madness of people.

—Sir Isaac Newton

The phrase "you're only human," is used almost daily in describing the foibles of life. Plenty of people make mistakes on a routine basis, but most people don't get too upset about this because, hey, you're only human. Part of our humanity is that we do things that we know we shouldn't. We persist because of entrenched habits or the feeling we get when we treat ourselves. In some instances, we procrastinate because we don't want to deal with certain responsibilities or obligations that we've been putting off.

One of the most interesting aspects of being human is that we sometimes focus on things that are fun, while ignoring other things that are more purposeful. For consumers and FSPs alike, this can manifest itself in some perverse ways. For instance, even though there is a mountain of research that shows many aspects of economics to be the "dismal science," since it is so often thrown off course by human behaviour, there are generations of people who have gone through our school systems to get formal training in "classical" economics. Markets don't always behave the way they're supposed to because markets are just the sum total of a large number of people and sometimes people make weird decisions.

The expectation economists have is that on the whole, markets are efficient and decisions are rational. Unfortunately, people are human, so many observable "macro" trends don't always play out neatly in a "micro" sense. This quirk of human nature certainly has applications in the field of financial advice. From a planning perspective, there are just too many things that people don't focus on because they seem like the sorts of things that "would never happen to me." Human nature is a major deterrent to life insurance purchases, for instance. It also explains why so many of us still don't have Wills and Powers of Attorney in place.

When it comes to investing, most people (consumers and FSPs alike) tend to focus on the headlines of the day, topical concerns like: What will the central bank do at its next meeting? Will lobbying efforts lead to tax breaks in the next budget? How did my favourite stock/mutual fund do yesterday? In the grand scheme of things, none of this matters.

Sadly, there's a circular logic going on here. People are interested in these sorts of things, so that's what newspapers write about. Then, because people see these things written about in newspapers, they delude themselves that they must be important, otherwise why write about them? A vicious cycle of focusing on things that don't really matter is perpetuating itself as we speak and we're all complicit in its continuation. This is the sort of thinking that Steven Covey talks about when he says people tend to focus on things that are merely urgent, rather than genuinely important in life. But if all these things are unimportant, then what are the things that are truly important regarding financial planning and advice?

Does Anyone Understand Gary Brinson?

Back in 1986, some groundbreaking work was done on the subject of the determinants of portfolio performance. Updated in the early 1990s, research done by Gary Brinson and his team delivered the following finding: "Data from ninety-one large U.S. pension plans indicate that investment policy dominates investment strategy, explaining *on average* 93.6% of the *variation* in total plan return." (emphasis mine)

The language used in the study was sufficiently imprecise, and the training of people who read it was so weak that it may well go down as one of the most misquoted pieces of scholarship in modern history. Everyone in the financial services industry wanted to quote the research, but few people really understood it. They talked about asset allocation, explaining mostly the return rather than average variability. They ignored the fact that investment policy includes deciding which asset classes to use in the first place. They twisted the research to get it to say whatever their marketing department wanted it to say, which usually had little to do with the actual findings.

Brinson's research broke down the investment management process into three decisions, made sequentially. They were:

1. Choosing the asset classes to be used
2. Choosing the normal weightings of those classes
3. Selecting the securities to populate the portfolio

When it comes to investment decision-making, he showed that the tail is wagging the dog and has been for as long as people have been investing. Brinson defined the first two decisions as the investment policy and third as the investment strategy. Since investment policy was comprised of both the asset classes used and the percentage mix of those classes, it was shown that there are two ways to increase returns while holding risk constant. First, one could alter the asset classes used to construct the portfolio. Second, one could alter the weighting of those asset classes.

Brinson demonstrated that the third and final decision explains very little in terms of the average variability of returns. Almost all the average variability in returns was explained by the first two decisions. Yet which of these three decisions does the media focus on almost exclusively? The third. Which of these three decisions do most of us generally focus on? The third. Remember that when I say "most of us," I'm referring to *both FSPs and consumers.*

A number of years ago, I had an epiphany of sorts. A wrap program I was recommending to many of my clients had just undergone a fairly significant product enhancement. New RRSP-eligible investment pools were being introduced to allow clients the opportunity to legally skirt the foreign content restrictions in RRSPs, which had just been increased to 30% of the book value of the amount invested. Pools are essentially like mutual funds, the asset class building blocks of portfolios. The newly minted higher foreign content limit for registered plans combined with new RRSP-eligible pools, meant a lot of clients went from just under 20% foreign content to over 50% foreign content in their registered portfolios. By adding these new pools, clients were able to *enhance their returns without changing their risk tolerance.*

Over the months that followed the introduction of these new investment pools, clients were sent revisions to their Investment Policy Statements that showed how their expected return (the "Managed Account Premium") would increase, while the expected standard deviation of their portfolios would remain unchanged. In effect, these new pools had extended the so-called "efficient frontier" of how well they could do on a risk-adjusted basis. More precisely, the pools allowed the program to develop an entirely new frontier that was superior to the old one at all levels of risk tolerance. Expected returns increased, while expected risk remained unchanged. Remember this diagram, we'll be referring back to it later.

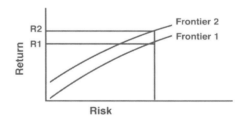

Best of all, the changes were entirely consistent with the responses given to the questionnaire used to design the original portfolio. My epiphany, therefore, was a direct result of the validity and importance of decision number 2. The same asset classes that had always been used were now being used *in different proportions than had previously been the case* and had improved the universe of possible client portfolios as a result. This all came about through the intrepid circumvention of Canada Customs and Revenue Agency's foreign content limits.

John J. De Goey

Most people in the financial services industry (but especially media pundits) still focus on decision number 3, while evidence suggests that decision numbers 1 and 2 are far more important. In fact, anyone who believes that asset allocation dominates portfolio return considerations should refrain from timing the market or engaging in either stock picking or fund picking. That's almost never what happens in practice. As a result, Professor John Nuttall at the University of Western Ontario has this to say about the repeated misuse of the Brinson research: "instead of being the knowledgeable experts that the marketing machine portrays them to be, thousands of professionals of many varieties do not understand the products the industry is selling."

Instead of understanding their own products, there has been an industry-wide dogma expounding the primacy of strategic asset allocation, whereby most people adhering to the dogma have likely never even read the Brinson research, much less understood it. Some of the most prominent consulting firms in the industry, including Ibbotson Associates, BARRA and William M. Mercer have inadvertently misquoted and/or misrepresented the Brinson findings, although Roger Ibbotson has recently revised his position.

What FSPs Shouldn't Be Doing

For most people, investing is about picking investments, be they stocks, bonds, Exchange Traded Funds (ETFs), mutual funds or anything else. At the end of the day, these decisions mean little. Often, FSPs focus on attributes like style diversification, rather than on asset class diversification, even though Brinson clearly shows that considerations like style diversification are also nearly useless since they're investment strategy (number 3 type) decisions. For instance, an FSP might recommend adding a growth manager to compliment a pre-existing value manager, rather than looking for entirely new asset classes that, when added prudently to the investments already in place, would serve to "extend the frontier" much further than the style diversification alternatives being considered.

In spite of this research, which has been cited almost endlessly for over eighteen years, the vast majority of FSPs hold themselves out as "adding value" by picking stocks and/or picking funds. The Brinson research showed that security selection accounted for less than 5% of any given portfolio's variance in performance and the effect was often negative. People in general, and FSPs and the media in particular, have simply been focusing on all the wrong things in their reading, writing and investing.

Real professionals don't engage in anything other than abstract discussions about the direction or timing of the market or the performance of individual funds or pools. Everyone who has even implied a predictive causality should offer a massive mea culpa and move immediately to rectify the misconceptions that they themselves have perpetrated as a result of their focus on investment strategy decisions. Consumers and FSPs alike should spend most of their time reviewing and adhering to Investment Policy Statements and looking for planning opportunities that go beyond specific products.

If the job of the FSP is to prevent clients from making "the big mistake," then any number 3-type decision falls into that category by definition. Making a mountain out of a molehill is a mistake. In short, FSPs should be doing everything in their power to assist clients in focusing on decisions numbers 1 and 2. Decision number 3 is simply unimportant in a relative sense (and possibly an absolute sense too), yet that's where the vast majority of discussions and ensuing behavioural errors occur. Considered differently, this means FSPs shouldn't care whether consumers buy fund X or fund Y, as long as it meets the criteria set out in decision numbers 1 and 2.

Instead of focusing on things that are controllable (cost, asset class purity, tax efficiency), the majority of us focus on the most random and uncontrollable element of portfolio design: performance as gained or lost through type number 3 decisions. In fact, there's a whole army of people from all avenues of the financial services industry who frequent websites, read entire magazines and newspaper sections and, worst of all, devour *annual* books devoted to perpetuating the myth of fund picking. They're like modern-day alchemists.

Perhaps it's more fun to focus on security selection and market timing decisions. Most consumers are generally unwilling to pay more than a few basis points for services that optimize portfolios with a wide range of asset classes and regularly rebalance those portfolios back to those targets. There's not much profit margin available in promoting decision numbers 1 and 2, even though they are highly important. On the other hand, there's a whole lot of money to be made in the monolith that is the industry focusing on decision number 3, even though doing so is almost useless.

No self-respecting professional would stoop to engage in decision number 3 type activity. Any professional who is serious about putting the interests of the client first, would simply have to acknowledge that the employment of active management is, to some extent at least, an exercise in profit maximization. The industry has shot itself in the foot. Having convinced all of society (and especially the media) that security selection is actually worth something, it can't kick the habit and come clean with the whole truth because this would pummel its profitability. Instead, the industry talks about the vital importance of investment policy decisions, charges additional fees for services that respond to the void in the marketplace and remains silent in the matter of investment strategy. Let's take a closer look at Brinson's three decisions.

Decision 1

The choice of asset classes matters greatly and the concept of how much one investment moves in relation to another is called correlation. Correlation is vital when contemplating which asset classes will be used in constructing a portfolio. Just as combinations of risky stocks exhibit less risk than individual securities themselves, combinations of asset classes can have less risk than individual asset classes. Two investments that move in lockstep have a correlation coefficient of 1.0. Those that move in exactly opposite directions have a correlation coefficient of –1.0. Those that move randomly, where movement in one asset class has no bearing on the movement of another, have a correlation coefficient of 0. These are said to be non-correlated. Asset classes that move similarly are said to be highly correlated, while those that move somewhat similarly are said to be weakly correlated and those that move in opposite directions (even if only modestly) are said to be negatively correlated. Most asset classes are at least somewhat positively correlated.

In general, the less asset classes are correlated, the more they lower portfolio risk. It is also important that these asset classes are not particularly volatile of and by themselves. Research done by Ibbotson Associates in Chicago shows that risk decreases as the number of randomly selected asset classes increases. Diversification improves the risk/ return trade-off and the best form of diversification is to add more asset classes.[4]

In most instances, any twelve-month period would see some asset classes go up and others go down. It is rare indeed to have all asset classes move in the same direction over even a relatively short time frame. According to information from Globe HySales, the decade from 1992 to 2002 saw only one year where major asset classes all went up. That year was 1996, when Canadian stocks, U.S. stocks, European stocks, Asian stocks, Emerging Markets stocks, Real Estate, Canadian Bonds, Foreign Bonds and cash all had positive gains. Is it any wonder that consumers had unreasonably high expectations of return and significantly underestimated portfolio risk in the 1990s? Risk can be thought of as the range of possible outcomes for any given asset class over any given period of time. We have no control over capital markets, only focus and discipline regarding our own behaviour.

As a general rule, the more asset classes available in the universe of investment options, the better off you are. Therefore, the old view of asset classes being narrowly defined as domestic stocks, bonds and cash is clearly a limiting factor. What amazes me is that marketing people talk about how having five or six asset classes is far superior to having three or four. That may be true, but wouldn't having eleven or twelve asset classes (including sectors and sub-categories) be better still? That doesn't mean all these asset classes have to be used, just that they should be available in case you choose to use them.

Decision 2

The second decision that Gary Brinson says investors need to make pertains to the proportions of the asset classes used by investors. As we saw earlier, changing the mix can go a long way to enhancing return and risk needn't necessarily increase as a result. The discipline of decision number 2 should be enforced through an Investment Policy Statement (IPS). The Japanese have a saying that applies: "A goal without a number is just a slogan."

Any strategic asset allocation needs to be formally written down so that it can be purposefully adhered to. Whatever number is chosen, there should be a written discipline to rebalance back to that target. It might be done automatically or manually. It might be done when there's a significant market movement (e.g., a 10% contingent model) or at a prescribed point in time (an annual meeting and portfolio review). How and when it is done is secondary. The important point is that once an asset allocation is set, there should be a system in place to keep it within those parameters.

Be extra careful when using actively managed mutual funds. One of the major drawbacks of the mutual fund industry today is that virtually none of the funds are pure; they all have multiple asset classes (including cash) within them. As a result, meaningful control over a precisely defined asset allocation can be nearly impossible.

Decision 3

The third decision is where virtually the entire industry lives: picking stocks and funds and timing the market. This is nearly useless. To begin, active management is not a precondition of strategic asset allocation, in fact, it can be a significant hindrance. Actively managed pools of capital are by definition less pure than asset class indices. In other words, the tendency to pursue decision 3 using mutual funds almost certainly compromises control over decision 2 to some extent. Since decision 2 is more important, why would a rational person skip over it just to get to decision number 3? The degree of compromise depends on how pure are the pools of capital in question.

As soon as an FSP recommends one manager over another, it automatically begs the question "Why did you recommend this manager?" If security selection is such a minor explanatory variable as to be nearly insignificant, one wonders why any serious thought should be given to manager selection at all. How professional is it to make a big deal out of something that explains very little? Why not just buy the asset class? At least that way, the FSP doesn't have to be bogged down in counterproductive debates about funds being in the third or fourth quartile, when they were in the first quartile for three consecutive years before the recommendation was made.

Obviously, FSPs have to recommend something. Since they should be logically indifferent between active and passive management, why not let the consumer decide? *Is there any better and more compelling way to communicate the relative unimportance of security selection?* If it was a big deal, surely the FSP would have a strong opinion. Since we all know now that it's not a big deal, why should an FSP care either way?

Anyone who looks at empirical research and then puts the interests of the client first would be hard-pressed to give a compelling answer. Anyone who is truly committed to the primacy of strategic asset allocation should be comfortable with using investment options that seek to replicate the index they are benchmarked against in the purest, simplest, cheapest and most tax efficient form available. Truly professional FSPs should be indifferent towards active or passive management. They should simply spell out the pros and cons, risks and limitations of each and then let the client decide based on his or her own comfort level.

In a court of law, those taking the stand are mandated to tell the truth, *the whole truth* and nothing but the truth. Virtually every firm in the industry today goes out of its way to downplay the incontrovertible fact that the fees they are charging for portfolio management as it pertains to security selection within an asset class usually do more to benefit themselves than their clients. They are deliberately telling less than the whole story. Obviously, these firms and the FSPs who work there do a number of very good things too and are quite concerned about the welfare of their clients. Nonetheless, when all the cards are not on the table, there is a crying need to clean up the system. We need to put an end to the misinformation that has willfully been allowed to take root by financial advisory firms, their employees and most of the media.

The surest ways to improve risk-adjusted returns are to either alter the mix of existing investment options or to add new asset classes that have favourable risk/return characteristics. These asset classes might be the kind that work well by themselves, but are particularly effective in improving trade-offs when combined with other asset classes. Alternative asset classes, therefore, are excellent diversifiers that belong in virtually all portfolios.

The logic involved with progress is often perverse. Before we become too self-satisfied with how previous generations resisted change, let's take a step back. We all need to understand that people often do things a certain way simply because they "were always done that way." Business schools have been teaching technical analysis for about as long as they've been around.

How many people go through life saying things like, "I don't believe in insurance," even though they never take the time to assess how the proper use of insurance might assist them in meeting their retirement objectives, estate planning needs and deal with latent tax problems? Old biases die hard and although we hate to admit it, everyone has biases of one kind or another, often based on actual life experiences.

The Big Mistake

It should be obvious by now that any focus on decisions about investment strategy is counterproductive. Since that's where the media and the world outside would have consumers look if left to their own devices, FSPs have a daunting task ahead of them. They have to keep clients focused on what's important, even as they are bombarded with unimportant information about what's topical, newsy and just plain more interesting.

Most investment errors are emotional errors driven by a lack of resolve that stems from societal pressure to act a certain way. Of critical importance, therefore, is the idea that FSPs need to be trained in how to constructively get their clients to tune out of the culture of CNBC's and RoB TV's investment pornography and to focus on things that actually matter. As soon as someone is seduced by investment pornography, they're prone to do something stupid with their money. Focusing on the wrong things can lead to making wrong decisions. If FSPs can just get their clients to keep their eyes on the things that matter, they will have likely earned their fees. The simple role of the FSP is to ensure his clients avoid "the big mistake."

Of all the advances in the field of personal finance, there is likely nothing more important than the discoveries of Behavioural Finance. Behavioural Finance is the study of how emotional decisions caused by human factors often lead to poor investment choices and reduced investment returns. There's a growing body of research that demonstrates how this "human side" of investment decision-making has a major impact on actual performance outcomes. In spite of this, there's no reference in any textbook for FSPs to teach them how to deal with the roadblocks associated with their clients' emotions and stay the course through constructive behaviour modification. *(teaching.)*

Daniel Kahneman and Amos Tversky are two of the most influential social scientists of the twentieth century, yet few people have heard of them. Their research into decision-making has precipitated a sea change in economics. These psychologists have conducted extensive research on how people perceive and react to uncertainty. In 2002, Kahneman was awarded the Nobel Prize in Economics together with experimental economist Vernon Smith. In essence, they demonstrated that people don't always think rationally and behave optimally regarding their decisions, especially when it pertains to their own money. People don't usually understand risk in terms of both the likelihood of something happening and the degree of damage that might be inflicted if it does happen. That's also likely one of the reasons so few people carry the right kind and right amount of life insurance.

Qualified FSPs can be useful in offering reasonable counsel that comes from a perspective that should mitigate these tendencies. In spite of this, FSPs receive *no formal training* in the field of behavioural finance. There are literally thousands of FSPs working today who had to demonstrate the ability to calculate intrinsic values of special warrants and to calculate the price of a security trading ex-dividend and cum-dividend. In reality, most never use these sorts of skills after writing their licencing exam. The course material did nothing to explain concepts like anchoring or loss aversion, even though these and other emotional and intellectual blind spots go a long way to explaining investment experience.

The financial services industry has trained an army of representatives to be salesmen, not true advisors. Any advisor worth his salt would understand that advice needs to be offered from the client's perspective and that (whether rational or not), that client is going to feel overwhelmed by some of the complexity and uncertainty of capital markets. The university courses leading to an advanced degree in financial planning, therefore, need to add an entire body of work to their course material dealing with tangible case study approaches on how to assist consumers in staying the course and avoiding "the big mistake."

Imagine the good that qualified FSPs could do if educators actually taught them how to apply solutions to these problems. It turns out that the best FSPs are like personal trainers. After all, anyone can workout on their own, but those who have someone with them to coach them and maintain a discipline just seem to do better.

Ironically, Kahneman and Tversky are also two of the biggest allies the fund pickers have. People engaged in the business of security selection argue that if people make repeated mistakes regarding risk and reward, then clearly capital markets must not be altogether efficient. This is only partially compelling. The behavioural finance research deals with discreet decisions made by individual investors, whereas "the market" is actually the sum total of all investors (private and institutional; large and small) that reacts to information as it becomes available. Even though individual investors might make inappropriate investment decisions, the market as a whole might not.

That's the essence of the problem. On the surface, many consumers have sufficient knowledge of capital markets to make adequate financial decisions. In spite of this, there is the irrefutable evidence that shows massive net redemptions when mutual fund values are dropping and massive net sales when markets are on fire. If the phrase "buy low; sell high" is such a trite little truism that any fool can understand, why do so many people ignore it and do just the opposite? Similarly, if the admonition to diversify is so basic that it is seen as a "motherhood" issue that everyone understands and agrees with, why were so many people wildly overweight in technology when the bubble burst in 2000?

Consumers, if left to their own devices, will frequently make emotional decisions during market swings and manias, even if they later acknowledge (usually with the "benefit" of twenty-twenty hindsight) that they were not making logical decisions at the time. In fact, people can make irrational decisions even when markets are behaving "normally," if such a phrase can be used at all. Professional FSPs should be able to save well-intentioned consumers from themselves in these times of weakness.

Dr. Meir Statman of Dimensional Fund Advisors is a leading authority on behavioural finance. He offers a number of examples of how our outlook on anything is really just a function of our vantage point relative to the thing we are observing.

Here's an example. At its origin in 1896, the Dow Jones Industrial Average stood at 41 (that's not a typo—it's forty-one). By the end of 1998, it stood at 9,181, a number exponentially higher. Here's the question: what number would the DJIA have stood at in 1998 if all the dividends paid were reinvested? Can you guess? It turns out that most people guess somewhere between 30,000 and 80,000, which seems plausible enough. The actual answer is 652,230. The simple reason most people guess far, far too low is a concept called anchoring. People use the figure of 9,181 as an "anchor" to their guess and make a significant cognitive error in the process. Most people never expect it to be possible for the actual number to be exponentially higher all over again.

We all make cognitive errors because the brain is designed to deal with the important problems in life, but the perspective the brain uses to deal with more complex problems isn't always accurate. Being mindful of behavioural finance, we can see how FSPs can be useful in helping people to see newer, more accurate realities.

Here's an example of how an FSP might utilize the principles of behavioural finance to give a client a better sense of perspective, which hopefully leads to a better decision. Let's say an FSP is talking to a client who wants to impulsively buy or sell an investment. The FSP could point out that there are two parties to every transaction and that (since investing is a zero sum game), only one of them can "win" in the assessment of the purchase or sale in question. Who's the buyer and who's the seller and why are you so certain you know more than that person? There's an old saying that if you're playing poker and looking around the table trying to figure out who the "patsy" is and can't figure out who it is, then it's probably you.

As a result, the professional FSP can play many vital roles. As an educator, she can teach clients how to frame their expectations. As a coach, she can help them retain a proper focus. As a financial physician, she can work to find the best treatment available *based on investment science*. Along with these important roles come a number of important challenges. These include convincing clients that their own brain often lies to them and keeping investors calm.

When I talk to friends who move up the corporate ladder and into management, many say their biggest challenge is "managing people." I think to myself that they don't know how easy they have it. *Professional FSPs have to manage people who are often irrational, emotional and unaware of their own biases in dealing with their life's savings!*

A 2001 Dalbar study came up with similar results regarding behaviour and performance. It showed that during the seventeen years form 1984-2000, the average U.S. stock fund investor earned returns of only 5.32% a year, even though the S&P 500 returned 16.29% over that same time horizon—a stunning testimony to the importance of behaviour in investing.[5]

We'll revisit this curiosity using more current data in a future chapter when looking at the things that do and don't add value for investors. For now, let's just recognize that emotional investment decisions based on seemingly logical objectives are often undermined by the biases and blind spots that all of us have. Poor investment choices are made all the time and they usually end up costing people money—even though the intent is to add value.

In fact, attempted market timing is a classic portfolio strategy error. Throughout history, market timers have come and gone, with no meaningful evidence of any capacity to predict things in a manner that is statistically significant. Market timing is simply the manifestation of a major cognitive error called "hindsight bias." After all, we all know that hindsight is twenty-twenty. There are now commercially available funds that attempt to time markets. Perhaps investors who want to engage in this practice could consider giving their money over to these people rather than trying to time markets themselves.

The world is full of stories about people who got into technology stocks because there was a sense that "this time was different." Books that talked about "new paradigms of security valuations" seduced people. One of the two primary drivers of human activity in capital markets, greed, had taken over in the late 1990s. Sadly, the third millennium brought a different storyline. In retrospect, many of the people who got in too late (and held on too long) admitted that they "should have seen it coming all along." That's hindsight bias. The past is always clear when viewed from the perspective of the present. By now, people should simply know that markets can't be reliably timed.

The most shameless element of the investment pornography industry (even worse than books that pick funds from year to year) is the raft of newsletters that forecast market movements from month to month. Independent research has shown that there is absolutely no relationship between newsletter forecasts and market performance. Some charlatans would have us believe that newsletters are actually a reverse indicator (i.e., that people would do well to do the opposite of what a newsletter suggests). Unfortunately, no relationship means just that—results are random. If newsletters were reliable negative indicators, they would still serve a useful purpose. Smart people would simply do the opposite of what the newsletters recommended.

Investors often behave badly due to any of a number of other behaviourally motivated biases: fear of regret, myopic loss aversion, cognitive dissonance, representativeness and overconfidence being the most likely remaining culprits. Research shows that *even those who do understand risk often act irrationally in spite of their comprehension of these concepts*. If the primary role of FSPs is to help their clients earn adequate returns while employing additional related wealth management services, then anything that assists in performing that role should be taught from the outset.

The New Keynesians

All this goes to show that the role of the professional FSP is both an interesting and unique one. On one hand, we're talking about people who know details about things that most people never think of. Most FSPs bombard clients with hard data, graphs, research reports and numerous more "serious" and quantifiable metrics explaining investment performance. Many can banter on regarding fixed income investments and the comparative merits of rate anticipation and relative value swaps the way most people talk about Saturday's hockey game. On the other hand, they have to stay tuned into their clients' deepest emotions if they ever hope to gain the necessary trust to get people to act in ways that are contrary to their natural instincts.

In short, a good FSP can be a valuable resource in understanding a number of concepts. Being a trusted financial professional goes well beyond managing money. Although FSPs know all about money, they have a particularly important role to play in educating their clients about themselves. Ironically, the word "educate" comes from the latin *educo*, which literally means to "draw out."

What is becoming increasingly clear in the context of financial advice is that most FSPs are left-brained people offering left-brained (i.e., logical and empirical) explanations for why things might happen and what to do in response. The trouble is, most people make financial decisions with the right side of their brain, the one that deals with the emotional aspects of decision-making. How much training do FSPs have these days to assist them in guiding their clients emotionally? The answer is usually none. In spite of this, behavioural finance is something most FSPs need to grapple with on a daily basis.

Let's use the ideas of another well-known economist to illustrate the coming together of both conventional economics and behavioural economics when explaining the role of a new age professional FSP. John Maynard Keynes was an extremely influential economist who posited that the primary role of governments was to mitigate the vagaries of the business cycle—to have highs that were less high and lows that were less low, while still growing the economy. His idea was sort of like portfolio design, in seeking adequate returns with acceptable levels of risk.

One of Keynes' most notable contributions to economics, was in the field of fiscal policy. He believed governments should spend more money (perhaps incurring a deficit) in order to stimulate the economy when things were slow *+ halt inflation* and then spend less (or tax more) when times were good to make up for any previously incurred shortfalls. One of the primary shortfalls of Keynesian economics was modern politics. Voters would be sure to throw out any politician who taxed more or spent less. In this context, no one should be surprised by first-world debt levels. *So it can't work in a democracy*

Still, Keynesian economics is a funny thing and more universal than you might otherwise think. Instead of looking at the financial stability of a nation, why not draw an analogy with an individual household? The most basic truism of investing is "buy low; sell high." Conceptually, FSPs have a role with their clients much like governments had in implementing Keynes's ideas. They have to get their clients to do things that they might not otherwise be inclined to do. Human nature being what it is, clients are inclined to buy when things are going up and to sell in a panic when the markets are heading south. Put another way, the role of a good Keynesian public policy administrator is to constructively temper the amplitude of the business cycle for the benefit of the greater public good. One might say that the parallel role of a good FSP is to temper the amplitude of client emotions. There's a distinct need to help people resist the temptation to buy just because the investment has been going up or to sell just because it has been going down.

To most people, money is an impenetrable topic that they wish someone could explain using plain language and simple concepts. There are still a large number of FSPs who consider it "beneath them" to employ techniques rooted in behavioural research, even if they were properly taught. Many FSPs who resist or are benignly ignorant of the findings of the behaviouralists, are probably still resisting the findings of Sharpe, Miller and Markowitz too. Give them time, they'll come around eventually. We might want to let the old school FSPs in on the fact that the allies won the war, too.

It is generally accepted (although there is little *reliable* empirical evidence) that good FSPs are usually useful in dealing with the concerns of behavioural finance. Pioneers in behavioural finance, like Richard Thaler at the University of Chicago, have done further academic research that demonstrates that when people are confused and anxious, they do irrational things like sell low and buy high, even as they profess to be sanguine, sensible, long-term investors.

Not everyone is behind the times though. One person who has been ahead of his time on this matter is Nick Murray. Murray is funny, witty, insightful and uncompromising all at once. He has written a number of books and counselled thousands of FSPs throughout a third of a century. One of his primary admonitions to FSPs is to stop watching markets and start watching peoples' lives. He tells FSPs to know their clients' anniversary dates, their children's and grandchildren's names, details about favourite authors, hobbies and vacation spots. He is, of course, entirely right—not because it's a good sales technique for FSPs to schmooze with their clients, but because the things most FSPs talk to their clients about are altogether the wrong things.

If FSPs really understood how most consumers of financial information think *before* they were allowed to go out and assist people in planning their financial futures, the world would be a richer place for it. In a business that's all about connecting and relating, we train our FSPs to be technically proficient in analyzing data that defies meaningful short-term analysis, yet we do a horrible job of training them in empowering the people they serve to take control of their lives by ignoring the investment pornography all around them.

Nick Murray is not talking about a triumph of compassion over competence here. He has argued convincingly for years that in order to be able to truly make a positive difference in peoples' lives, FSPs need to focus on things that are more important. He doesn't talk much about the vital importance of decision numbers 1 and 2, but he sure is adamant that decision number 3 is a complete waste of time.

Too often, people focus on things that are out of their control. Chasing a hot stock or a hot fund has another negative consequence: tax liabilities. A recent study showed that taxes eat up as much as 15% of the average mutual fund return, which is only 9% to begin with. Since approximately 54% of all mutual funds in Canada are held outside registered plans, this is a significant concern. Amin Mawani, Moshe Milevsky and Kamphol Panyagometh of the Schulich School of Business at York University in Toronto have researched the effects of taxation on mutual fund portfolios. In a recent study published in the *Canadian Tax Journal*, they conclude that "taxes exceed management fees and brokerage commissions in their ability to erode long-term investment returns." A responsible FSP can help consumers to resist making questionable trades.

In the United States, new legislation compels mutual funds to disclose after-tax returns. The York research turned up some interesting results, including the fact that when funds are ranked for their after-tax returns, the order generally differs from pure fund performance rankings. On average, funds moved up or down twenty-eight spots in the rankings compared to their peers, as a result of their tax efficiency (or lack thereof).

Research done by John Bowen of CEG Worldwide reinforces these ideas.[6] He demonstrates that "client-centred" FSPs are more financially successful on a personal level than "market-centred" FSPs. This is largely because the work being done is more meaningful to the client, who generally appreciates the more purposeful and customized approach that is invariably used by client-centred FSPs.

This is where the references to "life management" in chapter one come in. The financial services industry is morphing again. As old school "numbers people" within the industry become more and more in touch with the emotional side of investment and financial planning, there will be an ever-increasing need to rationally and purposefully bind the two together.

Looked at from a behavioural perspective, it seems FSPs generally do add value over time, but that this has virtually nothing to do with the products they recommend. Instead, it has more to do with the implementation of planning opportunities and constructive behaviour modification. The phrase *constructive behaviour modification* sounds awful to many people. In fact, many people think it sounds downright manipulative. *worthwhile teaching.*

What needs to be remembered is that the real manipulation is found in the culture of investment strategy (decision 3) discussions. When people talk about what the Central Bank is going to do at its next meeting, they are manipulating themselves into thinking the decision will have a material impact on their portfolio. It won't. When people read a magazine that talks about how reforms to corporate governance laws are too ham-fisted or proceeding too slowly or whatever, they are being manipulated. In the grand scheme, those things simply don't matter very much. In most instances, they won't matter at all. The role of the FSP is to get clients retired and to keep them retired in a lifestyle they have come to expect. Beating or predicting the market's short-term movements (or even understanding them) is simply not in the job description.

Among experienced and successful FSPs, the best clearly understand that there is a far greater need for an emotional connection than for a logical connection when dealing with clients. They pay thousands of dollars out of their own pockets to take courses that teach them how to draw out personal information about their clients that would be helpful in working with them. The "psychology of capital markets" is a nebulous and difficult subject and one that few are prepared to address directly.

Another person who is actively engaged in the alignment of life goals with financial planning objectives is Bill Bachrach. Bachrach has built a small consulting and training empire by catering to and teaching FSPs how to peel back the layers of the onion that are the human emotions associated with personal finance. He teaches courses and has written a number of books predicated on the simple "Values-Based" question, "What's important about money...to you?" The ensuing process of personal revelations allows FSPs to more deeply understand and respond to the values and dreams of their client base. Aspiring FSPs are not taught to do this kind of open-ended information gathering unless they pay the freight themselves *after* they start in the business.

If the term "financial professional" is ever going to be more than a mere catch phrase used by people in the financial services industry who don't want to be called salesmen, then it must certainly have to stand for something more. Calling someone a "financial professional" as a euphemism for "licenced financial product salesman," simply won't do.

On top of ensuring that our financial professionals need a comprehensive academic training in a wide variety of interdisciplinary fields associated with wealth management, there is obviously more reform needed. True professionals should certainly be able to understand the "soft," right-brained mechanics of personal finance too.

Remember that only the most recent generations of MBA graduates have been taking mandatory courses in ethics (look where the delay in bringing those educational reforms got us). Similarly, new university graduates with a degree conferring the right to practice as professional and holistic financial advice-givers will need to address the very real gap in the education system as it presently stands. Our number-cruncher FSPs are going to have to write some essays, role-play with their classmates and do some interactive learning in diagnosing both the financial *and the emotional* distresses afflicting would-be clients.

As with the previous problem of knowledge pertaining to passive investment products, FSPs have never been taught the importance of behaviour in investing. As with indexing, they have come to the conclusion that behaviour must not be very important since it isn't being taught. We need to set the record straight right away and to teach our newest FSPs that investor psychology is a very, very big deal.

PARTS AND LABOUR SOLD
SEPARATELY

There are risks and costs to a program of action, but they are far less than the long range risks and costs of comfortable inactions.

—John F. Kennedy

The essence of a genuine professional man is that he cannot be bought.

—H.L. Mencken

The neighbourhood auto mechanic is on to something. Say what you will about the price and quality of his work or the training required to perform it, at least there are no surprises when you come to pick up your vehicle. When the expectations are set out clearly and in writing before the fact, it is difficult to challenge what he's done if it is in accordance with those expectations.

The cardinal rule of the financial services industry is that the client comes first and FSPs are expected to subordinate their own interests to those of their clients. Part of that rule involves a "no surprises" commitment to professionalism. This is a noble objective, but one that is open to wide interpretation. If a prospective client sees two different FSPs on a matter and receives relatively different advice—either about planning concepts or products to be used—does that mean one FSP is being conspicuously negligent? Provided they are reasonable, each set of recommendations should be considered. But there is a problem with most investment recommendations—embedded compensation.

Separating the cost of the financial product from the cost of financial advice is known as "unbundling." Over the past three years, there has been a trend toward unbundling. The introduction of F Class mutual funds is allowing consumers to make a clear distinction between mutual fund management fees and expenses from FSP compensation. Now that virtually all mutual fund companies have released F Class funds (the "F" is for fee), this is the time to take a closer look to see what consumers are really getting. Most embedded compensation equity mutual funds in Canada have a Management Expense Ratio (MER) of about 2.75%, made up of trading and administrative costs of about 0.5%, a 1-2% fee for the mutual fund company, a 1% embedded advisory fee (called a "trailer fee") for the investment dealer and GST. Compensation is different if FSPs earn commissions. In that case, the commission is between 4% and 5% at the point of sale with an annual trailer fee of 0.25% to 0.5%.

F Class funds strip out FSP compensation, effectively offering the same investment products at a reduced cost; the cost is reduced by the exact amount of embedded compensation. As a result, these F Class funds generally cost about 1% less for equity funds and 0.5% less for fixed income funds, but require advisors to charge a direct fee on top. This is often more than 1% for small accounts, but less than 1% for large ones. Actually, since GST has to be charged on all aspects of mutual fund MERs, the client saves about 1.07% when buying an F Class fund, as compared to a traditional A Class fund.

But what about clients who don't want to use an FSP? Even if consumers go to a discount broker and do all their own research and execute their own trades (paying a transaction charge to do so), they will have to pay the same MER. Do-It-Yourself (DIY) consumers are not allowed to buy F Class funds at a discount brokerage. Doesn't this strike you as preposterous? Paying a fee for advice that is neither requested nor rendered? Remember that the fee is for the FSP's advice, wisdom, specialized knowledge, counsel and guidance. At a discount brokerage, there is no FSP to offer any of this, but the embedded advisory fee persists. Note that if you work with an FSP, it is not necessarily cheaper to pay a direct fee, compared to a DSC or no load (embedded trailer fee) format, and it may in fact cost you more.

The concept of unbundling reminds me of the famous scene in *Five Easy Pieces*, in which Jack Nicholson walks into a diner and orders toast. Speaking to a pleasant, but not particularly bright waitress, the conversation goes something like this:

> "I'd like an order of toast."
> "I'm sorry sir, we don't have any toast."
> "What do you mean? You've got bread, don't you?"
> "Yes, but toast is not on the menu."

Exasperated by the thickness of the lady he's speaking to, Nicholson continues:

> "Well then, what do you have?"
> "We've got a nice chicken sandwich."
> "Okay then, I'll have a toasted chicken sandwich—hold the chicken, hold the lettuce, hold the tomato, hold the mayo."

In the end, the waitress brings Nicholson a side order of toast. The point is that if some consumers want toast, why is the mutual fund industry forcing them to pay for the chicken sandwich?

The embedded compensation side of the mutual fund industry is so convinced that people need FSPs that they set up the system so that consumers have to pay for FSPs whether they use them or not. These same companies then tell FSPs (with a completely straight face) that they are firmly committed to the advisory channel. If this were really true, they would either prohibit discount brokers from selling their products or at the very least insist that if the discount brokers want their products on the shelf, that they use the F Class versions. In fairness, one company tried this and was forced to allow discounters to use its products and keep the associated trailer fee in the process. Embedded compensation mutual fund companies won't do that because they are interested in distributing their products as widely as possible. Maintaining market share supercedes loyalty to their primary distribution channel. It would be refreshing if just one embedded compensation company stood up and walked the talk by removing its products from the shelves of discount brokerages as an expression of solidarity with, and commitment to, qualified advice.

Discount brokers are also driven by profit. They're getting a great deal in this arrangement; the same compensation as qualified FSPs with none of the work or liability! Truly professional FSPs should never back down from the notion that qualified professional advice costs money. Other professionals don't back down from this and consumers accept the logic as a matter of course. The fact that most FSPs don't stand up for this concept illustrates clearly that most of them doubt whether or not they really do add value. At a time when people desperately need guidance in their increasingly complex financial affairs, advice-givers should resent the fact that their suppliers are talking about how their services are invaluable, while simultaneously paying other distributors—who do not offer advice—an identical level of compensation. It seems that advice-giving FSPs are not resentful, however. If embedded compensation companies can create a demand for their products, a large portion of the population will want to buy them. If it costs no more (i.e., the MER is identical) to buy them through an FSP than it does to buy them from a discount broker, people might as well buy the products from an FSP. It becomes obvious that these FSPs are thinking strictly about themselves if you follow their logic. Even if the advice rendered is worth only a fraction of what consumers are paying, it will be worth it, since the price is identical even if they get no advice. Since some advice is worth more than no advice and since consumers are free to disregard the advice if it is inappropriate anyway, why not have a second set of eyes looking over the situation?

Imagine if your auto mechanic tried this line of thinking. Let's say you need a new part and that part costs $140. You call the mechanic and say you will need it by the weekend and that you understand it will cost $140. You agree to come over on Saturday to pick it up, but when you do, the mechanic says it will cost $240 plus tax. You look puzzled and say, "What do you mean? When I called on Tuesday, you said it was only $140 for the part." At this point, the mechanic, full of self-righteous smugness says, "Well yes, the part does cost $140, but it will cost $100 to install it." You respond by pointing out that you were simply looking for the part and that it was your intention to take the part home and install it yourself in your driveway and on your own time. The mechanic says that is immaterial. The cost is $140 for parts and

$100 for labour and that is what you will have to pay, whether it is installed at the garage by a mechanic or in your driveway by you personally.

He is so confident that he and his staff will do a bang-up job and that you will mess it up somehow, that you'll need to pay for the service whether you request it or not. Any mechanic who tried this stunt would have consumers reporting his little operation to the Better Business Bureau in no time flat, and for good reason! With mutual funds at discount brokerages, this stunt is common practice.

The status quo suits both the advice and the DIY channels. The advice channel, with its inferiority complex about whether or not it can actually deliver what it purports to deliver, likes the fact that it "costs no more to use the very best" in positioning its services. Meanwhile, the DIY channel loves the fat profit margins that come with charging for services that are never delivered. Again, if you ran a garage and could consistently and legally charge for services that you proudly *didn't* provide, wouldn't you love it? That's exactly what discount brokers are doing and the embedded compensation mutual fund companies are letting them get away with it! Governments and regulators are guilty of complicity, since they're well aware of the situation, but do nothing to shut it down.

The question this begs is, "What would happen if discount brokers couldn't sell embedded compensation (A Class) funds?" For starters, discount brokers would be a lot less profitable than they are now. They would likely have to raise transaction charges or new account fees just to remain marginally profitable. The pricing gap between the advice and DIY channels would close, but it would never go away. Repeat after me: qualified financial advice costs money.

Direct fees are charged for tax preparation. You can do your own taxes and save yourself some accounting fees or you can delegate the task to a qualified professional. This professional will simplify your life, do a responsible job and charge you a predictable fee for services rendered. In the future, consumers are simply going to have to decide whether or not they are going to act as their own advisor or pay for advice and, if so, what a fair price might be. Extending the professional analogy further, there's a saying that the person who acts as his own legal counsel has a fool for an attorney. That's the idea FSPs want to ingrain in the public consciousness: that financial guidance is far too precious to be left to amateurs and Do-It-Yourselfers (DIYs).

With most FSPs, the level of "gross compensation" earned for product placement is identical regardless of credentials, experience or service. The wrinkle is that firms allow FSPs to keep different percentages of their income, depending on the firm's "payout grid" and the volume of sales done by the FSP. A higher sales volume means a higher payout. Note that FSPs don't get bonuses or pay increases by making more money for clients in good markets, losing less money in bad markets or saving an inordinate amount of tax—they get paid by volume of sales.

Some professionals cost more than others in the same field, so the notion of identical pay for identical product placement regardless of FSP seniority and sophistication will change too. In a fee-based environment, everyone knows instinctively that it costs more to get a partner at a specialized Bay Street law firm to do legal work than it costs to get a small-town generalist lawyer with a storefront office at the corner of Main and Elm. It stands to reason that FSPs with more experience, credentials, profile and aptitude will command a higher fee than raw rookies out of the chute once fees become the prevailing compensation model for FSPs.

Some consumers who are currently "on the fence" and use an FSP only grudgingly, might move to discount brokers, and the advice channel obviously doesn't want this, but the market segments itself pretty clearly. In general, people either want to work with an FSP or they do not, just as people either choose to do their own tax preparation or not. There should be an opportunity for consumers to engage in a meaningful self-selection process. If advice costs money, it should logically follow that it will cost more to work with an FSP than to do the work yourself. Under present circumstances, there is no real reason why people predisposed to investing in traditional embedded compensation mutual funds wouldn't want to use an FSP. Any value added is worth the inescapable fee that is being paid anyway. Obviously, this is not the case if portfolios are constructed with individual securities and ETFs. Bear in mind, however, that a lot more goes into financial planning than just portfolio management.

The system obviously needs to change. There are billions of dollars invested in mutual funds at discount brokerages that are paying these firms embedded fees while no value-added services are being rendered. That's tens of millions of dollars that discount brokers are earning annually, that rightfully belongs in consumers' pockets. As is stands today, you can file your own tax return, hope you don't miss anything and save yourself a few bucks in the process. You can defend yourself in court, take your chances with the judge and save yourself some legal fees. What you cannot do is invest by yourself using embedded compensation funds and reduce your advisory fees. The built-in preferential pricing biases simply have to end.

As an FSP myself, I obviously believe that FSPs add value. I also believe most consumers are better off using an FSP and wouldn't be in this business if I didn't believe that to be true. That said, I do not believe the system should condone pricing structures in which consumers have to pay for professional advisory services, even if those services are neither requested nor rendered. The most obvious and transparent solution is to abolish embedded compensation products (notably A Class mutual funds) altogether. The myth some FSPs perpetuate that mutual funds are "free" would be exploded. Those who want advice would pay advisory fees and those who do not want advice would be able to forego them.

If there are no commissions and no trailer fees at stake, FSPs are freed up to recommend whatever products they believe are best for their clients. If for any reason clients are unhappy with the service or advice they receive from their FSP, they will be free to either find another FSP or do the work themselves in accordance with their own preferences.

What Do Most FSPs Recommend and Why?

Most consumers have taken the view that if the cost is not visible, it doesn't exist. Studies show that the majority of consumers have no idea what a typical mutual fund costs on an ongoing basis (its MER). As a result, FSPs are loath to put compensation out in the open because it reminds their clients about something negative that they would never think about otherwise: the fact that FSPs have to earn a living and that the money is ultimately coming out of clients' pockets.

The incontrovertible fact that no one seems to grasp is that it is always the client who pays the FSP for services rendered. So many FSPs say they recommend embedded compensation funds because only embedded compensation funds pay them. That's hogwash. No funds pay FSPs. Only consumers pay FSPs. The difference is that embedded compensation funds have devised a seemingly benign way of collecting FSP compensation from the client and distributing it to the FSP. *Make no mistake. In one way or another, Financial Services providers are paid exclusively by their clients.*

In the past few years, many FSPs have struggled with the notion of moving to a fee-based arrangement in an attempt to be more transparent with the cost of their services. There are a number of so-called "wrap" accounts that do something similar.

The problem of course, is that the FSP's compensation is part of the wrap account "wrapping" and remains hidden. In the interests of true and plain disclosure, the wrapped investment program and the advisory fee should be charged separately, so clients can see who is getting what. While wrap accounts do some of the FSP's work (such as asset allocation, tax optimization and regular rebalancing), they typically charge the client more and pay the FSP more. That's probably reasonable for the client, because the client generally gets more, but it's absolutely great if you're an FSP, since there's more money for less work. Many FSPs are starting to behave like the mechanic we talked about earlier—charging for services that they don't even provide. The rationale given by wrap account proponents for this paradox, is that it frees the FSP to spend more time on more value-added activities, like looking for opportunities to deduct, defer or divide tax bills, do estate planning or set up more complex strategies. That's all fine and well if the FSP is qualified to do those things and actually does them. But what if the FSP only has a licence to sell products and no training to do planning?

Most FSPs fear the eradication of embedded compensation because the status quo protects their personal financial wellbeing. Making a voluntary transition from commissions to fees involves a painful restructuring of their business model—certain short-term pain for presumed long term gain. In spite of how FSPs blather on about taking a long-term view, FSPs are human and there is still the matter of short-term pain that has to be endured. If the transition is to occur with even a modicum of integrity, there will be a significant drop in income while it is being made. People instinctively move away from pain, so it should come as no surprise that FSPs aren't dealing with the disconnect between their positioning and their compensation method of choice.

Pain or no pain, the need for reform is obvious. A 2002 study entitled "Medium and Long-Term Retail Savings in the U.K.: A Review by Ron Sandler" made the following assertion:

Consumers rely heavily on advice from intermediaries, although they have almost no understanding of the costs of obtaining this, and are unable to gauge its quality. Moreover, the advice itself is often compromised by the incentive effects of commission paid by product providers... Commission-driven selling of these products remains the norm, leading to persistent concerns about consumer detriment and to consequent regulatory intervention. Recent research by the FSA (the British Financial Services Authority) found statistically significant evidence of FSPs recommending one provider's offering over another because it paid a higher commission.

Many of these same FSPs who earn commissions genuinely want to become true professionals, but given their past history, don't know how to make the leap. How do you tell a client who has been with you for twenty years and never paid you a direct fee in his life, that you now believe he will be better served by paying a direct fee? What if you've been telling that client that there are no costs provided the investment is held for the long term?

To make matters worse, it is difficult to "do the right thing" when competitors are making more money by picking the low-hanging fruit, preying off consumers who are sufficiently unsophisticated to know there are other business models out there. Perhaps more than anything else, the general lack of consumer awareness has allowed commission-based advice (read: sales) to flourish longer than it rightfully ought to.

Proponents of the commission-based compensation model argue that consumers are not demanding a fee-based arrangement from their FSPs and often don't understand important differences when (if) they are presented to them. If a large majority of consumers is essentially indifferent, why should anyone, including regulators and legislators, care? The answer is that consumers are blissfully unaware of how embedded compensation can cloud the judgement of FSPs who, after all, are only human. You can't be outraged by something you don't understand, only intimidated.

Since the industry allows FSPs to select their own business model, there is considerable resistance toward the total unbundling of parts (products) and labour (FSP fees) because the short-term pain is certain, while the long-term gain is anything but. Furthermore, behavioural finance teaches us that the pain of a loss is generally felt more than twice as strongly as the joy of an equivalent gain. Not only do FSPs have an emotional bridge to cross, there's the practical matter of paying the mortgage along the way.

Remember that there are also some FSPs, notably at banks, who receive a salary for their work. There is no conspicuously right or wrong model. Most independent FSPs choose commissions, but work on a fee basis if that's the only way they can land a "big account."

Many believe that the fees based on managed assets model is generally the most appropriate for those FSPs who want to make the transition from sales-people to genuine (entrepreneurial) professionals. In time, it may not even be a choice, as laws and policies motivated by consumer protection become more stringent. Ultimately, FSPs will be given a choice between moving swiftly, but willingly, to fees based on assets managed or being pushed into that same arrangement eventually. Assuming the FSP wants to move to a fee-based arrangement as soon as is practically possible (i.e., jump before being pushed), what would she and her clients need to know before starting?

On the client side, the most compelling reason to move to a fee-based arrangement is that it more closely aligns client interests with FSP interests. Because clients are paying fees based on the size of their portfolio, FSPs have a clear incentive to make portfolios grow and to mitigate portfolio declines. The more the account grows, the more the FSP makes; the more the account declines, the less the FSP makes. This is in direct contrast with a large commission payment up front, nominal trailing commissions over time and a potentially punitive DSC schedule that clients would have to endure if they want to change companies. The fee-based model might also allow for fee deductibility for non-registered accounts that otherwise would not be possible.

Given the lack of client demand for this transition at present, it should be stressed that even if FSPs firmly believe it is in their clients' best interest to switch, they cannot force any client to share that view. People (i.e. both FSPs and consumers) naturally resist change. Still, if you're a consumer who is working with an FSP you trust, ask yourself one question: "Would I be pre-pared to take a considerable *voluntary risk in my own career,* knowing that it would likely take six full years for me and my family to be as well off as a result?" Since most people tend to avoid pain if it can somehow be avoided, I suspect most people would honestly answer no. But six years is a reasonable time frame for FSPs to expect when running the gauntlet.

Eradicating embedded compensation should mean total product flexibility and independence. Any FSPs reading this and considering the switch should know that those who have already done so believe it generally takes about three years to accomplish this switch and three more years to regain the revenues that were foregone in doing so. In other words, if you begin in 2004, you'll be worse off financially until about 2010, at which point you will more or less break even and then do better afterwards. Any FSP contemplating retirement before 2010 wouldn't be inclined to work toward this transition.

People who understand the situation know that the status quo is not viable indefinitely. Within the industry, people talk about DSCs as not being long for this world. The only point of debate is whether commissions will be going the way of the dodo sooner or later. That they will be going is not even in dispute. Once they go, can trailer fees be far behind?

The Joint Forum of Financial Market Regulators has already made some proposals regarding transparency and disclosure. Their proposals revolve around a new system that focuses on four documents to be compiled by fund companies:

1. The Foundation Document provides basic disclosure about the fund and contains the "non-changing elements of the fund." The information would be posted on the government's and fund companies' websites.

2. The Fund Summary Document would contain more current information such as financial statements and performance data. The information would also be posted on the fund companies' websites.

3. Continuous Disclosure Documents would be used in the sale process and would include information like investment objectives, strategies and risks. It could be used as a kind of checklist for investment selection.

4. The Consumer's Guide would contain basic information without going into specifics. It would be available in both print and electronic formats.

Once there's a consensus on what needs to happen, people can turn their attention to finding practical solutions. Remember that this is an environment where neither FSPs nor their clients are pressing for any meaningful reform. Does anything really need to be done? Many believe the answer is a resounding yes, but in a discussion about the ethical and purposeful reform of an entire industry, all the stakeholders need to understand where the others are coming from.

Many clients remain deluded into thinking that mutual fund investments are essentially "free." I know of a number of unscrupulous FSPs who sell A Class mutual funds at no-load to unsophisticated clients using precisely that terminology. As a result of their fear of pain, FSPs and clients together instinctively avoid what is likely a better arrangement for both of them.

My advice to FSPs considering the switch before it is forced upon them is don't expect your clients to thank you for the sacrifices you make on their behalf. Most won't understand that you have made any sacrifices at all. Making a switch to a fee-based arrangement is not for the faint of heart. Nonetheless, it could be argued that part of the FSP's job is to facilitate an honourable and staged transition to a fee-based format for those clients who want it.

Ethics and Independence

Joe Killoran is a consumer advocate who believes that far more needs to be done to disclose FSP compensation and total client cost to consumers of financial products. He also believes this is best accomplished through a series of questionnaires and checklists, on which consumers initial all the salient points associated with cost and compensation prior to buying a financial product at the point of sale. Mr. Killoran runs a website where these documents can be found (www.investorism.com) and advises consumers to download the documents and to bring them to their FSP for completion before transacting business.

The lack of direct and simple disclosure of matters like cost, allows some FSPs to make interesting comments to unsuspecting consumers. For example: "Cost is not important; total returns are important. It may be that the average mutual fund lags its benchmark over time, but I do not recommend *average* funds. My clients benefit from my input and look to me to assist them in buying the best funds. When I recommend products to them, I am acting with complete integrity and professionalism." When I hear this, I generally ask these "professionals" if they recommend exchange traded funds or mutual funds with no commissions or trailing commissions to their clients. They generally look at me as if I have two heads and sniff incredulously that they do good work and deserve to be paid. I respond that I could not agree more. They usually tilt their heads as I ask them again if they recommend products with no embedded compensation.

"Of course not," they reply. "We need to get paid!"

"So ask your clients to pay you," I say, taking in the stunned, but sheepish silence on the other end.

Most FSPs don't ask for the payment they are clearly entitled to. Perhaps that's because they fear most consumers won't understand and perhaps it's because the FSPs themselves feel handcuffed by the tyranny of client complacency and the tactics of less scrupulous competitors. Time and again, most FSPs are mortified to go to their clients to ask them to open their wallets and pay them directly. Making an FSP's compensation transparent has a way of getting clients to focus on that FSP's "value proposition" in a way that nothing else can.

For example, let's say there are two competing mutual funds, each with good track records. One has a ten-year return of 11% with below average volatility and a record of above average year to year performance to boot. The other has a ten-year return of 9% with average volatility and some good and some mediocre short-term performance history. Which is better? The first fund of course. But if the first fund pays no compensation to the FSP and the second pays commissions and/or trailing commissions, which one do you think the advisor will recommend? In virtually all cases, it is the latter. This is true even though the FSP knows that the difference in long-term performance of the two funds is in excess of the compensation he might have received. In other words, even if the FSP subtracts a reasonable fee from the performance numbers of the first fund, it would still outperform the second if everything else were held constant. A true apples-to-apples comparison (controlling for compensation formats) would still make the non-recommended fund preferable. In spite of this, FSPs almost exclusively recommend funds with embedded compensation.

Independence is a curious thing, especially in the world of finance where so many firms are acting as both manufacturers and distributors. Let's use Loblaws as an example. Some time ago, marketing wizard Dave Nichol launched the President's Choice brand within the Loblaws chain. It was fabulously successful. In essence, all he did was fill niches for certain products where his research showed there was a strong demand.

Where the marketplace allowed for more products, he would develop them. Sometimes his prices were higher than the competition, but often they were lower. However, since President's Choice came to be seen as a quality brand, consumers began to buy President's Choice products and Nichol gained valuable market share. Loblaws was having these products made by major labels when their processing plants weren't running at full capacity, so he could buy essentially identical products, stick the President's Choice label on them and capture a higher margin for doing so. He would put his "in-house brand" on the shelf to compete with the major national brands, often keeping the number one and number two suppliers on the shelf and using President's Choice in lieu of the number three supplier. Consumers felt they were no worse off for the change.

The lesson is that independence is not compromised when proprietary products are put on the shelf, it is compromised when major competitive brands are deliberately left off the shelf. More choice is good, since consumers are free to judge the product based on price, quality and various other factors based on personal preference. Had Nichol gone around taking Heinz ketchup off the shelf when he was putting his President's Choice ketchup on the shelf, there would have been hell to pay.

What about investment products? There *are* mutual funds that do not pay FSPs, and many of them are cheaper than those that do. Is it reasonable that all the funds offered by the true no-load families (Phillips, Hager and North, Mawer, McLean Budden, Beutel Goodman, Chou, Sceptre and others) should almost never be offered by FSPs? On the one hand, there is the argument that there is still plenty of choice from amongst the funds whose products are found on the shelves of FSPs. On the other hand, since a prospectus can often be acquired in a day or two even if it isn't on the FSP's shelf at present, why are these companies effectively blacklisted by FSPs, especially if their products are sound?

With the recent introduction of F Class funds, consumers can now compare apples-to-apples; all funds can be compared before any FSP compensation is added to the cost side of the equation. This is important, because once one adds FSP compensation to the cost of a fund, the total return to the client is correspondingly reduced dollar for dollar. As a result, a fund with no embedded compensation might outperform a similarly mandated fund with embedded compensation, but still not be as good. In fact, if the performance is similar, the fulcrum may shift in favour of the embedded compensation or "load" fund in some instances.

FSPs tend to recommend funds from certain fund "families" for various reasons, but *from the shortened list of funds that offer embedded compensation*. In essence, they are reasonably independent *provided that* the companies whose products they recommend collect and remit both commissions and trailing commissions. Since all commissions and trailing commissions come out of the funds' MERs, it is the investor who pays.

The inescapable fact is that about 99% of all mutual funds sold (and I use the word "sold" deliberately) by FSPs come with an embedded compensation of some kind. Surely the companies that have no embedded compensation cannot be that bad. In fact, a feature article in the *Globe and Mail* in April of 2002 identified the top fund families in Canada and *all of them* were of the non-embedded compensation variety. If independent media sources can identify these products as being as good as, or better than the embedded compensation kind why do FSPs (most of whom are otherwise exceedingly diligent) consistently fail to recommend them to their clients?

In the coming world of fee-based financial planning, investment counselling and holistic advice, everything will be conspicuously on the table. With regulatory pressures becoming more of a reality with every passing quarter, FSPs will need to be more explicit in disclosing precisely what their recommended investment products cost. The thing that investors need to understand is that price is usually a negative indicator for expected long-term performance. Legislators should perk up and pay attention too, because the more money there is in personal retirement accounts, the less reliance there is on government pensions.

In essence, the more an investment product costs, the more "leakage" there will be in that product's expected long-term return. Most investors never think of this. Partially, that's because FSPs don't generally focus on cost when making recommendations or when doing planning. This is counterintuitive to the way most other products are sold.

People generally expect more expensive cars to be better than cars that cost less and they are generally right when considering virtually any similar product. There's an old saying in the sales industry that "you are what you sell," so people don't want to be seen to be selling "cheap" products. Furthermore, FSPs want to make as much money as possible for themselves and their families so they generally don't talk about price. As we saw earlier, their compensation ultimately comes out of clients' pockets either way.

Automobiles are depreciating assets and, with normal wear and tear, they will one day be worthless. Better made cars cost more, but generally depreciate less quickly, so spending relatively more may be a sensible consumer decision. Investment assets, on the other hand, generally appreciate over time, so the best value is often secured by using products that cost least, allowing for maximum appreciation of value over time. This is an important distinction.

Virtually all other consumer products add value by minimizing depreciation. *Honda!* Investment products add value by maximizing appreciation. *Acura.*

Exchange Traded Funds and F Class Funds—Building Blocks of the Future
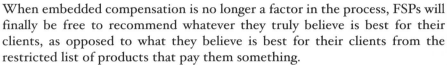

When embedded compensation is no longer a factor in the process, FSPs will finally be free to recommend whatever they truly believe is best for their clients, as opposed to what they believe is best for their clients from the restricted list of products that pay them something.

Since there are considerable risks and costs associated with portfolio construction using a traditional securities paradigm (individually held stocks and bonds), there is a need for products that offer a consistent mandate, affordable costs, diversification, the option of professional management and the absence of embedded FSP compensation. Fortunately, those products now exist. They are called exchange traded funds and F Class mutual funds.

ETFs are the harbinger of a new era in the financial services industry. These products are merely a basket of securities that trade on a stock exchange using an indexing strategy. They offer considerable benefits over traditional mutual funds. Specifically, they are purer, more tax efficient and considerably cheaper.

The cost for most ETFs available in Canada today is generally between 18 basis points and 55 basis points (a "basis point" or bp is 1/100 of 1%). Many American ETFs are cheaper still. ETFs can be purchased on margin and carry other trappings normally reserved for standard securities because legally, they are securities. They can be sold short, can have limit orders and stop-loss orders placed on them. They are repriced constantly, just like the securities within the ETF. Because they are securities, consumers will need to work with a securities-licenced FSP to purchase them and will likely have to pay a brokerage fee to do so. All told, ETFs are conspicuously superior to most traditional mutual funds.

As a complimentary product, F Class mutual funds are generally the same as the mutual funds people have come to know and love, with the singular exception that they do not have embedded advisor compensation. Equity funds generally have an embedded 1% compensation (trailer fee), making F Class equity funds 1.07% cheaper, since GST must now be included in MERs. Similarly, when discussing fixed income funds, the embedded compensation is generally set at 0.5%, so F Class funds are 0.535% cheaper. All other aspects of these funds are identical to their more prominent A Class cousins.

The excellent mutual fund families listed earlier have been running de facto F Class funds for some time. In fact, their MERs are often even lower than the F Class versions of the traditional "load" family funds they compete against. That's because they spend less on promoting themselves, so you can keep more of your money rather than having it bleed away slowly and relatively inconspicuously through MERs. In some instances, investors may need a certain dollar amount in order to qualify to use these products, but they would certainly merit consideration if the investor could meet the test.

Combining ETFs and F Class mutual funds, the total client cost, even with advisory fees tacked on, will likely be substantially less than a conventional mutual fund portfolio. If we're talking about a half-million-dollar portfolio with a 1% fee to the FSP and a 50% ETF/50% F Class weighting, then we're talking about cutting .5% (50 bps) from total client costs. That's $2,500 in annual, compounded client savings. It's absolutely huge! Here's a chart examining the cost of investment products depending on the blend of ETFs and F Class mutual funds. In the example, we'll assume a 40 bps cost for ETFs and a 140 bps cost for F Class mutual funds. Most F Class funds cost more than that, but let's be fair to both active managers and the people who recommend them, by assuming FSPs will recommend the cheaper funds since there's no compensation bias holding them back anymore.

Percent in ETFs (cost)	Percent in F Class (cost)	Total Blended Cost
100 (40 bps)	0 (0 bps)	40 bps
75 (30 bps)	25 (35 bps)	65 bps
50 (20 bps)	50 (70 bps)	90 bps
25 (10 bps)	75 (105 bps)	115 bps
0 (0 bps)	100 (140 bps)	140 bps

Still, it needs to be stressed that mutual fund MERs almost always understate the total cost incurred by investors. That's because their brokerage commissions are capitalized rather than expensed, meaning they don't show up in the MER. Let's say a manager buys 2,000 shares at $10 each, but pays a $300 brokerage commission. Rather than showing the $300 commission as a separate expense, it shows up in the cost of the shares. For instance, the 2,000 shares would go into the mutual fund's books as costing $20,300, not $20,000. The same idea applies when shares are sold and proceeds are deemed to be less than they otherwise might be. Fund analyst James Gauthier has determined that this quirk of accounting can add a full 1% to the cost of a fund, although the average was determined to be only 35 bps. Most FSPs aren't even aware of the practice.

The reason ETFs and F class funds work so well together is that clients generally give up no return when indexing those portions of their portfolios where active management is not likely to add value (i.e., where markets are "efficient"). A large majority of actively managed funds fail to keep pace with their benchmark in the long run. Besides, the handful of actively managed funds that manage to accomplish this feat cannot be reliably identified before the fact. This chart simply quantifies the approximate trade-offs involved in manipulating the mix from a cost perspective.

If you are of the opinion that active management makes sense all the time, then buy only F class mutual funds. If you believe solely in indexing, then buy only indexed products. The point is, there's room for both strategies. There's no definitive rule to be applied to active or passive investing, so you can mix and match all you want, just be mindful of the cost sensitivity along the way. It should be stressed that with very few exceptions, the only way that anyone has consistently outperformed an efficient market in the long run is to take on more risk than the market. Fund picking has been exposed as a mug's game. Stock picking was exposed as a mug's game long ago and it doesn't matter whether you're a professional money manger managing billions of dollars for fund unit holders and institutional clients or a hotshot broker with a corner office. Stock picking and fund picking are in essence the same game; one is played at the micro level and one at the macro level. Neither has been demonstrated to predictably and reliably add value.

The FSPs who are the most reticent to change are the ones who would be most conspicuously exposed as not having anything appreciable to bring to the table on behalf of their clients. They are primarily commission-based salespeople rather than holistic, professional advisors.

What Do Parts Cost?

The simple continuum we looked at earlier gives you a sense of what parts might cost. In fact, ETFs generally cost anywhere from 0.18% to 0.55% and F Class mutual funds generally cost anywhere from 0.53% to 1.90%, so there's considerable room for variability depending on the products you use. Hedge funds usually cost considerably more. In order to make a more meaningful disclosure to consumers, FSPs could offer a discreet listing of actual costs associated with each (unbundled) product. That way, consumers could see for themselves what the products cost and could simply add the FSP's fee on top. On the next page is a theoretical example of what a simple portfolio recommendation might look like in terms of the cost of the investment product "parts" as disclosed by an unencumbered FSP. The total cost of the portfolio is simply the weighted average of the sum of the parts. In this case, it works out to 93 basis points (0.93%), which is close to the 0.90% approximation listed above.

It should be noted that many FSPs will be justifiably worried that if they cannot earn commissions, they will have to make this type of disclosure. These transactional FSPs understand that they may well be forced out of business by more professional FSPs who are able to work in an unbundled environment. They will also likely resist the implementation of professional standards for the same reason. It's time the industry smoked out the salespeople, those FSPs who will fight financial services reform as if their life depended on it.

In a very real sense, the lives of sales-oriented FSPs depend on commissions. They will speak of the nobility and honour of earning commissions and of how many decent people have done so for generations. They will say that they themselves are beyond reproach in their personal business practices and will resent any inference to the contrary. These people miss the one

Active or Passive	Asset Class	Name of Investment	% Allocation	MER
Active	Global Fixed Income	CI World Bond F Class	10%	1.33%
Passive	Canadian Large Cap	iUnits S&P TSE 60 Capped ETF	10%	0.18%
Passive	U.S. Large Cap	iUnits S&P 500 RSP ETF	10%	0.30%
Passive	International Broad Market	iUnits Int'l Equity RSP ETF	10%	0.35%
Active	Global Small Cap	Templeton Global Small Co. F Class	5%	1.64%
Active	Emerging Markets	CI Emerging Markets F Class	5%	1.80%
Active	Global Value	Mackenzie Cundill Value F Class	10%	1.36%
Active	Alternative Strategies (Hedge)	Mackenzie Alt. Strategies F Class	10%	2.72%
Passive	Real Estate	iUnits Real Estate ETF	10%	0.55%
Passive	Canadian Fixed Income	iUnits Canada 5 Year ETF	10%	0.25%
Active	Canadian Fixed Income	TD Real Return Bond F Class	10%	0.80%

Ave. 0.93

inescapable fact that virtually all consumers understand intuitively: the term "professional salesperson" is an oxymoron.

What Does Labour Cost?

As we have already seen, most mutual fund investments are sold primarily in a "bundled" form, where the cost of the investment "parts" and the FSP compensation "labour" are blended together in the MER. Even when clients know what the MER of a fund is, they are often hard pressed to explain what portion of that goes to their FSP. They deserve to know. Consumers should be told how much an FSP is being compensated. Some products pay more than others and as long as the compensation is at least partially hidden and lacking in uniformity, how can consumers be assured that what is being recommended is truly in their best interests?

Again, it seems the answer lies in conspicuous, necessary disclosure. There are plenty of FSPs who make recommendations that are motivated at least somewhat by compensation issues. The first rule in the financial advice industry is that the interests of the client come first. But how is this monitored? At present, as long as the FSP can rationalize an investment as being consistent with client objectives, the investment choice goes unchallenged.

Generally speaking, a total advisory fee of somewhere between 1.5% (small accounts) and 0.5% (very large ones) represents reasonable value. There are two schools of thought on how fees should be charged. One is for services rendered (charged on an hourly basis) while the other is for ongoing holistic advice (charged as a percentage of assets being managed). The former certainly has merit, but the latter has been taking hold as the dominant approach for fee-based advice.

Once you settle on the notion of paying a fee based on the amount of household assets being managed, there are two ways to design a payment system. The first is to use discreet range-bound bandwidths. The second is to use "marginal fee rates," much like the government uses marginal tax rates. Note that some FSPs include GST in their quoted fees, while others quote their fees before GST. All FSPs charge GST, so be sure to ask whether the quoted fee is before or after GST. For purposes of comparison, the fees shown in the illustrations below offer both formats. The first format includes GST, while the second excludes GST. Here's a couple of possible fee schedules:

Format 1: Range Bound

Portfolios under $250,000	1.5%
Portfolios over $250,000	1.25%
Portfolios over $500,000	1.00%
Portfolios over $1,000,000	0.75%

Format 2: Marginal Fee Rates

Portfolios under $250,000	1.40%
Additional Assets up to $2,000,000	0.70%
Additional Assets over $2,000,000	0.35%

The benefit of the first format is that it is intuitively easy to understand and calculate. The problem is that there are inefficiencies at the margin. The second is a little more difficult to understand, but fundamentally more appropriate. Just think of how you pay your taxes. Once accounts are over $250,000, the annual fee becomes a blend of the differing marginal rates. This blended fee drops as accounts get bigger. Think of it as a "volume discount." The 1% benchmark that many media people think is reasonable, is reached at $583,333. Although accounts below that amount cost more than 1% per year, accounts above that amount would cost less. At $2 million, the fee is about 78 bps, just over three-quarters of 1%. Finally, although there aren't a lot of retail investors who qualify for the biggest discount, the savings would be truly substantial for those who do.

A fee based format recognizes three concepts: the alignment of FSP and client interests, the economies of scale implicit in the rendering of qualified advice and the need to weed out inefficiencies at various thresholds (price points). Of the three, the first point applies to both the range-bound and the marginal fee rate models. Because FSP compensation is now clearly linked to the size of the portfolio and not the placement of any product in particular, there is a clear consistency of purpose. If the account goes up, the FSP makes relatively more. If the account drops, the FSP makes relatively less.

Note that FSPs get paid even if accounts go down temporarily. This is entirely appropriate. Consumers need to be reminded from time to time that FSPs are not clairvoyant and cannot predict market movements. In fact, FSPs would not have to work for a living if they could do that.

Many FSPs have made the point that they need more than 1% as compensation for taking on smaller clients, since smaller clients involve nearly as much work as larger ones. The problem is that the logic cuts both ways. If small accounts should command a premium, large accounts should be accepted at a discount. The marginal fee rate format takes economies of scale into account quite nicely.

Finally, it could be somewhat unfair to clients who are on the margin of a fee range to pay a fee on a cusp. For instance, based on the discreet pricing model above, a $490,000 account would attract a fee of over $6,000 a year, yet an account of $510,000 would actually cost just over $5,000 a year. The absolute dollar amount should not go down just because a client went past an arbitrary threshold. If so, clients might be inclined to do inappropriate things (e.g., borrow an additional $20,000 to pass a threshold) in order to qualify for the preferred fee level. Such conduct is not necessarily in the clients' best interest, so artificial incentives should be avoided. See pg-133 -how to.

So far, this comparison has not looked at trading costs (i.e., brokerage fees). Although the marginal fee model shown is modestly cheaper for clients, let's assume it does not take into account brokerage trading costs. In contrast, let's assume the range-bound model includes a certain number of annual portfolio trades at no extra charge.

Under this scenario, the marginal fee model involves charging a small processing fee (say $50 per trade) on securities trades where the FSP receives no compensation. This wrinkle can more closely align the interests of the client, the FSP and the advisory firm. That's because trading costs money and if firms allow clients to execute a certain number of trades at no charge at all, there could be a tendency to make marginal trades because the cost of doing so is nil. This wrinkle is useful as a reminder to the client that trading should only be used to conspicuously improve the portfolio. Reduced trading activity passes the savings on to the client. Increased activity is charged to the client. The FSP, meanwhile, gets 140 bps either way, so there's no motive to churn the account. The firm the FSP works for is recovering most of the costs associated with placing the trade.

The processing charge would act like a user fee. Even token cost recovery charges can act as a forceful disincentive to marginal activities. Things that are too easily acquired are often not fully appreciated. This is a little like comparing the sixteen-year old who gets a new car from his parents on his birthday, with the sixteen-year old who works part-time to buy a 1989 model. Which child do you think is more likely to be in an accident? People tend to be more careful when their own effort is used to pay the piper. A similar concept applies to insurance where deductibles are concerned.

Modifying the format slightly to incorporate the concept of a user fee allows the client some nominal control over his cost structure. Fewer trades mean slightly more savings, while more trades could end up costing slightly more than the discreet fee model.

Research shows that excessive trading reduces long-term returns. The role of an FSP is not to trade actively (as some pundits and commentators infer), but rather to keep clients from tinkering unduly with their nest eggs. Don't just do something—stand there! Beyond purposeful rebalancing, trading activities should be kept to a minimum. The FSP of the future will work in concert with clients to ensure all aspects of their financial affairs are attended to. This partnership with the client should be aimed at attaining financial independence in a suitable time frame and then maintaining a consistent quality of life beyond that point. Achieving long-term returns in the mid-teens is not a reasonable expectation, since no one can control how capital markets will behave in the future.

On pages 136 and 137 is an example of a compensation disclosure document that all clients should be required to sign before investing. There would be no doubt as to how much an FSP is being paid if this letter were being used.

The Disclosure Imperative

Until the world of unbundled advice arrives, FSPs will be expected to make meaningful disclosures about how and how much they are being paid for the services they provide. This is best accomplished by having a single point-of-sale document that can be reviewed and signed by the client, who would get a

Explanation of Current Compensation Formats

FSP remuneration is dependant on two factors:
- Investable assets at the household level (through commissions and/or fees)
- Fee-based deliverables

New clients are accepted only after the FSP has explained how s/he is compensated and provides full disclosure in writing. Updated disclosures are provided for any changes to future renewal agreements.

The independent financial advice investment industry offers a choice of three primary non-salary compensation structures for clients working with qualified FSPs. The compensation methodologies are:

1. Transparent Fees Based on Assets Invested

Investments are made without any initial compensation, but with regular fees paid directly by the client.
- There are generally no acquisition or disposition costs, just regular fees that are charged to the client's bank account on a regular basis or charged as part of the ongoing management expense ratio (MER) of the underlying fund. This provides superior investment flexibility, leaving no impediments or restrictions for future transactions.
- Exchange Traded Funds (ETFs) require a $50 transaction fee be charged.

2. Embedded Commissions and Trailing Commissions
- The investor does not pay any direct commissions, but pays a portion of the mutual fund's management expense ratio (MER) to the FSP.
- The FSP's firm is immediately paid a commission by the mutual fund companies, at fixed rates of about 4% to 6% with an annual trailing commission of 0.5% to 0.25%. If the investor sells mutual funds within the first seven years (approx.), the investor may be required to pay DSC to reimburse the fund companies for commissions previously paid to the FSP.
- If the investor holds mutual funds, the DSC rate declines annually, typically from about 6% in first year to 0% in about seventh year.
- The investor pays annual management fees to mutual fund companies on a permanent basis. As such, the investor receives lower annual investment performance due to the annual management fee deducted.
- Future investment flexibility and transactions may be impeded due to DSCs being triggered.
- DSC commissions are at fixed rates as set by the fund companies (stated in prospectus) and are non-negotiable.

3. Fee For Service
- The FSP recommends that clients use a fee-based services model once he is confident the client will derive net benefits, based on portfolio size and personal circumstance. Professional services might include, but are not limited to:
- written recommendations regarding general planning objectives
- a written financial independence calculation
- a comprehensive financial plan
- ongoing, iterative planning to ensure that all elements of holistic planning are being attended to
- other questions or projects that might arise from time to time

Disclosure of Compensation

The FSP receives compensation in three possible ways: fees for assets under management, commissions and fees for services rendered. These are summarized below. Whereas the previous page explained the rationale to clients, this page quantifies payment to both the FSP's firm and the FSP. In all cases, the FSP receives 100-x% of the total compensation, while the FSP's firm receives the remaining x%.

1. Fees For Assets Under Management. For all clients using the fee-based program, fees are spelled out in writing. Fees are set in accordance with the amount of investable assets in clients' portfolios on a declining scale on cumulative assets under administration. Clients receive a customized Investment Policy Statement (IPS) with this program. Fees are 1.5% on the first $250,000; 0.75% on all assets above that amount and 0.375% on all additional assets over $2,000,000. These fees include GST. In instances when clients are not using the fee-based program, the FSP receives "trailer fees" for assets under management. These are paid directly by the company in question and vary depending on various factors. Therefore, where "wrap" programs are utilized, every effort will be made to set the compensation level at a comparable level, accepting that different companies have different methodologies for calculating fees.

2. Commissions. Some transactions may generate commissions. These can be summarized as follows:

Deferred Sales Charges (DSC) as defined in each mutual fund's prospectus are generally recommended for investment accounts under $100,000. These are generally set at 4% to 6% at the time of purchase. Such purchases also involve trailing commissions of 0.25% to 0.5% or no sales commission with an annual trailing commission of 0.5% to 1.25% if deferred sales charges are not used. There will generally be a penalty to the client of about 6% from the point of purchase declining to 0% over seven years with DSC funds. This is called a "load." Stocks, Bonds, Royalty Trusts and ETFs are purchased and sold with a flat transaction charge of $85. Other products such as life insurance, royalty trusts, labour-sponsored funds and limited partnerships also pay a commission to both the FSP and the FSP's firm. These products are recommended only when appropriate for the client and compensation may be highly variable. Please ask regarding compensation if you are purchasing a product such as this.

3. Fees for Services Rendered. These are clearly defined in scope and detail before beginning on the project and are set at $200/hour. The total fee charged depends on the services in question.

copy for her files once the account was established. Consumers of financial products often complain that they do not understand how the business of financial advice works. That's too bad. If they paid more attention, they might get FSPs to be more forthcoming, too.

Let's take a quick look at how a professional, qualified, fee-based FSP of the future might differ from the prevailing advice-givers of today. On the next page is a triangle that illustrates the differences in products, services and approach. Note that the illustration assumes the FSP of the future has all relevant licences (full securities and insurance) as well as all the necessary credentials necessary to perform planning activities.

The British Experience

In the late 1990s, Britain became the first country in the world to make compensation disclosure mandatory through legislation brought forward by the Financial Services Authority (FSA). The change in law has had a monumental impact on the financial services industry. Note that changing the law is about the only lever available to bring about a meaningful change in FSP conduct. Moral suasion simply doesn't work when the vested self-interest involves hard dollars and a livelihood.

Later in 2003, it will be mandatory for FSPs in Britain to allow consumers to pay by fee if they want to. More detail can be found by visiting www.fsa.gov.uk. The role of the FSA is fourfold:
1. maintain market confidence
2. promote public understanding of the financial system
3. protect consumers
4. fight financial crime

Cost Considerations

Over time, people will simply think of their investments as "parts," or building blocks for their portfolio. It stands to reason that since cost is a major factor in determining how well consumers do in reaching their financial objectives, then cost should be an up front consideration for all products and services that are purchased.

Management expense ratios (MERs) are widely disclosed in newspapers, websites and in the prospectuses of mutual funds themselves. This presupposes that the person buying the product knows what an MER is and where to look it up. Most still do not. Similarly, most brokerage and planning firms are fairly up front with stock commissions for those people who care to ask. Bond commissions, on the other hand, are far less transparent; they are embedded in the price of the product.

In order to make a truly informed decision about a product, the price should be an up front part of the discussion. Have you ever bought a car without asking what the price was? Of course not! Yet the amount of money spent on mutual fund MERs over the course of a lifetime will likely amount to a

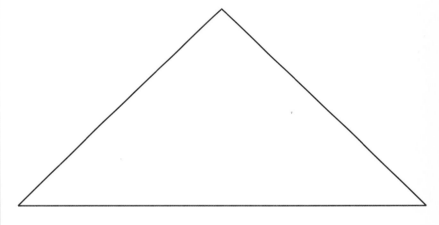

How A Professional FSP Differs

"Partnering to Secure Your Retirement Lifestyle"
Parts and Labour Sold Separately
Deductible Open Plan Fees
Access to Wide Product Selection
(Individual Securities, ETFs, F Class Funds)
Fully qualified to do Planning Work
Written Investment Policy Statement
Maximizes Risk-Adjusted Returns
Simplifies Client Lives
Mindful of Tax Implications
Considers All Things Related to Clients' Financial Affairs

Most Brokers Today	**Most Planners Today**
Embedded Compensation	Embedded Compensation
"Stock Pickers"	"Fund Pickers"
Relatively Expensive Products	No access to Individual
Corporate Underwriting Overlay	Securities, ETFs, Royalty Trusts
Ask about credentials	Ask about credentials

price that is in excess of *many* cars if you are anything more than an extremely modest investor.

Before placing an order, clients should be encouraged to go to a website run by the Ontario Securities Commission that has a fee calculator attached (www.strategis.ic.gc.ca/SSG/ca01457e.html). Use reasonable assumptions about your time frame and rates of return, but plug in your actual fee and see the impact of fees for yourself.

Problems Using the Current Format

There are a number of problems associated with embedded compensation for FSPs. Independence and impartiality are bound to be compromised when some products pay FSPs more than others, while still other products don't pay FSPs at all. Let's take a look at a few of the problems:

Problem #1: Deferred Sales Charges (DSCs) are often costly to clients. At present, most mutual funds are purchased through FSPs and about 75% of these are purchased using a DSC (also called back-end load) model. If a client sells more than 10% of any given DSC fund in any given year in the first seven years or so, there will be a penalty for having done so.

The average holding period for mutual funds currently stands at less than four years, which translates into a penalty of about 3.6%. Amortized over four years, this average consumer would have added 0.9% to annual costs. A fund with an MER of 2.4% would have effectively cost the client 3.3% over those four years.

Therefore, if a consumer chooses to redeem units of a DSC fund rather than switching to another fund in the same family to avoid penalties, the de facto cost of using the fund rises dramatically. Furthermore, some FSPs do not necessarily do all they can to dissuade clients from switching, because they can reinvest the proceeds of the sale into other DSC funds. That way the FSPs can simultaneously maximize their own revenue, while putting their clients back into the same bind they just paid so handsomely to get out of.

Problem #2: Balanced funds generally pay FSPs like equity funds. If a typical balanced portfolio is defined as being 60% stocks and 40% bonds, that asset allocation could be approximately replicated using balanced funds. When investments are sold as separate asset classes, there is more room for tax optimization, more precise asset allocation and cost reduction. Bonds (either when purchased directly or through a mutual fund) pay less than stocks. Balanced funds pay more than bonds and, not surprisingly, have higher MERs than bond funds. A 60% stock fund 40% bond fund split would have an asset allocation similar to a balanced fund, but the balanced fund would cost the client more and pay the FSP more. No self-respecting professional would ever use a balanced fund to construct a balanced portfolio, yet this is how many FSPs get a fixed income component into their clients' portfolios, by ceding discreet control over the asset allocation while being paid as if the mix was all equities.

Problem #3: Commission compensation is based on the day of the purchase. The ability to switch from a stock fund to a bond fund in the same family at no cost, means a cunning FSP can deliberately place an investment into a stock fund, earn a higher commission, and then switch the investment to a bond fund shortly thereafter. Since the bond fund pays less at the outset, there is an increase in FSP pay. By the time the client finds out what happened, the switch to the recommended fixed income product has been completed and an apology rendered. No harmdone—or is there?

Problem #4: Many clients don't understand that no load does not mean no embedded compensation and most equity mutual funds pay a 1% annual trailing commission when purchased in a 0% front-end load (i.e., no-load) format. Note that regulators call them "trailing commissions," but FSPs call them "trailer fees;" you be the judge of which stakeholder is more accurate. Some unscrupulous FSPs have been known to tell their clients that they are working on a fee basis and then charge anywhere from 1% to 1.5% while continuing to collect these embedded "trailers," effectively "double dipping" on their compensation. That's a total compensation of 2% to 2.5%, and that's usury, no ⟵ matter what the additional services are. Many unsophisticated clients are none the wiser. Some major firms have instituted policies that prohibit the use of funds with an embedded compensation in a fee-based program to combat this activity.

This has its own problems, however, since there are so-called I Class funds (the I stands for institutional), in which the fund company charges a lower management fee for clients who invest $500,000 or more with that company, but still pays a modest embedded compensation. After all, the notion of scalability applies to product managers too. If consumers have enough confidence in one company to place a large amount of money with it, it's only natural that the manufacturer would offer a 'volume discount' too. Here's the problem: if a client wanted to work with a fee-based FSP at a firm that had a policy precluding the use of embedded compensation products in a fee-based account, that client would not be able to take advantage of I Class fee reductions. This essentially defeats the purpose of I Class funds. In other words, consumers can choose between unbundled compensation products and products with reduced fund company fees. What is not available are funds with no embedded FSP compensation *and* reduced fees.

Problem #5: Some mutual fund companies have been known to offer "negotiable commissions." Here, FSPs can get a higher commission for some investments (e.g., RRSP assets, which are set aside for the long-term anyway) and less for others. The idea is for total compensation to be similar, but for clients to gain more liquidity than they would have otherwise. The trouble is, most FSPs manage to negotiate an up front commission in excess of the commissions set by traditional companies, meaning clients are even more restricted than they otherwise would be on their back-end load money. Furthermore, there is generally little or no recurring revenue associated with those assets that attracted the highest initial commission, offering no meaningful incentive for the FSP to continue to offer advice regarding those assets.

For example, let's say a client has $200,000 to invest, $110,000 in an RRSP and $90,000 in an investment account. The FSP could get a whopping 9% commission on the RRSP money (locking the client in to a nine-year redemption schedule in the process) and no commission at all on the rest of the portfolio. Trailer fees would be paid on the $90,000 in the open plan, but not for the RRSP account. The FSP would get a commission of $9,900 and a first-year trailing commission of $900 for a total compensation of $10,800, assuming the purchase was made on January 1 of that year. The client, in turn, would have total access to the $90,000 if needed without having to pay DSC penalties. Had the money been invested on a DSC basis, the FSP would have received $10,000 in commissions and $1,000 in trailing commissions for a total of $11,000, all else being equal.

The problems created here are many. First, the FSP receives no further compensation on the $110,000 in the RRSP ever and is therefore not likely to pay much attention to that money. The client, in turn, will have to pay massive redemption penalties if selling early and will have to wait longer than usual to get out at no cost. Second, most FSPs who "negotiate" their commissions, tend to do so in a way that is detrimental to their client, since negotiations generally favour the party with the strongest knowledge of the subject. Usually, the negotiation ends up with the FSP getting more money up front than would otherwise be possible. The rule of asymmetric information suggests that the party with a deeper understanding of the system is bound to win in any negotiation.

Problem #6: Sometimes clients move and FSPs have to give up the account as a result. Imagine someone from Toronto investing $500,000 in DSC equity funds. That would generate a commission of $25,000 for the FSP and her firm in the next pay run. A very good week! If that client suddenly chooses to move to Montreal, the Ontario FSP would have to surrender the account, since Quebec has a law stating that FSPs must live within fifty kilometres of the Quebec border in order to offer advice to Quebec residents. Let's say the client finds a new Quebec-based FSP, who dutifully takes over the account and offers all the advice and value-added services one would expect from a qualified financial professional. There's only one problem; the new FSP will receive only 50 bps per year (0.5%) for his trouble. Assuming no change in account size, it will take the new FSP a decade to earn what the original FSP earned in a week! That's not remotely fair to the new FSP. Of course, all of this is equally true if the client in question is simply dissatisfied with the first FSP and switches as a result.

Problem #7: Salespeople get paid the same. As noted previously, professionals charge according to expertise and experience. With FSPs, compensation is set and depends entirely on product placement. There is no room for clients to seek out better or lesser professionals on the basis of price. No matter which FSP they use, the cost is identical if they use identical embedded compensation products to plan for their future.

There are a number of other very real problems, but you get the picture. As long as there's compensation embedded in the product, there's potential for trouble, especially if that compensation pays a disproportionately high amount at the time of the original sale. No one is saying that FSPs working

with embedded compensation are inherently dangerous, merely that embedded compensation creates opportunities for outcomes that are not always in the clients' best interests, which are supposed to be paramount at all times. Moving to an unbundled format offers a number of very real benefits including:
- increased transparency and accountability
- elimination of conflict of interest
- the flexibility to switch investment products without paying penalties
- a potential for deductibility of fees in non-registered accounts
- an opportunity to improve compounding by paying fees without redeeming investment units
- access to cheaper investment vehicles than would otherwise be offered

Some of these additional benefits will be explored later. Embedded compensation doesn't necessarilly hurt clients, but FSPs who earn embedded compensation are routinely put into positions where they might hurt their clients if they have a momentary lapse of judgement or just plain bad luck. The vast majority of FSPs who use embedded compensation products do not do anything unsavoury, but the opportunity exists and can easily be removed. The surest way to eradicate these problems is to remove the circumstances that allow the problems to occur in the first place. If the only way an FSP gets paid is through fees paid directly from the client, based on a formal, written agreement, awkward situations like those listed above are far less likely to happen.

Understanding how most FSPs have been paid up until now will go a long way in finding an FSP who can help you do what is right for your money. There are few FSPs in Canada today who are truly independent and who offer the widest possible range of products and services to their clients. The time has come to press the issue. If FSPs are going to emerge from all the change the financial services industry is going through and hold themselves out as bona fide professionals, they will have to do away with embedded compensation. Anything less and their credibility would be too open to attack.

The conduct and practices necessary to transform the rendering of financial advice in Canada from a predominantly sales-oriented culture to a predominantly advice-oriented culture will have to be made mandatory. Now that the problems inherent in the embedded compensation model are more fully understood, regulators and legislators should be swift to rectify the situation and eradicate embedded compensation. How can this be accomplished?

THE RAMIFICATIONS OF UNBUNDLING

Integrity is when what you say, what you do, what you think, and who you are all come from the same place.

—Madelyn Griffith-Haynie

I can't understand why people are frightened of new ideas. I'm frightened of the old ones.
—John Cage

The majority of FSPs are decent people. This is true whether they are fee-based or commission-based. It is widely accepted that there is no meaningful correlation between FSP competence and any form of compensation model. Both models are generally thought to have equally thorough and creative practitioners too. As with any line of work, there are some who are better than others, irrespective of compensation model.

It needs to be said that no single business model has a monopoly on decency or competence and that improprieties may occur with either. Furthermore, the very question of what constitutes an impropriety is open to debate. Here's a list of things consumers should currently expect from an FSP, regardless of compensation model used:

1. New client application forms should be completed and returned to the client noting risk tolerance, liquidity, income and other salient points accurately.

2. Clients should receive a written investment policy statement (IPS) to govern the asset allocation decision and client expectations going forward. This is prepared based on responses given to a purposeful questionnaire that asks about risk tolerance, liquidity needs, time horizon, return expectations, frequency of portfolio reviews and rebalancing decisions, among other things. The IPS should be used to govern all future portfolio changes.

3. A letter of engagement should be used to outline precisely what services will be provided to the client and what the general expectations of the relationship are.

4. A compensation disclosure letter should be signed and added to the file. As with the previous point, clients should get a copy.

5. The clients' interests and those of the FSP should be linked to the greatest extent that is reasonably possible. With fee-based FSPs, compensation is

generally dependant on portfolio performance and growth. Presumably, there would be some comfort in knowing that independence and suitability are not being compromised when recommendations are being made. The more the account grows, the more the FSP makes. If the account goes down, the FSP makes less.

6. The FSP should have credentials to support whatever recommendations are being made. This is true both with regard to products and to the strategies and tactics used. The most widely accepted international designation for financial planning is the CFP designation.

7. There should be some coherent rationale supporting the investment recommendations and planning strategies being made. Whether the issue is one of mandate, track record, cost or some other generally accepted material factor(s), those considerations should be plainly spelled out. There should be a similar rationale for planning recommendations.

8. Both return and risk should be appropriately considered, from the client's perspective, when making portfolio recommendations. Often, FSPs allow their personal biases regarding risk tolerance to seep into their recommendations.

9. Proper consideration should be given to all related matters in portfolio design like tax efficiency, income splitting and pension integration. It is vital that the "big picture" be considered when making planning recommendations in general and portfolio recommendations in particular.

10. The FSP should demonstrate a commitment to professionalism through both continuing education and the purchasing of errors and omissions insurance. Both are traits of professionalism.

Although both fee-based and commission-based FSPs have coexisted for some time, each has been a little suspicious of the other. Some FSPs are so malleable as to be either fee- or commission-based, depending on what their clients want. In effect, these FSPs take the rationale outlined above to heart and say that the method of compensation is not nearly as important as the fact that it is clearly spelled out, that the client agrees and consents and that the format is in the client's best interests.

The future may well be different because of the problem of intellectual consistency. Professionals charge fees, whereas salespeople earn commissions. Since FSPs wish to be thought of as professionals, they need to charge fees for money management and financial planning services, even if there is nothing inherently wrong with the current practice of earning commissions.

The possible exception to this principle may be in regard to insurance advice. With insurance, commissions are likely the most appropriate and professional way to compensate people for providing insurance solutions to consumers. Just as commissions are the most appropriate way to compensate people for working as real estate agents, the insurance side of financial advice remains primarily transaction-based. Where there's generally one transaction and no meaningful relationship after the fact, commissions simply make more sense. Ultimately, the question of compensation structure revolves around suitability and common sense, not dogma.

One might even develop a "Continuum of Professionalism" regarding financial advice. There are three basic stages to be applied to financial services and advice:

<--->

Commission Based   Embedded Fee Based   Unbundled Fee Based

On the left, we have the least professional (most sales-oriented) compensation model. It provides FSPs with a big paycheque up front and a little bit extra for ongoing services. The compensation method involves penalties that are to be incurred by clients if they redeem their products in anything less than the long term, effectively constraining their decision-making along the way.

Moving right, we come to embedded compensation, in which products offer *indirect* "trailer fees" to FSPs for services rendered. These fees are collected by the company manufacturing the products through the management expense ratio of the products in question and remitted to FSPs. They are recurring, offering no appreciable "up front" commission and no corresponding penalty to clients should they wish to use another product and/or FSP. Disclosure regarding the total cost to the client and the total compensation to the FSP remains largely piecemeal. Compensation may or may not be scalable and fees may or may not be deductible for non-registered accounts.

Finally, we come to unbundled compensation, the most professional compensation paradigm. Similar to the embedded compensation model in that it involves fees being paid to FSPs (and commissions being foregone), it also involves a number of noteworthy differences. First, the FSP is paid *directly* by the client, so disclosure is never an issue. Second, fees are almost always scalable, meaning they taper downward as a percent of total assets as accounts grow. Third, they are most likely tax deductible for non-registered plans. Finally, they may be paid from outside the portfolios themselves, leaving more money to compound inside the portfolios that use this format. Virtually no FSPs are sufficiently confident in the services they offer to work using this format. One way to make decisions in life involves the question, "What would you do if you were not afraid?" That's a question today's FSPs need to look deeply into their own souls to answer.

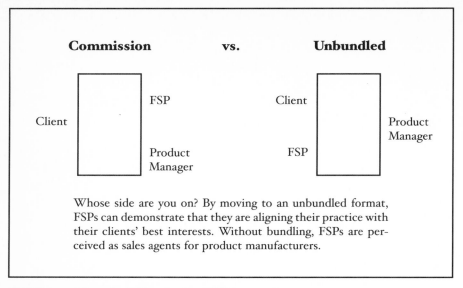

Commission vs. **Unbundled**

Client — FSP / Product Manager

Client — FSP — Product Manager

Whose side are you on? By moving to an unbundled format, FSPs can demonstrate that they are aligning their practice with their clients' best interests. Without bundling, FSPs are perceived as sales agents for product manufacturers.

MERs and Loads: What's the Difference?

No matter how much people in the industry like to think progress has been made in explaining how mutual funds work, most consumers still don't "get it." This struck me when speaking with a client recently. We had been investing money on a 0% front-end basis for a little while, but I was now asking her to move to an unbundled fee option. Since I had given her the 0% front-end option for some time (as a transitional situation between choosing from the aforementioned options), she was wondering if she could continue to work that way. In so doing, she would incur no DSC charges if she was to sell her funds early. I countered that this was not an option that I was giving to my clients. I wanted to make a clean break; clients were going to work on either an unbundled fee-basis or not at all and the time had come to choose.

She then surprised me. She said a friend had told her that it was cheaper to buy "no-load" funds. This, of course, is only true with a limited number of fund families. In most instances, clients who work with FSPs use traditional third party funds (names like Mackenzie, AIM/Trimark, AGF, AIC and C.I.). In this case, the MER is identical whether the fund is purchased on a 0% front-end basis (with no load for early redemption) or a back-end load basis.

The cost of a mutual fund is its Management Expense Ratio. This is generally the sum of FSP compensation, fund company compensation, trading and regulatory costs and GST. For most equity funds sold in Canada, MERs are between 2.30% and 2.95%. These are for so-called A Class funds and the total annual cost is absolutely identical whether the fund is purchased on a 0% front-end basis or a back-end load basis. Newspapers report returns net of MERs, so if a fund shows a 7.5% rate of return with a 2.5% MER, it earned 10% on the year, deducted 2.5% through the MER and passed the difference on to unitholders. The majority of consumers still don't understand that.

From an FSP's perspective, DSC funds generally pay a 5% commission (equities) with a 50 basis point (0.5%) recurring services fee (called a trailer fee), whereas bond funds pay a 4% commission with a 25 basis point (0.25%) trailer fee. In other words, when an FSP sells a fund on a DSC basis, he accepts more payment up front in exchange for lower payments in future years and is paid more for equity funds than for income funds.

From a client's perspective, DSC funds retain the identical MER as no load funds, but have a "charge" associated with them if they are redeemed early (generally within the first seven years after they are purchased). If the fund is held until the DSC charge expires, there is absolutely no difference between a DSC fund and a no-load fund, not in cost, content, tax treatment or anything else. It should also be noted that while investors may always switch from one fund to another fund within the same family at no cost, there may be tax consequences in non-registered accounts.

However, if it turns out that for any reason the client wishes to sell the DSC fund early, there will be a charge to pay. This drops over time. The friend of my client could potentially be right, if DSC funds were used improperly. In that instance, the client would have paid the MER along the way, but would have also incurred a DSC charge upon disposition.

It should be clear that the real difference here is how the FSP chooses to be paid. As in the U.K., this decision should not be unilateral and should always be made in consultation with the client. The options are either more money up front and less in future years (DSC) or some flat amount based on assets annually. Neither is right nor wrong, it is simply a matter of personal preference. Experts estimate that about 75% of funds are sold on a DSC basis in Canada, making it the most common way of doing business.

The difference in the two structures is how the FSP's compensation is amortized. If an FSP is paid 5% up front and the fund only costs 2.5% a year, it should be obvious that the mutual fund company is out of pocket in the short-term. As a result, it would want to recoup its payment to the FSP should the fund be redeemed prior to the DSC schedule running its course. Since the FSP has already been paid and the client has presumably been told that this is a long-term proposition and that there are virtually always options within the fund family that would forego these charges, the client is asked to foot the bill.

If she chooses to liquidate less than 10% of that fund prior to the amortization period (DSC schedule) running its full course, these charges do not apply, since this is considered a modest redemption made for liquidity/cash flow purposes and not a large-scale sell off. The 10% option can be exercised annually, but is non-cumulative. In other words, a client cannot redeem 20% for free in year two if there was no redemption the previous year.

Assuming the client understands that this is a long-term proposition, she should be indifferent to the compensation model chosen. However, FSPs tend to recommend the DSC option. It should be stressed that FSPs are required by their fiduciary duty as applied by the law to place the interests of the client ahead of any other interests.

Unfortunately, "no-load" is not the same as "no embedded compensation to the FSP." Moving to an unbundled environment would put an end to the misconception. The products would not pay the FSP in any way, shape or form. That's because FSPs will be paid for offering advice, not for placing products.

The GST of Financial Advice

The thing that keeps most people from working with a fee-based FSP is the fee itself. If consumers have worked with an FSP who didn't charge fees directly, the quantum of the bill was probably never openly discussed before. Sort of an "ask me no questions, I'll tell you no lies" kind of approach. Putting fees out in front changes that.

Perhaps the easiest way to understand the visceral hatred many people feel about paying fees (especially in years when markets are going down), is to consider how we reacted as a nation to the Goods and Services Tax (GST) when it was first introduced. I was working on Parliament Hill in the summer of 1990, doing a work term for my graduate studies co-op program in public administration. There was a special committee that was set up to look into the effects of the GST on consumer prices. All manner of people and organizations came forward to express fear and loathing about the proposed changes to Canada's fiscal policy. People instinctively resist change.

Members of the government of the day went to great lengths to explain that the tax would now be "transparent;" it would now be out in the open, whereas previously it had been embedded in the price of the final product (sound familiar?). Government members insisted that the GST would be replacing an outdated tax system that charged large amounts for some things (manufactured goods) and nothing at all for others (services). Again, many consumers today believe they are paying a load to buy a product (a "good" called a mutual fund), while they feel they are entitled to free advice (a service) along the way.

The position of the government was that all things, both goods and services, should be taxed equally and that the tax should be out in the open, making it politically difficult to raise taxes in the future. Consumers weren't buying it. Putting a tax on sales receipts where none existed before created the distinct impression that taxes were going up, even though the GST proved to be revenue-neutral. It was a measure that was tantamount to political suicide for the Mulroney government, even though the Chrétien government has done nothing to alter it and has won three majorities since. Perhaps now readers can get a better sense of why nothing has happened to unbundle products and advice in the past. Everyone in the financial services industry is scared of the backlash that is almost certain to follow.

By putting their fee right in the open, FSPs will be made to do business much like other professionals. There will be a constant assessment on the part of clients as to whether or not they are receiving true value for the services provided and advice rendered. This will be terrifying for many FSPs who do little to genuinely add value, but will assist consumers greatly in determining who the true professionals are. Until now, most consumers understood vaguely that they were paying their FSP indirectly, but had no real idea of how much money the FSP received as a result of various purchases.

Perhaps the greatest challenge for FSPs, especially in unsettling times, is to find a way to constructively get clients to do the things they likely wouldn't do otherwise—things like buying low, staying the course and focusing on a long-term future that seems perilously endangered when account values slip in the near term. There is no single way to monitor or quantify the power of ethical, purposeful persuasion. In this world, virtually nothing can be said with absolute certainty. Still, if you want to be as assured as is reasonably possible that your FSP is looking out for your best interests, you should ask some pointed questions before making choices. Of course, the transition to unbundled fees requires a high degree of disclosure, discussion and explanation about how this transition might reasonably be accomplished. The changeover must occur without undue damage to either the FSPs' welfare or clients' port-folio values. Both parties need to have their interests honourably represented as this transition moves forward.

Look Beside You, FSP

There is broad consensus in the financial services industry that all forms of commission are going away forever. Those FSPs who are intrepid enough to "change before they have to" have already begun moving their practices to a fee-based paradigm. This is a valuable and laudable step, but it is only an interim step in the ultimate evolution of financial advice. Like those "killer courses" in first year university in which the professor says, "Look to your left; look to your right. One of the three of you will be gone by the end of the semester," there will be a major weeding out process that FSPs will soon have to endure. No one can know for sure how many FSPs will have the drive and ability to "make it" as professionals, but the one-third benchmark used by most first-year university programs seems about right.

Virtually all of the FSPs who fail to make a career out of offering financial advice will be of the low value-added kind who probably never should have been allowed into the business in the first place. About one-third of all FSPs will be out of work once unbundling arrives, and one-half of the commission-based FSPs could find themselves in the unemployment line. Of course, this will leave more assets for the true professionals to manage, making them more profitable than ever. The new profession of offering financial advice is going to be a real-world test case of the popular reality series *Survivor*, with literally billions of dollars of client assets at stake.

How can this be accomplished? Note that this change will likely not occur without some client pain too. The biggest challenge we all face (indeed, perhaps the primary reason things haven't changed sooner) is how to "get there from here," in light of the very real sacrifices that both consumers and FSPs will need to make along the way. Like the Canada Pension Plan before its contribution levels were reformed, the problem was swept under the carpet and has now become chronic. The status quo cannot continue indefinitely, and there is no time like the present to take action. On the next pages are a couple of sample letters that might be used in completing the transition. The first deals with the disclosures that need to be made to allow clients to make a meaningful decision to make the switch to a true fee-based arrangement with all relevant details being covered. The second might be sent to the same client (who has been given the option to switch) requesting an acknowledgement of the client's decision if moving to a fee based arrangement is not the preferred course of action.

The problem that some people might see with these letters is that they give consumers the ability to "opt out" of a fee-based arrangement, which defeats the purpose of moving to fee-based in the first place. Of course, this is just one scenario. For now, let's just assume that professionals will ultimately have to coalesce around unbundled, fee-based advice.

It may well be that for those FSPs who are happy to call themselves "salespeople" as opposed to "financial professionals," it might be sensible for them to continue to work earning DSCs. In fact, it might well be doubly preferable if consumers are satisfied with the advice they are getting from these people. Consumers would be able to forego paying DSC penalties and the salesperson could continue to earn commissions. At the low-end of the financial services market (perhaps under $100,000 of investable assets), this might provide an entirely workable marriage of convenience.

The point is that FSPs can't be allowed to have it both ways. If you're an FSP offering financial advice as a salesperson, then feel free to call yourself a salesperson and to continue going on earning your commissions. If you want to be called a "financial professional" or "professional financial planner" or some such thing, you'll have to move to a fee-based format. You should then provide all the trappings of any established professional. Then consumers would finally be able to differentiate between salespeople and professionals.

Specialization and Mass Customization

Many people know about the Mayo Clinic. It's an ultra-high-end medical clinic in Rochester, Minnesota where a team of highly qualified specialists works together under one roof. Patients who go there have deep pockets and problems that remain unsolved by the medical professionals in their home community.

Once people are admitted, they are given an extensive questionnaire and run through an imposing battery of tests, the results of which are considered by specialists in a variety of disciplines in order to holistically diagnose and treat whatever ails the patient. The attitude is that if the best professionals at

Fee Conversion Deadline Rapidly Approaching!

Dear Client:

As you already know, I have been encouraging clients to switch to a fee-based arrangement since the middle of 2001. I have done a number of things to facilitate this transfer, including making all new purchases on a "no-load" basis and redeeming 10% of all DSC units annually and reinvesting the proceeds in identical funds. That being said, I can wait no longer for your decision. In essence, **you need to agree to a little short-term pain in exchange for what will likely be a substantial long-term gain**. If you decide to proceed with this switch, it needs to be completed by the end of this year.

Of course, if you prefer to work on a commission basis (which is how we were working prior to July of 2001), that is fine with me too. Although I believe it is in your best interest to switch to a fee-based arrangement, a decision to revert back to a commission arrangement is always an option. If this is your choice, I will be sure to refer you to a colleague who continues to work using a commission-based format. However, I strongly prefer that you stay with me and switch formats. I need a clear decision one way or another.

In this mailing you will find three enclosures to assist you:

1. A spreadsheet that quantifies our best guess of both the short-term cost and the long-term benefit (likely understated, since benefits only increase with time).

2. An article written by me that explains my rationale and the steps taken to date.

3. A letter that I would ask you to sign if you choose **not** to make this switch. If you choose this option, new purchases will be made on a DSC (back-end load) basis.

My assistant will be calling you this week to answer your basic questions and to see if a meeting can be arranged. I'm extremely excited about this. I cannot stress enough that this is an option that the vast majority of advisors are **not** giving their clients. I sincerely hope you give it serious consideration.

Sincerely,
ABC CAPITAL MANAGEMENT LTD.

Joe Brilliant
Senior Financial Advisor

Acknowledgement of Refusal to Pursue Fee Conversion Option

This is to provide formal acknowledgement that Joe Brilliant has recommended that I switch from my current commission-based format of portfolio management to a fee-based asset management program and that I have chosen not to follow his recommendation. This will also acknowledge that Joe has made every effort to educate me as to the ramifications of this conversion. Specifically, Joe has attempted to accurately quantify these items:

- DSC Charges that might be incurred as a result of a switch
- general tax ramifications for non-registered accounts
- changes in relative cost structure going forward
- the point in time where cost savings would make up for charges incurred (the "break-even date")
- annual savings beyond the "break-even date," assuming no change in portfolio size or composition

I understand that Joe has been making mutual fund purchases on my behalf on a "no-load" basis since July of 2001 and that he has offered to redeem 10% of all DSC units annually since that time in order to minimize DSC charges that would otherwise be incurred. In so doing, Joe has foregone considerable potential revenue.

Furthermore, I understand that by declining Joe's recommendation to switch, all future purchases will revert back to the traditional, commission-based (DSC) compensation. This development, in turn, will likely make a switch to a fee-based arrangement at a later date relatively more expensive than doing so now, although the 10% free conversion option will still be offered if that is my wish.

By signing and dating this acknowledgement, I hereby confirm that I have read and understood the contents outlined herein.

_____	_____	_____
Client	Joe Brilliant	Date

the Mayo can't help you, no one can. Sometimes urologists will know things that ear, nose and throat specialists won't and that cardiologists have never even heard about. By pooling their resources and considering alternative approaches and solutions to relatively uncommon problems, medical conditions that might otherwise be deemed untreatable are often successfully resolved at the clinic.

There is a parallel between the medical and financial advice professions. As financial planning and integrated wealth management becomes increasingly complex, the analogy becomes increasingly apt. Most truly professional FSPs are qualified to be diagnostic generalists first and foremost. They are the equivalent of small town general practitioners (GPs) and their focus from the outset is in understanding the situation.

That's where the Mayo Clinic analogy comes in. Financial advisory firms are increasingly setting themselves up in a parallel fashion, with an army of generalist professionals as the primary "relationship managers" dealing with individual households and an army of highly qualified specialists available in the background. Once the client's/patient's situation is thoroughly understood, treatment can begin. In most instances, the problems will be commonplace and the treatments correspondingly routine. However, from time to time, situations present themselves in which the highly skilled generalist needs only to make an appropriate diagnosis and then call in a specialist to perform an operation of some sort.

The in-house financial specialists can then brainstorm about how to solve the most challenging, interesting and potentially lucrative cases. These might involve estate freezes, corporate restructuring, creditor protection, buy-sell agreements, retirement compensation arrangements, will and estate planning, offshore planning, charitable gifting strategies, multi-generational planning, deployment of stock options and a host of other more complicated concepts. In fairness to FSPs, it would simply be unreasonable to expect them to know all the nuances of these often complicated and always specialized procedures.

Many ordinary citizens never have to think of such things and, perhaps mercifully, neither do most FSPs. But what if a client walks through the door where the FSP is absolutely certain that a sophisticated strategy would, if implemented correctly, go a very long way to solving a client's problems, but also that she does not possess the skill set to deliver that strategy? Acting out of self-interest, not all FSPs would refer that client to another, more qualified FSP because there are compensation issues at stake. Rather than risk looking foolish or give up a large income stream (complex cases tend to involve disproportionately large dollars) the normal course of action for an FSP might be to say nothing. That's not a professional thing to do when a client needs help.

In the medical profession, the failure to refer is also malpractice. In the financial services industry, it's usually just plain bad business, because it can undermine a primary relationship by allowing a competitor through the door.

Everyone in the industry wants to be the primary relationship manager for his or her client, but *none* have the training to truly do it all. Given that everyone is also going after affluent and wealthy households, you can see why integrated wealth management needs to be more than just a catchphrase.

The most forward-looking financial services firms are building their own regional "Mayo Clinics" in major urban centres so that there are specialists available to treat whatever ails their best clients. This provides a stimulating work environment and offers truly customized solutions for those who want, need and are willing to pay for it. It can be very good for the corporate bottom line, not to mention being the firm of choice when it comes to solving complex financial problems for high net worth families. These are the sorts of value-added services that the media never talk about when they give their "fire your conventional broker and do everything with a discount broker" pitch. Admittedly, it only applies to a small percent of the total population. Still, it is worth noting that most high net worth families would consider it reckless to use a Do-It-Yourself approach. Cost is important, but it is only one consideration. At the mid- to high-end of the financial services continuum, it's not as important a consideration as thoroughness and quality.

The concept that is strangely related to specialization is the seemingly polar opposite notion of "mass customization." To most people, a quixotic phrase like this seems contradictory. In fact, it is a natural extension of the principles most closely associated with branding. Mass customization involves having the company stand for something, a conspicuous identity in the consumer's mind that can be articulated and reinforced through consistent experiences irrespective of the initial point of contact. McDonald's is a strong brand, not because the food is exceptional, but because people know what they're going to get whether they're in Biloxi or Beijing. Mass customization does that.

If a financial services firm can articulate and then consistently deliver on a strong brand promise, there will be a considerable positive impact in the minds of consumers, which can lead to higher margins for the services offered, resulting in a higher stock price. One of the surest ways to get FSPs to "buy in" to this concept is to make them shareholders for the company they work for. Tying valuable corporate professional objectives to corporate profitability is a great way to get everyone on the same page.

As we will soon see, the conventional value proposition of most FSPs and the firms they work for is to pick stocks or pick funds in the implicit expectation of outperforming some benchmark—usually something wholly inappropriate. Since the performance of capital markets is unknowable in the short run, financial service firms and the FSPs who work there are trying to refocus their attention on the things they can actually control. These are not insignificant. In fact, the list pretty much includes everything *except* the short- to medium-term performance of capital markets. For greater understanding, these important elements of financial planning include tax minimization, asset allocation and regular portfolio rebalancing, reporting, investment manager selection and monitoring and any of a number of client-specific planning considerations that might crop up. On top of that, there's the whole universe of behavioural quirks explored in chapter four.

Aside from the ad hoc projects that arise unexpectedly and require specific time allocations for brain-hurting professional recommendations and solutions, these are generally all the things that can be standardized, just like a fast-food franchise. In other words, mass customization also involves an off-loading of specific duties, but this time the people working behind the scenes to support the FSP are not highly skilled professionals, but the financial services equivalent of burger-flippers.

Standardization and corporate liability for unsuitable recommendations are two prime reasons why so many companies are stepping forward with wrap programs. With a wrap account, clients are given a comprehensive questionnaire and then have a portfolio designed to meet their objectives in the form of client-specific risk-adjusted returns, implemented and monitored through a written Investment Policy Statement (IPS).

The problem, as is so often the case in the financial services industry, is that the nature of the compensation structure seems to contradict the rationale for the product. The stated purpose companies give in encouraging their FSPs to use wrap accounts is not only standardization from a corporate perspective, but also practice simplification for the FSP. The whole idea is that since certain things are relatively unimportant, FSPs should spend relatively less time worrying about them.

Who wouldn't want their work to be easier? What has happened is that companies have altered their compensation structure so that FSPs can make higher recurring revenue using wrap products, than they could on a recurring basis using conventional products. On top of life being easier, FSPs are being paid more for doing the same work, or if the manufacturers and distributors of wrap products are to be believed, *less work*.

Let's take a look at the logic that underpins wrap accounts. We can begin with a few embedded compensation assumptions: trailer fees are generally set at 50 bps (0.5%) for fixed income pools and 100 bps (1%) for equity pools. Furthermore, let's assume there is a wrap charge of 50 bps (0.5%) that is tacked onto the account and paid by the client. Setting aside the obvious perspective-mutilator of having equity pools pay twice as much as fixed income pools (and you wondered why so many FSPs were so keen on equities), who do you think the 50 bps "wrapper" benefits more, the consumer or the FSP? Well, there are certainly a number of benefits associated with these services and those benefits *might* very well be worth 50 bps to a consumer. What is beyond doubt, however, is that the FSP is *conspicuously better off on two counts*: less work and a higher income. For instance, if this idea were applied to a portfolio that is 70% in equities and 30% in fixed income without the wrapper, the FSP's compensation would be:

$$.7 \times 1\% = 0.70\%$$
$$+ .3 \times .5\% = 0.15\%$$
$$0.85\%$$

Add in a portfolio wrapper and the FSP's compensation becomes 1.35%. The FSP is no longer writing an IPS, assisting with tax integration, doing portfolio rebalancing or recommending managers to manage the pools that make up the portfolio. Remember, all firms are committed to putting their clients' interests first.

Imagine if your cleaning lady tried this. Normally, she comes once every two weeks and tidies, vacuums, dusts and scrubs all the basins in your house. In exchange, you pay her $100 for her troubles. One day, she comes in and says she's still going to vacuum and dust, but the tidying and basins are out. In exchange for this simplification of the working relationship, her charge will be an entirely reasonable $140 per visit. How long would you keep this cleaning lady?

Companies that actively encourage their FSPs to recommend wrap accounts steadfastly maintain that their FSPs are migrating to this kind of product because they believe it is better for their clients, not because of compensation. If the companies were truly serious, they would raise the compensation for the individual pools and then allow for a fee offset when the wrapping was put on the portfolio. For instance, the compensation could be 150 bps (1.5%) for equity pools and 100 bps (1%) for fixed income pools, with a 15 bps (0.15%) wrapper paid by the client and a 30 bps (0.3%) offset (compensation reduction) applied to the FSP. In sum, the client would be paying 15 bps more and the company would be making 45 bps more for the additional cookie-cutter services rendered. The FSP would be accepting 30 bps less in exchange for having had the company simplify and enhance his life through standardized procedures and processes. This revenue could be recovered by downsizing redundant staff who were doing the work that is now being done by the company.

Let's review so we're all on the same page with this. The consumer would pay 0.15% more because of the certitude associated with a consistent, purposeful application of financial planning principles, while the FSP would be accepting 0.3% less in favour of having the corporate burger-flippers take the work off his desk. The company providing this service, of course, would be earning the sum of these two, 0.45% per year, in exchange for consistent, repeatable services rendered. For example, here's the FSP compensation without the wrapper:

$$0.7 \times 1.5\% = 1.05\%$$
$$0.3 \times 1.0\% = 0.3\%$$
$$1.35\%$$

Meanwhile, FSP compensation with the wrapper would be 1.05% (1.35% - 0.30%). Less compensation for less work seems entirely reasonable to most people. The current bundling of financial advisory wrap account services involves FSPs getting more pay for less work.

Again, the best solution is almost certainly not to get into the trade offs involved in placing bells and whistles on financial advice at any price. Rather, the investment products and services should come with no FSP compensation at all, so that the services rendered, the decision about who performs them and the decision about how much it will cost, can all be customized to suit the consumer. The interests of the consumer must always come first. Someone needs to get through to FSPs that the question here is not about doing what is easiest, but doing what's right.

The logic is basic, but the implications are profound. If FSPs would truly have us believe they are moving to wrap accounts because of the imposed consistency and other ancillary benefits *for their clients* and that the compensation considerations are secondary, they should prove it by accepting less pay in the process. You shouldn't have to pay someone more money to do the right thing.

Independence: Rhetoric and Reality

Given the push toward consolidation within the financial services industry, there's been a sidebar debate raging for a number of years about the independence of FSPs in firms that offer proprietary products. This debate has missed the point entirely. So far, the media has focused on whether or not consumers are well served by moving from third-party products to in-house brands, even though most apples-to-apples comparisons show that the products are relatively homogeneous. *N.B.*

It's obvious why firms that offer in-house investment products want their clients to use them—profit margins. Many companies make only a few cents on the dollar when distributing products that someone else manufactures, but perhaps eight to twelve times that amount when they distribute their own products. To use conventional business lingo, there's a much larger profit margin in manufacturing than there is in distribution.

Think of cookies: if a consumer switches from Keebler or Dare or Mr. Christie's cookies to President's Choice cookies, does that mean the consumer has been duped? Some companies have found ways to leverage their distribution network in order to compete with the third-party products already on their shelves. If clients want the new products, it means more profit for the vertically integrated provider. If clients don't want these products, distributors are no worse off. Consumers are free to use whatever products they want; they can make choices in their own enlightened self-interest.

Because there's margin in proprietary products, there's a potential incentive for some FSPs to recommend a conversion into them if the FSP is a shareholder of the company that "manufactures" the product. Higher margins lead to larger profits, lead to higher share prices, lead to personal enrichment. *N.B.*

159

Motive could certainly be called into question, but no one should be an apologist for seeking profit. Every company in the industry has a business plan that involves some conversion of third-party products into the in-house brand. That's what capitalism is all about. That being said, the linkage should be made clear so that investors understand what they're getting before they sign on the dotted line. That's what professionalism is all about. Aligning interests is a very professional thing to do. At one time, it was permissible for companies to pay their employees more for in-house products—a flagrant transgression of the principle of independence. Before long, regulators stepped in and passed National Instrument 81-105, putting an end to this reprehensible practice.

The rhetoric coming from the financial services industry is that all products are essentially the same; companies have broadly similar products and they'll all get you to about the same place at the end of the day. The unspoken, but clearly implied, message is that it should not matter whether or not the products used are proprietary or independent, since they're all the same anyway.

The problem is that independence is not revealed so much by what is put on the shelf for consumption, but by what is effectively kept off. My dictionary offers the following definitions of the word "independent:" adj. 1: self governing; also: not affiliated with a larger *controlling* (emphasis mine) unit 2: not requiring or relying on something else or somebody else 3: not easily influenced: showing self-reliance and personal freedom.

Accepting that every FSP has to be affiliated with some firm in order to do business and ultimately will be expected to recommend some product or another to assist a client, the question really becomes one of undue direct influence. Sure, the house brand is being put on the shelf in order to offer more selection which, in theory at least, should be better for consumers, but what about products that are effectively left off the shelf in the process?

This brings us back to the notion of embedded compensation. Nothing compromises independence and professionalism more. Let's take a look at a simple example, Bissett Mutual Funds. Bissett was a small, independent mutual fund company with a solid track record and a strong and loyal following among Canadians in the know. On November 27, 2000, Bissett was purchased by a global colossus called Franklin Templeton Investments. This is the same Templeton that runs the massive Templeton Growth Fund, the largest mutual fund in Canada by assets, with over $9-billion under management. Templeton wanted to get in on the consolidation game like everyone else and there were only a limited number of quality firms around to be gobbled up. Furthermore, the longer companies waited to consolidate, the higher the sticker prices were getting.

Performance at Bissett was almost always better than most, but assets under management were modest. Support from FSPs was modest too. That's because Bissett had a philosophy of keeping costs low by not advertising and passing the savings on to clients in the form of better performance. Most notably, Bissett sold its funds directly to consumers and so avoided paying trailer fees (also known as trailing commissions) to FSPs. FSPs chose to ignore Bissett.

Shortly after buying and rebranding Bissett, Templeton began to offer its funds with embedded FSP compensation. Guess what happened to sales? They exploded. The little company that FSPs had ignored until the Templeton organization came along, was suddenly a darling within the FSP community. According to Bissett, there were 7,317 FSPs who supported its products at the time of the merger. By January 1, 2003, just over two years after the merger, that number more than doubled to 15,283 in spite of a horrible grizzly bear market.

The same thing had happened a few years earlier when Mackenzie Financial purchased the Cundill family of funds from industry stalwart Peter Cundill. Cundill had a reputation to die for, but poor sales figures. When combined with the brilliant marketing savvy of Mackenzie and the embedded compensation that it brought, sales increased rapidly.

In spite of exemplary performance for many years prior to the Mackenzie acquisition, the Cundill funds toiled hard in relative obscurity with fairly low sales. Why was no one buying the funds if they were performing so well? The answer is that mutual funds, to this day, are not so much bought by consumers seeking suitable investments, as they are sold by FSPs who are seeking personal profit maximization. Cundill hadn't been paying FSPs, so FSPs simply refused to recommend Cundill funds. Of course, that didn't stop FSPs from insisting they were independent.

The lesson is that FSPs were not suddenly recommending these products because they were proprietary (because they weren't proprietary at all); they were suddenly recommending them because the majority of FSPs prefer to sell products that offer embedded compensation. There's a game of half-truths going on that virtually no one is talking about. The game is that FSPs will recommend almost anyone's mutual fund products (good or bad; third-party or proprietary) *provided that those companies pay them commissions and/or trailer fees.* Otherwise, FSPs will just pretend the other companies don't exist and continue to hold themselves out as independent professionals offering the widest possible range of investment choices for their valued clients.

When a consumer comes across an FSP who says that all managed products are essentially the same and that, furthermore, he is independent and will happily use whatever mutual fund product the consumer wants, the consumer should ask that FSP about McLean Budden; Beutel Goodman; Mawer; Phillips, Hager & North; or Chou Funds. These are five of Canada's best mutual fund companies, yet most allegedly independent FSPs would never be caught dead recommending their funds. These companies continue to do what Cundill and Bissett used to do—sell excellent products that offer no embedded compensation to FSPs. Better yet, ask about ETFs and watch the typical "independent" FSP squirm. (Andy 2004)

— *you often said most FSP's have client interests foremost!*

Most FSPs actively do everything they can to dissuade clients from buying these types of funds because they offer no embedded compensation.

In making the transition, consumers will need to acknowledge that if the FSP says he needs to be paid, there should be an agreement to pay, provided the payment requested is fair. Most FSPs are simply too frightened to ask their clients to pay them directly and will go so far as to recommend inferior products in order to avoid having that conversation. These same FSPs still call themselves "independent professionals."

Even if the companies that offer no embedded compensation had "best in class" products, those products would be tacitly blacklisted because FSPs are afraid to go to their clients and ask for direct payment. That's the saddest part of this situation. Everyone agrees that FSPs need to be paid for the important work they do. The need for payment misses the point just as much as the debate about proprietary funds versus third-party funds does. *The real point is that FSPs hold themselves out as true professionals, yet consistently act like the commission-based salespeople they were trained to be.* Eliminating embedded compensation would change that once and for all.

The companies that employ FSPs play along too. They approve products with no embedded compensation for sale and point to that fact as evidence of independence. Can they help it if none of their FSPs actually recommend these products? After all, these companies will argue, the FSPs are not being denied access.

Independence and Advice

There are many tricky situations tied to embedded compensation for people who offer financial advice. From a FSP's perspective, the primary issue has always been the need to be able to earn a fair and reasonable living. Of course, many do exceedingly well. Ironically, the question of real independence is often secondary.

For instance, many FSPs in the same firm, or even the same office, may use entirely different products when making recommendations to the public. Traditional third-party (embedded compensation) mutual funds, while diverse, are still quite similar in that the FSP gets paid simply and consistently, irrespective of which fund they recommend. Other products, which may or may not be more suited to the client's objectives, are never really considered, because they do not offer embedded compensation and FSPs are loath to ask clients to open their cheque books to pay directly.

From a client's perspective, when working with an FSP the issue is getting *unbiased advice*. From where clients stand, it all comes down to "Can I trust this person to recommend what is truly appropriate for my circumstances?" No matter how ethical, empathetic, competent and professional the FSP seems to be, clients instinctively wonder if the products and strategies being recommended are what's best—and for good reason.

That's the irony of the industry. On the one hand, there are literally thousands of embedded compensation mutual funds that offer a mind-numbing assortment of asset classes, sub-classes and strategies for consumers. On the other hand, there is an equally broad range of products—individual stocks and bonds, Exchange Traded Funds, true no-load mutual funds, royalty and income trusts—that pay the FSP nothing. The two types of investment products coexist as almost entirely mutually exclusive product lines, since embedded compensation mutual funds, primarily those sold with a commission, are the vehicles of choice for the majority of FSPs.

How can consumers be absolutely certain that what is recommended from the universe of embedded compensation mutual fund products is what's most appropriate and that there's nothing else available that makes more sense for their circumstances? In short, there is no way. Specifically, how can the consumer be assured that there isn't a non-embedded product out there that suits them better? As long as one set of products offers FSPs a form of compensation in which they do not have to do what they desperately do not want to do—insist on direct payment from clients—there will always be an inherent bias toward those products.

Some product choices are justified and defensible. FSPs have made a living holding themselves up as being totally independent when in fact they are independent only if one uses a narrow definition of the term.

The concern about FSP income is particularly true where mutual fund commissions are concerned. Most FSPs have come to rely on commissions as the primary driver of their own viability. As a simple matter of practice economics, many would not be in business if they could not earn commissions. Forcing FSPs out of a commission environment will force many FSPs out of the industry. Perhaps even more disconcerting is that those who have the biggest and most established client base are best positioned to weather this transition. For survival, size matters. Unfortunately, the size of a practice does not *necessarily* correlate with the professionalism of that practice.

Those FSPs who have fewer and smaller clients, but perhaps are more academically and professionally qualified, may not make it. In the past, and probably in the short-term future, benefits accrue disproportionately to the "big producer," rather than the "qualified professional." This is starting to change. As consumers become more discerning, the fulcrum will shift and there will be a tendency to move toward either working with a truly competent FSP or simply doing it themselves. With both primary financial services stakeholder groups, consumers and FSPs, we're looking at a scenario of "short-term pain for long-term gain." Both FSPs and their clients will likely have to endure a period when they are temporarily worse off, before things can become conspicuously better. For both parties, there are definite risks and limitations associated with making the change away from embedded compensation.

Leaving the Hotel California
The transition is not necessarily part of a "zero sum game" in which FSPs are better off after six or more years at the expense of consumers, who are somehow

worse off. Instead, both parties will endure some short-term pain in exchange for a long-term gain through the appropriate use of cheaper, index-based products.

The incremental profitability of FSPs down the road is not coming at the expense of consumers, who will be paying less in sum. Instead, it will be coming from the profit margins of mutual fund companies who weren't adding value for the fees they were charging. Even if an FSP charged 40 bps more, client costs could be reduced by using ETFs. Of course, if the client used only active funds, the total cost could rise incrementally, but only if the account was relatively small. Depending on the active/passive mix, there's enough room for both consumers and FSPs to be better off as a result of the switch.

This still understates how long it takes to break even from an FSP's perspective because it essentially assumes no new assets are being added to the portfolio. If new assets are added in a commission-based format over the original six year time horizon, the break-even will likely extend to ten years or more, depending of course on the rate at which new assets are added. The actual inflection point depends on how much is added and when. If someone suggests it will take a decade for an unbundled format transition to bring the FSP to the point where she is as well off as if she used commissions, many people in the industry would not disagree. That does not mean that a dysfunctional system should be allowed to exist in perpetuity.

No matter how good things are "on the other side" (i.e., after the transition), most independent small business owners (FSPs very much included) are not prepared to voluntarily put themselves and their families through many years of financial hardship, even if the long-term rewards are substantial. That's because FSPs are human. There is a substantial risk that the FSP won't survive the hardship to see the good life that awaits as a qualified, professional fee-based FSP.

But think about it logically. All FSPs tell their clients to take a long-term perspective. Credible FSPs walk the talk. If there is a genuine belief that the long-term perspective is best for their clients, wouldn't it be disingenuous to take anything but a long-term view regarding their own businesses?

In the long run, fee-based advice giving is almost certainly more profitable for FSPs, but few have the steely will to endure the short-term pain necessary to realize that long-term gain. They most certainly need and deserve to be paid for their efforts in guiding their clients toward financial independence, but their prevailing business model may not be the most suited for that purpose.

What about consumers? They could simply make the transition in one fell swoop and incur any DSC costs associated with the switch. Depending on when the back-end load funds were purchased, this could be an expensive proposition indeed. Other material factors, such as taxable capital gains and losses in non-registered accounts might also be major factors. Once again, the actual circumstances would vary from investor to investor. Some would be at banks where there are no DSC charges. Others might have purchased DSC funds, but their redemption schedules would have completely run their course, so there would be no DSC costs associated with a transition.

Most, however, will have purchased some DSC funds in the previous seven years or so. For these people, there are some very real costs associated with getting out of their back-end loaded mutual funds. They can do so whenever they wish, but the cost may be punitive. As a result of this reality, DSC funds are a lot like the Eagles' song "Hotel California," "You can check out any time you like, but you can never leave." The cost of divestiture will depend on the redemption schedule of the fund family you're in, the date of purchase, whether or not free units were redeemed in the interim and actual investment performance. The inescapable point is that consumers can't get out at no cost.

What will have to follow is a negotiation. Both sides will feel they are being asked to give up more than is reasonable. All concerned will need to look for compromises that respect the legitimate interests of affected parties and try to bring about reforms that will make things better in the future.

The FSP will have received a commission up front which, together with his trailing commissions, will have compensated him for his trouble. Ignoring the time value of money, which can be discounted at varying rates depending on what you believe are reasonable assumptions, a substantial period of time has to pass before an FSP will be as handsomely compensated on a fee basis as on a commission basis.

Ignoring taxes for the time being, if a consumer sells his equity DSC mutual fund fewer than seven years after buying it, he will be worse off than buying it on a no load basis. Meanwhile, the FSP will be better off. If the consumer sells more than seven, but fewer than ten years after buying, he should be indifferent, but the FSP will still be better off. If the consumer sells on the tenth anniversary of his purchase, both he and the FSP will be indifferent. Any time after year ten, the consumer will still be indifferent, but the FSP would have done better having made the recommendation on a no load basis.

With fixed-income DSC mutual funds, client costs and benefits are nearly identical to DSC equity funds. The FSP break-even, however, is pushed even farther down the road. For FSPs the point of indifference is a whopping sixteen years. Any consumer divestiture in fewer than sixteen years would mean the FSP would have been better compensated using a DSC model than a no load model.

Let's look at the mathematics of both models, ignoring the time value of money. Before we do, there is one caveat. There is a definite time preference of money. Anyone, given the choice, wants money sooner rather than later. Therefore, although the exact time-weighted monetary value of being paid more up front is debatable, the fact that a relatively larger up front payment in exchange for a relatively smaller stream of payments down the road is preferred. The net benefit is obvious. What is in dispute is the precise value of being paid more up front.

Equity Fund
$10,000 Invested FSP Break-even in Year 10
Option A, DSC: commission: $500; annual trailer fees: $50 = $1,000 in 10 years
Option B, No Load: commission: $0; annual trailer fees: $100 = $1,000 in 10 years

Fixed Income Fund
$10,000 Invested FSP Break-even in Year 16
Option A, DSC: commission: $400; annual trailer fees: $25 = $800 in 16 years
Option B, No Load: commission: $0; annual trailer fees: $50 = $800 in 16 years

Two observations spring to mind when looking at these facts:
1. If FSPs are paid more for equity investments as opposed to fixed income investments, doesn't that create a bias toward recommending equity investments?
2. Why does it take ten years to break even with no load equities, but sixteen years with no load fixed income? Shouldn't the break-even point be identical, irrespective of the asset class used?

Both consumers and FSPs have constraints above and beyond the simple break-even point. Consumers will have to concern themselves with taxes for their non-registered accounts. On the other hand, FSPs will need to consider the time value of money and time preference of money when making their own self-interested decisions. How much money do I need to make now in order to accept less down the road?

This exercise has led most FSPs to a DSC model and to recommend equities disproportionately relative to what responsible pension funds and endowments use. Even if the time horizon in question turns out to be more than ten or sixteen years, there is a natural preference to make more money sooner. That way, if another career opportunity opens up eight years down the road, the FSP will have maximized personal income before moving on. Is that the kind of thinking you want your FSP to engage in before making a recommendation to you? In the short, medium and even the long run, the DSC model seems to favour FSPs.

Ironically, the consumer being indifferent to compensation models after seven years and the FSP being better off with DSC under ten years leads to an interesting three-year window in which one party is better off, while the other is no worse off. Economists call this "Pareto Optimality," after the famous thinker Vilfredo Pareto. The idea is that if there are multiple parties involved in a transaction and at least one can be made better off without the other being made worse off, it would be an improvement. As a result, advisors can sell funds on a DSC basis and make 8.5% over seven years, after which, the consumer might be indifferent to selling and incurring no DSC charges for doing so. This allows the FSP to reposition the proceeds into the identical or at least similarly mandated fund and pocket the difference.

In the real world, this is especially prone to occur in RRSPs, in which there are no negative tax consequences. Regulators look for egregious transactions that are not in the client's best interest. Since they are no worse off from a DSC perspective, there is no obvious transgression. Still, any transaction is only supposed to be undertaken if it is believed the client will be better off and it is in the client's best interests to proceed.

One might say that there is no harm in this instance. Taking such a cavalier approach means such repositioning can go on with impunity. Fair-minded people can differ and impropriety is in the eye of the beholder. The point is that transactions can be manipulated to benefit the FSP. Note that in this scenario, the consumer spends seven years being somewhat constrained and "worse off" as a result. The FSP, however, never makes it to the point where he is worse off. As soon as the client is indifferent, the FSP can capture the market inefficiency and pocket the spread for himself. Had the client started off in a no-load scenario, there would have been no temporary constraint for that client and the FSP would have no financial incentive to make the switch after year seven.

The FSP can then recommend the redemption of a fund that has no further DSC penalties associated with it and buy another DSC fund with the proceeds. As a result, the FSP simply recommends a similar fund for some seemingly legitimate reason. That's how some unscrupulous FSPs rationalize their behaviour. Remember that people who rationalize often tell rational lies.

The technical term for this behaviour is "churning," defined as an activity that is undertaken for the sole purpose of generating a commission to the FSP. It is illegal, but difficult to prove. The FSP can point to a new fund (there must be one somewhere that had a better record over some time horizon) as a solution to all the client's problems and sell it on a DSC basis. If the FSP recommends the top fund in its category and the client is delighted with the performance, there is always a suggestion that the client's objectives or tolerance for risk have changed in the previous seven years, thereby necessitating a change. Regulators would be unhappy but would likely be unable to make any defensible assertions against the FSP.

This is not to suggest that the practice illustrated above is commonplace, merely that embedded compensation allows circumstances to persist in which this kind of unsavoury conduct can, and therefore might, occur. Commission-based FSPs are a little like the gun lobby in the U.S., which contends that "Guns don't kill people, people kill people." The fact that it's people using guns is immaterial to them.

The challenge is to find an honourable way for all stakeholders to make the switch without feeling they've been hard done by. How does one leave the "Hotel California" of back-end loads? If FSPs are simply encouraged to make the transition on a firm by firm basis, there will almost certainly be a flight of talent from firms who make this kind of transition mandatory to firms that do not.

What is required is a government and regulator-sponsored "damn the torpedoes, full speed ahead" approach, that institutes a mandatory, staged transition from commissions to fees. The nature of the problem requires that this take place over a number of years, perhaps five or six. This will allow enough time for the more unsavoury aspects of the switch to be muted, while still allowing ample time for discussion, explanation and decision-making. Until now, the political will for this kind of wholesale reform has been absent. That may no longer be the case, so here's how the transition might work:

Stage 1: Seek input from all affected parties. Many of these ideas have already been put forward in the form of two groundbreaking reports by Glorianne Stromberg in the late 1990s (see Further Reading). Public hearings need to be held to determine how to affect the necessary changes without being unduly hard on any of the legitimate interests along the way. Expected elapsed time: six months.

Stage 2: Communicate the final recommendations clearly to all parties with sufficient lead time for preparations to be made—no surprises. Expected elapsed time: six months.

Stage 3: Eliminate embedded compensation that leads to penalty charges on all products, except for those that allow consumers to redeem their units in two years or less with no adverse consequences. These sorts of mutual funds are called "low load" funds. Expected elapsed time: two years.

Stage 4: Eliminate commissions entirely on all products so that any can be redeemed at any time without penalty. Continue to allow for embedded trailer fee compensation. Expected elapsed time: two years.

Stage 5: Abolish all embedded compensation in all financial products. At that point, consumers will, *for the first time ever*, be able to rest assured that whatever product is recommended to them, is genuinely believed to be in their best interest by the person making the recommendation. It will be the first time in Canadian history that the FSP's compensation is not allowed to cloud the issue. Expected elapsed time: 1 year.

Total expected elapsed time: 6 years.

Over the years, many FSPs have talked about how they have entered into, and continue to seek, meaningful relationships with their clients. The FSP/client relationship is discussed in reverential, almost matrimonial terms, but actions speak louder than words. The investment portion of the financial services industry has grown up with an "eat what you kill" mentality of earning commissions as soon as a new account walks through the door.

Industry speakers and consultants like Nick Murray and Bill Bachrach talk about this being the golden age of financial advisory services and how the industry is being transformed from one of salespeople to one of trusted advisors. This is great in theory and there is little doubt that those who subscribe to the ideas these industry thinkers promote are doing precisely the things that ought to be done. The problem, however, is that FSPs self-select whether or not they are going to "raise the bar" to be more professional in both word and in deed. Most simply choose to do nothing, because the industry allows them to do nothing. The implicit question is, "How much should consumers trust

FSPs' advice if there's a commission involved?" Shouldn't "raising the bar" be done across the board rather than on a piecemeal basis? How else can consumers feel assured that they are working with a true professional?

In a commission-based compensation model, the legitimacy of advice will always be called into question. People looking at this arrangement from the outside might suggest that back-end loads are a bit like a one-sided prenuptial agreement, in which one party gets a disproportionate stake in the assets should the relationship go awry. No one is suggesting that the status quo is evil or unfair. Simply put, the status quo allows for illogical and sometimes unfair developments to arise, because of the way things are done. If these unfortunate developments can be eradicated, why not do it?

Checkout Procedure

Let's take a look at how the five-stage scenario might play itself out using an actual consumer example. It would take at least five years to move from the status quo to a world in which the motives of the FSP are totally beyond reproach. Let's consider a consumer with $100,000 invested in DSC mutual funds over the past five years. For simplicity's sake, let's assume further that $20,000 was invested annually and that there has been neither any growth nor decline in portfolio value over that time. The client will continue to add $20,000 a year for the foreseeable future. We can pick up the story near the end of stage two, when everyone knows the elimination of back-end load mutual funds is imminent.

The FSP and the client should have spent some time going over the ramifications of this move. They should have been involved in a meaningful discussion about what the next steps should be. The steps ultimately taken should reflect the legitimate interests of both the FSP and the client. They should seek a win-win scenario, one in which both believe they are better off in the long run.

Since the client has all the money invested with a back-end load, penalties would be substantial if there was to be a wholesale liquidation up front. Specifically, those penalties might be 2% on the first batch of $20,000 and up to 5.5% on the last DSC redemption. Mathematically, this would amount to a penalty of about 4.9%, assuming equal parts invested with 2%, 3%, 4%, 5% and 5.5% in redemption charges (19.5% divided by 5). ⟵ *3.9*

However, since 10% of any fund can be sold in any year at no cost, the de facto cost to the client would be about 4.41%. That means the account would drop from $100,000 to $95,590 the week after the liquidation and repositioning was completed. The FSP is no worse off—she would be free to charge a full fee on the entire amount—but the client sure feels the difference. The result, as you might imagine, is no deal.

Instead, the two parties must try to come up with a way to honourably maximize revenue for the FSP, without adding to the consumer's MER or DSC charges. Since 10% can be redeemed annually (i.e., over any calendar year), they agree to do that as a first step. Remember that FSPs continue to receive annual trailer fees on their existing "load funds." In spite of this, revenue for the FSP drops precipitously, as an entire year passes without earning the traditional 4% to 5% commission up front. It's like trying to quit smoking. The FSP knows this has to happen, but the reality of a significantly reduced income stream leads to professional "withdrawal symptoms." There is a craving for a commission "hit" that will never come again.

There may also be legal implications for the owners of mutual fund limited partnerships, the tax deferral vehicles that were sold over the past two decades that helped to finance DSC commissions in the first place. In the interim (i.e., during this transition), the absence of traditional DSC funds will cause virtually all traditional independent "load" companies to come up with a "low-load" option for all their existing funds. These so-called low-load funds offer a 1% commission and a 1% annual trailer fee to the FSP.

Consumers will pay no redemption charges whatsoever if they have held these funds for two years or more. If, for some reason consumers can't hold the fund for a two-year period, the DSC charge will be a more palatable 2% and the consumer will deserve to take the hit.

The client *should* agree that this arrangement is fine. The $10,000 from the free units, along with the $20,000 of new money, is invested on this basis, generating an up front commission of $300 for the FSP. The FSP receives a further $300 over the course of the year in trailer fees on this amount. A small portion of the portfolio is now paying the FSP more than ever before on an annual, recurring basis, but the client is no worse off as a result.

The next year, the same exercise is repeated. To begin, $9,000 comes from the remaining pool of "load" assets. Remember that the original $100,000 is still there, but that 10% of it was repositioned the previous year into the "low-load" fund. Next, the additional $20,000 is added to the portfolio on the "low-load basis" explained earlier. This generates an up-front commission of $290 and an annual trailer fee of an additional $290.

In the third year, we enter stage four. Everything is the same as stage three, except that "low-load" funds have now been abolished too. Intrepid mutual fund companies, ever-determined to hang onto market share, are now offering trailer fees of 1.25% on their no-load funds. The most decent ones do this without changing their MERs. Both FSPs and clients need to be careful that there has been no change. Where there has, they ought to have a full and frank discussion about whether or not they will continue to use the original fund or switch to a similarly mandated fund that has not raised its MER.

On the next page is a quick summary of how it would look, in terms of both the FSP's income stream and the client's asset placement, assuming all changes occur on January 1 every year. As you can see, the FSP makes marginally more than in year two, but because there is no more commission (even 1% can make a big difference), FSP compensation expressed as a percentage of client assets actually goes down in year three. This will be a major concern.

Transition Detail and Effect on FSP Revenue

	Year 1 $120K	Year 2 $140K	Year 3 $160K	Year 4 $180K
DSC Trailer Fee	$360	$324	$291.60	$262.44
Low-Load Commission	$300	$290	$0	$0
Low-Load Trailer Fee	$300	$590	$590	$590
No-Load Trailer Fee	$0	$0	$351.25	$692.38
Direct Client Fee	$0	$0	$0	$0
Total FSP Revenue	$960	$1,204	$1,232.85	$1,544.82
Average Percentage	0.80%	0.86%	0.77%	0.86%

Client Asset Placement

	Year 1 $120K	Year 2 $140K	Year 3 $160K	Year 4 $180K
Original DSC	$90,000	$81,000	$72,900	$65,610
Low-Load	$30,000	$59,000	$59,000	$59,000
No-Load	$0	$0	$28,100	$55,390

The FSP invests $8,100 (10% of the remaining $81,000) plus the additional $20,000 on the new fee basis and earns a respectable $351.25 in annual recurring income on that portion of the portfolio for having done so. If, at any time, the client is unhappy with the fund(s) selected in this go-round, those funds can be redeemed with no penalty whatsoever.

Remember that by year three, the portfolio has grown to $160,000. The original DSC assets (about $72,900) are paying the FSP about 40 bps (0.4%)

on average, while the other assets are paying anywhere from 1% (about $59,000 in assets) to 1.25% (about $28,100 in assets) annually. Cash flow for the FSP is starting to stabilize, although it is still nowhere near what it used to be. The blended average revenue for the FSP in year three is now about $1,232.85 on $160,000 or about 77 bps (0.77%) per year.

One more year to go and everyone checks out of the Hotel California! In the fourth year, 10% of the remaining DSC funds are redeemed and invested along with the $20,000 of additional assets on a no-load basis. Once again, the FSP earns 1.25% on this amount, while the client remains no worse off. I might add that virtually all fund companies agree that it is both easier and cheaper to introduce new classes of funds than to create totally new funds with separate investment mandates.

That's over $27,000 of additional assets now paying the FSP a respectable 1.25% per year. Still, for the fourth year in a row, the FSP has made less money than would otherwise have been the case, a huge commitment to the industry and the clients being served. Remember that in the year prior to making the switch, the FSP earned 1.4% on $100,000, a 5% commission on the $20,000 invested that year ($1,000), plus 0.4% in trailer fees on $100,000 ($400) for a total of $2,800.

By day number one of year number five, there are no DSC charges on the low-load assets and no DSC charges on the no-load assets. Perhaps best of all, the DSC charges on the original traditional DSC assets themselves, are quite nominal. The investments that were made a number of years before preparing to check out have no redemption penalties. It should also be noted that some of the DSC funds would have begun to wind-down their DSC schedules and might also have no penalties associated with them by this time. Practically speaking, it may take the entire year for all clients to check out.

In year five, an additional and final free 10% can be withdrawn and the penalties on what is left are quite modest. Remember that this illustration assumes fairly large annual contributions, given the size of the account. However, if the client was not adding money as quickly, it would be more difficult on the FSP, as income would likely drop even further. The cost to the client in year five would be identical in dollar terms.

Also, it would seem pricier to the client if the cost was expressed as a percentage of assets, given that the account would not have grown as quickly. Either way, my math puts the total DSC penalty at somewhere around $826. Obviously, individual experiences will vary, but if the companies in question charge 1% for redeeming in year seven, 2% for redeeming in year six and 3% for redeeming in year five, that's what it comes to. Given the revenue that the FSP has foregone to get to this point, that amount of pain is the least that can be asked of the client.

As a result, the agreement is reached that the time has come to check out. The last of the DSC Funds are sold and repositioned into investments with no embedded compensation whatsoever. The no-load and low-load funds can be switched to F Class versions of the same fund to eliminate embedded compensation. Our task is complete: we'll be living in a world with totally unbundled investment products. With these two types of funds, there are no tax consequences, either. Selling DSC funds, however, would involve a disposition and associated tax liability—even if the proceeds were used to buy the identical fund in an F Class format.

After selling the DSC funds and paying the remaining DSC charges, the client is left with just under $65,000 in cash, just under one third of his portfolio. Repositioning that dollar amount means that if the client were to use the proceeds of the DSC funds sale to purchase ETFs, the total cost would remain essentially unchanged. The client in the example would have made a complete transition, while incurring a total cost of less than $1,000 along the way. It should also be noted that investors would be able to switch from a DSC fund that has no penalties to an F Class fund without it being considered a taxable event. The underlying fund is identical and limited partners are not adversely affected. In truth, the concern for the rights of people holding mutual fund limited partnerships is likely the only consideration that could cause the transition to take more than six years. Having created the monster, the industry must now devise a practical way to kill it off.

There are many other factors that will impact on the actual results of this transition, which can vary considerably from client to client. These include, but are not limited to:

- the client's marginal tax bracket
- whether the assets are held in a registered or cash account (this affects taxes when switching and deductibility thereafter)
- capital gains or losses that might be triggered in the switch
- whether or not the client has any capital losses being carried forward
- the MERs on the original funds as compared to the MERs of new funds
- whether or not the client's asset allocation has changed over the years
- whether or not the client and FSP use cheaper products after the switch
- the FSP's fee once the transition is complete

From the FSP's perspective, it took until year five just to earn as much as would have been earned had the status quo been maintained. Or did it?

Remember two things. First, if we assume that FSPs currently get a 5% commission and a trailer fee of 40 bps, compensation in year five would have been $1,000 on the $20,000 invested with another $720 in trailer fees on the pre-existing $180,000. Had there been a continuation along the path that the FSP and client had started on, the FSP would have made over $1,000 less in year five ($2,800 via fees as opposed to $1,720 via commissions). By year four, the FSPs compensation would be nearly identical.

Second, four years of earning approximately 0.8% should bring some longer term rewards for the FSP too. In year four, the income is nearly identical and the FSP is clearly better off from that point onward. The "short-term pain" for the FSP, therefore, lasts about thirty-six months. However, it will generally take another few years to recover the foregone income before the FSP is about as well off under either format. Beginning around year seven, the FSP is better off, too.

There probably isn't an FSP in the country with any reasonable amount of assets under management who wouldn't love to start anew from a position of having already left the "Hotel California" of commission-based compensation. For FSPs, the philosophical question is, "What would you recommend if embedded compensation had no impact on your recommendation?"

If an FSP could magically turn time ahead by seven or more years, with the assumption that she would ultimately make an identical income under either scenario in the interim, which would she choose? Arriving in or after 2010 would be an interesting experience. Given the choice, FSPs will either come to in a world like we know now with commissions and trailer fees or in a world where FSPs are receiving recurring annual fees for assets under their management. I bet the vast majority want to arrive in the second world. Most consumers want to be there too. They do not want to have to second-guess the motives of their otherwise trusted FSP and they love being out from under their "loads" once and for all.

There are a number of variations on the theme of moving from embedded, primarily commission-based income to unbundled and unbiased fee income. In essence, it comes down to how long the transition should take, whether the costs should be borne primarily by clients, FSPs or split evenly, whether or not "incentives" such as early switching discounts should be used and the unique circumstances of individual consumers, especially surrounding taxes. The "costs" are incurred either through DSC penalties for consumers or foregone income for FSPs, but are a very real impediment to moving forward either way. Let's look at these variations:

The Indefinite 10% Shuffle

Some observers believe that if 10% of all DSC funds can be switched into no-load funds annually, then most accounts will have significant (although not complete) liquidity available to them in relatively short order. New money is still invested on a DSC basis.

Pros: No DSC charges to clients at all if used properly and no reduction in income for FSP at all.

Cons: The process doesn't get you out of the infernal trap of having at least some of your money invested in DSC funds all the time.

The Cold Turkey Approach

Everyone wakes up one morning and commissions no longer exist. Obviously, there is discussion and warning, but the idea is that the switch is implemented instantaneously.

Pros: Would reduce the confusion that is bound to occur with a longer, more complex and staged transition. Some FSPs would take steps in advance on a client-by-client basis.

Cons: Would likely result in FSPs charging some fees on assets where commissions were originally earned or asking clients to absorb a significant loss in the liquidation of DSC assets when making the switch to fee-based.

The Discount Turkey Approach

This would be much the same as above, except that FSPs might offer a short-term transitional fee discount, perhaps in the first year or two, to offset the DSC charges incurred in moving to a fee-based arrangement. This would effectively "share" the transition costs.

Pros: As above, except with some latitude about how the costs of transition are split between the FSP and the client.

Cons: Incurs substantial short-term costs that could be largely avoided if the transition is phased in over a longer time frame.

One of the biggest reasons why no real change has happened yet in the eradication of embedded compensation, is that no one can agree on how best to do it. Very few people want to incur needless cost and turmoil if it can be avoided. The result is sort of like a New Year's resolution: everyone agrees it is good if the thing committed to can be accomplished, but no one is all that keen to swallow hard and do what is required.

The Consequence of Not Leaving

One thing that any fair-minded person can agree with is the notion that the status quo is untenable and needs to be reformed. The cost of doing nothing is very high indeed, since the integrity of the entire financial services industry is now being called into question. Figuring out an honourable way to leave the "Hotel California" of embedded compensation for FSPs is job one. Everything else regarding the establishment of a true profession flows from it. The current situation cannot continue indefinitely; there are simply far too many dysfunctional investment decisions being made due to the compensation overlay.

Here's an example of what can happen if no action is taken. Consider the AGF International Value Fund. In 2001, the fund had realized net sales of $1.6 billion, easily outpacing all rivals. Investors vote with their wallets and this was clearly a place Canadians wanted to be. When Charles Brandes, the influential fund manager, announced he was terminating his relationship with AGF in early 2002, unitholders were left wondering what to do. They had bought the fund from FSPs who sold (I use the word deliberately) the fund based on Brandes' perceived superior stock-picking abilities.

The fund had about $7.1 billion in assets at the time of the announcement, making it the second-largest mutual fund in Canada. Only the aforementioned Templeton Growth Fund was bigger and Templeton had a head start of about forty years. Other funds managed by Brandes within the AGF stable represented another $2.8 million for a total of nearly $10 billion of the $28 billion in AGF's assets under management. At the time, Brandes meant the world to AGF. In fact, according to one industry analyst, Brandes' funds represented 48% of AGF's net sales in 2000 and 79% of net sales in 2001.

But where did all this leave the investors in these funds, particularly those invested on a DSC basis? Clients could either sell the AGF fund that Brandes used to manage, pay their tax liabilities (open accounts only), their back-end loads and make the move or they could simply stay with the fund under new management.

Since virtually everyone who bought the fund bought it for access to a presumed world-class manager who was no longer available to AGF unitholders, it came down to a determination of whether or not the unitholders thought it was worth paying the DSC penalty to follow Brandes across the street. It was a tough choice and a number of personal factors had to be considered.

People had been handed a choice between keeping the same great manager, but paying up to 5.5% in penalties, or almost certainly getting inferior management from a fill-in, but foregoing the penalties. Since very few people switched, it seems consumers were prepared to stick with a familiar company and a new manager, as opposed to switching to a new company with a familiar manager. Remember that the latter would likely have involved some costs to most unitholders. In a fee-based arrangement, those who wanted to follow Brandes to his new company could have done so with no additional charge.

Once again, consumers clearly demonstrated that the pain of loss can be a major motivator. Never underestimate the power of behavioural finance in explaining consumer conduct. Shouldn't people be free to pursue the best investment options in a manner that is unfettered by previous decisions, especially when circumstances beyond their control cause them to shift their preferences? The bottom line is that right now, financial decisions are being made based at least somewhat on compensation factors that clearly compromise true independence and professionalism. This also forces people to consider the actual value of the various inputs that go into financial decision-making.

Ironically, Brandes has taken the lead in offering an automatic 10% fee redemption of DSC units. A large number of FSPs have been doing manual 10% fee redemption for years now (the writing really is on the wall), so Brandes made the simplification of the process as automatic, painless and consistent as possible. Both consumers and FSPs are believed to benefit from this service. It's likely only a matter of time before other companies begin to offer an identical service in order to keep up with the Joneses.

The longer-term problem for mutual funds, however, is not the competition they will feel from one another. Rather, the strong challenge put forward by index-based products, notably ETFs, will mean that it will be mutual fund companies, not the FSPs who recommend mutual funds, who will have the steepest hill to climb in staking out their value proposition in an ever-changing, but ever more rational marketplace.

MOST FSPS ADD VALUE; MOST ACTIVE MANAGERS DON'T

All great truths begin as blasphemies.
—George Bernard Shaw

To think is easy; to act is difficult; but to act as one thinks is the most difficult of all.
—Johan Wolfgang von Goethe

Personal beliefs are funny things. Creationists are adamant that their world view is right, while Darwinists are equally convinced that they have it right. Agnostics are the Switzerlands of the religious world; they don't take sides. In many ways, agnostics are prudent, since neither the Creationists nor the Darwinists can offer incontrovertible proof that their view is correct, or that the opposing view is conspicuously wrong. There are precious few agnostic FSPs when it comes to money management in the ongoing spat between active and passive money management.

Pension funds have been aware of this for years and have governed themselves accordingly. Most use elements of both active and passive strategies in designing portfolios, so we might call them portfolio agnostics. They're not interested in taking sides and being right, so much as doing whatever they can to avoid being conspicuously wrong. Like atheists who go to church regularly, they hedge their bets.

In spite of the fact that the brightest pension funds act equivocally in this debate, the dogmatists in both the active and passive camps act as though they are conspicuously and incontrovertibly right when dealing with retail clients. There is some evidence that can be analyzed on this matter, so people can look at the details and draw their own conclusions, but that evidence is far from conclusive, which brings us to questions of belief. The one thing we should all respect when living in a pluralistic society is that it is inappropriate for anyone to impose his or her religious beliefs on others, yet that's what so many FSPs do regarding how investment assets are managed.

People have a tendency to believe things based on what they were taught in their formative years. Finance textbooks talk about the various strategies and techniques that portfolio managers might employ in attempting to add value by improving risk-adjusted returns (lowering risk, increasing returns, or both). True scientists, of course, are more interested in how things actually work and what is accomplished in practice, rather than how things ought to work in theory. Theories are nice, they say, but they have to hold water in the real world of actual testing. The scientists' mantra is, "Can you prove it?"

There is a further difference between honesty and full disclosure that also needs to be considered and in spite of these fairly obvious criteria, both sides have managed to make strong cases for themselves over the years. Still, if economics were a religion, the ivory towers of academia and the gleaming towers of Wall Street would be waging a vicious war right now. The two camps essentially hate one another because each is a proponent of a specific doctrine (i.e., their proponents have been indoctrinated) that runs contrary to the views of the other. Academia is mostly for passive management and portfolio managers are entirely for active management.

How can this be? Aren't FSPs mandated to do what is in their clients' best interests at all times? As such, shouldn't they work to identify the strategies that are the most likely to be successful and then pursue those strategies exclusively? Using a medical analogy, what if your physician said the odds of success were 60% for one procedure and 95% for another. Would you be indifferent regarding the procedure you pursue since the odds are in your favour either way?

The False Dichotomy Between Active and Passive Investing

Part of the discussion around unbundling has to focus on the merits of the constituent parts. This is tougher than most people think. For instance, there are many Christians who simultaneously possess a low opinion of organized religions and their weekly services and therefore don't attend. Casual observers might think that this form of Christianity is insincere, based on activity. But this isn't necessarily so. Belief in God and respect for the Church are different things. Bundling them together makes it possible for people to come to erroneous conclusions based on simplistic assumptions.

In late May 2002, the U.S. federal education act was interpreted in Ohio through an addendum stipulating that, "Where topics are taught that may generate controversy—such as biological evolution—the curriculum could help students to understand the full range of scientific views that exist." It seems a similar amount of open-mindedness might do FSPs some good regarding active and passive management. At present, virtually all FSPs are strict proponents of the active approach, even though scientific evidence is largely, but certainly not entirely, against them. Not surprisingly, virtually all FSPs have been taught in the "traditional school" of active management. Least surprising of all, active management features embedded FSP compensation while passive management does not.

Similarly, the media would have many of us believe that consumers can fire their FSPs and pocket the savings, as if the FSPs add no value, but only cost. This is a simplistic view that is only sometimes true. The part about cost is usually true and the part about added value is usually false, although there are exceptions in both directions. *Under the current structure, there are some highly qualified FSPs who are actually cheaper than discount brokers*. It is equally fair to say that there are some FSPs who, no matter how reasonably their services are priced, do more harm than good.

It bears repeating that virtually all FSPs recommend active management since it involves embedded compensation while passive management does not. There's no logical reason why FSPs wouldn't recommend passive products based on merit. In other words, active management and traditional financial advice are joined at the hip. As such, FSP recommendations can be explained more by prevailing compensation structures than by any form of compelling or overriding logic.

The academic case for indexing much of a portfolio is quite strong. Many of the most highly respected economists in the world including Eugene Fama, Rex Sinquefield and Nobel Laureates William F. Sharpe and the late Merton Miller are proponents of indexing as a core element of portfolio construction. Perhaps the most evangelical proponent of indexing is Vanguard founder John Bogle. His views are readily available at www.vanguard.com.

The position taken by all these proponents is that markets are efficient and that costs for fees, commissions, risk exposures and trade execution all deplete returns. As a result, most active managers will ultimately "regress to the mean" and put up returns approximately equal to the returns of the market minus their fees. Sharpe (for whom the Sharpe ratio measuring risk-adjusted returns is named) has gone so far as to call active investing a "negative sum game." The average active manager is going to have a return that is less than the index because the average active manager incurs higher costs relative to the index itself.

So much for averages. People have drowned in rivers that are, on average, less than a foot deep. The point that all indexers concede is that there will always be a handful of active managers who beat their benchmarks handily just using the laws of probability. If coin-flipping were a skill and the whole world started flipping fair coins at the same time, someone out of the more than six billion people would come up heads thirty or forty times in a row. Would that outcome make that person a skilled coin-flipper or a lucky one? This is a simple probability based on something statisticians call "The Law of Large Numbers."

To be fair to those managers who have developed superb track records over very long time horizons, there certainly does seem to be a substantial element of skill involved. People like Sir John Templeton, Warren Buffett and Peter Lynch have all developed intelligent adherents over the years. It would be disingenuous to say there's overwhelming evidence that most markets beat most active managers most of the time, without also acknowledging that some active managers beat the market handily, over long time horizons and after fees. Investment gurus seem to have clearly demonstrated their skill. What is more, they regularly articulate how they do it.

There's only one problem. If what these gurus do can be so readily *explained*, why has it never been effectively *taught*? In other words, if Warren Buffett's value style of investing is so compelling, why has he never had a protegé who has put up similar numbers? It's certainly not because he has a lack of protegés (he likely has tens of thousands). For a "system" to be worth anything, it has to be repeatable. Otherwise, it's not really a system.

Here's a quick summary of the key points associated with each strategy:

	Active	**Passive**
Market timing:	Some	None
Asset Class Purity:	Almost never	Always
Typical turnover:	25% to 100%	5% to 8%
Unbundled Cost:	1.00% to 1.95%	0.08% to 0.90%
Performance:	Some beat; most lag	Market index minus cost

The debate about performance is the big bugaboo. Most active funds lag their benchmark index in the long run. Proponents of active management say that passive strategies need to acknowledge that they will never beat their benchmark. This is absolutely true. Of course, the other side of the coin is that in *trying* to beat their benchmark, most active managers most often fail and lag *as a direct result of having tried.* Most proponents of active management never get around to explaining this equally true part of the story to retail clients. How professional is that?

Purity and turnover are also major concerns in gauging performance. Active funds almost always have cash or other asset classes in their funds. For instance, almost all have some cash component beyond the 5% or so required to meet redemptions and buying opportunities. I know of one fully invested Canadian equity fund that has had a 20% stake in U.S. equities for over five years, but still markets itself as "pure" because there's no meaningful cash component. Given the importance of the purity decision, surely this should be a source of concern. Any portfolio that uses impure products in implementing decision 3 (security selection) is compromising decision 2 (strategic asset class weighting). Therefore, any IPS written under these circumstances is incorrect the moment it is implemented.

Finally, in a world where integrated wealth management is the overarching objective, tax efficiency becomes a primary concern. The higher the portfolio turnover, the higher the tax liability in a non-registered account, all else being equal. Any FSP who is truly conscientious about the delivery of total wealth management needs to give serious consideration to those products that can accommodate this reality. In the U.S., mutual funds are reported not only in absolute returns, but also in absolute, after-tax returns. Tax considerations often play a major role in the rankings, with the more efficient (i.e., lower turnover) funds often moving up considerably.

The Reality of FSP Recommendations

The proponents of active management state that if you have an army of highly educated, intelligent, motivated and competitive people assisting you in analyzing individual companies and overall market trends, you are likely to outperform the market as a whole. The market for any given asset class, after all, encompasses everything—the good, the bad and the ugly. Surely, cherry-picking the cream of the crop can't be that hard. Most investors agree with this notion, since there is more money invested in active products than in indexed products worldwide.

That's only part of why the vast majority of retail investment assets in Canada is actively managed. There are two other factors at play. First, FSPs want to be perceived as "experts" in picking either mutual fund managers or individual securities; that way, clients will continue to come to them for their "expertise" in selecting investments. There is no "expertise" involved in recommending an index (or so they say). The other reason, of course, is that actively managed products generally feature embedded compensation, while indexed products generally do not. FSPs need to provide for their families, but don't think there is professional credibility in recommending passive, indexed products.

Is active management actually delivering on the promise of superior returns? Ideally, these returns would also come with lower portfolio risk. Offering returns that are identical to an index with less volatility, should also be considered a value-added activity, but it is debatable as to what that value-added is worth.

This leads directly to a concept I'll call the Active Management Premium (AMP). People pay mutual fund managers a fee to manage a portfolio with a mandate to outperform a certain benchmark. If the manager is outperforming the benchmark after fees, consumers should say thank you very much and not begrudge the fee. If, on the other hand, the manager lags his benchmark, either a new manager should be hired or the consumer should cut his losses by simply buying the benchmark, or it's nearest facsimile, an ETF or index fund that tracks that benchmark.

Obviously, the higher the fee, the harder it will be for the manager to beat the benchmark. However, any manager that can consistently beat his benchmark after fees is worth the money and should be paid with a kind thank you. Similarly, any manager that lags his benchmark, no matter how reasonable the fee seems to be. is, by definition, charging too much. That's because anyone could do better by simply buying the benchmark.

As long as the manager posts a return (net of fees) that exceeds the benchmark, he's delivering an AMP. The bigger the AMP, the better the manager. The better the manager, the higher the fee that can be charged. Presumably, the manager could charge the same as his competitors and still be handsomely rewarded, since investors would be pleased to give him a disproportionate percentage of total assets to manage. In other words, savvy consumers should not be opposed to high fees of and by themselves, they should be opposed to any fees (high or low) that are worth less than they cost. It's not about cost; it's about value.

Intuitively, there shouldn't be much to dispute. Empirically, however, evidence suggests that in most instances, investors would be better off with a passive strategy than an active one. Furthermore, the degree by which an actively managed mutual fund lags its benchmark is primarily determined by how much that actively managed fund costs. The more it costs, the more it lags, all else being equal. The lower the cost, the greater the likelihood of out-performance. Low cost merely increases the likelihood of better performance. It should also be stressed that there are exceptions in both directions: cheap managers who consistently lag their benchmarks and expensive managers who beat their benchmarks.

Remember that since most actively managed mutual funds feature embedded compensation and most index-type investments in Canada don't, there is an added performance burden for active management. Active management proponents argue that it is unfair to compare one strategy that generally pays FSPs (active management) to another that generally does not (indexing), since FSP payment further compounds the difficulties inherent in relative performance comparisons. Of course, they are right. Ironically, this is another reason to eliminate embedded compensation A Class mutual funds and get on with unbundling. Without unbundling, a true apples-to-apples comparison is impossible for all funds with similar mandates, but different compensation models.

What if we took out the embedded compensation in order to make a more meaningful comparison? How do true no-load company funds and F Class company funds fare when compared to their benchmarks in the long run? They would be that much closer to matching their returns. For instance, if an index returned 12% and the MER of a fund benchmarked against it was 2.5%, one might expect the long-term return for that fund to be about 9.5%. If unbundling were used, the fund manager would look better and the return might be more like 10.5% after accounting for fees. Closer, but still no cigar.

At the end of the day, FSPs should be ideologically indifferent to the debate between active and passive investing, because a case can be made for either or both. As long as the risks and limitations of each strategy are clearly spelled out from the outset, the integrity of the recommendation should never be called into question. It should also be noted that some asset classes can only be accessed through active management if one wants a diversified holding in that asset class. Venture capital, hedge funds, real return bonds, global bonds and diversified high yield debt are all examples of asset classes in which there is no reputable index currently available. Anyone who wants those asset classes in their portfolio will have to use active management to get them.

Most Active Managers Underperform

A small library of books exists that demonstrates how the average actively managed mutual fund will lag its benchmark after fees and over time. The research also shows that although there are actively managed funds that have outperformed their benchmark consistently and over long periods of time, those managers who have outperformed could not be identified reliably before the fact. To make matters worse, Gary Brinson teaches us that security selection doesn't explain much in terms of the variance of the expected returns on average anyway.

Most FSPs wish the findings were never released. They continue to misrepresent them and to solicit business based on the spurious presumptions that active managers consistently outperform and also that they can reliably identify the cream of the crop. Unfortunately, most consumers buy into the routine. Any FSP who purports to be able to *reliably* identify superior managers is not telling the truth and not telling the truth is not professional.

Truly professional FSPs make no such assertions about fund performance and fund picking because they know they cannot reliably defend them. Most consumers still think the primary role of the FSP is to pick funds (or stocks, if you're working with a conventional or discretionary broker). FSPs compete against one another to be the preferred advice-giving alternative and if the public has misconceptions about their work, but those misconceptions lead to increased business, then they do nothing to rectify (and frequently do much to perpetuate) those misconceptions.

The media is complicit in perpetuating the problem by interviewing managers. "How did you get those fantastic results?" The question presumes that the answer is something more than "I just got lucky, I guess." Has anyone ever read an interview with a money manager who attributes his (or anyone else's) performance to random chance? Over a one year time horizon, approximately half of managers will beat their benchmark. If we had a coin-flipping contest (with no fees involved) about half the contestants would demonstrate superior performance there too. As time wears on, the number of statistically significant outperformers becomes smaller still, creating the illusion of true skill. The illusion of presumed skill is not the demonstration of actual skill. Looking at American data for the S&P 500, what percentage of active funds have beaten the index over the past number of years?[7] Let's have a look:

Year	% of U.S. Equity Funds Outperforming S&P 500
1995	16
1996	21
1997	10
1998	16
1999	43
2000	42
2001	26
2002	30

ave. 25½ %

¾ lag index

Taking a somewhat longer perspective, over a five-year period, the S&P Mid Cap 400 Index outperformed 93% of Mid Cap funds. Going back further still, and using Large Cap data, *Fortune* magazine recently reported that only 27% of all U.S. Equity Funds with a ten-year track record managed to beat the S&P 500, their benchmark. Again, the results are even worse for small caps and micro caps and considerably worse when the time horizon is extended even further. In the very long run (three generations), there are virtually no active managers left standing who beat their benchmark.

Fun Picking Funds

To demonstrate just how difficult it is to reliably identify funds that will out-perform their peer group or their benchmark index, I asked Steve Kangas, perhaps Canada's foremost expert on mutual funds and managing director of www.fundlibrary.com, to do some analysis for me. Steve reviewed copies of one of the mutual fund rating books from each of 1998 and 2000. I asked him to track the one hundred funds recommended in each, to determine which quartile they fell into for the three-year and five-year periods ending on December 31, 2002.

The authors used three-year periods as the minimum required, gathering enough information to be "statistically significant" when writing the book. Most students of statistics would know that thirty-six (monthly) data points lies at the extreme low-end of the range of statistical significance, but what else can the authors do if they have funds that are only three years old that they really, really like? Having all one hundred funds fall into the top quartile would have meant perfect predictability. Similarly, twenty-five funds falling into each quartile would have meant totally random predictability. The latter result would mean the mutual fund ranking book was (and is) essentially useless.

If the authors believe three years is long enough to evaluate the funds, then it should be considered fair to use a three-year time frame to evaluate the authors. The problem is something known as "short-term persistence." Most investors will do okay if they buy the most recent winners. That's because "the trend is your friend" and winners in the recent past are slightly more likely to be winners in the near future.

Books like these tend to do reasonably well if you check results against recommendations over a short time frame, provided the trends that prevailed at publication persist a little longer. Authors are quick to point out that any-thing less than three years would be "statistically insignificant." What they don't tell you (in fact, what they count on), is that you would need about ten years of quality data to be truly meaningful in your modelling.

The authors are betting that no one will take out their recommendations from ten years ago to see how the funds they recommended actually per-formed. If the results turned out to be relatively random, that would be all right, since there's a big disclaimer on the inside sleeve that says in future, performance may not be repeated. The people publishing these books are counting on not having anyone going back to look at the funds recommended years ago. It's amazing how conveniently ephemeral these books are, even though they talk about products that should only be used with a long-term perspective.

Using the one hundred funds that were rated in each book, we find that the three-year numbers, from January 1, 2000 to December 31, 2002, identified forty-two funds that ended in the first quartile, twenty-six in the second, seventeen in the third and only twelve in the fourth. It doesn't sum to 100 because a few funds were discontinued altogether in the rash of mergers and acquisitions over that time horizon. Still, at first blush, that seems quite impressive.

Next, we looked at the 100 funds ranked in the 1998 book for the period from January 1, 1998 to December 31, 2002. In this case, 35 funds were in the first quartile, 29 in the second, 16 in the third and only 12 in the fourth. Again, there was some attrition due to M&A activity. In future editions of this book, we'll look at the ten-year numbers and see how good these funds really were, as we head into a long-term time horizon.

The trend of regressing to the mean already seems under way and my guess is that by the time we get to a decade of performance data, we'll have about one-quarter of the funds in each quartile. In other words, the results will have become randomized; you may as well have been using darts to make your picks. Remember that since most funds lag their benchmarks, even first quartile funds may turn out to be laggards. If a fund can be reliably identified as a first quartile fund before buying it, is that a good thing? Most people would say 'yes!' What if that fund simultaneously lagged its benchmark? After all, no 'skill' is required in buying an ETF or index fund that tracks a benchmark.

Poor funds tend to be merged out of existence or just plain discontinued, creating a "survivorship bias," in which only the relatively good funds are left in the universe, making the survivors look better than they really are.

Late in 2001, I had a company wholesaler for a wrap product in my office. "I don't know about you," he said, "but I don't think anyone can pick funds reliably." He then launched into a routine about his program and how it regularly rebalanced and did all these wonderful things to maximize risk-adjusted returns. I stopped him fairly quickly and told him that I agreed more than he knew. In fact, I said, I believe it is so difficult to predict which active funds will outperform, that I often don't use active funds in instances when ETFs are available. It seems he had never thought of that.

Maximizing risk-adjusted returns is all about strategic asset allocation and you don't need active management to set and adhere to it. In fact, using active management often compromises purposeful asset allocation through asset class impurities and style drift. If you're genuine about your commitment to the primacy of asset allocation, you should use pure asset classes.

Here's another example of fund picking running headlong into investor behaviour. There's some fascinating research in the *Financial Analyst's Journal*, in which Matthew Morey looks at the techniques used by Morningstar to derive their ratings.[8] Since these ratings began in 1980, they have become a staple in both fund company advertising and investor decision-making. Looking at the calendar year 1999, Morey noted that funds with four or five stars received inflows of $223.6 billion, while funds with three or fewer stars suffered net outflows of $132 billion. Scoring their three-, five- and ten-year performance numbers, Morningstar arrived at the overall ranking of funds. Morey demonstrated that the methodology used showed a time bias that favoured older funds over younger and middle-aged funds. This bias caused people to invest in funds more for their longevity than their performance.

Anyone with an Internet connection or a newspaper with a business section can identify those managers who have outperformed in the recent past. The future, however, is a different story. Why do you think all mutual fund prospectuses come with a disclaimer that past performance is no guarantee of future performance? The longer the time horizon, the lower the likelihood of an active fund outperforming a benchmark. That's because active managers give the index a head start by way of an MER that must be overcome before any "value-added" can be realized.

There is simply no compelling evidence that past success leads to future success. If the majority of funds lag over one-year time frames and longer time frames are simply the sum of a number of one-year time frames laid end to end, then it stands to reason that the percentage of outperformers will be quite modest over the very long run.

Historically, only a small number of funds will beat their benchmark in any given year. Did you catch the nuance? *In any given year.* If, for instance, a fund was to beat its benchmark only three or four years in ten, it is almost certain to underperform over the decade (unless the years of outperformance outstrip the years of underperformance). As time marches on, fewer and fewer funds are able to maintain records of outperformance. The tendency to lag becomes greater and greater over time and FSPs always encourage their clients to take a long-term view.

Interestingly, the poorest performers tend to remain the poorest. Therefore, it might be more useful for the people writing mutual fund rating books to identify the one hundred worst funds in the market place. If you can't reliably select winners, you might as well stay away from losers. It wouldn't be nearly as much fun, but at least it would have a real purpose.

Eugene Fama, one of the great investment minds of this century, looked at twenty years of U.S. data from Morningstar for the period from 1976 to 1996.[9] He split performance into two chronological halves, taking the top half of funds from 1976 to 1986 and then testing how they did from 1986 to 1996. The result was that exactly half were up and half were down over that second decade, after accounting for three primary explanatory variables: market risk, small vs. large cap and value vs. growth.

If one assumes that markets are efficient, then the only way to beat the market is to gain information that no one else has, analyze its significance (quantifying the impact on stock prices) and act on your (hopefully accurate) analysis *before anyone else can.* This last point is vital, because there are thousands of pieces of information being thrown out daily (some more valuable and relevant than others) and millions of market participants receiving this information simultaneously. For one participant to be able to claim that she or he can dissect and act on information more swiftly than *the broader market as a single entity* is rather far-fetched.

Rex Sinquefield is the chairman of Dimensional Fund Advisors in California. He says that in the social sciences (i.e., fields like economics and capital market trends), predictions are more general than specific, because they involve people who might change their beliefs and objectives at any point in time. As such, Sinquefield says the "burden of proof" rests with active managers to demonstrate that they are regularly and predictably adding value. Trying really hard isn't good enough.

Active managers try really hard to impress people with what they are doing. I was at a professional development conference hosted by a prominent mutual fund company last autumn, where there were no fewer than twenty-one "wholesalers" (product specialists with a sales mandate) lined up—and that's only for the Toronto market. The intent was to show off the strength and solidarity of the company to FSPs before the session started. The clear message to the FSPs present was, "We've got a strong, dedicated army backing you up and helping you in your sales process." In looking at them, however, I couldn't help but think, "How much are they paying these guys and what is that doing to my clients' MERs?"

In spite of the best efforts of some of the brightest people around, cost overhead leads directly to higher MERs, which leads directly to lower consumer returns. A few months later, I overheard a representative from another company say that they were boosting their sales force from eighty-five to 165 inside sales representatives. Again, I wondered about the net effect on MERs and did some digging to find my answer. According to Morningstar Canada, MERs in Canada have been on the rise for the four years from 1999 to 2002. In 1999, the average equity fund MER was 2.50%. By the end of 2002, it had risen to 2.76%. Even when accounting for the recent inclusion of GST in mutual fund MERs, it is clear that mutual fund companies have not yet moved to make cost a priority.

The aftermath of the 2000-2002 bear market is a wonderful case in point. Many active managers will correctly proclaim that (for the first time in a long time) a majority of active managers were beating their benchmark in this environment. Bubbles have a funny way of making active management look good when they burst, usually because impurity works in favour of active funds as large cash components often reduce the damage of a major downdraft. However, since markets go up about seven years out of ten, this cash component ends up being a drag more often than not.

What results is much like that scene from the 2001 remake of *Ocean's Eleven,* in which George Clooney and Brad Pitt are talking about the people currently playing at the casinos they're about to knock off. Pitt mentions that 90% of the people playing will lose money, 5% will break even and 5% will make money. Apparently, this has been proven statistically. That's pretty close to how it is for active managers trying to beat their benchmarks. The vast majority lag, but a few talented or lucky managers end up either keeping pace or, better yet, ahead when all the chips are counted.

Embedded Compensation as Tied Selling

Money can also compromise principles and most FSPs earn a living recommending investment products that feature some form of embedded compensation. Eliminating embedded compensation would also eliminate the temptation to compromise principles. Most traditional financial planners don't hold a licence to sell individual stocks, bonds or exchange-traded funds and couldn't legally sell them even if they wanted to, so they are pretty much limited to recommending mutual funds. Perhaps licencing courses could be altered to allow FSPs with a mutual funds licence to take a special course allowing them to recommend and sell ETFs, much like the additional requirements for selling labour-sponsored funds.

The concept of tied selling is well known in the financial services industry; access to a product or service is denied unless the purchaser also buys another related, but different, product or service. The latter becomes a precondition for access to the former in an all-or-nothing gambit. An example might be an RRSP loan. Banks used to be happy to lend you $5,000 to make an RRSP contribution, but only if the money was invested in their products. If you wanted to buy some other product, your loan was denied. Regulators stopped this, but tied selling soon gave way to "relationship pricing," in which that same bank would give you a loan, but it would be at prime if you used the bank's products and at prime + 1% if you used someone else's. While technically legal, many people still see such conduct as an unscrupulous abuse of position.

Here's the similarity. FSPs offer advice. If a consumer comes to an FSP and indicates that she would like to use his services and could she please get some advice on the best index fund available, the FSP might politely ask that would-be client to leave and not come back. Advice is currently predicated on embedded compensation. No embedded compensation to the FSP, means no payment upon implementation, means no advice in the first place. This is generally true unless the consumer goes to a discount brokerage, where the situation is often worse. At discount brokerages, you can pay for advice that is never received or even requested, since the embedded compensation in most mutual funds remains.

It is rather humourous how the industry has changed. In the middle of the last decade, popular industry motivator Nick Murray coined the phrase "no-load means no advice." This was never true in an absolute sense, but true enough at the time since most FSPs were competing primarily against no-load providers, like banks. It was a way of legitimizing the tied-selling aspects of mutual fund sales since many consumers were focusing on the handicaps of back-end load penalties rather than the very real benefits of qualified advice. It was a cute way of turning the tables on those companies that were gaining market share by trumpeting their no-load "value proposition."

Murray even had a little vaudeville routine that drove the point home. It was called the "no-load cardiologist," in which a "professional" cardiologist would be happy to do whatever you wanted and best of all there was never any load! People who come to cardiologists generally have no training in physiological matters and so are looking to a trusted medical professional for advice on problems that are vitally important to them personally. It didn't matter if they asked about CAT scans, EKGs, arrhythmia or any other ailment or treatment, the advice was always the same; the no-load cardiologist would always do what you wanted and there would never be a load.

The routine poked fun at the notion that "no-load" could somehow trump "no advice" in a professional environment. The paradigm has certainly shifted. Today, there are a number of qualified FSPs who are happy to offer their services for a fee, without any "loads." Their value proposition is "no-loads with excellent advice." There have always been FSPs out there who offer this kind of service, but they're relatively rare. At present, people needing advice are choosing between whether a fee or a commission (which establishes a load) is the best way to pay for that advice.

In time, everyone who holds herself out as an FSP will charge fees like any other true professional. Murray is still a much-loved speaker and author across North America, but his newest book talks about FSPs working for fees and it has been years since he has performed his "no-load cardiologist" routine.

Why Work With an FSP?

Most consumers want to work with a qualified FSP. A recent Ipsos-Reid poll showed that 59% of respondents said this about FSPs: "It is important that I talk to someone face to face. Regular contact is important to me." There is a sizable minority of consumers who feel using an FSP is redundant. These people choose to do their own financial planning and advising. They're known as the Do-It-Yourself (DIY) crowd. The same poll showed that 50% of respondents defined financial advice as what is offered by someone who provides a financial plan, and that 86% of respondents said it was important that their FSP understand their goals. These are motherhood findings, but crucial for any FSP that wants to work without a written game plan or to "wing it" by offering advice in a vacuum.

Similarly, research done by a major mutual fund company has determined that consumers are becoming more sophisticated in the past five years. By tracking incoming calls, fund companies can determine trend lines for various areas of interest. Analysis shows that consumers have moved along the continuum from performance, to account adjustments, to tax information to information about accounts for minors to division of asset/divorce details, to income-splitting to asset protection to estate planning over that time frame. The good news is that consumers are becoming savvier. This means that a qualified FSP might be more necessary than ever, since the things consumers want information about are becoming increasingly complex and specialized.

Here's one of the great ironies of the financial services industry. Financial service providers generally add value. They do it, for the most part, while using actively managed mutual funds that generally subtract value relative to passive products and strategies. Mutual fund companies know this and continually tell FSPs how great they are. They also pay their FSPs through embedded compensation in their products. Index providers only talk about cost because without an embedded payment mechanism for FSPs, that's all they have to go on. In short, there's no financial incentive for FSPs to recommend passive products. *It might be said that an often inferior product line has co-opted the complicit loyalty of those FSPs who recommend these products through what amounts to bribery!*

In case you think this is an unduly strident stance, let's look up the word "bribe." The dictionary says a bribe is something (money or a favour) given or promised to a person *to influence conduct*. No one is suggesting that FSPs are all being bribed, only that FSPs function in an environment where it might fairly be said that de facto bribery could enter into the decision-making process regarding the products FSPs recommend. Where the potential for conflict of interest exists, shouldn't steps be taken immediately to eliminate the mere possibility of abuse?

A recent study by Mark Warywoda of Morningstar Canada surveyed Canadian mutual fund MERs. It showed that MERs are rising. According to Morningstar, the average MER rose from 2.02% in 1995 to 2.62% as of April 30, 2003. In fairness, a number of factors led to that jump. For starters, there are now more segregated funds in the marketplace. These are the insurance industry equivalent of mutual funds, but they cost more because of insurance overlays and features. Second, there are now more specialty funds, which are inherently more expensive. Finally, GST was added to the stated MER of all mutual funds in 2000. In spite of this, analyst Dan Hallett has calculated that the average dollar-weighted MER has risen to 2.13% in 2003 from 1.93% in 1995.

The Morningstar study also demonstrated that investors have paid over $10 billion in annual fees to the mutual fund industry over the past few years. Not surprisingly, the study once again confirmed the well-known fact that funds with lower costs performed better on average. To get a sense of just what a gravy train the mutual fund industry has been in the recent past, the study revealed that the industry has grown from about 1,000 funds in 1995 to over 4,600 in 2003. That's astounding given that a number of companies have been consolidating their offerings after a spate of merger activity.

Perhaps the most damning finding of the study was that among those funds with reported MERs as of the end of each of 1998 and 2002, only 12% of them experienced a reduction in MERs. Meanwhile, fully 78% of the funds in question saw MER increases. This finding was independent of changes in asset size.

Although fund picking doesn't work on a discreet fund by fund basis, it certainly works in aggregate. Morningstar assigns star ratings to funds in 23 fund categories. In 22 of them, the average MER among funds with above-average star ratings was lower than the category-wide MER. The lone exception was the science and technology sector. It seems clear that cost matters. Phillips, Hager and North, which is Canada's 14th largest mutual fund sponsor with almost $10 billion under management, is responsible for 2.3% of all mutual fund assets invested in Canada, but for only 0.9% of all annual management expenses. Is it any wonder that PH&N is consistently ranked as a top company by independent observers?

It should be clear by now that most, but certainly not all mutual fund managers fail to live up to their end of their value proposition of outperforming relevant benchmarks after fees. What about FSPs? For most people, mutual funds and FSPs are seen as two peas in a pod. What if we took the unbundling idea one step further and tried to determine whether or not FSPs are actually adding value in excess of the fees they charge?

Do FSPs Add Value?

Although the question is a contentious one, there is a strong consensus that FSPs do add value, just not the way most people think. For instance, working with an FSP does not increase the likelihood that an investor will beat an index, but it does reduce the risk of having that person substantially lag it. In essence, FSPs reduce losses more than they maximize gains. This is actually a massive value-added attribute by itself, since research shows that people feel the pain of a loss more than twice as strongly as they feel the joy of a gain. Interestingly, the mathematics of capital markets means that a 49% market decline from a previous peak like the one that ended in October of 2002, requires about a 98% rise just to get back to that previous level.

When discussing financial matters, it is generally accepted that fear and greed motivate people. No one likes to admit it, but research in the field of behavioural finance demonstrates that people are far more emotional than rational when it comes to their money, especially when they are living through wild swings in values.

Ironically, most FSPs promote their services as offering return maximization (playing to people's collective greed) when in actual fact, the value of working with a professional FSP is usually gained through the peace of mind that comes with loss minimization. This is especially true as accounts grow in size. Research also shows that people with small portfolios are more interested in return maximization, while people with large ones are more interested in risk management. There's nothing surprising here. Poor people may as well swing for the fences; what have they got to lose? Meanwhile, people who already have money are keenly aware of what a significant loss could mean to their quality of life.

Moreover, individual investors generally make decisions based on a multiplicity of inputs, including family, friends, popular media, co-workers, online research and gut instinct. Other more personal factors like self-esteem and personal life experiences are also thought to be major contributors to decision-making.

Investors Behaving Badly

A study conducted by CEG Worldwide examined investor behaviour for the period from January 1990 to March 2000. The research study, aptly entitled "Investors Behaving Badly," showed quite compellingly that FSPs have a positive impact on their clients' financial lives.[10] It showed that the traditional foundations of financial planning, such as setting financial goals, were often not in place for DIY investors, who were more inclined to be moved by short-term influences as a result. How many DIY investors do you suppose have an Investment Policy Statement?

Specifically, DIY investors were more likely to trade too frequently, which more often than not led to poor market timing. It is well documented that portfolio turnover correlates negatively to returns. These DIY investors often chase a hot stock, hot fund or hot asset class effectively buying near the top of the market when they do so. In forty-two of the forty-eight Morningstar mutual fund categories studied, higher net inflows occurred when performance was best. In doing this, they often focused unduly on immediate past performance and ignored the principles of diversification, something any qualified FSP would pay primary attention to when designing a portfolio. As a result, the study found that many DIY investors missed out on potentially better results through failed attempts at market timing. Investors are supposed to buy low and sell high, while it seems that most are naturally inclined to buy high.

What about DIY investors' sell discipline? Not only are DIY investors unduly confident in their own investment selections when they are dropping, they frequently delay in returning to the market after getting out. They reason that they need to be confident that the market is indeed moving upward again. Research shows that investors need to be right more than half the time when engaging in this kind of market timing (both when to get out and when to get in) in order to do as well as simply buying and holding. Most truly professional FSPs are sufficiently humble to know that predicting the future is a daunting task that should not be undertaken casually. In fact, except for highly extenuating circumstances, it should not be undertaken at all.

In 1996, 5.5 years was the average holding period for mutual funds, with a redemption rate of 17.4%. By 2000, with markets on a veritable tear, the typical long-term holding period had dropped to 2.9 years and the redemption rate had risen to 32.1%.

Furthermore, the study showed that since DIY investors had consistently higher redemption rates and shorter holding periods, higher tax bills naturally followed. By not staying invested, they often missed those days when markets moved ahead strongly, something FSPs could have helped prevent. The average DIY mutual fund investor realized a return of 8.7% versus a market average of 10.9% over similar time frames. *(−2.2% vs. mgt. fees)*

Therefore, the mathematics of this study implies that an FSP is worth 2.2% in fees. That may be a bit of a stretch, but the trend should be clear. Most DIY investors unwittingly take on more risk than those who work with an FSP, setting themselves up for self-destructive behaviour when things go awry. *(DIYs incur some costs to buy + sell.)*

This is an especially important consideration coming out of the bear market that began in 2000 and ended in October of 2002. FSPs add value by helping their clients to understand and cope with market fluctuation, putting movements into a historical context and keeping them focused on long-term objectives. The primary role of an FSP is to help clients achieve their financial objectives—whatever they may be and however they are defined. Beating a market index (or some composite of multiple indexes) is not how truly professional FSPs should position their services. Rather, they should tell their clients that it is their role to get them retired and keep them retired with the least trouble by making smart financial decisions along the way. Good FSPs help to prevent their clients from making "the big mistake."

In fact, FSPs add value in other, more subtle ways. Information is ubiquitous, but the added value of strategy, context and discipline only comes from qualified FSPs. "Wisdom Sold Separately," is a phrase many people in the industry use to make that distinction.

There are three reasons why investors generally behaved as badly as they did in the 1990s: the market, the marketers and the media. The market at the turn of the twenty-first century was a seductive temptress. Everyone seemed to be making money and people who took a "rear-view mirror" approach (expecting the near future to be much like the recent past) jumped in as the fear of loss was replaced by the fear of being left behind. Marketers capitalized on both disintermediation the notion that information that was once only available from a controlled source (e.g., stock quotes in the 1970s) is now readily available to the general public and the seemingly endless stream of good news. Investors took comfort in the ubiquity of all the positive spin they were bombarded with. Finally, the media created a mania. People extrapolated the "good news" from independent sources and believed the music might never stop.

What Else Might a Good FSP Do?

A whole raft of "value-added services" from yesteryear is now being given away as financial information becomes a disintermediated commodity. The middleman (i.e., the broker) is being bypassed in this process and therefore needs do other things in order to truly add value for those who want to use his services.

Let's take a quick look at some of the things traditional brokers used to do and in some cases still do. These services include stock quotes, consolidated statements of holdings, asset allocation, proprietary securities research and trade execution. Do you notice anything about this list? All these services can now be accessed by anyone who has a computer with an Internet connection. All of them are absolutely free, save for trade execution, which is almost free.

What does this mean in the context of "wisdom sold separately?" To many, it means that FSPs are required to assist their clients in maintaining a sense of focus and an even keel, particularly in uncertain times. For instance, the great bear market of 2000-2002 has led to a considerable misattribution of blame. Consumers were upset that their portfolios were dropping at an alarming rate and needed to blame someone. As a result, many FSPs got it on the neck.

Some (those who allowed, or worse, encouraged) their clients to load up on technology, deserved it, but FSPs are no more responsible for the events of September 11, 2001 or corporate malfeasance than anyone else. There was no way anyone could have foreseen the two latter events. Although FSPs were in no way responsible for these events, their clients were looking to them to "fix" the problems that these events caused. In a situation like that, the wisdom of perspective is crucial.

Consumers can have a perverse sense of perspective regarding what FSPs do. Many consumers resent paying their FSP if they have lost 10%, even if markets have lost 20%. Conversely, many don't mind paying if their portfolio has gone up by 10%, even if markets on the whole have risen by 20%. Neither is a particularly sensible or healthy approach. Consumers tend to look at portfolio performance in isolation, with a tendency to focus on loss aversion. A more appropriate approach would be to look at portfolio performance relative to life goals, accepting that some years will be better and some worse than others. The notion that FSPs have a mandate to "beat the market" (and there are literally hundreds of "markets") is simply not tenable.

Life Goals

Research has affirmed over and over that the great life goals most people strive for are not financial. People strive to be happy, to be healthy, to see their children have a better life. Financial independence, in turn, allows people to secure a better quality of life for themselves and a better quality of life for their children. The professional FSP of the future will not only be able to make linkages to these sorts of objectives, but also to talk to clients in terms of their life goals and the financial trade-offs required to meet them. The great goals in life are highly personal and highly emotional and the kind of relationship-based advice required to address personal and emotional goals cannot be found on any website. The web will come to be seen as the provider of a wide series of product offerings, while FSPs will be seen as providers of customized solutions or relationship offerings.

Asset Allocation

Asset allocation is the decision of what proportion of a given portfolio should be invested in various asset classes. Asset allocation can be strategic (i.e., written down formally and changed relatively infrequently) or tactical (i.e., allowing the manager to move between asset classes and or sectors that are expected to outperform in a given time frame).

The division of stocks, bonds and cash within a portfolio can be further subdivided by region, sector, management style and market capitalization on the equity side and by geography, management style and credit quality on the fixed income side. Various specialty and alternative investments can also be added. One might also wish to consider allocating assets between active and passive management products. At any rate, most credible FSPs today focus primarily on getting the asset allocation decision right.

A written Investment Policy Statement (IPS) that sets out client objectives, circumstances and associated allocations, best governs this decision, once made. Regular meetings are then held to rebalance portfolios back to the initial target allocation. At present, most people with FSPs don't have an IPS in place.

Research covering the twenty-year period from 1981 to 2001 produced some fascinating results regarding the application of simple asset allocation decisions.[11] Looking at six simple equity asset classes, the results were as follows:

Investing $10,000 each year on January 1	End Value	Standard Deviation
In prior year's top-performing asset class *growth*	$732,992	14.1%
In prior year's worst performing asset class *value*	$752,187	15.6%

Investing $1,667 in each class on January 1	End Value	Standard Deviation
Equally weighted among asset classes	$913,808	14.1%
Equally weighted and rebalanced every three years	$953,024	13.8%

Of course, this is data that applies simple methodology without any intervention from human emotion. How many among us could stick to any of these strategies (even the worst isn't that bad) *on a consistent basis over a twenty-year time horizon?*

Purity

For a number of years, the people at Ivory Soap ran an ad that touted their product as being 99.44% pure. Although I confess to being uncertain about why purity should matter when choosing a cleansing agent, it certainly should be a factor when choosing an investment.

This is an area in which mutual funds and Exchange Traded Funds (ETFs) are conspicuously different. One of the reasons forward-looking FSPs use ETFs extensively, is that they are invested in one asset class only. This gives the person designing and monitoring the portfolio far greater control over the strategic asset allocation, the most significant determinant of portfolio variability. When combined with strategic asset allocation, it becomes quickly apparent that pure asset classes need to be used, otherwise control of the allocation can be easily watered down or lost.

The simplest and most compelling way to demonstrate a commitment to the Brinson research is to buy asset class pools in their purest, cheapest, most tax efficient and generic form. That means index funds and ETFs. Picking active funds not only presupposes a heightened importance for security selection, but also that the products employed are as good or better than the alternatives in dealing with constraints like purity, style drift and tax efficiency.

In essence, standard mutual funds are typically a dog's breakfast of asset classes and ill-defined mandates. The most obvious example is balanced funds. Recent research has shown a massive variance in the underlying asset allocation of some of the biggest and most popular balanced funds in Canada today. Some have 25% in bonds and 75% in stocks. Others have 50% in bonds and 50% in stocks. Some have 25% in cash. Others have essentially no cash position.

Again, no self-respecting proponent of thoughtful portfolio design would ever use a balanced fund as a portfolio building block. This is especially true since the managers of balanced funds are often given carte blanche over the asset allocation within the fund, so that the mix within any given fund often changes dramatically based on the sentiment of the manager. This is not to say that the manager isn't trying to add value, merely that investors had better be careful about what it is they are buying. They must be conscious that what they buy today may become substantially different with time.

Balanced funds are the most conspicuous transgressors in the asset allocation game. "Balanced" isn't even a real asset class. Still, funds in other asset classes are far from lily white. For instance, most Canadian equity funds have 20% or more of their holdings in foreign securities, usually American positions. One prominent (i.e., large and successful) Canadian equity fund has about $5 billion in assets, but has nearly one-quarter of the portfolio in U.S. stocks and a similar amount in cash. Only 52% of the fund is invested in Canadian stocks. There's nothing wrong with having a cash position in most portfolios, but is it really appropriate to charge a full management fee on a fund that is only three-quarters invested most of the time? If a consumer had $40,000 to invest, wouldn't it be better to put $30,000 into a quality fully invested fund and $10,000 into a cheaper, more purposeful money market fund? The de facto asset allocation would be identical.

The dictionary defines pure as "unmixed with any other matter; free from taint." There are some people who promote mutual funds that are fully invested at all times (i.e., the manager has no discretion to put even a small portion of the fund into cash) as being pure. That manager might then go ahead and put 20% of the fund's money into another asset class. The fact that 20% of the money in the fund is in an entirely different asset class is lost on marketing departments, compliance departments and regulators. Industry players act as though the terms "pure" and "fully invested" are synonymous. They most certainly are not. Everything is relative, but having something that is purer than the rest of the universe is not the same as being pure in an absolute sense.

Imagine if the people at Ivory Soap ran an ad proclaiming that the product was 80% pure. It wouldn't have the same compelling message, would it? Impurity allows manufacturers to keep on pursuing their inexorable quest for top performance for market share. As with any war, the first casualty is truth. Meanwhile, responsible FSPs and consumers who are trying assiduously to maintain a meaningful portfolio strategic asset allocation, have to deal with this environment.

The same research that demonstrates the primacy of a strategic asset allocation shows that market timing explains virtually nothing in terms of risk and return and that attempts to time the market often have a negative impact. In spite of this, mutual fund managers frequently put a large portion of their fund into cash (especially when markets are flat or headed downward) under the pretense of "adding value." Note that they never admit to "subtracting value" when they have large cash positions while markets are rising.

These managers are engaging in a form of market timing and merely looking for a way to justify their fees, repositioning their conduct as something ordinary consumers would likely find acceptable. It has been said that the surest way to win first prize for your tomato at the county fair is to bring in a cantaloupe painted red. If you get away with it, there can be no disputing that your entry is the biggest, it just isn't what it seems.

Similarly, putting foreign equities into a Canadian fund is a legitimate and useful way to circumvent an unnecessarily restrictive foreign content rule for RRSPs. American equities have historically offered returns that are 1% to 3% higher than Canadian returns and the two are only about 80% correlated. In other words, sneaking some U.S. stocks into a Canadian fund allows managers to simultaneously increase returns and lower risk. These two pursuits are entirely worthwhile. In fact, the quest for improved risk-adjusted returns is what modern portfolio theory is all about.

The trouble is that since Canadian equity funds are generally benchmarked against the TSX, we're often left with an apples-to-oranges comparison. What is worse, managers will sneak in other asset classes to improve the risk-adjusted return of the fund and then try to pass off their outperformance (when it happens) as superior security selection and/or market timing.

Let's extend this analogy. If you have six or eight mutual funds in your portfolio and most of them incorporate some form of impurity, what is your actual strategic asset allocation? Remember that anything, in order to be truly strategic (defined as "a plan or technique for achieving some end") needs to be consistent and measurable. If people were to dig beneath the surface to find out what some funds actually invested in, they would likely be shocked by their findings.

Back to ETFs. When you purchase an exchange traded fund, you know exactly what you're getting, every time and all the time. Simply stated, ETFs track an index. They do so cheaply, accurately and extremely tax effectively. There are a number of ETFs in the Canadian marketplace today that are entirely RRSP-eligible. So, if an investor wants to exceed the normal 30% foreign content limit in an RRSP, that investor can buy an RRSP-eligible ETF that might cost 30 to 35 bps (0.3% to 0.35%) as opposed to an RRSP-eligible foreign mutual fund that might cost 3%.

Market Timing

There are two ways to look at market timing: that done at the micro level (i.e., by individual investors) and that done on the macro level (i.e., by fund managers). Both conventional wisdom and considerable research hold that market timing doesn't work. Research done by Dalbar from January of 1984 to December of 2000 compared the annualized returns for the average investor to the index that investor's investments were tracking.[12] The results were depressing for market timers. In all cases and for all asset classes, individuals did far worse than their investments.

In fact, the average fixed income investor had a 6% return, while the long-term government bond index returned 11.83%. Similarly, the average U.S. equity investor earned 5.32% while the S&P 500 Index returned 16.29%. Finally, the average money market investor returned 2.29% while T-Bills returned 5.82%. Investments perform more or less how they're expected to, but investors who use these investments do poorly.

That's because most investment decisions are made on an emotional level. In spite of the well-worn mantra of buy low, sell high, people just can't buy enough investments when they're already expensive, but are all too willing to ditch them when they fall out of favour.

Let's say we're looking at a fund that has a track record of five to ten years and has been a first quartile fund over the most recent one-, three- and five-year periods. That's the sort of fund most consumers would want to buy and that many FSPs would be likely to recommend. Let's say this fund hits a "rough patch" in which its style falls out of favour. Perhaps it's a value fund trying to avoid the temptation of style drift in 1999 and 2000 when growth is all the rage. What would investors naturally be inclined to do, given the Dalbar data? They would want to sell. They would be seduced by talk of a "new paradigm" and views that the old metrics of security valuation no longer hold. If investors are so fickle as to sell an actively managed fund with a strong and long track record and an *established discipline*, can they be trusted to make their own investment decisions? Good FSPs can temper these tendencies.

One could even argue that these investors are inclined to sell precisely because the manager is sticking to his guns and not engaging in style drift. Many consumers think that smart managers suddenly become stupid when their numbers head south. In fact, managers are no smarter or dumber when markets move. However, since markets do in fact move, there is an implied attribution that falls back on the mutual fund manager that may not be justified. If, on the other hand, investors can be convinced that they have a suitable weighting in the asset class that is out of favour and all other asset classes to boot, wouldn't there be a reduced inclination to sell because of a short-term rough patch? What could be more convincing as a demonstration that fund picking is unimportant than to simply refuse to engage in fund picking? Again, if it's about the asset allocation, then let's put the emphasis squarely on the asset allocation.

Obviously, the lesson is that market timing doesn't work when left to individual investors. What about program trading, the use of computer models to get in and out with absolutely no human emotion being brought to bear? Can a methodology be dispassionately constructed to engage in market timing for profit without the harmful effects of human decisions, which are by definition emotional, even if only at a subconscious level? New kinds of mutual funds have recently been released into the marketplace that aim to do precisely that. Using historical back-tested data, these funds have developed computer models for getting the entire fund into and out of markets quickly. This is obviously a high turnover strategy and is therefore only suitable for registered accounts. The jury remains out on these funds.

Funds like these are also an interesting weigh-station en route to a more intriguing product offering called hedge funds. Traditional mutual funds are long only, meaning they can only invest in the hope that markets go up, while hedge funds can be long or short in any given asset class, commodity or currency in which the manager believes there's money to be made. Market timing funds are never short; they're either fully invested in the market (passively, there's no security selection going on here) or they're sitting in cash while the market is going down. At least that's the premise. The variations on how money managers might manipulate products in an attempt to add value for consumers are almost endless.

Holding Periods

The great problem in getting people to act is human nature. We are simply not very logical creatures. When there's a "buy two cans, get one free" sale on tuna fish at the local supermarket, we buy more. However, when financial stocks are down by one-third, we're scurrying to the exits. It's the same discount on a different product, except that the stocks will eventually go up in value and the tuna will not.

We all know that the phrase buy low, sell high has merit, yet we find it difficult to act accordingly. Research done in 2001 vividly demonstrated the inconsistency between basic logic and human nature. It showed that in 1996, in a bull market, DIY investors had a redemption rate of 18.0%, while in 2000, the redemption rate ballooned to 30.5%. Why were people almost twice as likely to redeem when markets were dropping? Didn't they understand that to be successful investors they had to buy low and *sell high?*

In contrast, the 1996 redemption rate for FSP-assisted clients was 13.8% and the rate in 2000 was 25.4%. In other words, redemption rates are generally about 20% higher for unassisted DIY investors than they are for FSP-assisted investors, irrespective of market conditions. Emotions, not fundamentals, are what drive stock prices. That's why people were buying Nortel at $124.10 in July of 2000 and selling it at .67¢ in October of 2002. Had the company really become worth less than 1% of what it was trading at just two years earlier?

Perhaps Nortel was never worth either $124.10 or .67¢. Perhaps people just got ahead of themselves and overpaid irrationally on the way up and then made the same mistake in reverse and oversold the stock irrationally a little later on the way down. Fear and greed drive markets in both directions, and quality FSPs can help to mitigate both the euphoria and the depression that less disciplined and less experienced consumers of financial products might otherwise be prone to. This, of course, is exactly what active managers profess to be able to discern often enough to justify their fees. In the end, even a small dose of sanguine wisdom can go a long way in a complicated and volatile marketplace.

Research led by Moshe Milevsky from the Schulich School of Business at York University has shown that portfolio turnover can often have a material effect on portfolio returns.[13] Furthermore, Milevsky and his team found that the erosion of wealth can be significant when comparing a high-turnover mutual fund to a low-turnover fund in a taxable environment. They suggested that taxes can eat up as much as 15% of an average mutual fund's return, which they calculate to be only 9% to begin with. Since 54% of all mutual fund assets are held in taxable accounts, this is clearly a major concern. Milevsky's research goes so far as to say that taxes exceed both management fees and brokerage commissions in their ability to erode long-term investment returns.

Of course, passive products like ETFs have lower turnover rates than all but the most slothful of active managers and are therefore usually more tax effective than virtually all mutual funds on the market today.

Background Noise

In the late 1990s, a phrase was coined that neatly captured the whole swath of information that the business media preys on; the phrase is "investment pornography." It's information that gets you hot and excited, but ultimately doesn't lead to anything productive. Ironically, it is these unimportant but interesting tidbits of information that grab financial headlines on most days. These stories are ultimately nothing more than background in the busy hub-bub of life for a person seeking financial independence. Part of the job of a good FSP is to act as a filter and to ensure that clients are not unduly swayed by these seemingly important sound bites that don't usually add up to anything. Investment pornography can include the following items:

- interest rates, employment, inflation and GDP changes
- fluctuation in currencies
- the price of oil, gold and other commodities
- where the TSX, Dow, S&P 500, Nasdaq, Nikkei and FTSE closed
- yield curves
- housing starts
- consumer confidence
- anything uttered by Alan Greenspan
- news about mutual fund sales or redemptions
- hot stocks, funds and sectors
- new highs and cyclical lows for the markets

Anyone with a time horizon of twenty years or longer isn't going to care much about the day-to-day, week-to-week or month-to-month gyrations of any of these items. But people read about them nonetheless (newspapers have to print something!) and people watch the business news daily (CNBC has advertisers to satisfy, don't you know?). Again, to quote Nick Murray, "In the short run, returns are virtually unknowable. In the long run, they are virtually inevitable." Truly professional FSPs are aware of market developments in most, if not all, of the areas listed above, but won't make predictions about what any of them mean or will lead to. That's because they don't genuinely matter. Professional FSPs focus on things that matter and are within their control.

Simplification and Perspective

There are a couple of FSP functions that, on a good day, might be worth a little more than investment pornography. These include monitoring funds for management changes, style drift and ultimately making recommendations on whether or not to fire an active manager. Generally speaking, if the attributes of a fund's discipline and personnel are the same now as what they were when you hired that fund manager, you should continue to retain that manager's services, even if he was once a first quartile manager and is presently mired in the fourth quartile. Regression to the mean is a very real phenomenon and firing a manager after a bad year or three is often a style-specific way of buying high and selling low. Professional FSPs wouldn't let their clients go there.

The main job of the FSP is to help consumers remain focused on their most heartfelt goals and to pursue them with steely determination and a sense of calm and context. Perhaps the easiest way to describe the function of an FSP is to *assist investors in overcoming their own irrationality.*

Therefore, FSPs also add value through simplification. To the extent that an FSP can simplify and enhance your life by doing spade work, filtering data, developing shortlists, calculating adjusted cost bases, securing T3s and T5s, interacting with other professionals or simply coaching you to "top up that RRSP," there is a benefit. Putting a price on it is virtually impossible, but it would be hard to deny that these activities are worth something.

Actual Financial Planning

Everything in this chapter has been about investment design, discipline and monitoring. This is not a book about financial planning, but rather a book about professional financial advice. The most conspicuous aspect of this is the need to reform compensation structures for investment products. However, investment planning is just one part of financial advice and often not even the most important part.

The majority of people reading this will not have the tools to purposefully implement all the required aspects of a comprehensive financial plan, many of which require specialized knowledge that qualified (i.e., CFP) FSPs themselves might not have.

A comprehensive questionnaire should be required that goes into great depth on matters of tax and estate planning, business succession, proper use of insurance and advanced financial planning solutions. The point is that in order to make the most of qualified financial advice, the person offering the advice needs to be completely thorough in practicing his craft. These other planning-oriented skills are often more specialized and therefore more valuable, although many people might not need that level of advice if their situation is relatively straightforward.

Applied Financial Planning

Most people should expect long-term average returns of 3% to 7% above inflation. This is made more difficult if one considers the additional erosive effects of taxation. The only possible way to do better in the long run, is to have a portfolio that is almost entirely invested in foreign equities and also in a tax-sheltered (RRSP) environment. For planning purposes, a time horizon of four years or less might be the short run, while four to ten years is the medium run and anything over ten years is the long run.

Once people have been invested for ten years or more, returns should begin to approach the long-term real return targets stated previously. Similarly, as one increases a planning time horizon, risk falls away. Remember that risk is not variability of returns, but the likelihood of losing money. Otherwise, periods like October of 1998 and July of 2002 would be depicted as "risky" months because of substantial market advances! Since people generally become slightly more conservative as they age, portfolios may be modified over time to be more conservative.

There are three primary ways to increase investment returns.*

1. reduce fixed income exposure and increase equity exposure
2. increase foreign equity exposure (perhaps using derivative products in RRSPs)

3. increase exposure to small and mid-sized companies

There are three primary tax reduction strategies.*

1. deduct all allowable expenses
2. defer taxes until a later date (when you may be in a lower marginal bracket)
3. divide taxes so that family members in lower brackets can pay less tax

Clients may also wish to consider the appropriateness of universal life insurance policies to meet tax obligations upon death and to provide tax-free growth while clients are alive.

Finally, consumers should remember that financial independence projections are made using the best and most reasonable assumptions available. If it turns out that someone falls short in their independence projections, there are really only four possible assumptions that can be altered:

1. savings rate: clients could save more on either a monthly or annual basis
2. rate of return: returns are fairly predictable provided one takes a longer view
3. retirement date: waiting longer increases savings and delays depletion
4. reducing lifestyle in retirement: this is only to be considered as a last resort

Clients have noted that they are not always aware of the various services offered by FSPs. That's likely because these things do not come up in regular conversations and communications with clients. Listed on the next page are areas where expertise should be either directly or indirectly available through a qualified FSP.

Investment Philosophy

Although the Prudent Investor Rule is not a governing standard for investment strategy at the FSP level (in fact it relates to trustees under the Ontario Trustees Act), it is appropriate to treat client assets with the same level of responsibility that formal trustees are held to. Hence, the following guidelines serve to bring focus to any FSP's philosophy, investment process and overall responsibilities.

- portfolio diversification
- matching of risk and return
- active manager selection
- management of active risk
- investment-related costs

minimize

---

* Please note that the concept of "leverage" (borrowing to invest) can both lift returns and provide additional tax deductions, but is only recommended for people who have a strong cash flow, stable income stream and high tolerance for market volatility.

Investment Planning

- Asset Allocation
- Reviews and Written Recommendations
  - Tax Efficiency
  - Estate Freezes
- Written Financial Plans
- Investment Policy Statements
  - Short-Term Budgeting
  - Offshore Planning

Debt Management

- Appropriateness of Level
- Tax Efficiency (deductibility)
- Appropriate Management
- Consolidation and Financing

Tax Planning

- Comprehensiveness
- Income Splitting
- Introductions to Professionals
- Shelters, Deductions/Deferrals

Estate Planning

- Review of Wills (transfer wishes)
- Powers of Attorney
- Suitability of Beneficiaries
- Documentation of Location

Disability and Income Protection

- Life Insurance (amount and type)
- Disability Insurance
- Pensions (public and private)
- Critical Illness Insurance

Asset Protection

- Amount and Type of Insurance
- Estate Preservation
- Business Interests
- Creative Planning

Principles of Prudence

1. Sound diversification is fundamental to risk management and is therefore ordinarily required of trustees;

2. Risk and return are so directly related that trustees have a duty to analyze and make conscious decisions concerning the level of risk appropriate to the purposes, distribution requirements, and other circumstances of the trust administrator;

3. Trustees have a duty to avoid fees, transaction costs and other expenses that are not justified by the needs and realistic objectives of the trust's investment program;

4. The fiduciary duty of impartiality requires a balancing of the elements of return between production of current income and the protection of

purchasing power;

5. Trustees may have a duty as well as having the authority to delegate as prudent investors would.

The overriding philosophy is a belief that investment returns cannot be predicted and that they are only a by-product of other factors. The thorough, diligent application of prudence will enhance performance in a more stable manner. Many people who forego the services of an FSP remain dangerously underdiversified.

Diversification

There are two risks that one can mitigate through diversification, market risk and active management risk (uncompensated risk). Uncompensated risk is pervasive in the active strategies employed by the money manager and mutual fund manager.

The most practical way to isolate market risk and control uncompensated risk, is to blend passively managed index funds and highly regarded active management. Portfolio design considerations should not use active management unless there is a high level of confidence in the ability to increase portfolio return and/or reduce portfolio risk. Investors should be compensated for taking market risk. In other words, the more market risk the investor takes (the greater the allocation to stocks), the higher their expected return. Two additional factors exist within market risk: company size (market capitalization) and valuation measures. These additional factors cannot be diversified away and investors should be compensated for taking them. Differences in risk and return characteristics are what define asset classes.

Fortunately, these additional risk factors are not totally correlated; the returns for various asset classes tend to vary over time. As a result, the higher risks and returns of relatively volatile asset classes can be moderated in a prudently diversified portfolio.

The Prudent Investor Rule makes frequent reference to the importance of viewing investments in the context of the total portfolio, rather than judging them in isolation, which is clearly sensible in the context of a highly structured portfolio, diversified by asset class. Diversifying beyond a single broad market index has historically resulted in significantly greater return with significantly less volatility if approached intelligently. The very nature of risk suggests that these relationships do not exist for every period and in all circumstances, but the underlying principles are sound and should serve an investor well over the long-term. By approaching portfolio management in this way, tailored solutions are offered to individuals, reflecting their specific objectives.

Having considered the various things an FSP should be doing, let's turn our attention to the one thing that they should not be doing: picking funds.

Benchmark Appropriateness

Given how impure many of the biggest and most prominent mutual funds in Canada are, is it any wonder that there are questions about "value-added" advice that may be going unasked? For those funds that do outperform their benchmark on either an absolute or a risk-adjusted basis, how much of that outperformance is attributable to being allowed to muddy the mandate of the fund in question?

It stands to reason, given the Brinson research, that those managers who are allowed to put wine in their water through asset class impurity will also be the most likely to beat their benchmark. The differences are largely attributable to the strategic asset allocation within the fund itself, something fund managers don't generally acknowledge. Ben Johnson was not given his Olympic gold medal back, even though he undeniably was the fastest man on the track in Seoul in 1988. The recent discovery that Carl Lewis was likely also on steroids does nothing to exonerate Johnson. Unfortunately, in money management as in track and field, there's a strong temptation to cheat—if for no other reason than the suspicion competitive rivals have that the other side is also cheating.

Some observers would say that a manager's mandate is to outperform the TSX 300, and the actual ten-year return is 1% higher than the benchmark, then critics should stop carping about impurity, say "Thank you very much" and get on with their lives. The problem is, if the U.S. stock market outperformed the Canadian stock market by 4% annually over that ten-year period and the manager had 25% of the portfolio in U.S. stocks over that time horizon, then the 1% "outperformance" has just been explained. Furthermore, the explanation has nothing to do with security selection and everything to do with the strategic asset allocation of the fund. The fund company's marketing department, of course, will position it differently and will have unwitting investors believing this track record was built on shrewdness and insights rather than the portfolio management equivalent of steroid doping.

Since there are few managers who are required to be fully invested in one asset class, most overall portfolio mandates and Investment Policy Statements are flawed from the outset. They set out a strategic asset allocation that doesn't reflect the true portfolio mix. As a result, even those FSPs who try to design and manage a portfolio more scientifically are constrained by the building blocks available to them. The end result is often a portfolio that is substantially different from what was contemplated and signed off on at the outset. This is a flaw with active management products in general and has nothing to do with whether a person uses an FSP or acts as a DIY investor.

To the extent that manufacturers can add "pure" funds to their product offerings, they should be encouraged to do so. Having funds with various permutations and variations certainly allows for choice, which is good. However, when those same permutations allow manufacturers to cloud the question of their own performance and the subsequent monitoring of that performance, you've got a problem. Good FSPs are far better equipped to deal with the problem than DIY investors.

The other element of benchmarks is the comparison of funds to one another, as opposed to a relevant benchmark. The industry is sneaky that way. Since the vast majority of funds lag their benchmark in the long run, the industry has chosen to score itself against itself. Mutual funds are rated according to their performance relative to other mutual funds, rather then in relation to a suitable benchmark.

For instance, if there are one hundred funds in an asset class and sixty lag their benchmark over a five-year period, one might get a false impression when looking at quartile rankings. There would be twenty-five funds in each performance quartile, yet approximately ten funds in the second quartile would have lagged the benchmark. It gets worse. In the very long run, fewer than 25% of all funds beat their benchmark. As a result, one could go to a ranking book to find a fund with a ten-year track record that is ranked in the first quartile and *unwittingly buy that fund even though it may have actually lagged its benchmark!*

By comparing one product with another, the financial services industry has created the impression of a balanced, apples-to-apples comparison. This comparison is fair in a relative sense (i.e., we can see which funds have been *better than the others in the past*), but that's as far as it goes. In fact, the industry is establishing a kind of kangaroo court where no comparison is being made to the real challenger, the asset class that the portfolio is benchmarked against. That would be far more meaningful to consumers and far more damaging to the mutual fund industry.

The Four Quadrants of Financial Services

Although nothing is absolute, it seems that *most of the time, passive trumps active and people with FSPs trump DIY.* There are four combinations of active/passive and FSP/DIY. Let's explore the underlying assumptions that lead to each:

1. Active with an FSP

This is where most people are today. They work with a trusted FSP who will hopefully add value through insight, discipline and planning opportunities and use actively managed investment products to do so. The presupposition is that both active security selection/portfolio management and the input of a trusted FSP are expenses worth incurring in the pursuit of one's financial objectives.

2. Passive with an FSP

There's virtually no one in this quadrant today, even though it is the quadrant that generally makes the most sense based on research. It acknowledges that working with a qualified, trusted FSP is well worth the potential additional cost, but also that using active managers to implement the strategy is often a waste of time, energy and money.

3. Active DIY

A somewhat curious quadrant, especially for those people using A Class mutual funds. The assumption here is that the consumer doesn't need an FSP for investment advice (or advice regarding taxes, estate planning or myriad other financial issues), but believes not only that active management adds value, but that superior active managers can be reliably identified.

4. Passive DIY

A respectable quadrant if you are reasonably astute, have a simple situation and are remarkably disciplined in your investment approach. Anyone with the time, temperament and training to manage their own financial affairs *should* be in this quadrant and pocket the savings in the process.

The problem with the second quadrant is the presumptive nature in which investment products are sold today. Active investments generally come with embedded compensation and passive ones do not. Furthermore, research shows that FSPs generally do add value, but since they will only recommend active products if they want to meet their mortgage payments, emphasis is put on the value of active management as provided through the careful guidance of a trusted advisor. This is as if passive management accessed through the careful guidance of a trusted advisor wasn't an option. Practically speaking, retaining bundled compensation effectively precludes passive management with qualified advice from ever becoming a real option.

	Advice	DIY
Active	1 Active Advice	3 Active DIY
Passive	2 Passive Advice	4 Passive DIY

blended →

Financial Service Providers engage in what is called a "presumptive close." In sales, when an agent says, "Great, I'm free Tuesday. Will the morning or the afternoon be better for you?" she is presuming that you'll take the bait and set a meeting, even if you're not sure you want to proceed. With FSPs, it's more like, "So it's agreed you need a 20% stake in large cap equity value. I recommend either the (embedded compensation) Mackenzie Fund or the (embedded compensation) CI Fund." It is presumed that an actively managed fund with embedded compensation will be employed to implement the strategy, as if there was no other option. Want proof? Next time your *independent* FSP makes a recommendation like this, ask for a Beutel Goodman, Sceptre or a Perigee fund instead and see what she says. Bundled compensation gives way to bungled logic.

The above chart is a simplification, since it assumes an investor is using either entirely active or entirely passive investment products. There remains a legitimate case to be made for both approaches. As a result, the two passive quadrants might be renamed "blended" or "indifferent" to more accurately reflect the nuances and uncertainties of the great dichotomy. I'm showing it this way to more clearly differentiate the differences, not to advocate using an all-passive portfolio. Some of the most useful asset classes around are only available in an actively managed format.

Nonetheless, it should be clear by now that a quasi-religious belief in active management has necessitated making the simple complex. Ironically, the role of a truly professional FSP is to make the complex simple. This is best accomplished by not attempting to pick funds and focusing squarely on what can be controlled.

Bob Veres, an American financial writer, summarizes it quite neatly. He says there are only three attributes that are important for FSPs to have. They should be able to:

1. spot problems and identify solutions
2. motivate people to act/change their behaviour
3. emotionally detach from investment markets

That's a pretty clear synopsis of what FSPs can and should do. It should also be stressed that they should not be doing any of the other things that consumers and the media seem to think they should be doing. The three things above add value; everything else is just noise. The role of the FSP is to help the consumer navigate the emotional minefield of financial decision-making. Active money managers generally don't add value to the process, but responsible FSPs generally do and that process has absolutely nothing to do with picking mutual funds.

We'll leave the last thought on this mater to Jamie Golombek, Vice-President Estate and Tax Planning at AIM Trimark Investments. He told me that "an April, 2003 survey found that Canadians were willing to pay for tax advice if the advice saves them more in taxes than the cost of the advice. The same can be said for financial advice. Clients are willing to pay, but there must be both perceived and real value added."

EXTENDING THE FRONTIER

'Tis the part of a wise man to keep himself today for tomorrow, and not venture all his eggs in one basket.

—Miguel de Cervantes

Where there is an open mind, there will always be a frontier.

—Charles Kettering

Risk and return: the yin and yang of portfolio management. No one wants the former, everyone wants the latter and the two are inextricably linked. People simply cannot get one without the other. The primary purpose of investment management is to improve returns without compromising risk unduly, within each individual's personal comfort level. Although the world has many people who amassed their personal fortunes by "betting the farm" on one investment idea, the preponderance of evidence lies with the sentiments of the diversifiers.

Over a little more than a half century, portfolio management has evolved from two separate paths. Let's call them the conventional world first articulated by Harry Markowitz and the alternative world as first articulated by Alfred Jones.

Markowitz demonstrated how risk could be reduced in a diversified portfolio. He got the world to focus on asset class returns and thought very little of security analysis. Although he never said so explicitly, many people familiar with his work believe that it implies a purely passive approach.

Jones is the grandfather of modern hedge funds. He aimed to isolate analytic talent from market forces. In so doing, his focus was on talent, security analysis and underlying events.

Most of the industry today follows the teachings of Markowitz, although there is a strong and increasingly vocal contingent of Jones proponents that is making a lot of noise in getting hedge funds accepted as mainstream vehicles for portfolio construction.

The terms diversification and professional advice are virtually synonymous, since all FSPs extol the virtues of diversification. But how well do they understand the benefits of diversification? Always remember that risk and return are related and that it is unprofessional to talk about returns in isolation, as if risk was not a consideration in portfolio design. Many people (including some FSPs) don't give it proper consideration. Too often, there's a focus on those elements of portfolio design that, while interesting, are not necessarily purposeful. The majority of investors (both those who work with FSPs and those who work without them) are likely under-diversified.

If there is considerable research that demonstrates how a portfolio can be constructed to improve risk-adjusted returns by adding more asset classes, why is so little done to actually add more asset classes to most portfolios? In particular, shouldn't the primary means of improving risk-adjusted portfolio returns be to add more asset classes, rather than to add new styles to pre-existing asset classes? If FSPs believe (as I do) that the value style offers superior returns, on both an absolute and a risk-adjusted basis, why would they want to compromise that attribute by adding growth, diversified, sector rotation or momentum styles? Style diversification is interesting, but asset class diversification is where the real value-added lies.

Modern portfolio theory clearly suggests that adding more asset classes to a portfolio will allow one to improve risk-adjusted returns. As an example, a portfolio with eight asset classes can probably deliver better risk-adjusted returns than a portfolio with five. That being said, a portfolio with ten or eleven asset classes would likely offer superior risk-adjusted returns than the one with eight.

Practically speaking, this principle could, and probably should, be tempered by the size of the portfolio in question. Portfolios under $100,000 might get by with five to eight asset classes. Those between $100,000 and $500,000 might be well served by eight asset classes. Those with over $500,000 might well require even more asset classes. The marginal utility of each additional asset class goes down as more classes are added. In other words, adding a third asset class does more to improve a portfolio than adding a fourth. Adding a fourth does more to improve risk-adjusted returns than adding a fifth. Each additional asset class improves the risk-adjusted returns, but by an ever decreasing amount. At some point, the addition of yet another asset class adds little value. Diversification has a diminishing marginal utility.

Focus Squarely on Diversification

Most FSPs are focusing on the wrong things. By extension, retail investors end up focusing on the wrong things too. Most FSPs attempt to "add value" by choosing investments that will beat their benchmark, even though that is virtually impossible to do on a consistent, predictable basis. They might combine value and growth managers within the same asset class as a means of lowering risk. However, if they truly believed that one style (e.g., value) outperforms others on both an absolute and risk-adjusted basis, they would not be adding other styles of the same asset class. They might lower risk marginally, but they would lower returns marginally too.

The net effect would move the portfolio in question downward along the frontier, rather than extending the entire frontier upward as a permanent improvement over all points on the initial frontier. Instead of adding inferior styles of pre-existing asset classes, FSPs should be looking for other asset classes that can be added to offer superior diversification by virtue of being weakly or negatively correlated to the pre-existing asset classes without compromising long-term expected returns.

Remember my epiphany earlier? It struck me at the time that the financial services industry was doing a disservice to FSPs and consumers alike, by constantly referring to *the* efficient frontier, as if there was only one. In fact, there are multiple "efficient frontiers" that maximize risk-adjusted returns for individual consumers who have their own personal and discreet risk-return trade-off choices to make. The big "aha" moment came in recognizing that risk-adjusted returns could be improved by altering the percentage mix of the asset classes employed in portfolio construction (decision 2). (*allocation*)

But there are two ways to improve risk-adjusted returns. The other was to add to the asset classes available for portfolio construction in the first place (decision 1). Portfolio design permutations are almost endless when determined primarily by the universe of asset classes that can be drawn upon. Any FSP should want to improve returns while reducing risk or at least holding risk constant. The whole (risk-adjusted portfolio) is better than the sum of the parts (the expected return from the weighted average of investments).

Too often, consumers and FSPs rush off and start buying investments for portfolios before being certain about their long-term investment strategy. The strategy in this case consists of determining the asset classes to be used and the proportion in which they will be used. Doing anything else ahead of these two things is like putting on your shoes before putting on your pants. It makes no sense. Furthermore, building better portfolios means making sure that different asset classes work together to reduce risk. People should think of personal risk thresholds: how much risk can a person reasonably be expected to bear in pursuit of higher returns? *low correlation.*

In spite of the research, there has been dogged resistance to adding alternative asset classes to retail portfolios on the grounds that the asset classes are "risky" of and by themselves. Marketing people, who don't understand the academic framework for maximizing returns within specific risk constraints, imply that there can only be one solution to optimize returns. Compliance people don't want the liability associated with having FSPs recommend asset classes that no one else is recommending in case something "goes wrong." One of Keynes' more prescient assessments of human nature is that it is often better to be conventionally wrong than unconventionally right. As a result, no one in the financial services industry really wants to "go first" in employing alternative assets in their clients' portfolios.

There are literally hundreds of potential *efficient frontiers* that would dominate current optimized portfolios if only more asset classes could be included. Extending the efficient frontier is finding a way to improve client-specific, risk-adjusted returns with the tools we already have—additional asset classes. We can do this by adding to the universe of asset classes with a primary interest in those classes that have strong returns of and by themselves, but are weakly or negatively correlated to the asset classes already in the portfolio. At least that's the ideal. Sometimes only one or two of these attributes is enough. Even a volatile asset class can be of great help *in stabilizing* a portfolio's overall returns, if it is also negatively correlated to the other asset classes in the portfolio.

Modern Portfolio Theory Revisited

A well thought-out investment strategy naturally serves as the foundation for a properly constructed portfolio. Consumers often focus almost exclusively on security selection (decision 3), while ignoring associated risks and underlying asset allocation.

In the late 1950s, a bright graduate student at the University of Chicago named Harry Markowitz theorized that a total portfolio approach was more appropriate than one that looked at a portfolio as a series of discreet parts. Portfolio design began a shift from art to science that is continuing to this day. Markowitz's research into portfolio optimization wasn't actively taught until much later. In fact, the research didn't gain real credence until 1990, when Markowitz, Bill Sharpe and Merton Miller won the Nobel Prize in Economics for their research in this area, collectively referred to as Modern Portfolio Theory (MPT).

There are many potential explanations for why it took so long for cutting-edge academic research to enter the mainstream, ranging from healthy skepticism to sloth to hubris to nefarious suppression to benign oversight. Most believe that the Capital Asset Pricing Model (the basis of MPT), if taken to its logical and complete conclusion, would cripple the profitability of conventional financial services firms. Nobel prize winning research revealed the dirtiest little nuance the financial services industry has ever miscommunicated. Security selection means virtually nothing in explaining the average relative variance of similarly mandated portfolios. Security selection, therefore, is largely a waste of time and the fees expended in doing it are being squandered.

Although it took over a generation for Markowitz's work to be appreciated, it has since become the hallmark of prudent portfolio management. People are striving to build portfolios that maximize returns, but hope to do so by taking on only as much risk as they can personally tolerate. Unfortunately, his ideas are still not truly appreciated, since virtually all applications of his logic involve the use of active management, something Miller and Sharpe have been particularly disdainful of.

Thinking on MPT

The offshoot of this thinking is that portfolio development now focuses primarily on reducing risk. Recent advances in portfolio design have rested almost entirely in the realm of risk reduction rather than return enhancement. Consumers often put too many eggs in only one or two baskets, rather than diversifying properly. Those who work with FSPs generally do a better job of diversifying, but there is still considerable room for improvement. Diversification means not only adding securities within certain asset classes, but also including additional asset classes.

There are two primary types of risk within any given asset class: systematic risk and unsystematic risk. The former is simply the risk of being in the market—any market. The latter is the risk associated with individual securities. Unsystematic risk can therefore be diversified away, while systematic risk is inescapable.

Simply "buying the market" is the surest and simplest way to eliminate unsystematic risk. By buying an individual stock, an investor is assuming a high degree of unsystematic risk within a single asset class. Buying a mutual fund offers considerable diversification, especially if there are a broad number of holdings within the fund. Buying the market (or an index that tracks it), all but eliminates unsystematic risk.

Buying the market still leaves one exposed to systematic risk, which can be considerable. Fortunately, the ability to hedge one's portfolio against temporary declines can go a long way to mitigate this risk. Unfortunately, the world of retail investment management hasn't yet found a way to dovetail hedge funds into mainstream product solutions like wrap accounts.

The notion of purposeful diversification and ethical disclosure come together in one crucial area that no one in the industry wants to talk about: adding value. Remember, active management usually does not add value, but good FSPs often do. Asset allocation is what drives risk and return above all else. People tend to forget about allocations and strategies when markets go haywire and tend to pay very little for asset allocation services and advice. That's a shame, because they are worth far more than what they are presently paying. These same consumers simultaneously overpay for portfolio management that is generally worse than worthless; they would be better off simply buying and holding the market and pocketing the savings.

Imagine a mutual fund wrap program where the total cost is 3% + GST. In exchange, clients get a comprehensive offering: advice, active asset class management, consolidated reporting, tax optimization, the works. Here's the rub. If the service includes all those elements *except* active asset class management, the cost will (or at least should) be about 1% lower, provided that all else remains constant.

Economics Nobel Laureate William F. Sharpe has shown quite conclusively that investing is at best a zero sum game. The returns of an average manager in any given market are, in aggregate, equal to the returns of the market as a whole *minus the costs charged by the average manager.* Technically, that makes active investing a negative sum game. The preceding statement should be obvious, since the managers in question comprise, in aggregate, the market in question.

Even in the very long run, some managers meet or exceed their benchmark after deducting their fees. These managers are as rare as hen's teeth. They would have to consistently outperform the market by more than their fees *in perpetuity* just to "add value." This assumes there are no taxes due in the actively managed portfolio, which would almost certainly experience a higher turnover than a passive one.

Since fees for actively managing money were introduced, firms have come to rely on their "pound of flesh" and the profit margins that go with it. Ironically, there are many excellent programs available today that strategically maximize risk-adjusted returns and regularly rebalance the portfolio to ensure that it remains on the efficient frontier (again, as if there is only one). This is a huge value-added service, yet one that is practically given away.

The net effect is that companies and FSPs are overcharging for services that add no value while simultaneously undercharging significantly for those services that do. Why? Neither the average consumer nor the media "gets it." Both are focused on the "investment pornography" of market gyrations, be it in the form of market timing or from a manager or an asset class, rather than the primacy of a strategic asset allocation. In fact, the relationship creates a vicious cycle. The more the media focuses on the narrow matters that explain next to nothing, the more consumers are led to believe these factors must actually be important. After all, why else would they be newsworthy?

The media is in the business of selling advertising space and advertisers pay for readers and "top-of-mind, newsy" stories are what people generally want to read. It's a form of presumptive sale, much like the training FSPs get in active management. If the media talks about market gyrations often enough and long enough, the average person will be effectively brainwashed into believing that market gyrations are somehow relevant to their situation.

Often, FSPs are sucked into the charade of investment pornography. Rather than setting their clients straight about what it is they do, they delude their clients (and ultimately themselves) into thinking they have a better sense of where the market is headed, when it will change direction and which stocks and mutual funds will outperform their peer group. Once they have played the game for a while, it becomes difficult to "come clean." Only the most professional FSPs have the decency to avoid claiming any ability to predict these sorts of things. Most FSPs still rely on sales tactics to get new business. In fact, most still seriously believe that top performing managers can be reliably identified and spend an enormous amount of time trying to do so. These are precisely the sorts of FSPs who are not long for this industry.

The Prudent Expert Rule

In 1974, Markowitz's work began to gain practical credence when the Employment Retirement Income Security Act (ERISA) was passed in the United States, forcing all fiduciaries to uphold the standard set out in the Prudent Expert Rule. This rule mandated those offering professional management to manage the entire portfolio in consideration of overall risk-adjusted return. Over time, pension plans, endowments and ultimately individual investors in the U.S. came to accept this line of thinking as the most suitable approach.

Prudent investment principles are also beginning to seep into the Canadian marketplace at the retail level. First up are trust accounts. On July 1, 1999, Ontario (the de facto regulatory standard-bearer in Canada) joined the group of jurisdictions that replaced the "legal list" basis for trustees' investment powers with a "prudent investor rule." This mandated that trustees exercise the same standard of care, skill and diligence that a prudent investor would exercise in making investment decisions. A trustee must consider the following criteria in planning the investment of a trust property, in addition to others that are relevant to the circumstances:

1. general economic conditions
2. the possible effect of inflation or deflation
3. the expected tax consequences of investment decisions or strategies
4. the role that each investment or course of action plays within the overall trust portfolio
5. the expected total return from income and the appreciation of capital
6. needs for liquidity, regularity of income and preservation or appreciation of capital
7. an asset's special relationship or special value, if any, to the purposes of the trust or to one or more of the beneficiaries

There is a specific mandate for the trustee to diversify the investments within the trust property to the extent that it is appropriate. Both the requirements of the trust and the general economic and investment market conditions need to be considered. These requirements are making their way to the retail level and will almost certainly be enacted over time. How many stories have you heard about consumers who have been hurt through lack of diversification or inappropriate investments?

It's happening already. Society is slowly coming around to the notion of risk as defined at the portfolio level. We still haven't reached the point where individual asset class investments can be accepted (even in modest amounts) simply because they are good diversifiers. For instance, FSPs have to complete New Client Application Forms (NCAF), itemizing all the salient points of their clients' circumstances. Colloquially known as a "KYC" (for Know Your Client), these forms force FSPs to itemize individual *investment asset classes* as low-, medium- and high-risk rather than to depict entire *portfolios* as low-, medium- or high-risk.

A more enlightened form of thinking might be all that's required. For instance, hedge funds, if added prudently to an already diversified portfolio, will almost certainly lower the risk or increase the returns of that portfolio. If the fund is used properly, the risk of the portfolio will likely diminish, but will certainly not increase. In spite of this, regulators insist that the hedge fund component of the portfolio be depicted as high-risk. *in itself.*

If regulators were restaurant owners, they would not put "house salad" on their menus. Rather, they might depict it as a medley of fresh vegetables, 76%

lettuce, 7% tomatoes, 6% cucumbers, 9% green pepper and 2% radishes. Regulators are not interested in the portfolio as a whole, but prefer to depict the whole as the sum of the parts and then itemize those parts.

This needs to change and is, in fact, changing. Portfolios might one day come to be seen as soups rather than salads, where the various elements of the portfolio are mixed to the point where they are nearly inseparable and indistinguishable from the other elements. If one were to insert the phrase "balanced diet" and then talk about food, rather than the phrase "balanced portfolio" as it pertains to investments, people would think differently. They would quickly agree that a diet of only green peppers is unhealthy of and by itself, irrespective of the undeniable benefits of eating green peppers in reasonable proportions. In portfolio design today, even if the whole is demonstrably greater than the sum of the parts, FSPs are in for a potential lawsuit if any one of those parts is deemed unsuitable when viewed in isolation, irrespective of its overall portfolio role.

An investor may have a conservative portfolio of blue chip stocks and investment grade bonds in a portfolio and wish to add a small allocation (say 5%) to emerging markets stocks or small company stocks. The NCAF forces the FSP to depict the 5% portion as high-risk even though the net effect on the portfolio as a whole is to add stability, since these asset classes are relatively weakly correlated to the asset classes that are already in the portfolio, although they are admittedly more volatile on a stand-alone basis. The idea of adding a "risky" investment in order to make a portfolio more stable seems perverse to many, but research has proven the soundness of this concept many times over.

Combining multiple asset classes reduces portfolio risk. By utilizing asset classes that are weakly correlated, non-correlated or, best of all, negatively correlated to one another, risk can be reduced even further. An appropriate correlation analysis can be used by FSPs to shape portfolios, taking into account actual correlations over long-term time horizons and expectations for shorter time horizons in the future. Additional asset classes can be added to more conventional classes that normally make up the core of any portfolio, improving overall risk-adjusted returns.

Three Little Pigs

To distill this academic theory to a familiar analogy, let's look at a fairy tale. Consider the story of the "Three Little Pigs." The story is simple. There are three pigs who, being good capitalists, venture out into the world to seek their fortunes. The first builds his house out of straw, the second out of sticks and the third out of bricks.

If portfolio design advocates were to play the parts of the pigs, the dominant portfolio paradigm from a generation ago would feature building basic portfolios out of stocks, bonds and cash: a modern-day "house of straw." People from the wrap account world of today, using additional levels of style, geographical and market capitalization diversification, would effectively be building houses of sticks. These people are totally oblivious to the considerable benefits offered by adding alternative asset classes to their portfolios.

Today's wrap account proponents are so self-satisfied with their little houses of sticks and their superiority to previous portfolio models (the houses of straw) that they never stop to consider if a good thing can be made better still. There is evidence in dozens of books and learned journals about how the prudent use of alternative asset classes can improve risk-adjusted returns. Still, the modern-day wrap account little pigs are so proud of their collective houses that they spend all their time and energy chastising their peers in the house of straw paradigm. They tell the house of straw piggies to get with the program, not recognizing that they too are being left behind by progress.

It never occurs to the manufacturers of modern-day wrap accounts that there's a state-of-the-art house of bricks that uses alternative asset classes as portfolio building blocks just waiting to be built. There's a whole world of portfolios with superior risk-adjusted returns out there being built for pension funds, family offices, foundations and endowments around the world. Retail clients, however, have been systematically denied access to some of the best portfolio building blocks. In this little fairy tale world, the regulators are the construction safety board. Unfortunately, we've already seen that the current regulatory patchwork isn't working very well. Regulators claim to hold the interests of consumers at heart, but they're really on the take from the lobby representing stick houses (conventional wrap accounts). The bottom line is, the houses of bricks (superior portfolios) never get built because the construction safety board regulators are not letting the construction workers (FSPs) get access to bricks (alternative asset classes) on the pretense that bricks are too dangerous for most consumers, even though there is considerable evidence that the premise is false.

Want proof? Until late in 2001, hedge funds were only sold to "sophisticated investors." Most people had to have at least $150,000 to invest, in order to put money into a hedge fund. The actual number varied depending on which province you lived in. Then, in late 2001, the law changed and access was allowed for "accredited investors." All you had to have was either $1,000,000 in investable assets or a personal income of $200,000/year (verified by two years' tax returns) or an annual household income of $300,000/year (again, verified through past returns) and you too, could buy a hedge fund, in increments starting at only $25,000. In other words, rich people got the regulators to pass laws allowing them to build houses of bricks for themselves and forced the rest of the world to make do with stick houses.

Using this logic, the fourth line winger of your favourite pro hockey team is considered a "sophisticated investor," while the finance professor at the local university is not. What passes for sophistication these days? Surely, there must be better tests. Under the current rules, a person can inherit $20 million, turn it into $2 million in no time flat and still hold himself up as being sophisticated.

Before turning to alternative assets, let's take a moment to review the primary asset classes that are frequently used in constructing a basic portfolio. Standard portfolio building blocks generally include cash, fixed income (bonds or GICs), Canadian, U.S. and international equities. A couple of the asset classes below are somewhere between mainstream and alternative, so they might appear on both lists. Accepting that return expectations need to be standardized and that no consistent standard presently exists, let's extrapolate some numbers for long-term expected returns and use something midway between the historical averages and the lower projected expectations.

Asset Class Summary

Listed below is a quick appraisal of the primary asset classes: what each is, what portfolio role it plays and what its expected long-term returns might be. Note that since inflation is assumed to run at 3%, the real returns (actual return minus inflation) for these classes are far lower. A total portfolio rate of return is simply the weighted average of the rates of return for various classes.

Inflation

Not an asset class, but an enemy to investors. Inflation erodes purchasing power over time. People should always look at performance in terms of real return; how well they are doing after tax and inflation. **Historic inflation rate: 4.0%. Expected future inflation rate: 3%.**

Cash

Includes Canada Savings Bonds and Treasury bills. Cash is seen as a "parking lot" or "anchor" to a portfolio. A "risk-free" investment, it is a liquid, conservative vehicle for both minor emergencies and market opportunities. It is also used as a benchmark for the "risk-free rate" that people could get in any account. Savings accounts will produce lower returns. **Expected long-term real return: Inflation + 0.8%.** $\approx 1\%$

Canadian Fixed Income

An asset class that includes bonds (both government and corporate) and GICs. This is a conservative way to increase yield over historical cash returns. Bonds can show negative returns when interest rates rise quickly. **Expected long-term real return: Inflation + 3.0%.**

International Fixed Income

Like its domestic cousin, this asset class has an inverse relation to interest rates. It is also a great diversifier because of its weak correlation to other asset classes. **Expected long-term real return: Inflation + 3.6%.**

Canadian Equities

Stocks appreciate more in value than other asset classes, but also fluctuate more. They earn capital gains and are therefore taxed at only half of your marginal tax rate. Large corporations pay a regular dividend, which is taxed even more preferentially, due to the dividend tax credit. **Expected long-term real return: Inflation + 5.1%.**

U.S. and International Equities

These are like Canadian equities, but often realize even higher returns at the expense of even greater fluctuation. Canada represents just over 2% of the world's stock market capitalization. Therefore, nearly 98% of the world's stock market investment opportunities are outside Canada's borders. A must for any growth-oriented portfolio. **Expected long-term real return: 7.3%.**

Tangibles and Real Estate

These asset classes include oil and gas, precious metals such as gold and real estate investment trusts (REITs). They play the critical portfolio role of "inflation insurance policy," since values usually rise when interest rates rise (or when there is inflationary pressure). As such, these are great hedges against inflation. Demographic influences may dampen future performance. **Expected long-term real return: 4.1%**

Asset Classes that Improve Risk-Adjusted Returns

Turning our attention to those asset classes that are somewhat less conventional (the ones that can convert a house of sticks into a house of bricks), we can get a better sense of how to build a better portfolio. The formal term for maximizing risk-adjusted returns is called "optimization," and the goal of optimization is either to achieve a return objective with as little risk as possible or to set a threshold risk tolerance and to maximize returns for that tolerance. The expected return of any multi-asset portfolio is the weighted average of the sum of the portfolio's parts, whereas the risk of the portfolio is always lower than the weighted average of the parts, since asset classes are never perfectly correlated.

Correlation is one factor in looking for additional assets to add to a portfolio, but there are other attributes that you might intuitively expect these additional asset classes to have in an ideal world. They should offer reasonably strong returns of and by themselves. They should be liquid (easily converted to cash), unless the portfolio can tolerate a certain degree of temporary illiquidity. Finally, if there are any additional benefits, like preferential tax treatment, that would be nice too.

It follows that if it is uncommon outputs (results) you seek, you may need to utilize uncommon inputs. Most wrap account programs do not use *any* asset classes other than the most conventional ones. There is a fear that "serious money" would be frightened away by less conventional asset classes.

This perception is a little odd, when one considers that the most "serious money" in the world—that of pension funds, foundations, endowments and family offices—has been making extensive use of alternative asset classes for some time now. Perception is vitally important to professional money managers. No one wants to be seen as being too different from the rest.

True professionals should be encouraged to do what is right based on the best information available and in spite of any derisive comments from their peers. In medicine, if someone is dying and conventional methods aren't working, caregivers and medical professionals may well ask the patient if he would be willing to undergo experimental tests that have shown considerable initial promise in the lab. The choice is the patient's. Most money managers don't make similar offers regarding alternative asset classes, because their peers would think of them as the financial services equivalent of a mad scientist. This is the case even though diversification within the standard asset classes has become less useful, due to higher correlations realized through globalization, twenty-four-hour trading and the like.

In the laboratory of scientific money management, there are many asset classes that have been shown to improve risk-adjusted returns fairly conclusively, yet are not used much. "Leading edge" can become "bleeding edge" quickly in a hyper-competitive industry where reputations are precious and vast sums of money are at stake. Innovation is encouraged, provided it isn't too radical. There is a saying in the industry that "you are what you sell." As a result, no one wants to be the first to recommend anything that's too different, because if it doesn't work out, a reputation could be seriously damaged.

Still, if the primary objective of FSPs is to construct portfolios that improve returns without taking on additional, undue risk, then the single most useful concept must surely be diversification. As fate would have it, this is also a strong argument for active management. Some asset classes are simply not available in a meaningful way outside an actively managed environment. Since there's a pre-eminent importance associated with adding additional asset classes to portfolios, there's *an extremely compelling need for active management in a number of circumstances*. Asset classes like venture capital, hedge funds, high-yield debt, income and royalty trusts and real return bonds are not generally available to ordinary retail investors in anything other than an actively managed format.

If you can find ways to improve on this situation, you should do it. Generally speaking, the more layers of diversification you add, the more stable the portfolio becomes. Nonetheless, let's have a look at some of the best asset classes for improving risk-adjusted returns.

Hedge Funds

Intellectually, people can't have it both ways. Markets are either efficient or they are inefficient. If they are efficient, then people should only use passive investment products to build portfolios, since passive products are by definition designed to allow capital market efficiency to do all the work. If markets are inefficient, then extensive use should be made of hedge funds. That's because hedge funds are the ultimate instrument to capitalize on market inefficiencies. If employed properly, they can reduce risk dramatically. Virtually any view about market efficiency can be made to accommodate hedge funds, but those people who are proponents of active management should inherently be most receptive.

Alfred Winslow Jones devised the original idea of a hedge fund in the late 1940s, so please don't let anyone tell you that hedge funds are "too new" to be credible or some sort of passing fad. The concept developed out of the notion that since analysts couldn't agree on whether a bear market or a bull market was around the corner, both outcomes should be considered. Anyone who listens to the popular media today still suffers from this affliction.

As a result of this thinking, Jones decided he would simply buy undervalued stocks and short overvalued stocks, shifting his holdings throughout the market cycle. The objective here was risk management, effectively hedging away the risk of a market downturn, hence the name. Hedge funds are not really an asset class, but a professionally managed pool that is focused on absolute returns, rather than relative broad market indices. They came to utilize the widest possible range of strategies in the investing universe, so wide that many are called "alternative" strategies. These include such seemingly esoteric concepts as market neutral, long-short, convertible arbitrage, event-driven, global macro, fixed-income arbitrage, distressed capital and managed futures. The primary aim for most hedge funds is to reduce volatility, while attempting to preserve capital and deliver positive returns *under all market conditions*.

At their core, hedge funds are quite similar to various forms of insurance, since they offer risk management as applied to a wide range of possible outcomes. In this case, the offering consists of various types of "portfolio insurance" against trends that might otherwise be damaging. Hedge funds can make market volatility (especially the negative kind) work in the investor's favour.

Although they have been around for decades, hedge funds are only now making their way into mainstream retail portfolios. Because they seek to earn maximum absolute returns and are not a true asset class unto themselves, they can really only be benchmarked against similarly mandated funds. Given the lack of reporting standards in the hedge fund community, this has been a major problem.

One thing that hedge funds have going for them is that virtually all of the best ones were started with the manager's own money. This takes the "alignment of interests" concept discussed earlier to a whole new level. With hedge funds, the manager not only "feels the pain" of reduced fee revenue when the account drops in value, she actually loses principal along with the unitholders and usually on a much larger scale!

The quest for absolute returns requires that risk is isolated and hedged. This is often accomplished with leverage techniques, yet virtually every manager has a different definition of leverage. The current trend is to develop "fund of funds" hedge funds that mitigate the risk associated with any particular strategy or manager. Let's have a quick look at why a focus on absolute returns with low volatility can be so compelling by illustrating what goes into an 8% target return under different scenarios.

Year	Scenario 1 Return	Investment Value	Scenario 2 Return	Investment Value
		$100,000		$100,000
1	8%	$108,000	8%	$108,000
2	8%	$116,640	(8%)	$99,360
3	8%	$125,971	26.8%	$125,971

Starting with $100,000, we have two fictional portfolios, both aiming to return 8% compounded annually. The first compounds at exactly 8% a year, while the second is variable. It gets 8% the first year, but then loses 8% the second. Given that 8% of $108,000 is more than 8% of $100,000, the portfolio is actually negative after two years. It would also be negative if it lost 8% the first year and then gained 8% the second. But here's the truly remarkable point; in order to catch up to the first portfolio that earns a simple 8% annually, the variable portfolio will need to earn nearly 27% in the third year for investors to be as well off. Some people call this "winning by not losing."

Because hedge funds can do virtually anything with the money that is entrusted to them, they often pursue strategies that other funds don't or can't. For instance, they can sell stocks short or buy put options, both of which are essentially bearish strategies. They can profit from fluctuations, not only of major capital markets and the securities within them, but also on things like commodities and currencies, things very few investors ever think to invest in. They can use arbitrage strategies, look for distressed companies trading at a deep discount or use convertible debentures. In short, if a hedge fund manager spots a potentially profitable trend, he'll have an opportunity to capitalize on it on behalf of unitholders. In capital markets, any trend—up or down, commodities or currencies—will do.

Managers can genuinely add value by using their wits and preying on market inefficienies. Furthermore, many hedge fund managers charge substantial fees for their services. Where these managers have genuine track records of offering strong risk-adjusted returns, investors would be well advised to pay the fee and say thank you very much. Unlike conventional mutual funds, there is considerable evidence that *responsible* hedge fund managers can and do add value, generating superior risk-adjusted returns even after accounting for their industry-leading fees. Perhaps more than anyone else in the portfolio management side of the financial services industry, hedge fund managers really do focus on adding value.

A primary example of this added latitude is that hedge funds do not correlate to other asset classes. Non-correlation is crucial. Even if total net returns were identical, this would be a major benefit unto itself. In a nutshell, non-correlation means that the performance of other investments does nothing to explain the performance of hedge funds. This is exactly what one would intuitively expect. After all, if it is possible to make money, irrespective of the market's direction, then there is a reasonable opportunity to make money under any prevailing circumstances. As a result, hedge funds are superb diversifiers. The only thing a standard portfolio manager can do in a bear market is to put a disproportionate part of the portfolio into cash and ride out the storm. In contrast, hedge fund managers often relish bear markets. *[selling low?]*

As globalization becomes more and more entrenched, it would be reasonable to expect that stock markets around the world will become more highly correlated than ever before. Indeed, a number of research papers over the past decade have demonstrated this concept.

Now that all the basic levels of diversification have been attended to in most portfolios, hedge funds stand out as the obvious "next step" in constructing portfolios that can offer superior risk-adjusted returns. Typically, people get higher returns only by taking on progressively higher levels of risk, especially if their portfolio is already deemed on the efficient frontier.

Hedge funds are perhaps the only products that can be added to virtually any portfolio with the net effect of lifting returns, lowering risk or both. Be sure to ask about leverage, since that one simple concept is the single greatest cause for most hedge fund blow-ups. Most experts either do not recommend using leverage or recommend that it be used judiciously and when it is circumstantially advantageous. Leverage can lift returns, but only by increasing risk correspondingly. Again, the objective most people should be aiming toward is risk reduction, not return enhancement. *[not what you've been saying!]*

Of and by themselves, they *can be* risky investments, so they are not a panacea. Most hedge funds are actually more stable than conventional long-only stock mutual funds or ETFs. When adding a reasonable hedge position to a pre-existing portfolio that is already reasonably balanced and customized to client circumstances, the net result is virtually certain to be higher returns and/or lower risk. This is what management consultants call a "win-win situation." The rest of us would call it common sense. *[short-term view]*

Given the hardship investors have endured at the turn of the millennium, the ability to profit from falling markets and alternative asset classes and strategies should be given every serious consideration when moving to the next level of true portfolio diversification.

This is clearly an area where current investor restrictions need to be further relaxed. Regulators seem to think that since hedge funds use sophisticated strategies, they are only suitable for "sophisticated investors." Precluding investors from participating in this kind of investment option simply because they don't have or earn a lot of money is a dangerous form of financial elitism.

Another practical barrier to using hedge funds is their compensation structure. Although there are a few that are unbundled, offering no commissions or trailing commissions, most hedge funds feature performance bonuses above and beyond any embedded compensation that pays the FSP if performance is above a certain threshold. No payments are made if the threshold isn't met or exceeded. The only problem with performance-based compensation (which is just another way of aligning the interests of the hedge fund manager with

[goal is always best (safe) returns.]

the client) is that sometimes bonuses can be paid that substantially increase the FSP's compensation, even though that compensation cannot be quantified before the fact. Some would say this is not an issue—"Don't complain if you're beating the market"—whatever you define it to be. Others would say it compromises professionalism by allowing for a kind of back-door FSP compensation.

60+ - 1/4's Since January of 1988, there have been nineteen quarters in which the Morningstar Average Equity Mutual Fund lost money. In every one of those quarters, the average hedge fund did noticeably better. Over the same period, U.S. hedge funds have more than tripled the returns of equity mutual funds since 1988, representing a 950% total return for hedge funds, as compared to a 280% return from conventional funds. Furthermore, the annualized Sharpe Ratio of the Van Hedge Fund Index has been 1.4%, as opposed to 0.4% for conventional equity funds. In plain English, that means hedge funds have offered superior risk-adjusted returns.

There are also some very real risks and limitations to hedge funds that need to be taken into account. One such example is the hurdle rates that conventional hedge funds build into their modelling. They'll generally charge a 1% annual management fee, plus 20% of all returns over a certain hurdle (say 10%). If a manager is performing poorly the hurdle will be missed and the bonus won't be paid. Again, this is touted as a clear alignment of interests between the investor and the manager. But what if we're approaching the year's end and the manager is just a little below the hurdle? Wouldn't that create a situation where the manager might engage in a little style drift in pursuit of a little more return so that the bonus target is more attainable? The pursuit of absolute returns can still be a slippery slope and due diligence is more necessary than ever where hedge funds are concerned.

There are other limitations. For instance, there are problems with the quantitative methods stemming from the misuse of statistics, sometimes causing people to buy at the wrong time. The quality of information surrounding hedge funds remains poor and unlike conventional long-only mutual funds, historical returns are essentially useless. There are a whole series of factors that might result in tantalizing, but statistically insignificant, track records. These include survivor bias, creation bias, reporting bias, perception bias, changing personnel, changing processes, game theory, non-replicable events, misrepresentation and outright fraud.

Let's use one simple example from game theory. Since there are low barriers to entry in the industry (it's not formally regulated) and people tend to give money to "hot new stars" who produce stunning results, there's a major incentive for a manager to launch an aggressive new fund. Here's what could happen: the fund gets launched and if it does well, everyone makes money. However, if the fund does poorly, the manager will simply close the fund, choose not to report the results (lack of reporting standardization is part of the overall regulatory problem) and simply start a new fund. Better luck next time for the manager; *caveat emptor* for the unitholder.

Due diligence is vital. Get reference checks, look for steady communication from the manager and do meaningful audit reviews. Be very careful about checking third-party service providers like the custodian, administrator and net asset value calculator. You don't want the hedge fund manager "marking his own papers."

The framework that hedge funds operate in will be standardized with formal audit controls soon enough. In the meantime, there is a movement afoot to offer specific training and credentials for hedge fund advice in Canada. This would ensure a minimum level of FSP competency, which in turn would imply a reasonable amount of due diligence being performed on behalf of investors. Another good reason to work with a qualified FSP.

Think of hedge funds as seat belts for your portfolio. Seat belts don't prevent you from being in an accident, just as hedge funds don't prevent markets from dropping. If an accident happens, however, wearing a seat belt might just save your life. Furthermore, if the bear market of 2000-2002 was the equivalent of an "accident," does that mean we can't have another accident some time down the road? Is it prudent not to wear a seat belt *after* you've been in an accident, as if you have a quota that's been used up?

Serge Simone is the founding President of the Canadian Chapter of the International Hedge Fund Association. He says that one day, virtually all portfolios will include a hedge fund component and that people will look back disbelievingly at the archaic attitudes of our past when consumers invested in long-only portfolios. He has also suggested that there's a far greater need for accredited FSPs than there is for accredited investors.

Venture Capital

For over a decade, Canadians have been allowed to invest in a special kind of mutual fund. Labour-Sponsored Investment Funds (LSIFs) allow people to gain access to the diversified, professionally managed portfolios of very small, or micro-cap, companies. Many are simply too small to be publicly listed. There are many funds available (registration is province by province), and there are a number of benefits to using these funds for a small portion of a balanced portfolio.

Micro-cap stocks tend to offer returns that are greater than large company stocks. The price of this higher return, of course, is higher volatility. However, since micro-cap stocks often dance to the beat of a different drummer and have a relatively weak correlation with larger companies, they are great diversifiers and can lower portfolio risk when used judiciously.

There are at least two other major benefits associated with venture capital. One is that it automatically increases the de facto foreign content limit in RRSPs from 30% to up to 50%. Still anyone can get up to 100% de facto foreign exposure by using derivative funds that synthetically gain exposure to foreign markets, without going offside with Canada Customs and Revenue Agency.

Third, Labour Funds allow investors to claim either a 30% or 35% non-refundable income tax credit, depending on the mandate of the fund.

Although the maximum purchase in any given year is only $5,000, getting an additional $1,500 or $1,750 back every spring is a very compelling proposition. It's like a 30% downside risk protection. Your $5,000 investment could drop to $3,500 and you would still be breaking even on an after-tax basis.

In the 2000 annual report of the Canada Pension Plan, investment head John McNaughton said that up to 10% of the CPPs investment assets will ultimately be invested in private (i.e., venture) capital projects and substantial CPP investments have been rolling into private equity ever since. That's a stunning vote of confidence for an underappreciated asset class.

At present, there is a problem on the compensation side for FSPs. Those who wish to recommend venture capital on a fee basis cannot do so. It is impossible *not* to earn a commission on this type of investment vehicle, since it is only available as a commission-based product. Hopefully, this will also change along with some of the concerns about embedded compensation mentioned earlier. Today, the problem is one of "double dipping," in which FSPs can receive both a direct fee from the client and a commission and trailer fee from the company that promotes the fund. The only ethical way around this conundrum at present is to use the fee offset concept where the embedded compensation is fully disclosed and the FSP reduces his fee dollar for dollar so that the inclusion of the asset class is 'revenue neutral.' Some FSPs are ahead of the rest of the industry by such a wide margin that the industry hasn't been able to come to terms with how they place these trailblazers into a precarious position, just because they want to recommend the best solutions to their clients. Does this circumstance seem like the industry is thinking through the full ramifications of its policies?

High Yield Debt

In general, the asset classes with the highest historical rates of return are also the most volatile. Diversifying within and throughout asset classes is therefore the closest thing the investment community has to a "free lunch."

Perhaps the most misunderstood asset class with a fixed income pedigree is high yield debt. Consigned to the margins after the Michael Milken junk bond phenomenon of the 1980s, high yield debt has regained some credibility. In the brave new world of shareholder rights, many companies have gained the respect that is owed to them for their fiscal responsibility. As corporate profitability becomes more sustainable, corporate debt becomes more respectable. Historically, corporate debt provides investors with returns that are only slightly below stock returns, with a variability that is only slightly more than conventional investment-grade debt.

I would certainly never recommend that an investor buy an individual corporate bond. However, a mutual fund that is professionally managed containing a basket of forty or more bonds might be an excellent way to get a little more return out of your fixed income portfolio without adding unduly to your risk.

The great irony of corporate bonds is that they are so often disparaged, while their equity cousins get all the glory and attention. Most people know that if a corporation is faced with insolvency, it is the bondholders who need to be paid first. Stockholders are paid from whatever is left over. However, there are many companies whose stock trades at high multiples, while the same people who buy that stock stay away from corporate debt on the grounds that it is "too risky." How can this be?

Let's use Rogers Cable as an example. The company is stable and has a very wide customer base with a product that has a reasonably high inelasticity of demand. If the price of cable services went up by 5% or 10% tomorrow, it is highly unlikely that Rogers would lose 5% to 10% of its customers, so the cash flow is pretty secure. Equity usually has more long-term upside than debt. But how does it make sense to stay away from the debt because it is too risky, while simultaneously loading up on the stock?

These are the sorts of market inefficiencies that good money managers look for. Indeed, these are the sorts of inefficiencies that all investors should look for, but generally do not consider. When building a portfolio, it is important to consider a wide variety of both strategies and asset classes. For many people who want some form of fixed income but are disillusioned by today's low interest rates, high-yield is a good place to start.

Emerging Market Equities

Buy low, sell high. Emerging market equities have been low for most of the past decade and all asset classes move in cycles. Irrespective of where we are in the economic cycle and what happens in the short- to medium-term with emerging markets, there is little doubt that this is a part of the world where investors should want to be, if only to a small extent.

Remember that Sir John Templeton was laughed at when he started buying Japanese stocks half a century ago. After all, Japan was an economic backwater that could at best cobble together a copycat economy while the real innovation occurred elsewhere. Templeton proceeded based on fundamentals and he and his investors were handsomely rewarded for doing so.

Look at the fundamentals for emerging markets today and tell me if you see a pattern. GDP growth is substantially higher than in the developed world. Price/earnings for stocks in emerging markets stand at less than half those of their Canadian, American and European counterparts. Emerging markets generally march to the beat of their own drummer since they are relatively weakly correlated to developed markets. Are these circumstances where a small exposure to this part of the world might be prudent? How many wrap programs in Canada actually have emerging markets as a separate pool?

Real Estate Investment Trusts

Real estate is the one asset class that has the greatest total worldwide market capitalization. Most people reading this will have more equity in their home than in their portfolio of financial assets, and by now everyone knows that the real estate market and the stock market often move in different directions. By using REITs, investors may gain from both capital appreciation and a regular income stream. The appreciation comes from selling property at a profit, the income stream comes from the rental income earned while owning it. Like other "hard assets" (oil and gas, gold, precious metals), real estate tends to do well in an inflationary environment. As long as inflation is relatively benign, there is relatively less benefit in having investment real estate in your portfolio. That being said, real estate has enjoyed a major resurgence in the early 2000s, just at the time when stock markets have begun to tumble. Weak correlation is a wonderful thing.

Royalty and Income Trusts

Consumers want yield, safety and tax-efficient income. Quality royalty trusts and income trusts provide all three through a regular, reasonably predictable income stream. Royalty and income trusts give unitholders an opportunity to share in a company's profit from a specific income stream, by distributing the cash flow from that company back to the owners on a pre-tax basis. Investors purchase an interest in an operating company or a series of producing oil wells, which in turn distributes income to all unitholders. They are neither stocks nor bonds, but share many of the same attributes (potential capital appreciation, potential income, liquidity).

Moving a small portion of a portfolio into royalty and income trusts offers consumers yet another asset class and will not appreciably add to risk. In fact, depending on what asset classes the money for royalty and income trusts comes from, the risk level for the portfolio as a whole could very well be reduced.

Small Company Stocks

Small companies have historically outperformed large ones over time, but have been more volatile in the process. Like anything else, they can be further sub-divided into domestic and foreign holdings. The general thinking when adding asset classes like small-cap stocks to an already diversified portfolio is that, all else being equal, they will add to return, but also add to risk. People obviously need to be compensated to take on higher risk. Why would anyone want to invest in something that is riskier, unless that riskier asset class also offered higher returns?

This is generally a fair assessment, except that the additional risk may be more modest than you otherwise think. Small companies do not always move when large companies move, meaning they are not too highly correlated to large company stocks. The seemingly perverse outcome of this is that one might actually make a portfolio more stable by adding this inherently volatile asset class. Having small-cap stocks zig while large-cap stocks zag could very well lead to a less volatile total portfolio.

Global Bonds

Foreign bonds can be another good way to get a reasonably steady return without taking additional risk. There have been global bond managers plying their trades for decades, yet most people have never seriously considered using the asset class for their own portfolio. These have many of the same attributes as domestic bonds, but since other parts of the world are on different interest rate cycles, they can lower portfolio risk. Furthermore, results can vary depending on how foreign currencies perform relative to the Canadian dollar. This, of course, is yet another form of diversification. Depending on the countries involved, global bonds might be more akin to corporate, high-yield debt, since some countries are less creditworthy than those of North America. This, in turn, might allow for higher yields.

Real Return Bonds

This is another asset class that has been around a lot longer than people think, having first been issued by the Government of France in 1952. A real return bond is one that pays a rate of return adjusted for inflation. These novel products currently represent about 8% of the American Treasury Bond market, but could well represent 20% of the market by the end of the decade.

Unlike regular (nominal) bonds, the real return feature means that purchasing power is maintained, regardless of the future rate of inflation. Real return bonds represent the only asset class that provides a *guaranteed* hedge against inflation. Others, such as tangible assets have traditionally performed that role, but their performance is not guaranteed. To understand how real bonds are valued, we'll need to consider the break-even rate of inflation. Here's an example:

10-year treasury note yields	5.29%
10-year RRB yields	3.53%
Necessary inflation rate	1.76%

In this scenario, inflation need only exceed 1.76% over the next decade for a real return bond to outperform a treasury note. Furthermore, real return bonds have a relatively low correlation to traditional asset classes. Here's a look at a few of the more relevant correlation coefficients for real return bonds:

Scotia Capital Bond Universe	0.19
S&P/TSX	0.02
S&P 500 (C$)	-0.10

Even a relatively small amount of inflation can be devastating over time. If inflation averages 3% annually over five years, for instance, then $10,000 today will have the purchasing power of only $8,600 in today's dollars at the end of the half decade. Over eighteen years, an inflation rate of 4% would cut a person's purchasing power in half. Seniors and those on a fixed income are typically highly concerned about maintaining purchasing power. For them, real return bonds are an excellent vehicle to add to their portfolios since they are contractually linked to the rate of inflation.

Here's what Robert Bertram, Executive Vice-President of Investments at the Ontario Teachers' Pension Plan has to say about them: "More and more, we are trying to take a long-term view for investing. We are trying to pull away the short-term market volatility... We (aim to) take positions on which we have a longer view that will give us the stable absolute return. That's what we're looking for...to make sure we cover off the inflation indexing and to produce a higher return with more stability."

There are many people who believe a period of more than twenty years of disinflation starting in the early 1980s (a long-term time horizon when bonds outperformed stocks!) is drawing to a close. If a modest reflationary trend asserts itself by the middle of the decade, this asset class could be a big winner. Even without renewed inflationary pressure, there's a strong case to be made for real return bonds. Secular trends, like the decline in real rates due to the falling debt to GDP ratio through both enhanced growth prospects and control of the deficit might make them even more attractive.

Tangible Assets (Oil and Gas or Gold)

It is generally accepted that a stake in tangible assets (also called hard assets or inflation hedges) can substantially lower portfolio risk. Oil and gas is actually negatively correlated to traditional asset classes, making it a superb diversifier. Notice that no one is saying there will be any appreciable return enhancement as a result of including this asset class in your portfolio. Sometimes, however, a penny saved is worth more than a penny earned. Ibbotson Associates in Chicago have gone so far as to say that a stake of between 10% and 25% in direct oil and gas investment can improve the risk-adjusted return of a portfolio, depending primarily on what was in the portfolio in the first place. (hi-risk - hi-return)

Prior to the most recent bear market, the most turbulent downturn in most peoples' financial lives was the bear of 1973-74. It was a vicious downturn, brought about by the energy crisis. Ironically, anyone who had even a modest (perhaps 10%) exposure to oil in 1973-74 actually did reasonably well.

Gold has historically played the portfolio role of "store of value" and has preserved wealth better than most asset classes in times of real or perceived insurrection. Given that many people are talking about how the world is becoming an increasingly uncertain place in which to live and invest, it would seem prudent to consider a small allocation toward gold as an "insurance policy" against war, runaway inflation and other man-made scourges.

Earlier on, we examined how the primary role of the professional FSP was to prevent clients from making "the Big Mistake." There is a broad consensus that FSPs can assist people in framing their thinking since most peoples' thinking is often checkered by short-term, random movements in capital markets. Therefore, wouldn't it stand to reason that anything that could be done to minimize portfolio fluctuation would by definition also assist professional FSPs in doing their jobs?

This behavioural finance concept is called loss aversion. Research shows that the pain of a loss is more than twice as powerful as the joy of a gain. That's because gains are generally expected and losses are largely unexpected. To that end, shouldn't all constructive steps to limit negative fluctuation be heartily embraced? They would certainly go a long way toward helping consumers sleep better at night!

The Difficulty in Implementing the Concepts

All of the above information about asset classes, risk, return, co-variance and standard deviation is nice, but it doesn't matter one bit to typical investors. They would rather leave the logic and portfolio design to FSPs. More than anything else, that's why regulators and legislators need to step in to protect investors. The system, as it is currently constituted, puts all the power in the hands of the FSP.

Most FSPs do not want to cede the mundane elements of portfolio design to mathematicians or portfolio optimization software, because their whole "value proposition" is predicated on fund picking, stock picking and knowing more about the minutiae of capital markets than their clients. Today, almost all of the aforementioned security selection information is readily available to anyone on the worldwide web and is essentially worthless anyway.

Another difficulty is that optimization inputs are only estimates; they are unavoidably going to be subject to some degree of error. Correlation coefficients are not static. As the world has become more closely integrated, the covariance of different economies has increased. That means certain types of diversification that were effective in the past might be less effective going forward. Consumers and FSPs alike will need to consider the answers to two questions:

1. How sensitive are portfolio allocations to changes in estimates of return, risk and correlation?
2. Which portfolios are efficient, or nearly efficient, under a variety of possible circumstances?

Any portfolio should be compared against the resulting band of possible *efficient frontiers*. Remember that the FSP mantra is "people don't care what you know until they know that you care." More than anything else, consumers look to a trusted FSP to ensure that all elements of their financial affairs are being attended to practically, thoroughly and professionally. We are only now getting to the point where meaningful optimization software is available to FSPs across the country. Any FSP who resists using this kind of software does so at his own peril. Real professionals don't recommend products or product mixes based on which wholesaler took them to the ballgame most recently.

Professional investment managers' efforts to beat the market have almost always failed. In any given asset class, the only consistently superior performer is the market itself. As a result, people should employ active management only once they have been apprised of these facts or when passive products are otherwise unavailable. Investing using primarily passive strategies for asset class exposure will dramatically alter the way individuals invest their money in the future. Those people who wish to pursue active strategies, in spite of the evidence against them, could even be asked to sign a written disclosure document spelling out the unlikeliness of their success. Again, one would expect compliance departments to support these kinds of initiatives.

Most major brokerage and financial services firms aren't in the business of truly educating the public, since a well-informed public would cut into their profits dramatically. They talk about asset allocation and professional management as if they are inseparable. One adds value to the consumer. The other adds profits to the firm.

Passive management rests on the sound theoretical framework that free and competitive markets work, and that assets are priced fairly and reflect all known information. In essence, the concepts of Modern Portfolio Theory are not widely understood, even by FSPs.

In the financial markets, you cannot determine what is going to happen by analyzing historical price movements. Short-term movements are too random. Those professional FSPs who specialize in asset class investing should be paid a predetermined fee, not a commission. This fee would usually be a percentage of assets under management, paid annually according to account size. The fee should be transparent, scalable, directable and potentially tax deductible.

Many of the brightest minds in the world of finance today are projecting real returns (i.e., returns above inflation) for equities at no more than 5%. Warren Buffett and Jeremy Siegel are two of these people. Others, like Sir John Templeton, have already actively embraced alternative assets in light of this expectation. In an October 2002 interview in *Wall Street Week* with Louis Rukeyser, Templeton disclosed that although half his money was in long-term treasury bonds, the other half was in market-neutral hedge funds. The fact that one of the great money managers of history is completely out of traditional long-only stock positions shows us how much credibility alternative assets in general and hedge funds in particular have gained among people in the know in today's marketplace.

A physician who stubbornly refuses to utilize new procedures or medicines is considered unprofessional. Blatant refusal to "stay current" can lead to malpractice suits, since physicians are bound by the Hippocratic Oath to protect the health and welfare of patients. Full professional disclosure is simply a part of how true professionals conduct their day-to-day affairs.

In a similar vein, it would be difficult for an FSP to hold herself out as a true professional if the advice she offered did not incorporate the fullest breadth of products and services currently available. Alternative asset classes are precisely these sorts of products. The majority of retail portfolios are presently built with little or no exposure to these asset classes, but any FSP who hopes to be viewed as a professional in the future needs to be familiar with and actively recommending these alternative asset classes to their retail clients, in sensible amounts. *China?*

An integrated approach includes insurance, cash management, estate planning, investment management and other related concerns. At present, many FSPs don't always do what's best for their clients at all times and under all circumstances. Often, this is simply because they have a predisposition to work with only one set of product solutions and don't have the full breadth of skills with other products. This is especially true with insurance. The "to do" list for regulators, legislators, self-regulatory organizations and all related stakeholders in the financial services industry is a long one. It is time we got to work. Insurance is a great place to start.

CONSTRUCTIVE REFORM FOR INSURANCE

Nothing astonishes men so much as common sense and plain dealing.
—Ralph Waldo Emerson

It is the mark of an educated mind to be able to entertain a thought without accepting it.
—Aristotle

Until now, most of the discussion surrounding financial advice has revolved around investment options. Real integrated wealth management needs to cast a much wider net. It should encompass financial planning, estate planning, tax planning, risk management and investment management. Any client of an FSP who is genuinely trying to integrate advice on all aspects of her financial life will find the process conspicuously incomplete if it does not consider the proper use of various forms of insurance.

Insurance provides financial risk management. It comes in various forms, but at its core is used to mitigate the financial risk associated with an unfortunate event such as a death, disability or critical illness. Many consumers have come to think of insurance as either a necessary evil or an unnecessary money pit that offers nebulous benefits to the purchaser. Either way, few consumers have a high opinion of those people who recommend insurance as a viable planning tool. Insurance in its many forms is a product that offers fuzzy "lifestyle" benefits that are often difficult to quantify, largely because people have different impressions and values surrounding the notion of quality of life.

The poor cousins of the insurance world, home and auto insurance, are thought of in particularly unsavoury terms. They are seen as necessary evils imposed by governments as a means of mitigating liabilities that would otherwise almost certainly go unfunded. While these are certainly important considerations when engaging in life planning, they are beyond the purview of this discussion.

Those who make a living "selling" insurance are often thought of as anything but true professionals who have their clients' best interests in mind. When going through a life insurance illustration, much of the discussion surrounds emotional "hot buttons" associated with something going horribly wrong. The image of people crossing the street in order to avoid coming into contact with an insurance representative holds true. There are many people working in the insurance industry in a highly responsible and professional manner, offering solutions more appropriate than anything else available. These solutions are often highly complex and specialized.

The appropriate use of insurance is a vital part of integrated wealth management. This is especially true for affluent people, because the applications are almost endless. The wealthy might need to shelter money from the tax man, protect their human capital (earning power), control the risks inherent in small businesses, make charitable gifts or pass a meaningful estate on to future generations. Insurance is often the most effective and tax efficient means of doing so.

From a wealth management perspective, there are four primary types of insurance: life insurance, disability insurance, long-term care insurance and critical illness insurance. The former comes in various formats: renewable term, term to one hundred (T-100), universal life (UL) and whole life. These are all predicated on the inescapable fact that after centuries of medical advances, the long-term human mortality rate remains unchanged at 100%.

The last three types of insurance are somewhat less likely to be part of most peoples' planning, largely because they are relatively misunderstood. They are based on the probability of someone becoming disabled, critically ill or unable to care for herself later in life and provide financial assistance for those who ultimately come to need it.

It's a particular shame that critical illness insurance and disability insurance are not more widely accepted, partly because they are more expensive than life insurance. Of course, there's a perfectly good reason for the cost; both outcomes are far more likely to occur than *premature* death. What is amazing about both of these products is that there is a return of premium option available. If you don't need the insurance, but pay into the system long enough, you can get your money back. Try that with your local home insurance policy.

In many ways, long-term care (LTC) and critical illness (CI) policies are the easiest to understand, since they offer what might be called "pure insurance," i.e., insurance and nothing more. As a result of this purity, compensation is more predictable and easier to calculate and disclose before the sale is transacted.

Long-term care does two things; it protects the client's quality of life and it protects a client's assets. It pays out when it is determined the client is unable to care for himself. The test lies in how well the insured can perform basic daily activities like eating, dressing and toileting. Statistics Canada predicts that by 2011, one-fifth of the Canadian population will be age sixty or older, and that 1.5 million of those people will suffer from some kind of disability during their retirement years. Combine that with the fact that a recent Ipsos-Reid poll found that 47% of Canadians are concerned about becoming a burden as they get older, while simultaneously finding that 49% have never heard of long-term care insurance, and you can clearly see both the need and the opportunity.

Right now, elderly people who do not use long-term care insurance and are unable to live independently face two choices: they can either accept a very basic level of care offered through government programs or they can deplete their own savings in order to pay for additional support necessary to maintain a suitable level of human integrity. Where appropriate, LTC can bridge the gap. As a rule, LTC comes in three formats: per diem plans, reimbursement plans and income plans. The exact services covered can vary widely, so be sure to ask about varying levels of institutional and home care, adult daycare, and respite and palliative care.

Much like LTC, critical illness insurance is a particularly vital product that is often not presented to clients. Astonishingly, 43% of all mortgage foreclosures in Canada are due to critical illnesses, while only 3% of foreclosures are due to death. Furthermore, there are only four critical illnesses that make up about 95% of all claims: cancer, heart attack, stroke and coronary artery disease. Therefore, before some FSP tells you about how the policy recommended has twenty-four different illnesses covered simply turn to that FSP and say, "That's nice. Please tell me about the *definitions* the company you recommend uses in making payments to victims of the big four." That's not a question most people would think to ask, but it is far more relevant than rhyming off a laundry list of esoteric illnesses.

Standardization is a big issue in the insurance industry too. Almost everyone in the field agrees that we need identical and consistent wording around the definitions of ailments that can be easily understood in layperson's terms. If the terminology is easier to understand, it will be easier to explain and easier to help people get the coverage they need. Until now, every provider has had its own definition of the threshold needed to constitute a critical illness. Imagine having a mild heart attack (or "infarction" as some companies call it), and having the claim denied because it was "too mild." Imagine the law suits from people who thought they were covered.

Consumers need to understand that there is no free lunch. If one CI provider is conspicuously cheaper than another, it is likely not because that company is ultra competitive or because the company actuaries have mispriced the product. The most likely explanation is that the company's definition of what constitutes a critical illness is narrowly defined and therefore less likely to trigger a payment. In insurance, as in life, you get what you pay for. Professional conduct requires consistent, plain and professional disclosure of the matter at hand.

The other contentious wrinkle in critical illness coverage is that there remains some uncertainty about whether or not the "death benefit" (paid out to a living person upon diagnosis of a critical illness) should be tax-free. You'd think the tax people would be clear on this one way or another. In spite of this, critical illness coverage is rapidly becoming a major tool in the professional FSP's tool kit. In 2002 alone, critical illness premiums were up 48%, benefit amounts were up 59% and policies sold were up 40% from 2001.

Even a passing consideration of disability, critical illness and long-term care coverage would go a long way toward meeting the test of providing life management to people who need it. Life happens. People often make financial decisions without fully contemplating the consequences of things not going exactly as planned. Truly professional FSPs will insist that all bases are covered. On the whole, a good principle to apply when considering insurance is that there needs to be a genuine insurance need, otherwise it is almost certainly not right. The corollary of this principle is that insurance does have a valid place in many portfolios and might even offer the best possible solution to a person's financial problems. The appropriateness and type of insurance depends primarily on the situation.

Segregated Funds

The insurance industry features a mutual fund counterpart called segregated funds. They are similar to mutual funds because they offer investment options to clients, but different because they feature an insurance component so that 100% of the investment is guaranteed if held for ten years. At least that's how it used to be. At present, most insurance companies generally only protect 75% of the amount invested if held for more than ten years, although some still offer guarantees over ten years. Segregated funds also offer a 100% principal guarantee if the unitholder passes away in the first ten years with the ability to lock in and reset a (presumably higher) value with a death benefit if the unitholder passes away within ten years. Practically speaking, people don't really need both the 100% principal protection and the reset feature. One or the other should suffice. Segregated funds also offer creditor protection in case of professional liability or insolvency, and generally cost about 50 bps more than similarly mandated conventional mutual funds Consumers need to consider whether the benefits outweigh the costs.

Unlike conventional investment products, however, licenced representatives are allowed to sell segregated funds without ever completing a "know your client" form to ensure suitability. In other words, there is no requirement to demonstrate that the funds being recommend correspond to the lifestyle or general objectives and needs of the person making the purchase. This represents a massive gap in the overseeing and regulation of the financial services industry. There are simply no quality control assurances for how segregated funds are sold in the marketplace. Even more disconcerting is that there are no requirements for branch managers to oversee segregated fund recommendations and no requirements for audits to ensure suitability. There is also no such thing as an unbundled, F Class segregated fund. Anyone who wants the product will have no choice but to purchase it in a bundled, embedded compensation format.

Many life-licenced agents have little training in investment planning. Of course, the opposite is equally true; most investment specialists have little training in insurance. A little knowledge could be a potentially dangerous thing. Many life-licenced FSPs began holding themselves up as holistic financial planners once segregated funds hit the marketplace, while having very little training on investment products. Having a life licence allows people to sell segregated funds, even though they are de facto mutual funds and require a rather different knowledge base.

Some FSPs with an insurance background have been known to recommend highly concentrated investment mixes in pursuit of maximum returns. This would almost certainly not be permitted in the more closely regulated investment industry. If putting 100% of your investment portfolio into the Nasdaq index in 1999 makes little sense, how does doing so within the context of an insurance policy make it any better? As with investment planning, there is no one to make sure that client illustrations are reasonable, so recommendations like this can be and have been made, with virtual impunity. Brokerage firms and mutual fund dealers have branch managers to review trading, but insurance Managing General Agencies (MGAs), the counterpart to an investment firm, have no analogous person in the hierarchy.

A similar concern might be raised about leverage (borrowing to invest). If you leverage using segregated funds, there is some certainty regarding protection of principal if held for ten years or longer. Obviously, the principal protection isn't reason enough to consider leverage, but it does remove one level of risk.

On top of this, there is no mandate to complete segregated fund trades in anything other than a paper-based transaction system. This lack of mandatory electronic order execution means that trades can be placed many days after the original order is placed with potentially damaging consequences if investment options are moving up smartly. Unlike standard mutual funds, there are added problems when redeeming the annual 10% free units from segregated funds. This is one more reason why the insurance side of the financial advice industry will find it difficult to move to an unbundled, fee based business model in a practical manner.

How Life Insurance Works

Anyone who thinks ordinary investment options are difficult for the average consumer to understand ought to look at life insurance. If you want to see convoluted products, applications and marketing, then these products are for you, especially the complex and divergent bonus structures put in place by various companies as they compete for business on the life side. By trying to "add value and flexibility," they often add cost and complexity. Perhaps most shockingly, many FSPs are at a loss to proficiently explain the terms and conditions associated with many bonus structures. If the person recommending a product doesn't truly understand how it works, what is the likelihood the person buying it will ever understand?

Almost any meaningful comparison between competing Universal Life (UL) illustrations involves calling in experts to "reverse engineer" the options. Insurance companies actually like this, since they can honestly say "there's nothing else on the market like this product." Differentiation using complexity is good for insurance companies, since there's no meaningful way for consumers to make apples-to-apples comparisons. People are left to make decisions based on whether or not they trust their FSP, not on the relative merits of competing products. Similarly, there are often major problems associated with trying to rerun in-force policies (i.e., illustrate them again). The software that allows this is constantly being updated, making it difficult for conscientious FSPs to take meaningful information to their clients.

Right now, insurance is available only as a commission-based product. There are rare instances in which companies strip out all commissions and simply pay FSPs a fee, but the case size needs to be truly massive. When this occurs, it is difficult for competing FSPs to offer something comparable on a pure cost of insurance basis. Many feel a commission-based compensation format is appropriate, since the purchase of insurance is more like the purchase of real estate than other financial products. When the planning implementation is largely predicated on a single up front purchase, commission is widely seen as the most appropriate form of payment for the person assisting with the decision-making. Even this concept can be a delicate one to manoeuvre, since renewable term life policies offer pure insurance, while whole life and UL policies have embedded investment options that should be reviewed just like any other investment portfolio. Although real estate may be the best analogy, it doesn't capture the nature of the problem, either. Today, a person can sell his own home without using the services a real estate broker. Aside from whether or not this is a prudent course of action, it should be obvious that there is no analogous alternative for insurance—yet.

Another matter to be considered is that insurance often involves the sale of a "concept" or strategy. In some instances, the FSP making the recommendation might have only a cursory background in the applied nuances surrounding the concept in question. Certain concepts, like Retirement Compensation Arrangements, are highly complex. Other concepts, like insured annuities, might involve inherent conflicts such as having the same company offering both the annuity and the life insurance, effectively doubling compensation for the FSP. The concept in question might be entirely appropriate for the client's circumstances, but care should still be taken that at a minimum, perceived conflicts be acknowledged and explained.

As in real estate, where three or four agents might be representing different clients and only one can ever get paid, insurance is based on contingent outcomes. Real estate agents are paid shortly after the closing of a deal, even though the purchaser may well be making payments on the property for the next twenty years. With insurance, there's no guarantee that the purchase will be allowed to proceed since there are always underwriting issues that might prevent this from happening. The fact that approval is not automatic means a lot of spade work might go for naught.

Here's how it works: after successful underwriting, the purchaser acquires a policy, signs a contract and ultimately begins making installment payments until the policy is totally acquired. This is a lot like a mortgage. The person making the sale is paid in a lump sum shortly after the contract is signed and the first payment is received. Many people in the industry feel that offering an annualized compensation system for ongoing support and advice is inappropriate. Some would argue that there's still the matter of managing the investment side of the account, but since the primary role for insurance is risk management, commission advocates believe the primary compensation is quite appropriately placed on the front-end of the deal.

Unlike most mutual funds, different insurance companies pay different commissions (remember, it all comes out of the client's pocket in the end) and the quantum of commission is seldom disclosed to the purchaser, even after the fact. Still, insurance companies are fairly homogeneous in pricing their product offerings. Many companies are now revisiting compensation structures to level out and standardize FSP compensation, regardless of the concept solution presented. Otherwise, FSP motive can always be called into question, just as it is with investment products that sometimes pay more than others. The product may in fact be the best for the client's needs, but that client will still have a voice in the back of his head wondering if perhaps the recommended solution didn't have more to do with the FSP's compensation than his own circumstances.

When it comes to whole life and universal life policies, the surrender charges are directly analogous to DSC charges—they are punitive. The analogy extends to FSP compensation too. Even if a client switches FSPs shortly after buying a policy, the FSP who sold the policy will continue to receive compensation. As with mutual fund loads, the "eat what you kill" mentality is alive and well in insurance. *(sometime agent is debited on early cancel)*

Even more than with DSC mutual funds, there is little incentive for most FSPs to offer ongoing advice on insurance policies once they are in force. Consumers need to be mindful of this. Responsible FSPs will point out that UL policies still need to have their investment components managed and that term policies might need replacing. Replacement often makes more sense than most insurance companies let on. Many people who have purchased life insurance might also have an unmet need for living benefits and critical illness insurance.

Once the initial sale is made on a UL policy, there's not a lot for the FSP to do. There is a prevailing sentiment that post-sale service is not particularly important in the insurance business. In light of this, there's a related concern of switching FSPs if service or advice turns out to be poor. No matter how much a client wants to switch FSPs, the FSP who sold the original contract and the MGA he works for both need to sign off on their agreement to pass the client's account to a new FSP. Switching is a client right and even if the original FSP refuses to return phone calls or provide basic service, the client

John J. De Goey

will be stuck with that FSP forever unless he consents to the switch. How's that for consumer choice and protection?

The insurance side of the financial advice business generally takes a dim view of "replacement" policies, but offers only nominal compensation to new FSPs who take over for the one who sold the policy in the first place. In terms of equity, this is a tough nut to crack, since an argument can be made for paying the FSP more on the front-end, without harming a new FSP if she takes over later.

The Ultimate Bundled Product

People in marketing departments realized that insurance wasn't the easiest product to sell long ago. This is a result of the complexity of the products, but also because people are resistant to dealing with their own mortality and have difficulty dealing with intangible products, especially if they won't be around to enjoy the payoff.

The intellectual gap has been bridged somewhat with the release of life policies that combine life insurance with investment benefits. Known as Whole Life, these are a sort of black box investment where all the money seems to go into one pot to cover both investments and insurance. This is the original financial services version of bundling. The problem with these products is that they are highly inflexible. Consumers are paying for insurance and investments simultaneously. At any point, they can access the investment portion and forego the insurance (for instance, if they live) or keep the insurance in place and forego the investments (for instance, if they die). Since people are paying for both and haven't figured out how to be dead and alive simultaneously, the products have fallen into disrepute. This is a little unfair, since policyholders can always access the paid amount through the cash surrender value once the whole life policy is in force, but the general limitations remain a very real concern.

Still, whole life policies can be useful for affluent people who are certain they will not need to access the money they are putting into the policy over the course of their lifetime. Obviously, some people bought whole life in the past when it might not have been the most appropriate solution for their circumstances. In these cases, sensible FSPs looking at the situation often advise policyholders to keep these policies, but stop paying into them once there is sufficient cash reserve to meet future obligations. Whole life isn't a bad idea unless people continue to pump money into the policy.

This lack of flexibility has some roundabout benefits. The major benefit is that insurance is now self-funding and that no money will be required later, when insurance may be prohibitively expensive, if you can get it at all. The second reason is that there might be a modest amount of growth in the face amount, allowing for de facto protection against inflation. The third reason is that people can borrow against the cash surrender value of whole life policies, allowing them to leverage out a tax-free income.

Of these three reasons for continuing to use whole life policies, only the first is particularly compelling. Inflation is fairly benign these days and the "Insured Retirement Plan" or IRP of borrowing against the cash surrender value makes less sense now that there are lower marginal tax rates than before. Besides, there are other retail investment alternatives that are far cheaper, yet comparable in tax efficiency, namely ETFs.

Somewhat Unbundled Insurance

Not wanting to be depicted as dinosaurs, actuaries and marketing people got together to revamp their "permanent" (since it could not be outlived) insurance products to make them more responsive to consumer wishes. The investment side fund that would ultimately be called upon to fund premium payments, was separated from the insurance portion so that access to the money could be permitted while keeping the insurance in place. Unbundling! The new generation of insurance products, released in the 1980s, was called Universal Life insurance. It was far more flexible, since it allowed policyholders to manipulate their funding patterns to better meet their needs and to have more say in investment options within the policy. In this respect, insurance representatives are light years ahead of their investment representative cousins. Of course, just because the product's bells and whistles are unbundled doesn't mean the products are transparent in their compensation structure. The commissions for a "buy term and invest the difference" and a UL policy should be identical, since one is effectively a bundled version of the other. Unfortunately, they are not.

Increased flexibility can also mean reduced discipline. The phrase "you can pay me now or pay me later," has truly frightening consequences when the choice to pay later means risking default.

Insurance contracts are like mortgages; it's generally best to pay as much as possible up front. Paying more early on mitigates the risk of vanishing premiums that don't actually vanish. A Universal Life insurance contract allows for premiums to be paid and growth to be credited to the policy in the form of the account value. That value can dwindle as monthly deductions and withdrawals are made. There are a number of options to consider:
- death benefits can be level or increasing
- cost of insurance can be yearly renewable term (YRT) or level
- investment options are available both as active and passive strategies
- premiums are flexible regarding amounts and timing
- the availability of withdrawals
- the availability of leverage
- riders to enhance coverage
- the ability to change any of the above once the policy is in force

The insurance industry would have us all believe that "flexibility" is the same as unbundling. Although the compensation aspect of insurance products is not unbundled, the industry would argue that the considerable flexibility of a modern-day UL contract is effectively unbundled, since it involves exact charges for fees and mortality and exact charges for premiums and growth, with a wide array of combinations and choices between them. This complexity can lead to a number of problems that are fairly unique to the insurance side of offering financial advice. These need to be considered fully and addressed in a way that dovetails with the red flags that have already been raised on the investment side.

Whole Life and Universal Life policies give the insured person the ability to deliberately overpay premiums in order to establish a tax-sheltered investment account that will grow and ultimately pay the premiums at a later date, thereby offering "permanent insurance" once the policy is fully funded. It is this unique feature that has caused many wealth management experts to sometimes refer to permanent insurance as the "last great tax shelter" or "the best kept secret in personal finance" due to the preferential tax treatment of death benefits.

Compensation Disclosure

Just as FSPs tend to recommend equity mutual funds over fixed income funds when equity commissions are higher, there's a perception that the insurance advice being offered may not always be the most balanced and in the best interests of the consumer. Not surprisingly, commissions tend to be much higher for more complex products like Universal Life and Whole Life than for Renewable Term. Think of term insurance as insurance that is rented and other forms as insurance that is permanently owned. Which type do you think FSPs are more likely to recommend to their clients?

The inference of compromised independence is unfortunate because there are a number of circumstances in which a clear and compelling case can be made for a permanent insurance solution over a renewable term solution. For example, everyone acknowledges that term is cheaper. But think about it from a logical perspective. Renewable term insurance is designed to expire before the client and relatively few families ever collect on these policies. In contrast, permanent insurance policies, if used properly, are *guaranteed* to pay out potentially huge sums to the insured's next of kin. When approached from this perspective, isn't it entirely sensible that permanent insurance should cost more?

Technically, FSPs do not have to accept a commission, but cannot reduce the premium to the client by the amount of the commission being paid. If they could only reduce the client's premium as an offset against not receiving a commission, there might be a way to charge ongoing fees for insurance in a way that is similar to ongoing fees for investments.

To further complicate matters of compensation and disclosure, insurance payment to FSPs depends not only on the type of coverage, but also the quantum of coverage and number of lives being covered. As with the above premiums, there are overrides that might affect FSP compensation considerably, but are seldom discussed or disclosed.

For instance, the FSP might recommend a term to one hundred (permanent insurance) option that seems to suit the client's needs very well. What might not be disclosed is that although the first-year commission might be 40% of the premium, there might also be an override from 100% to 200%. Overrides are like a hidden quota system. Companies pay them for increased business. As a result, an FSP might be given an incentive to put all business through one insurance provider in order to qualify for the largest override possible. That's fine if that company has competitive products in all fields of insurance, but what if there's another company that can provide superior coverage? In that instance, the FSP might recommend the company with the bigger override (what's best for him) rather than the company with the best coverage (what's best for the client). How professional is that? As with embedded compensation on investment products, independence can be called into question.

The surest way to accurately disclose compensation for insurance at present is after the fact, since there are a number of variables that affect compensation along the way. That being said, there is certainly an opportunity to offer a best guess of what the compensation will be with illustrated assumptions.

Consumers can be shown what the anticipated FSP compensation is for alternative proposed solutions and can ask for an explanation from the FSP if the most strongly recommended solution is also the most lucrative for the FSP. If the FSP can make a compelling case for why that solution is being recommended, then the client should give it serious consideration, in spite of the fact that the FSP stands to earn more. There are many examples in life when the best products cost the most. BMWs cost more than Yugos for a reason: they're better products.

In spite of the obvious benefits of compensation transparency, there is a very real concern in the industry that consumers might recoil in horror when they learn how much FSPs stand to make if placing a large policy. It would be a shame if people resisted a solution simply because they fear it is somehow wrong that someone could make so much money in meeting that need. If an FSP can demonstrate that the market will bear a high level of compensation for meeting a client need, you'd think the client would find that reassuring (it must be hard and meaningful work if it pays *that* much). The financial services industry needs to comes to terms with the effects that "sticker shock" might have on consumers' buying patterns and product choices.

As with investment products, disclosure and full client education are vital in making an informed decision on placement or rejection of insurance. The average consumer, however, has no clue about how to read and understand an insurance quote. In spite of this, consumers are asked to initial and sign these applications and illustrations, verifying both the formal explanation and personal comprehension of the contents. There is usually nothing about the compensation of FSPs in these illustrations, yet the actual dollar amount could easily be included in the illustration.

The notion of appropriate but unavoidable commissions can be partially mitigated through improved disclosure at the point of sale, but also through the idea of a "fee offset." Let's say a client's annual fee for financial services rendered by an FSP is $5,000. Furthermore, let's assume this FSP earns a $4,000 commission when selling a life insurance policy to that same client. Now the FSP has some options. She could say that the fee is for ongoing advice and since the $4,000 commission is unavoidable (which is absolutely true), the full $5,000 annual fee is still due. Alternatively, the FSP could say $5,000 is all she expects to earn in any given year from that account and if there is a $4,000 commission involved with the placement of an appropriate insurance policy, then the fee will be only $1,000 that year. Finally, some middle-ground alternative might be reached. For instance, the FSP can charge a lower minimum annual fee of $2,500 if commission-based products are purchased that year.

This is another example of the brokerage and insurance industries not being up to speed with the practical modern application of comprehensive wealth management. Mutual fund companies require FSP firms to have letters in place with all clients, verifying that fees are being charged to all clients using unbundled products. As a result, FSPs who waive their fees entirely in an attempt to avoid "double-dipping," could be in trouble. In attempting not to double-dip (i.e., earn commissions and fees simultaneously), they would technically be in breach of their obligations and in serious trouble with those companies that manufacture unbundled managed money products.

Until the mid-1990s, FSPs could be licenced to sell either insurance or securities, but not both. Earnest people trying to solve financial problems on behalf of their clients by using the widest possible array of tools were constrained by regulators who insisted they could only go to work with half a tool kit.

The brokerage and insurance industries grew up as "silos," each disdainful of the other prior to the days of comprehensive wealth management. Until recently, FSPs had to choose what kind of products they would offer and often had to force a "product solution" on to their clients based on what they were legally permitted to recommend. Insurance people sold insurance products even if investments made more sense. Investment people sold investment products even if insurance made more sense. Mutually exclusive licencing arrangements made for numerous inelegant planning solutions and needlessly forced consumers to work with multiple FSPs.

Clients were largely oblivious to the silliness of separate licencing arrangements and the planning solutions they spawned. They simply assumed that the person they were talking to would recommend whatever was appropriate, as opposed to what was expedient and what they were permitted to recommend. Ethical FSPs referred clients to other professionals if they were not equipped to deal with the situation properly. Many, however, did what they had to do to feed their families, and their clients were none the wiser. Regulators still expect FSPs to have separate files for insurance and investments for the same client, even though their member firms promote one-stop shopping for financial services.

Illustrations

Looking at how insurance policies might be employed reveals some interesting things, but conceals a number of vital things too. Cynics call this selective information and questionable use of assumptions "Illustration Games."

The trouble with illustrations and assumptions is that fair-minded people can differ. Although there is no single, unequivocal "right answer," there should at least be a well-thought-out analysis that shows the client the alternatives in a way the client can understand. Insurance policies might then be employed as a solution to a client's situation, simply by changing variables that many clients might not consider.

For instance, if an FSP shows an illustration that features a level cost of life insurance, instead of a yearly renewable term, less money will be kept in the investment side fund for supplemental income in early retirement. As a result, the yearly renewable term (YRT) might be seen as the superior alternative from the client's perspective. Although YRT would be better for the client for the first fifteen years or so, the FSP's pay would be cut by about two-thirds if that option was employed. How many clients do you suppose ask to see a YRT illustration for comparison? How many FSPs take the initiative to illustrate the YRT option to the client?

Perhaps that's just as well. Critics of YRT suggest that it is a dreadful policy that "illustrates well" because it seems "cheap" at the outset. They also say that YRT is a ticking time bomb that may not be the most appropriate insurance option under any circumstances, since term is better if you die early and level cost permanent insurance (either UL or whole life) is better if you die late. With YRT, costs rise in perpetuity, making insurance prohibitively expensive and highly prone to lapse later in life when it is most needed. Level cost permanent insurance allows the consumer to overpay in the early years of the policy being in force in order to save a gigantic amount later on. As a result, YRT almost never makes sense unless the client is very young, is not concerned about the death benefit, can significantly overfund the policy in the early years and uses a conservative illustration to benchmark expectations.

Therefore, even illustrations can be deceptive and the problems discussed earlier about probabilistic forecasting and reasonable assumptions are equally applicable to insurance illustrations. Probably more so, since no permanent insurance policy can be placed without an illustration signed by the client. Illustrations are also why costs matter. The additional fees within an insurance contract are applied to things like investment expenses, mortality costs, taxes, capital costs and administrative costs. The 2% provincial new premium tax also applies to permanent insurance policies with an investment component. It's like a 2% front-end load on investments, meaning that only

98¢ of every dollar invested in an investment side account actually goes into that account.

As with investment accounts, it is of paramount importance that the assumptions used be reasonable. There are many people in the industry today who believe it inappropriate to illustrate returns higher than 6%. We'll be getting into the actual cost of investment options within a life insurance context in a few moments, but suffice to say that it is not unreasonable to expect returns of 2% less than what one might ordinarily expect a similar investment in a non-insurance environment to produce. If we assume a mid-range 4% cost, this means the investment would have to come in with a 10% nominal return in order for the illustration to be remotely accurate at 6%.

The MERs on insurance investments are also considerably higher in insurance vehicles. An asset allocation in a conventional investment account generally costs about 2% less than in an insurance contract using identical investments. The MER on index funds in Canada is usually a little below 1%. The MER on index pools in UL policies is usually about 2.85%. There are three reasons for these higher MERs:

1. insurance companies have been known to pay a 1% bonus to clients who stay invested for sufficiently long periods
2. insurance companies have to pay investment income tax on the money in the UL policy (usually 50 bps to 70 bps), which is passed on to the policy holder
3. capital taxes are also due

That's an extra 2% in insurance product MERs. Some of the more enlightened companies are finally getting on with the unbundling required. They're abolishing the bonus structure and reducing their MERs by 1% as an offset. These companies now charge as little as 1.60% for index pools in a UL environment. Given the ultimate tax treatment of these investments, this might turn out to be cheap in the long run.

Looking at the drag of an extra 2% MER, a portfolio that returns 9% in an investment account will show an insurance illustration for that identical portfolio of about 7%. How many actively managed investments can return 9% after taking off the 2.5% standard fund MER? If the expected return is indeed 9%, but total costs are 4.5%, the total return after costs will still only be 4.5%. Illustrations need to reflect the impact of costs. Forward-looking FSPs working in insurance have been ahead of FSPs coming from an investment environment in acknowledging cost as a factor in actual results.

Consumers will be better served if they can see a range of outcomes in their insurance illustrations, giving them a better feel for what they're getting into. Illustrations are nice, but remember that the consumer is buying a *contract*, not an illustration. There are many who believe that the key to good disclosure is to find, to the greatest extent possible, what the required gross rate of return is, in order to fund a specified illustration rate. For instance, some policies pay guaranteed bonuses, while others only pay a bonus if the client achieves a positive rate of return or a return above a certain prescribed amount. Again, costs matter. So does disclosure.

Illustrated disclosure began a generation ago, when the world was mired in a historically high interest rate environment. The term "vanishing premiums" became well known in many households. Whole Life policies had been sold using the concept of a limited payment period, with the notion that by paying more early on, there would be enough money in the contract to carry it until the policyholder's death. When rates dropped, the money being generated within the policy dropped with it, causing the "vanishing premiums" to reappear in order to prevent the policy from lapsing. *Bin dare–Bun dat!*

Today, no one would be so foolish as to offer an illustration where interest rates remain sky-high indefinitely. Still, the possibility of having to pay massive premiums in one's autumn years (when insurance often becomes prohibitively expensive) just to keep a policy in force, is a frightening thought. Offering misleading illustrations is hardly behaviour that is becoming of a true professional. Just as with Monte Carlo simulations on the investment side, many believe it should be mandatory to offer a variety of illustrations to demonstrate that due consideration is being given to a variety of possible outcomes when using insurance. Illustrations should show a range of premiums, a range of payment periods and different growth scenarios.

Keeping with the notion that financial planning is an ongoing, iterative process, illustrations should be rerun every few years to account for changes in circumstances and for comparison against the original plan. In essence, this is what the Canada Pension Plan Investment Board did when it increased premium payments over the past number of years; it allowed for changing circumstances and took those new circumstances into account when revising public policy. Citizens didn't like it at the time, but it represented sound thinking and purposeful planning.

Truly comprehensive FSPs will also want to offer IPSs for their permanent life products. The principles are identical to those discussed earlier in considering investment account IPSs. In fact, a client might want to have a single IPS that governs *both the life insurance contract and the investment accounts simultaneously*. After all, the two should be combined when considering the holistic nature of comprehensive, professional wealth management advice. Alternatively, if the consumer chooses to view the two accounts as separate silos, this can be accommodated with two separate IPSs reflecting different objectives (e.g., investment IPS for retirement income, insurance IPS for charitable giving). Each works in concert with the other on related matters like tax planning.

Universal Life policies and Whole Life policies are unique in the financial planning world because unlike RRSPs that limit annual contributions to 18% of earned income up to the prescribed maximum, people are allowed to shelter potentially large amounts of money from the taxman. This option is especially attractive for people who have "redundant assets," i.e., more money to their name than will be required to maintain their quality of life until they pass away.

What's the best way to invest money for the next generation while keeping it in the hands of the current generation? Life insurance often provides a solution, because it offers a tax-free cash amount immediately upon the demise of the life insured. If the life-insured passes away prematurely, the imputed internal rate of return for the policy beneficiary can be massive.

Term to one hundred is also technically considered permanent insurance and is often an outstanding investment in its own right. For instance, a seventy-year-old might buy a T-100 policy, knowing his actuarial life expectancy is fifteen years. The odds are about fifty-fifty that this person will live to see his eighty-fifth birthday. Although the effective rate of return upon death on the eighty-fifth birthday might be a mid-range single-digit return, the payout will be made in after-tax dollars, making the return equivalent to something in the double-digit range when compared to other alternatives that are necessarily taxed at a higher rate. This is also the sort of disclosure that real professionals should make when discussing alternatives with clients.

As a general rule, people are allowed to purchase either market indexes or actively managed investments within a permanent insurance policy. There are variations on the theme, since some index options cost substantially less than active investments. In these instances, the indexes often don't include reinvested dividends. As with so many things in life, it helps to check the fine print.

In general, an investment purchased within a permanent insurance contract costs 2% more per year simply to cover additional insurance costs. If the TSX 60 index could be purchased for 50 bps as an investment, it would likely cost 2.5% if purchased within a permanent life contract. If it costs 2.5% to buy the Ivy Canadian fund as an investment, it might cost nearly 5% within a UL contract. Remember that some companies are backing out the bonuses and reducing MERs accordingly.

Active vs. Passive Insurance Investments

If a consumer invests in an index through an FSP, it might cost 0.5%, but the FSP receives no compensation unless he charges for it separately. If the consumer buys an actively managed mutual fund, it will cost perhaps 2.5%, but the FSP receives a 1% trailer fee. There's a 1% saving to the client when holding FSP compensation constant. In other words, an apples-to-apples comparison of active and passive investment options might involve a choice between an index at 0.5% and an F Class mutual fund at 1.5%, since neither pays the FSP anything.

In an insurance environment, the FSP gets paid the same whether the client buys an active or passive investment vehicle within the permanent life policy, *but the client pays 2% more*. Passive investments in an insurance contract might cost 2.85%. Active investments in an insurance contract might cost

4.85%. We've already established that insurance products cost about 2% more than identical pure investment products. We've also established that unbundled active products cost about 1% more than comparable passive ones. Doing the math, an unbundled active investment might cost 1.85%. Add on 2% for insurance costs and we get an expected MER of 3.85%. But active insurance products generally cost about 4.85%. Why the extra 1%?

In the world of DIY investing, consumers are forced to pay a 1% trailer fee to discount brokers who offer no advice. In the world of insurance, that 1% trailer fee equivalent is found in the form of higher consumer MERs. The FSP gets the same compensation irrespective of the investment vehicle chosen. The net effect is that insurance companies are padding their pockets by comparing costs of active management *with compensation* to passive management *without compensation.* They keep the missing 1% as pure profit, effectively double charging the consumer and paying the FSP only once. Many FSPs recommend passive strategies within insurance policies, even though they recommend active strategies in investment accounts. It is highly instructive that in an insurance environment, FSPs are happy to recommend the cheaper product and pass the savings on to their valued clients *provided it does not involve taking a personal pay cut.* Most UL products feature the use of indexes for the investment component. As a result, FSPs have some explaining to do. Why do they typically recommend actively managed products on the investment side, but index investments on the insurance side? If the FSP sincerely believes that one format is better than the other, shouldn't he recommend that format in both cases?

Insurance companies need to be held accountable for their product pricing. One possible solution is to pay the insurance compensation and the investment compensation separately. This, of course, is another form of unbundling. In almost all permanent life policies (these include Term to 100, Universal Life and the Whole Life versions) there is an investment component. As a result, there could be a simple commission, based on both the insurance cost and the investment component, itemized separately. The investment component might even be unbundled, in a conventional investment sense, with direct fees applying. Note that with Whole Life, no such unbundling is possible and FSP compensation is one big black box.

Other Considerations

Remember that investments inside an insurance policy grow tax deferred until withdrawn at a later date, exactly like an RRSP. Therefore, given the choice between both active and passive investments, in which a person has both a permanent life policy with a discreet investment component and an investment account (non-registered), the active portion of the portfolio should be held in the insurance policy. That way, the portfolio turnover associated with ongoing buying, selling, and rebalancing will not trigger tax liabilities that could be a potential concern in an investment account. This is not rocket science, but it is remarkable how few FSPs integrate the details of their clients' insurance policies with their various investment accounts.

Most insurance product purchasers never ask about the little "enhancements" that are often tied to bonuses. What they don't know certainly *can* hurt them. A person can buy the same policy with no bonus option. When this occurs, the potential for a bonus is foregone in exchange for the certainty of a lower cost. Most people prefer the unbundled, simplified approach, leaving the complex bonus structure out of the policy. Neither is right nor wrong, but the illustration clearly reflects the implied assumptions.

Today Universal Life and Whole Life insurance products are perhaps more complex than anything else in the financial services world, with the possible exception of hedge funds and their underlying options strategies. Given the understandable reticence most people feel when discussing life insurance, there's a natural tendency to ask, "Where do I sign?" without looking at the fine print. It may not be a pleasant thing to discuss, but it certainly is important.

In many instances, the spadework for insurance requires even more due diligence (on the part of both the buyer and the FSP) than for other investment vehicles. What is the current status regarding buying insurance directly? It simply doesn't exist at the retail level in Canada. Rather than debate whether or not that ought to be the case, let's just accept it for now. If you know you need comprehensive planning anyway (and insurance is a part of it), you may want to work with a qualified FSP. The FSP may give you a discount on the investment side if there's an insurance commission to be earned.

Insurance is the sort of financial product that is often purchased once and then forgotten about. This is often a mistake, because insurance needs can change drastically with life events such as increased income through promotions, additions to the family and gaining significant equity ownership in a company. Like other aspects of your life, it should be reviewed at least sporadically, to ensure nothing has changed too much in the interim.

Leaving registered accounts aside for the time being, consumers should recognize that UL policies are tax shelters, since the money inside grows tax-free. That's not as good as an RRSP (where you also get a deduction for making a contribution), but tax-deferred growth is certainly not a bad proposition.

Anyone who has money in both an investment account and a UL policy should use active management in the UL policy, since there are no taxable distributions on the securities traded within the account. Conversely, index products in the open account attract nominal tax, due to low portfolio turnover (provided they are bought and held). How many FSPs have a philosophical discussion with their clients about the most tax-efficient positioning of insurance products within their broader portfolio of financial assets? Similarly, anyone buying life insurance with redundant (non-registered) assets, should be using highly taxable assets like bonds and GICs to pay the premiums, because the money inside an insurance contract is tax deferred. If you can't stuff your fixed income investments into an RRSP or RRIF, an insurance policy is the next place to go.

DIY Insurance

Dealing with the need for insurance is far more complex than many people realize. Still, there are ways an unscrupulous FSP can make an extra few bucks without having the client catch on. Consumers have no real alternative but to purchase these products from someone who stands to earn a commission for recommending them.

Another element of offering professional financial advice that is inconsistent when comparing insurance with investments, is that there is no Do-It-Yourself (DIY) market in insurance. Although there are discount brokers for investments, there are no discount brokers for insurance, even though potential client savings would be enormous since virtually all of the premium a client pays in the first couple of years goes to paying the FSP. Wouldn't it be nice if a consumer could go to a website, answer a suitability questionnaire, compare relevant quotes and ultimately get insurance coverage, while saving the embedded commission? That's essentially what they can do with their investment options. This option for DIY insurance already exists in the United States.

Obviously, there's a lot of room for human error and it remains a very real possibility that the consumer in question might buy the wrong kind or the wrong amount of insurance. However, the same can be said for investment options, yet no one bats an eye when people buy investments without corresponding advice. There are even ads from some discount brokerages that try to shame people into doing it themselves, as if working with an FSP means being uninformed or weak. There has to be room in the marketplace for an intrepid company to offer unbundled insurance products to the wider population. After all, what's good for the goose ought to be good for the gander.

If the parts and labour are sold separately, either for investments or insurance, then consumers should have the capacity to opt out of advice for any and all products and save the corresponding compensation for non-existent advice in the process. Consumers will have to understand that although they might save a considerable amount in premiums, they might do an even greater amount of financial damage to their personal affairs if they take this approach. Liability is like that; once you take matters into your own hands, you have no one else to blame if things go awry. Advice costs money. Foregoing advice, therefore, should cost less. Yet it doesn't. There is simply no truly unbundled insurance option available to consumers today.

The problem with disintermediation of specialized knowledge and services is one of information pilfering. For instance, since automobiles have been offered online through "no haggle, no hassle" providers, some cost-conscious consumers have done their due diligence by speaking with their local dealership about the makes and models they are most interested in and then have gone online to buy that vehicle at a lower price. This is an abuse of the system. People who offer advice should be paid appropriately for their insight. That's one of the ongoing problems with commissions and advice. No matter how much value is added along the way, if there's no sale, there's no paycheque for the person with specialized knowledge. Good advice that fails to result in a sale (for whatever reason) is not paid for, while poor advice that results in a sale comes with a paycheque attached. The world is littered with thousands of FSPs who didn't "make it" because they effectively engaged in unpaid consulting in their early years in an attempt to jumpstart their businesses.

Insurance options can be exponentially more complex and specialized than investment options, so the number of people likely to engage in information pilfering is nominal. Still, controls should be in place. A legally binding "best efforts" clause could be inserted into the letter of engagement used by the FSP to guarantee the FSP that any insurance pursued within a reasonable time frame (say ninety days) will be purchased through that FSP. If the prospective buyer wants to wait ninety-one days before making the purchase elsewhere, he can. Ethics cannot be enforceably legislated.

One area in which the insurance side of the financial advice industry is ahead of the investment side is in FSP taxation of purchases for the FSPs' own account. We have already seen that with investments, FSPs often inadvertently charge themselves. They pay trailer fees on mutual funds, earn those same trailer fees as income and then pay tax on that income. The insurance industry has eliminated this silly circumstance. When an FSP buys a policy for himself or a member of his family, the commissions on that purchase are tax free, as they should be. Accountants don't send themselves a bill when they do their own taxes. Why should insurance agents bill themselves when they purchase insurance?

Given that current tax law already reflects a more enlightened view of FSP compensation for disclosure, one would think FSPs who recommend insurance would also favour a similar tax treatment for DIY insurance purchasers. If it is unreasonable to pay tax on services provided by yourself, it should be equally unreasonable to pay for services at all if they are never provided. In spite of all the grand talk of integrated financial advice being a reality, the insurance and investment elements of financial advice are clearly not yet running on the same track. In fact, the logic of FSP compensation and consumer choice on the investment side seems diametrically opposed to the logic used on the insurance side.

There are still a number of clear inconsistencies between the logic underpinning FSP compensation when comparing insurance and investments. Many believe this is also an illustration of why the wealth management industry needs one single regulator and one single set of standards. Without common ground rules and a consistency of purpose, there will always be a disconnect between the rhetoric communicated to consumers and the products they are being offered. The products should be seamless and in order for that to happen, the compensation rationale behind them will need to be seamless too. Becoming a holistic, integrated profession will not be an easy transition. One of the most difficult realities the industry needs to face is that no matter how useful its services purport to be, there will always be some members of society who will choose to go without.

USING AN FSP OR GOING IT ALONE

God grant me the <u>serenity</u> to accept those things I cannot change, the courage to change the things I can, and the wisdom to know the difference.

—The <u>Prayer</u> of St. Francis

People do not know what they do not know...because they do not know what they do not know!"

—Benjamin Franklin

I never try to do anything with my car, other than drive it. It's not that I'm particularly slothful or negligent, just that I have no personal aptitude or training in automotive repairs and maintenance. That being said, I certainly understand that it is important that my vehicle receives regular care and attention: tune-ups, winterization, tire rotation, oil changes and so forth.

Sensing that I was more of an academic and less of a "work with your hands" kind of person, my parents insisted I take a basic car maintenance course when I was in high school. Their intentions were entirely good, but their money was entirely wasted. I didn't have the interest to internalize anything I learned. I found the topic distasteful and didn't have the discipline to apply the things I had learned. Over time, I forgot everything I was taught. Use it or lose it.

I mention this to illustrate that in a world of "different strokes for different folks," we can't all be good at everything. Generally speaking, people are good at what they know and know what they are good at. Not everyone wants to know about financial planning and portfolio management. Others do want to know, but their interest does not translate into aptitude.

Most people know intuitively whether or not they want to work with an FSP. Still, what sorts of things should be considered when deciding? When the price of advice is made explicit where it was previously hidden, some consumers will naturally reconsider the value proposition being offered. How to decide?

An Ongoing, Iterative Process

The production of a financial plan should not be thought of as a one-time event. Instead, financial planning is an ongoing, iterative process. People graduate from school, find work, get married, start families, pay off debts, take on mortgages, get promotions, acquire stock options, have children, endure disabilities, buy second properties, suffer temporary setbacks and myriad other things. Life happens. Circumstances change and so should the plan.

Consumers need to be able to change with the times in managing the various developments in their lives, and FSPs should enable their clients to focus on all aspects of their financial lives, with the most important things being addressed first. A financial plan is usually done at the beginning of a relationship in order for an FSP to win an account but then it is not reviewed. There isn't a formal plan, just a brief written action plan focused on narrow investment matters and perhaps the provision of insurance. Brian Mallard, the inaugural President of Advocis, is fond of saying that if financial planners were charged with planning as a crime, most would be exonerated because there wouldn't be enough evidence in their files to support the charges.

Planners, advisors, brokers and other FSPs who go by similar titles, should all be engaging their clients in regular processes and procedures to make sure they are on track with their plan. This assumes there is a financial plan in place to begin with. The internationally accepted six-step process to planning is:

1. understand the client's situation
2. clarify goals and objectives
3. identify any particular barriers or unique circumstances
4. make written recommendations with clear alternatives
5. implement the chosen route
6. review the plan regularly

Clients can work together with their FSP to complete self-diagnostic checklists on a wide variety of financial matters like client awareness, investment planning, investment policy statement monitoring, debt management, tax planning, estate planning, disability and income protection and asset protection. A qualified, professional FSP has a pivotal role to play in this instance. Let's have a quick look at each of these financial matters.

Client Awareness

This is an extension of the six-step process. Clients need to understand that financial professionals cannot help without complete information. No one goes to the family doctor and says, "Doc, I'm sick and I need you to make me better," then answers, "I'm not going to tell you," when the doctor asks where it hurts. If clients want the full benefit of professional help, they need to understand that full disclosure is required. Of course, the information gathered should always be held in the strictest confidence.

General Investment Planning

This can include diversification (by geography, asset class and investment style), risk (featuring illustrations and probability forecasts), asset allocation (as set out in the investment policy statement) and tax implications.

Investment Policy Statement Monitoring

It has become a generally accepted practice to set expectations and parameters for portfolio design, monitoring and evaluation. If financial planning is going to be more than a series of one-off ad hoc decisions, then a framework for portfolio construction needs to be a given. People get blueprints before they build a house and an Investment Policy Statement (IPS) is like a portfolio blueprint. Like so many things in life, what gets measured gets done.

Pension funds and money managers the world over set parameters to ensure they have a clear mandate to benchmark their individual managers and the portfolios they design and manage. However, most people (including many who presently work with FSPs) make ad hoc investment decisions based on emotion and current events. Research into mutual funds has shown that new investment dollars flow disproportionately into hot funds and hot sectors. If one of the cardinal rules of investing is "buy low, sell high," why do so many consumers do the opposite, at least on the buy side? If the best and most serious money managers, managing pools of capital so massive that most of us cannot even fathom the amount, use written guidelines to set and effectively manage expectations for their money, why don't ordinary retail investors do the same?

It may one day become mandatory that everyone have an IPS for his or her investment portfolio. An IPS is like a contract between the client and the FSP regarding the most critical matters of portfolio design and management, including expected real (after inflation) rate of return, return variability, asset mix, tax optimization, liquidity, frequency of face-to-face meetings and thresholds for rebalancing. It is crucial for those FSPs who are serious about maximizing long-term, client-specific, risk-adjusted, after-tax returns, that an IPS be used to maintain focus. People get respect when they inspect what they expect.

Other factors can be considered too. For instance, to the extent that cost is a concern, steps can and should be taken to reduce and disclose them. Similarly, there may be a desire to have the family member in the highest marginal tax bracket pay all the fees associated with the account, in order to make the best use of tax laws.

Debt Management

Debt management can be further sub-divided into three areas: personal debt levels, interest rates charged (including mortgage rates) and tax deductibility. Not everyone has to worry about debt, but for those people who have debt, it certainly does merit specific attention.

Tax Planning

Most people do most of their tax planing in April, long after the end of the calendar year in question. Ideally, people should aim for income that is as tax effective as possible. Are clients doing all they can to deduct, defer and divide their respective incomes? What about RESPs for children? Are records being kept for matters such as capital losses, allowable expenses and similar considerations? In many instances, an FSP can add value in these areas, areas that do not show up explicitly in portfolio performance reports.

Estate Planning

Estate planning is no longer seen as the preserve of the wealthy. It is important that consumers name proper beneficiaries on investment accounts, select and name guardians for their young children, choose an executor, set up trusts for minor children and have powers of attorney in place in the event of incapacitation.

Disability and Income Protection

Would it be prudent to set aside a small sum of money regularly in order to deal with the unlikely, but potentially devastating impact of a premature death or disability? Consumers should give this serious consideration, since the correct answer is almost always yes. Practically speaking, this should be co-ordinated with benefits offered by employers, much like pension benefits. Critical illness coverage is also gaining considerable attention.

Asset Protection

For some, life insurance is part of an income replacement strategy, while others use it for estate creation, estate preservation or tax minimization. Does the family in question have the right kind of insurance and the right amount of coverage? How flexible is the policy if circumstances change? Business owners have the added issues of succession planning, risk management and creditor protection. These all need to be explored fully by those people who fall into this group.

The bottom line is that qualified FSPs should be able to find ways to add value for consumers if they are doing their job. In spite of this, there is a prevailing sentiment in the media that many FSPs should be fired because they cost too much. Choppy capital markets between 2000 and 2002 made it difficult for many FSPs to justify their "value proposition" to clients and potential clients alike. This is because the media tends to focus only on investment results, rather than integrated wealth management and financial planning.

The trouble is, real returns are more or less constant over time. Over the past decade, the Bank of Canada has set and adhered to an inflation rate target range of 1% to 3%. Taking the midpoint leaves us with a 2% inflation rate, which is almost precisely what we have experienced over that time frame. But if real returns are constant and expected inflation drops from 4% to 2%, nominal returns will drop from 10% to 8%. Add in the possibility of heightened volatility as a result of high valuations and the new transparency of fees, and it becomes difficult for many investors to justify the use of an FSP. If consumers fire their FSP and do all aspects of financial management themselves, they can save money, which adds to their bottom line. The media's thinking, however, tells only the cost half of the story.

Financial journalists tend to focus on FSP costs and all but ignore the very real benefits of qualified advice. Many FSPs only tell consumers their side of the story, which, not surprisingly, is the other half. They say clients *benefit* from advice in the form of improved discipline, reduced taxes, reduced stress, total integration and a number of other important objectives. Since consumers should want these things for their portfolio, they should gladly pay what it costs and simply ignore the media noise about cost.

The truth is somewhere in the middle. Cost is one half of the story and benefit is the other. Ultimately, this is a discussion about *value*. Everyone needs to recognize that different people define "value" in different ways. A new compact Hyundai might cost $15,000. A new mid-sized Toyota might cost $25,000. A new full-sized BMW might cost $60,000. Which is the best value? The notion of "value" depends on whom you ask. All three models are profitable for their manufacturers, while fulfilling different niches in the marketplace. People who buy the Hyundai focus primarily on cost. People who buy the BMW focus primarily on benefits. A large number of people fall somewhere in between. None of them is right or wrong, they're merely expressing a preference for their definition of value. What's your measuring stick?

If you think your FSP is adding value that is at least equivalent to what you are paying, keep your FSP. If not, have a clear and frank discussion about expectations. If they cannot or will not be met, find another FSP. The person you choose should meet all your terms. If you can't find anyone who can add sufficient value for your purposes, then be prepared to go it alone. If you are correct, the savings will exceed the costs associated with the benefit of having an FSP and you will be better off.

But be sure you think about all the costs, including opportunity cost and the value of your time when making your decision. How many consumers consider the superficial loss rules when doing their investment planning? Consumers can sell an actively managed mutual fund and reposition the proceeds into another investment such as an index fund or exchange traded fund with a similar mandate and it is not considered a superficial loss. Similarly, they can sell one actively managed mutual fund and buy another similarly mandated fund and accomplish the same objective. Applying this simple concept allows many consumers who have been burned by the recent downturn in capital markets, to both trigger capital losses and redesign their investment portfolio for the future. How many consumers actually do it, though?

Earlier, we looked at how fee scalability offers considerable benefits, especially for accounts over certain thresholds. Once you get over larger thresholds, it can actually be cheaper to work with a fee-based FSP than to use most actively managed A Class mutual funds at no-load. Obviously, scalability offers disproportionate benefits for larger accounts, but since we have already looked at fee scalability as one of the primary features of professional financial advice going forward, what are the others?

Consumers need to be able to make a meaningful comparison between what they're paying and what they're getting in return for their advice dollar. The cost differential between using an FSP and going it alone as a DIY consume, will not likely be as great as the media would have you believe, even if you consider only investment management and set all other planning concerns aside.

The Added Benefits: Fee Transparency, Deductibility and Directability

While it will certainly cost more to work with an FSP than to do it yourself, it will often be worth that added cost. As the cheeky saying goes, "If you think education is expensive, try ignorance." Without knowing what questions to ask, how will we ever come to the answers we seek? Professionals can help to identify those areas that require attention and ensure those areas are suitably addressed.

There are other benefits that clients need to understand about working with FSPs in a fee-based arrangement. The first is transparency. There is no direct economic benefit to working with someone who charges a direct fee to a client, as opposed to being paid by a product supplier.

However, there is usually an added level of comfort in having all the cards on the table. When the only way an FSP is paid is directly by the client, you get a sense that reasonable efforts are being made to do the best job for that client. The mind tends to focus when the chequebook is pulled out. This, of course, is how most other professionals get paid, so consumer understanding and acceptance should be high once the transition is complete.

Deductibility

The second additional benefit is deductibility. This is a misunderstood and often improperly quantified benefit. The Income Tax Act (ITA) allows for the deductibility of investment counselling fees under section 20 (1) (ii). Although the matter is contentious and ill-defined, the prevailing and conservative view is that financial planning fees (e.g., those associated with a financial independence calculation and illustration) are not deductible. As a result, many FSPs have taken to doing their financial planning work for free, provided the investment counselling fees are sufficiently large.

The problem is that professional counselling fees are only deductible if they do not apply to registered accounts. Counselling fees for RRSPs, RRIFs, LIRAs, RESPs and the like are not tax deductible. Only the fees associated with non-registered accounts (also known as cash accounts or investment accounts) are tax deductible. If a consumer has both an investment account and a registered account with an FSP, the deductibility is prorated and allowed on a proportional basis. There are many people who feel the ITA needs to be rewritten in order to clarify the issue of deducting financial planning fees and whether or not deductions should be allowed when F Class mutual funds are used.

Both opponents and proponents of direct fees have been known to misrepresent deductibility. Opponents say that since there is a de facto deduction through the reduction of gains in an MER, there is no benefit whatsoever. This is true only if talking about instruments that earn interest income. Conversely, proponents imply that the benefit of the deduction is absolute and applies in all circumstances. This, too, is erroneous. As is often the case when two sides try to persuade relatively unsophisticated consumers about the merits of their way of doing business, the first casualty is truth.

It is true that products with embedded compensation already offer a de facto deduction through the reduced income or capital gains realized through MER deductions. This reality is ignored by some less scrupulous FSPs who overstate the benefits of deductibility in the furtherance of making a sale. A $100,000 investment in a bond fund that earns 6% (5.5% after backing out an embedded 50 bp trailer fee) leads to $5,500 in taxable income at the client's top marginal rate in a cash account. If the same fund is used in an F Class format and an identical fee is charged, there is no benefit to the consumer from a tax perspective, because the deduction occurs at the same marginal tax and inclusion rates.

What about vehicles that earn capital gains? The recent lowering of the capital gains inclusion rate from 75% to 50% is a major boon to many people working with fee-based FSPs. Let's say we have a mutual fund that earns 10% before backing out the 1% trailer fee. A $100,000 investment would render a return of 9%, which would be taxed at 50% of the owner's top marginal tax rate, currently around 46% in most jurisdictions, but varying slightly between each of the provinces and territories. In the embedded format, the gain (assuming the top marginal rate) is 9% x 50% x 46%. The total tax bill is therefore 23% of the 9% gain or 2.07%. This yields an after-tax return of 6.93% to the client.

Now let's look at the situation in which the fee is charged separately. Assuming an identical 1% fee, it can be charged as an expense against all sources of regular income. As a result, it is deducted at the full 46% rate, rather than at half that rate. This results in the following sequence: (10% x 50% x 46%) – (1% x 54%)—the reciprocal of 0.46%. In this instance, the client gets a gross return of 7.7% minus 0.54% for a real return of 7.16%. The difference of 23bps is the difference between 1% deducted at the top marginal rate (i.e., against regular income) and 1% deducted against capital gains (i.e., at 50% of the top marginal rate). The larger deduction derived from claiming investment counselling fees against all sources of income leads directly to higher after-tax client returns. There is therefore a very real and substantial benefit to charging client fees directly, provided a number of factors are considered. These include:

• the fee needs to pertain to a non-registered account or deductibility is lost

• the fee needs to pertain to capital gains or dividends, which are taxed at a preferential rate, allowing the investor to capitalize on the inclusion spread

• the actual amount of the benefit depends on the client's marginal tax rate

If either of the first two circumstances exists, there is no benefit either way. If the third exists, the benefit of direct fees may be reduced if the client in question is not in the highest marginal tax bracket since the *spread* between any given rate and 50% of that rate goes down as the rate goes down. For example, at the 46% rate, the benefit is 0.46% - 0.23% = 0.23%. At the 38% marginal rate, the spread is reduced to 0.38% - 0.19% = 0.19%.

More Fun With Fees

Applying the concept of Pareto Optimality, we see that an FSP can charge 1.25% directly and the client will still be better off, provided the three conditions noted above are met. For instance, 1.25% x 0.77% (the after tax rate) = 0.9625% which is less than 1% if embedded.

Ironically, this little quirk is even more pronounced when using a wrap account, in which traditional investment management fees (such as those charged by F Class mutual funds) and investment counselling fees (those normally charged directly by FSPs) are often combined (i.e., remain bundled). In this scenario, the larger combined fee makes for a larger total deduction.

For instance, if the combined investment management and investment counselling fee is 2.5%, then the benefit for equity investment advice in a non-registered account for a person in the top marginal bracket would be 2.5% x 0.23% or 57.5¢ on a $2.50 fee! That's a de facto (after tax) cost of less than 2% for investment management *and* qualified advice. It is for this reason that wrap accounts may well be able to justify their relatively high fees for those clients who meet the above criteria.

As an aside, this feature can make the concept of leverage particularly compelling. No one has a crystal ball, but many experts believe that the period immediately following the uncertainty of the 2003 Iraq War will go down in history as one of the great opportunities to borrow to invest. That's because of two factors that have come together: a deep and prolonged bear market and a cyclical low in interest rates. It should not be too difficult to recognize the opportunity. *Now you are "predicting"*

When talking about leverage, it should be stressed that investors have a time horizon of at least ten years and that they should be reasonably secure in their work to ensure they can make ongoing payments. There is very little difference between borrowing to invest and buying a house. Two things are required. First, you need to know that there is no guarantee that your investment will be worth more than what you paid. Second, you need to ensure that ongoing payments won't be beyond your means, whether those are mortgage payments (usually principal plus interest) or payments on a leverage program (often interest only until the investments are sold). A third requirement might be the commitment not to panic if the market goes down, but that depends more on emotions than anything financial.

There are a number of reasons why people tend to do better in real estate than in the stock market. The real estate market is illiquid and it is not priced daily. These two attributes mean that real estate investors are less likely to panic than capital market investors.

If you use a leverage strategy and pay investment counselling fees separately in a non-registered equity account, the benefits can be huge. Let's say someone borrows $100,000 and adds it to a larger portfolio worth $500,000 where the investment counselling fee is 1.0%. That's an additional $1,000 a year in fees with another potential $230 a year in tax deductions. If the $100,000 is borrowed at a 5% interest rate, that's $5,000 a year in payments, but only $2,700 in annual after-tax payments, since there would be $2,300 in interest deductions at the top marginal rate. That's $6,000 in total annual fees, but only $3,470 ($6,000 minus $2,300 minus $230) in after-tax costs. Combining traditional leverage interest deductibility with investment counselling fee deductibility can create a fascinating opportunity.

Directability

The final additional benefit in working with a professional, fee-based FSP is directability. It is the flip side of deductibility. If fees associated with a registered account are comparable (through scalability), there is no benefit from a cost perspective. Transparency is nice, but does not add to the bottom line, since fees aren't deductible for registered accounts. While fees for a registered account cannot be deducted, they can be paid from an investment account or bank account; they are "directable." This is highly relevant because it can maximize tax-deferred compounding in a registered plan.

Let's say you're fifty-nine and have $600,000 in family RRSPs growing at 9% a year before fees. If you can pay a 1% fee from outside the plan, it will compound tax free until age sixty-nine at 9%, rendering a total portfolio size of $1,420,418.00. However, if the fees come from the investments while inside the plan, the de facto growth rate is reduced to 8%, rendering a portfolio worth $1,295,354.80. The amount paid by the consumer is essentially the same throughout (1% on the annual portfolio size), but there will be an additional $125,063.20 available when the RRSP is converted into a RRIF in a decade.

Of course, the benefits continue later in life. Even though the RRSP matures and is converted into a RRIF once the client is in his or her seventieth year, the benefits continue for as long as the client lives; there is merely a need to redeem a small portion of that portfolio on an annual basis. Still, if the client lives to be ninety years old, there will be an additional twenty years in which the RRIF earns a de facto return that is 1% higher than it would be using conventional billing methods.

What if the client is much younger, say twenty-nine years old, with a forty-year time horizon before retirement and perhaps a fifty-five year time horizon before passing away? Two primary assumptions will likely change. First, the client is likely to be a little more aggressive, so the difference in return might be between 10% (paid separately) and 9% (paid within the account) as opposed to 9% and 8% for the older person. Second, the account is likely to attract a fee of more than 1% in the early years, but because of scalability and superior tax-deferred compounding, might still attract a fee that averages out to 1% per year over the life of the relationship with the FSP.

Let's say this client is starting out with a modest portfolio of $50,000. Taking a forty-year time horizon and using 9% and 10% as return assumptions, we get a portfolio differential of $692,492.

For those who don't have a financial calculator (or don't know how to use one), a simple way of approximating the growth rate is to use the "Rule of 72." This states that the rate of return divided into 72 gives you the length of time in years it takes to double your money. A portfolio earning 10% doubles in about 7.2 years, while a portfolio earning only 9% doubles in about eight years. Big deal you might say; after nine or ten months, both portfolios reach roughly the same point. But when the time horizon is forty years, that 1% difference in compounding is absolutely massive.

The 9% return doubles roughly five times, so the portfolio grows to about $1.6 million ($1,570,471). The 10% return doubles just under 5.5 times, growing to about $2.3 million ($2,262,963). This twenty-nine-year old with a modest portfolio just added about $700,000 to his retirement portfolio by paying his FSP fees separately.

Let's also assume that this young financial independence seeker is also maximizing his annual RRSP contributions. Since the limit is now being raised and will ultimately be indexed to inflation (how many financial plans have you seen that reflect this assumption?), let's assume that his annual RRSP contribution is $18,000. Now how does this young fellow fare? The results are staggering and well into the millions of dollars. Directing fees to be paid from outside one's account provides a major benefit to consumers that most people simply never think of tapping into.

This even works for non-registered accounts. Not only can consumers reduce their tax bill by deducting fees, they can minimize portfolio shrinkage by paying fees from their bank account. There are also applications for income splitting. If one spouse is in the top marginal bracket while the other is a homemaker, the high income spouse can pay fees for all family accounts (including children, trusts, etc.) and deduct the fees (where deductible) at her top marginal rate. This is really a combination of deductibility and directability, but you can see that there are potentially large benefits here, too.

All this leaves more money in consumers' pockets. The best thing about fee directability is that it represents a win/win scenario for FSPs and consumers alike. In this case, the FSP is no worse off (receiving an identical level of compensation), but the consumer is better off because there is more money left in the account at the end of the relationship.

Investment planning and tax planning are often seen as separate matters. Taking a comprehensive approach can offer considerable benefits. The ever-changing landscape has made it imperative that people consider the implications of all decisions so that nothing is overlooked and maximum benefit is gleaned when choosing to work with a qualified FSP. Taken together, deductibility and directability are a powerful pair. Anyone who has registered accounts can benefit from improved tax-deferred compounding. Anyone who has non-registered accounts can claim tax deductions that would otherwise not be available. Simply put, there are substantial benefits that apply to all consumers in all circumstances when working with a fee-based FSP.

Unbundling for DIY Investors

One of the best kept secrets of the financial services industry is that discount brokers aren't really offering discount products when it comes to mutual funds. In fact, the term "discount brokerage" might be one of the great marketing ploys of our time. Simply put, if you're buying an A Class mutual fund at a discount brokerage, there's no discount.

We've already looked at the difference between A Class mutual funds and F Class mutual funds and how they're the same product, except that the embedded compensation normally found in the A Class version has been stripped out (unbundled) in the F Class version. Guess which version consumers *have to* use when buying funds at a discount brokerage? The A Class version. Remember that this is the version that pays the FSP for advice, which may or may not be offered as part of the relationship. With discounters, there's no doubt about what you get: no advice with the same embedded compensation going to a non-existent FSP. How's that for a value proposition? If one were to use other investment vehicles (for instance individual stocks, traditional no load funds, bonds, royalty trusts and ETFs), there would certainly be a substantial cost saving to the consumer.

One of the major regulatory reforms that has to take place is that discount brokerages should not be allowed to operate this way. It's simply disingenuous. Clients pay FSPs a fee for advice. If there's no advice being offered, there shouldn't be an additional fee associated with buying (or simply owning) a product. Of course, some mutual funds are true no-load funds, meaning they never had an A Class version. Buying one of these funds is the equivalent of buying an F Class fund. Anyone working with a discount broker should be extremely careful to buy A Class funds through their discounters only when they are absolutely certain that a similar fund can't be found in a true no-load format.

There have been verified stories of discount brokerages that charge 75 bps (0.75%) when consumers purchase true F Class funds. The rationale, one presumes, is that the brokerage house needs to earn a profit too. In the grand scheme of things, a one-time shot of three quarters of one per cent is not terribly onerous. Ironically, if an A Class fund were purchased instead, there would be no acquisition fee at all. A valid question people need to ask themselves before signing on with a discounter is, "How often do I expect to trade in this account?" More trading means more acquisition charges.

One way the discounters might be able to reconcile their stated position in the marketplace with what they actually do is to create yet another class of mutual funds with the help of some regulatory overseeing. These funds would only be available to clients of discount brokerages and not available to the wider public.

Because they would be manufactured exclusively for the use of DIY investors, these might be called DIY or discount units, so we'll call them D Class funds. If A Class funds feature embedded compensation, I Class funds offer a manufacturer's discount and reduced compensation and F Class funds offer totally unbundled compensation, cynics might think another means of slicing and dicing compensation isn't necessary. But what about fairly compensating the discount distributor of the product? It would be unreasonable to charge clients for advice not rendered (A Class), but unfair to the discount brokerages to allow them to sell funds without getting any money for themselves. What if there was a smaller embedded compensation going to discounters for their trouble? Perhaps 25 bps (0.25%) would be suitable payment in this circumstance.

It should be obvious that for a buy and hold investor, paying 75 bps once and then never trading the account again is cheaper. The problem is that discount brokerages are charging different acquisition costs for different mutual fund products when there's no logical reason to have different rates. The cost of buying a mutual fund as an administrative transaction is the same whether that fund is offered in an A Class, F Class or D Class format. The system should be fair to everyone. Charging consumers for non-existent advice is exorbitant and patently unfair, but allowing them to buy and sell mutual funds completely free of charge isn't fair to the discounter either. The price of the service offered should fairly reflect the quality of service rendered.

At 25 bps, the discount brokerages would at least be getting something for their trouble. They would be offering consumers real choice in the marketplace without feathering their nests as if they were offering full-service advice. It would cost some consumers more, but only modestly, and would still allow discounters to offer a real, credible value proposition to consumers who want to forego paying for advice when none is required.

Unless and until D Class funds are introduced, it is entirely possible that certain mutual fund investors will actually save money (and gain a potential tax deduction) by working a with a fee-based FSP as opposed to doing it themselves. For instance, a $1,000,000 all equity mutual fund account in A Class funds at a discount brokerage might involve paying the discounter $10,000 a year in trailer fees (in exchange for what?). If working with a fee-based FSP, the fee might be less than $9,000, but the consumer would also be getting *a potential tax deduction and qualified advice that could save money, time and aggravation.*

I don't know how many millionaire mutual fund investors are currently working with discount brokers, but those who are need to know that there's a better game in town and that fee-based advice is a plausible alternative.

The Three Ts

There are two primary consumer segments in the financial services market-place: delegators and Do-It-Yourselfers. Many people have a quick, intuitive, gut reaction about which camp they fall into and work in accordance with that gut feeling. There are a number of consumers who simply don't need an FSP. Nonetheless, the generally accepted principle is that people should, at a minimum, possess the "Three Ts" necessary to manage their own financial affairs: time, temperament and training. Here's a quick ten-question self-diagnostic exercise to help you determine which group you fall into:

Time
- Do you review your portfolio at least annually, even if you change nothing?
- Do you need to be reminded of major deadlines (taxes, RRSPs, RESPs, etc.)?
- Do you put off planning considerations because they seem too distant?
- Are you a procrastinator (not just with personal finances)?

Temperament
- Did you maintain your asset allocation from Q2, 2000 to Q3, 2002?
- Did you maintain your savings rate over that time frame?
- Did you sleep as well as usual over that time frame?

Training
- Do you have the capacity to handle the complexity of your own circum-stances?
- Are you certain about how complex your situation is and what you need?
- Have you taken courses in order to follow anything other than basic strategies?

If you honestly answered yes to all ten questions, you probably don't need an FSP. If you answered no only twice, you might already need an FSP. If you answered no three or more times, you almost certainly should be working with an FSP. There are people who can honestly answer yes to all ten questions. Most people, however, cannot.

The need for qualified professional advice becomes even more obvious when you consider account size. Since qualified advisory fees can be scalable, there are disproportionate benefits that accrue to households with larger pools of investable assets. The bigger your portfolio, the less advice costs on a per dollar invested basis. Some people are delegators as a practical matter, rather than because of natural predisposition. Furthermore, the bigger the portfolio, the bigger the absolute dollar consequences of an unfortunate error or untimely oversight. There are many people who are wealthy, but not par-ticularly sophisticated. Going it alone might save a few dollars, but won't make much sense, all things considered.

The idea of having unbundled investment products available to consumers is seen by many FSPs as a huge threat. They fear that some of their clients will leave to go to a discount brokerage if the artificial level playing field of mutual fund cost is eliminated, making it cheaper for DIY investors. Essentially, what these "professionals" are saying is that their advice is worth less than it costs. At least that's their inference with the current pricing structure. Today, if a DIY consumer can get the same product at the same price and forego the advice by going to a discount brokerage, the implication is that the FSP's advice is worth zero and might even have a negative impact on returns and/or convenience. These FSPs fear that if it becomes conspicuously and *consistently* cheaper to go to a DIY environment, there will be a mass exodus of clients to discount houses.

I sometimes ask other FSPs if they do their own taxes. Some do, some don't. For those who use a tax professional, I ask them if they don't realize they can save money by doing their taxes themselves. Of course, they do, but they also find it both convenient and comforting that they have a professional looking after their tax matters. For the record, I use a tax professional to assist me in my tax planning. Many FSPs are doubtful that other consumers might reach the same conclusion for the services that they offer. I also ask those who proudly do their own taxes about whether or not they send themselves a bill for doing so. When they incredulously respond that they do not, I ask them why it is that they bill themselves for their investment management services.

Financial planning and advice, like tax preparation, is the sort of thing some people don't mind doing themselves, while others simply loath it. People are either Do-It-Yourselfers or delegators and changing the price structure associated with the task doesn't alter that fact. Anyone who is a delegator by nature will continue to delegate even if there are cost savings that can be realized by doing the work alone. The fact that many FSPs are themselves delegators with their own tax returns demonstrates this quite vividly.

Know Thyself

This advice is still true and applies to many of life's challenges, including whether or not to work with an FSP. People need to decide. Do they want cost savings or value-added assistance in arranging their financial affairs? It comes down to whether or not you believe an FSP can add value through planning, discipline, insight, additional services or just piece of mind.

Financial wisdom will soon be sold separately. If you already have what it takes to plan your affairs and manage your portfolio, then off you go. Consumers need to be honest with themselves. They shouldn't either rush off to find an FSP or blindly stick with an FSP if they believe they can do just as well on their own. One other yardstick of need, especially for people with smaller portfolios, is found in consumers' attitudes regarding their tax returns. Those who file their own might be savvy enough to handle other aspects of their financial life too. On the other hand, those who rely on professional assistance in aspects of financial life like tax planning, probably need help in other fields too.

It would be wonderful if there was a simple, reliable way to determine whether or not any given individual would be better off working with an FSP or going it alone. There isn't. It comes down to whether or not they have the confidence in their own abilities to do the necessary work for their unique circumstances. However, there is some broad societal research on the subject.

Every year, a large national financial planning and advisory firm asks Canadians to take a simple ten-question quiz regarding financial literacy. In 2002, 4,083 Canadians were polled. Fully 61% of respondents said they considered themselves knowledgeable, yet they gave incorrect answers to at least six of the ten questions asked. Only one third of all respondents managed to get five right. It seems investor overconfidence is certainly alive and well. People seem to think they know more about money than they actually do and what they don't know can hurt them, even when the questions are relatively basic. Here's the quiz (without answers).

1. Suppose you have invested in a mutual fund containing bonds or mortgages. If interest rates go up, what would happen to the value of your fund?
a) Decrease in value
b) Increase in value
c) Stay the same

2. What is the maximum percentage of RRSP investments that can be put into investments outside Canada?
a) 10%
b) 20%
c) 30%
d) 50%
e) 100%

3. Suppose you had a choice of receiving $1,000 in bank interest, $1,000 in rental income, $1,000 in dividends from a Canadian stock or $1,000 as a bonus from your employer. Which of these would give you the most dollars after deducting the taxes owed?
a) Bank interest
b) Rental income
c) Dividends
d) Bonus
e) All the same after taxes

4. Let's say you've been investing in shares typical of those sold on the Toronto Stock Exchange for the last twenty years. To the best of your knowledge, in how many of those twenty years did the stock market go up?
a) 5
b) 8
c) 10
d) 12
e) 14

5. Imagine that you had a $200,000 five-year GIC with a chartered bank. If the bank that you held the GIC with went out of business, what is the maximum

amount of your funds that would be protected by the government through the CDIC?
a) None of it
b) $25,000
— c) $60,000 *used to be*
d) $75,000
✗ e) $100,000
6. Are investments in mutual funds guaranteed by the Canadian Government's CDIC Depositor Protection Plan?
a) Yes
b) Only if the fund manager goes out of business
c) Only if the fund was sold by a bank
— d) No
7. Which of the following investments, over the long term since 1950, provided Canadians with the best returns, before taxes which were due? To the best of your knowledge, is it:
a) Canada Savings Bonds
— b) U.S. stocks
c) Long-term corporate bonds
. d) Canadian stocks
e) Five-year GICs
8. And which of those same investments, over the long term since 1950, provided Canadians with the worst returns before any taxes that were due?
—. a) Canada Savings Bonds
b) U.S. stocks
c) Long-term corporate bonds
d) Canadian stocks
e) Five-year GICs
9. Which of the following best describes a "capital gain?" Would it be:
a) The annual increase in your net worth
— b) The profit you make when you sell stocks or bonds
c) The interest your receive on an investment
d) The increase in value of your RRSP investments
e) Financial gifts from another family member
10. Over the long term, from 1926 to the end of 2001, what has been the average annual rate of return on shares of large companies in the U.S. stock market (including both increases in the value of shares and dividends received by shareholders)?
✗ a) 6.3%
b) 8.7%
— c) 10.7%
d) 12.8%
e) 15.6%
f) 20.3%

This quiz should prove fairly sobering for most people. It is likely particularly eye-opening for people who are doing things themselves with larger accounts. In general, a portfolio of $100,000 means consumers should probably give serious consideration to using an FSP. At that point, the stakes are high enough that cost becomes a less vital consideration. Once a portfolio reaches $500,000, consumers had better be extremely sophisticated and have a lot of time to devote to personal financial affairs if they want to continue on a DIY path, because there are usually a host of related planning considerations that arise. At a half-million dollars, integrated wealth management is almost a necessity. Many people need even greater comprehensiveness in their planning once their portfolios reach that point.

In fact, at $500,000, it could be said that a truly holistic approach is absolutely vital, allowing a series of financial management professionals to work together to make sure everything is addressed and co-ordinated. This might involve getting a team of related professional advisors—insurance specialists, estate and corporate lawyers, tax specialists, offshore investment advisors—working together to ensure they are all "on the same page."

Research shows that wealthy individuals are increasingly turning to qualified professionals precisely because of the complexity and interrelatedness of financial management The value of advice becomes more obvious.

Less wealthy people have less need for advice, given the relative simplicity their affairs might require. They may end up paying a higher proportional cost for whatever advice they receive. Portfolio size is just one factor in deciding whether or not to work with an FSP.

The key for consumers is to know what matters to them and to know their own strengths, weaknesses and tendencies. Given that most consumers have already decided whether or not to work directly with an FSP, it is unlikely many will reach a different conclusion when the cost of doing so is brought into the open. Obviously, there will be a handful of consumers at the margin who switch, but generally speaking, the expectation is that those who are currently with an FSP will stay with an FSP and those who are DIY consumers will be happy to remain DIY consumers.

The reasons for this type of seemingly dysfunctional behaviour are rooted in behavioural finance, the study of how human emotions, biases, tendencies and perceptions shape investment decisions, seldom for the better. To the extent that we know these quirky tendencies can checker our thinking, we need to take action to effectively curb them. You can tell people not to panic when markets are temporarily down, but not panicking is something that is often easier said then done, especially when your life savings are at stake.

Anyone who is still uncertain about whether they should be working on their own, or with an FSP, might re-examine the chapter on behavioural finance. Think of market gyrations as the equivalent of a cheesecake buffet to a person on a diet. If you can resist its temptations on your own, then perhaps you don't need additional assistance. If, on the other hand, you think you'll need the financial equivalent of a personal trainer to keep you honest with your resolutions of disciplined good health, then hire one.

Consumers need to seriously consider the complexity of their personal financial affairs. Are they basic and predictable or complex and erratic? No matter how disciplined you are, there's no sense in doing things yourself if your situation requires a deeper level of preparedness. Think of the continuum we looked at earlier, moving from empowered Do-It-Yourselfer to collaborator to delegator to abdicator. Consumers need to determine where they fit. There is absolutely nothing wrong with being a Do-It-Yourselfer, as long as you know yourself and can be certain there will be no regrets if you work this way.

It is ironic that FSPs generally make more money when markets are going up (when they are less necessary from a behavioural perspective) and less money when markets were going down (when they are actually more necessary). When markets are going down and clients are spooked by it, FSPs often have to work harder to keep clients from making "the big mistake." On the other hand, as long as things are going well, it might be argued that FSPs are less useful, since clients are naturally inclined to stick with the original plan. This is not to suggest that people should use an FSP when markets are headed downward, but can feel free to do their own planning when things are all right. And it certainly doesn't mean that financial planning is only about investments either. All it means is that some serious introspection is required before deciding whether or not to work with an FSP.

In case you're wondering, here are the answers to the quiz:

1. a	6. d
2. d ✗	7. b
3. c	8. a
4. e	9. b
5. c	10. c

90% – Dec.'03,
80% in Jan. 07

WINNING WITH ETHICS

Conditions are never just right. People who delay action until all factors are favourable do nothing.

—William Feather

Not everything that is faced can be changed, but nothing can be changed that is not faced.
—James Baldwin

[handwritten: eg. central + East? can.]

We conclude where we began—grappling with change, which is never easy. Change is especially difficult to achieve when powerful interests resist it because it undermines their business model. We've all heard the cliché: the more things change, the more they stay the same. There are justifiable reasons for people to harbour this kind of cynicism. Inertia often seems like the safest way to go.

For about a decade, regulators, thinkers and consultants have been earnestly telling FSPs to change their business model from commissions to fees and to get the credentials necessary to have true legitimacy with consumers as bona fide professionals. Many FSPs have done precisely these things. Sadly, the majority has not. Moral suasion, no matter how logically and compellingly applied, cannot overcome human nature. For the sake of all stakeholders involved, more forceful actions are required. Changes will have to be imposed and it is only natural that they will be opposed by those who stand to lose because they are either unwilling to change or incapable of changing.

We expect many things from our professionals, including a dedication to clients' best interests, real independence, professional training and ethical integrity. In spite of generally high standards and lofty expectations, there have been instances in which these expectations have not been met in the financial services industry. But the financial services industry is by no means alone in this.

Doctors have been hit with malpractice suits. The Governor of New Hampshire recently banned tied selling because physicians were getting free trips tied to their prescriptions and calling them due diligence trips. Lawyers have been sued for a number of reasons. Accountants are currently held in wide disrepute due to a string of recent corporate malfeasance scandals. With Tyco, Enron, Adelphia, Worldcom and others, people only got up in arms after it was too late and far too many innocent people were hurt. We can't let it happen again.

We see the signs of societal wear and tear in the other professions already. Lawyers are dealing with increased divorce rates. Doctors are treating more people due to stress brought on by financial concerns. The clergy all over the world have to deal with stresses, many of which are financial in nature. Newspapers are full of stories of seniors getting bilked out of their life's savings. Those with large sums are even bigger targets, yet regulators continue to equate the possession of capital with the possession of a sophisticated investment mind.

White-collar crime is no different than any other crime. People get hurt and lives are ruined. As with any ailment, prevention is the best prescription. To date, no one has replaced the policy of buyer beware with a policy of full and necessary disclosure. That needs to change.

Being a professional means being held to a higher standard than other members of society. Virtually every MBA program and professional school has courses on ethics and many have become mandatory for graduation. Still, the temptation to "fudge the rules" in order to pad the bottom line remains as inexorable as ever. Perhaps most unfortunately, this lack of a moral compass seems to extend to all levels of society, not just to desperate people turning to desperate acts just to get by.

We all know how it works. You take a buddy out to lunch to talk about old times and then, just as the bill comes, say, "So, do you think we could do some business?" just so you can "honestly" claim a deduction for the meal. You pay a contractor less money in cash to do some work on your kitchen and he either falsifies the income on his tax return or claims it was never earned in the first place. It happens all the time. Some financial advisory firms even go so far as to put out newsletters encouraging their clients to "get it in writing" before engaging the services of a contractor or similar service provider, even though they see no reason to have their own FSPs put their own obligations and fees in writing. It's this "do as I say, not as I do" attitude that has caused the industry to fall into disrepute.

That's the thing about ethics—they cannot really be imposed. Integrity is either earned through years of reputational spadework or not earned at all. Every industry and profession has some bad apples. The intent of this book was to offer clear examples of what the more established professions practice and to uncover some of the inherent inconsistencies in the field of financial advice. That way, the most appropriate concepts can be applied to the field of financial advice in the hope that a new profession might be born.

The stakes are often higher and more personal with financial advice than with other professions, so it's only natural that some consumers will be surprised at certain elements of how the industry works. Similarly, there will be resistance on the part of many FSPs who have clung to a "value proposition" that doesn't dovetail well with a paradigm of professionalism. Corporate governance is a very real issue. People are rightfully leery of what professionals are saying and doing. They've been burned too often in the past. Some within the industry don't feel a sense of urgency. "It's not about how people are paid, it's about how people are made," they sniff—as if integrity can be discerned a mile away. The situation has become as dire as it is precisely because of how "people are made." It's human nature to look out for number one. Capitalism enshrines the attribute as an unqualified virtue.

We expect things from other members of society too. Salespeople, for instance, are expected to know all there is to know about the products they sell. Generally speaking, society has no problem with salespeople earning a commission. The difference is that people who sell shoes or cars or aluminum siding are not so brazen as to call themselves "professionals." Although we have no problem with salespeople in general, we do have very real problems with people who call themselves professionals when their conduct and lack of training belies their posture.

As a society, we have done almost nothing to meaningfully address the inconsistencies in the field of financial services and advice. We have come to tolerate FSPs who have passed a course or two, allowing them to sell certain products, to consider themselves true professionals. We've done a poor job in other ways too. We teach our children about sex at a young age in our homes and schools, yet do virtually nothing to teach them to be savvy consumers of financial products and services. Is it any wonder, in this context, that salespeople can call themselves professionals and get away with it?

So much needs to be done. There is no standardization of realistic expected rates of return. No required written client disclosure of how much one product pays *in comparison to other similar available products*. No consistent requirement for ongoing FSP education. No requirement for errors and omissions insurance. No requirement for probabilistic forecasts about the possible outcomes associated with a strategy. No requirement for FSPs to use a letter of engagement.

There are two solutions: either FSPs can call themselves salespeople or FSPs can act like the professionals they consider themselves to be.

This brings us back to the "change imposed is change opposed" conundrum. The truly professional FSPs of the nation have transformed themselves, but virtually no one has noticed. At the corporate level, profit margins have been squeezed by a debilitating bear market and increased regulatory costs, so that the focus has been placed squarely on the bottom line, sometimes at the expense of meaningful rules of conduct and best practices.

It's a little like the NHL's crackdown on obstruction. The rules have always been in place, it's just that no one ever meaningfully enforced them. Over time, this meant certain teams of lesser calibre were allowed to compete on a somewhat level playing field, by willfully ignoring the very rules that were put in place to ensure fair competition and the merit principle of having the best team win.

The only way to truly ensure that the financial services *industry* will be fully and ethically transformed into the financial services *profession* is to legislate the necessary changes. Otherwise, the least professional FSPs will always find a home somewhere and the clients of that company will be susceptible to the same questionable practices that have plagued the industry since its inception.

Other related matters might also be legislated into effect. For instance, although investment counselling fees are tax deductible, financial planning fees are not. Therefore, someone with a huge pregnant capital gain in Coke shares can seek advice on whether or not to sell the stock, trigger the tax liability and pursue other strategies. If an investment counsellor offers advice for a fee, that fee is deductible (assuming the shares are not held in a registered account).

On the other hand, if a CFP offers a twenty-page planning report that discusses the triggering of gains or losses, the calculation of each, strategies to carry these forward or backward, associated opportunities for the redeployment of proceeds, transfer to holding companies, attribution rules, superficial loss rules and the like, the fee associated with this report is not deductible. Perhaps if the CFP makes the recommendation to buy or sell the security as a stand-alone recommendation and then attaches the twenty-page report as an appendix, the fee might be at least partially deductible.

Obviously, financial advice is more comprehensive and, if done correctly, more of a value-added activity than mere investment counselling. So why is the low value-added activity deductible while the high value-added activity isn't? Shouldn't the Income Tax Act be written in such a way that it offers clear incentives to engage in suitable activities? At the very least, shouldn't it remove disincentives? Furthermore, wouldn't the eradication of embedded compensation and the resulting advent of universally accepted and often deductible fees be a step forward? Again, so much needs to be done.

The rationale behind all financial advice needs to be reconsidered. In the current environment, it is important for clients to have some choice regarding FSP compensation and absolutely vital that proper disclosure is made before transacting business. In time, there will be no choice; commissions and trailing commissions will be relegated to compensation options that are only available to salespeople. They might be totally wiped out. Either way, true financial professionals will be charging fees.

In the meantime, consumers should have the right to both understand the differences in various compensation models that exist today and to choose which one best meets their needs. All models have some merit and none are inherently or conspicuously inappropriate. Commissions have been suitable compensation vehicles for certain segments of the industry. There may be very few professional FSPs who will work with households that have less than $100,000 in investable assets. In fact, it is reasonable to expect that many will set the thresholds for their practice higher, say $250,000 or more. Ultimately, FSPs might only work on an hourly basis, just like the more established professionals. That's even farther away, but it's coming. In the meantime, let's just say that different clients have different value sets and that there's room for all three methods.

Still, there can be little doubt that the industry is coalescing around an unbundled fee-based model. Everyone agrees that this is where holistic financial services are headed. The disagreement seems to revolve around how to get there. But if everyone pretty much agrees on the state and shape of the industry at present and the approximate shape of the industry in the future, isn't this the ideal time to get all stakeholders involved in a purposeful dialogue?

Disclosure is a difficult thing to do with verifiable evidence when people don't want to acknowledge what you are trying desperately to tell them. Qualified financial advice is not free, in spite of what an army of "independent" FSPs would have you believe. FSPs are often guilty of not correcting obvious misconceptions and misunderstandings. Mutual funds are not free. No-load does not necessarily mean no advice. No-load never means free. As a whole, industry players could do more to disclose exactly how and how much they are paid. Right now, the financial services industry is resisting transparency because it is convinced it will cost in terms of sales and profit margins.

Hopefully, consumers will recognize that every reasonable effort needs to be made to capture all material aspects associated with the services of an FSP. Some day soon, every FSP will have to make all material compensation disclosures as a matter of course.

In the world of business, the Sarbanes-Oxley Act was enacted to strengthen corporate disclosure, certitude and audit trails, to reduce investor uncertainty and vulnerability. If capital markets need trust to be restored about the accuracy and diligence of underwriters, analysts and corporate executives, isn't there a need for the same degree of certitude about FSPs? After all, it is the FSPs who are on the front lines of the relationship with retail consumers, and examples of financial illiteracy are all around us.

Scientific Testing and Necessary Disclosure

FSPs want to be thought of as professionals. They refer to themselves as such constantly. Actions, however, speak louder than words. The time has come to align the rhetoric and the reality. The acronym that can explain how to bridge the credibility gap is STAND, for Scientific Testing And Necessary Disclosure. True professionals are careful to use both. At present, most FSPs do neither.

Scientific testing means recommendations are made based on the best research available on probable outcomes. Physicians do not make recommendations based on which drug supplier last visited them; recommendations are based on clinical research that demonstrates cause and effect and most likely outcomes. That doesn't mean every prescription will work wonders, only that it is the most sensible prescription available for the diagnosed ailment in question.

Similarly, people do not engage the services of an accountant if they are not told explicitly (and hopefully in writing) what that accountant will be charging in exchange for the services rendered.

Consumers of financial advice often don't want to ask about compensation, largely because they fear it will expose their own lack of comprehension of how things work. They hope they can trust their FSP and don't want to ask annoying, embarrassing or "stupid" questions. Besides, clients fear that if they get too nosey, that might just compromise their relationship with their FSP. Both phobias are largely irrational. People should always feel free to ask how much they are paying the people who work on their behalf and should be entitled to an answer that is both clear and understandable.

What FSPs Can Do

Any FSP who is serious about being a true professional needs to "get with the program" immediately. That means implementing as many of the best practices employed by other professionals as soon as possible and with all clients. It means getting credentials that demonstrate a capacity to offer holistic advice and no longer making do with merely having licences to sell products. Having a licence is not sufficient background to call oneself a "professional." It means talking to clients frankly to explain how the industry is changing and that positive, necessary reforms are just around the corner. After explaining the rationale to clients, begin making 10% free mutual fund redemptions immediately and place the proceeds into low-load, no-load or F class funds.

Almost no one has had the courage to stand up and categorically do the right thing voluntarily. Many who have tried have been labelled heretics and have been made to suffer financially and emotionally for their efforts. As other stakeholders become more comfortable with how the industry works and what needs to change, these FSPs will be disproportionately rewarded. Newly informed consumers of financial services will radiate toward those FSPs who demonstrate true professionalism in their practices.

Regulators have put "snitch lines" in place to allow FSPs to come forward when they believe their peers are engaging in unsavoury practices. Coleen Rowley, Sheron Watkins and Cynthia Cooper were *Time Magazine's* "Persons of the Year" in 2002 for their willingness to step forward about wrongdoings at the FBI, Enron and Worldcom respectively. No one should apologize for having high standards and for not tolerating peers who do not share them.

There will be a major debate about the amount of DSC penalties a client should reasonably be expected to absorb in making the transition. Whatever time frame FSPs determine is best for their practice, there should be little doubt that full disclosure will be required if the principles of openness and integrity are to be upheld.

What Consumers Can Do

More than ever, an informed consumer is a good consumer. There are already enough FSPs in the marketplace who espouse professional principles that a little due diligence shouldn't make finding one too difficult. Good places to start are www.advocis.ca and www.cfp-ca.org. This is particularly important for people who are currently dissatisfied with their existing FSP.

As everyone knows, the business of offering financial advice is predicated primarily on relationships. Relationships, in turn, are predicated on the usual hallmarks of professionalism—honesty, integrity, experience and a genuine concern for the welfare of the client. If the FSP you're working with today possesses those qualities, you would probably be well advised to stick with that person. Of course, constructively encouraging that FSP to get credentials, unbundle and disclose fees and implement a number of professional best practices wouldn't hurt.

Don't be too surprised if your FSP who has historically talked almost exclusively about investments is a lot more interested in insurance over the next little while. If insurance makes sense, have a serious look. After all, more holistic services and products are where the industry (soon we'll be able to call it a profession) is heading. Just make sure that insurance isn't being offered as a gratuitous product that will generate a commission as embedded investment commissions disappear.

Perhaps most importantly, consumers need to understand that any FSP who begins a conversion toward true professionalism will be making a huge financial sacrifice that will likely take the remainder of the decade to overcome. How many consumers would be willing to take a pay cut in their own career over the next six or seven years, just so that society can be better off as a result?

What Legislators Can Do

The financial services industry is largely broken and desperately needs a fix. Sadly, the primary stakeholders don't want to admit that, because it would be seen as a condemnation of past practice. In a world where both the mutual fund and insurance companies that manufacture products, and the planning and brokerage firms that recommend them make money from investors who do not fully understand what they are paying and what they are getting in return, meaningful systemic change from within is nearly impossible.

Legislators could bring about the necessary changes, but to date, they have lacked the necessary courage. That's because of the logic behind yet another saying: "change imposed is change opposed." What political party would willingly upset the entire financial services industry when there is no clamour from consumers for fundamental reform? Making a whole slew of well-financed enemies, without picking up a correspondingly large or powerful cache of supporters, is a fast track to political ruin. Or is it? It seems the winds of change may be blowing after all. It may now be more politically dangerous to do nothing in the face of broad societal outrage.

What if consumers of financial advice across the country banded together and demanded that something be done? What if people used petitions and letters to get politicians to take notice and made submissions at committee hearings about legislative reform? What if we all forced policy-makers to give a damn and to realize that the greatest political risk was in *not* imposing legislative reform?

Forcing change when the system is self-evidently dysfunctional, should not be a stretch for politicians. Given that embedded compensation compromises both professionalism and independence, it's a wonder politicians haven't been more ham-fisted in the past. Public policy is supposed to be about implementing meaningful reforms and any politician who wants a legacy ought to stand up and do the right thing: eliminate embedded compensation as soon as is reasonably possible.

That's the biggest conundrum about change; people know they have to go through it, but resist it and procrastinate shamelessly nonetheless. People with legislative authority are human too. Knowing something needs to be done and actually doing it are very different propositions. Think of New Year's resolutions. Any changes in law must also contemplate meaningful sanctions for non-compliance with professional standards.

Regulatory reform is clearly required. "Ottawa won't act to create a national regulator if the industry itself is not demanding it," says Jim Peterson, former secretary of state for International Financial Institutions. "We need to mobilize industry players," says Mark Daniels, president of the Canadian Life and Health Insurance Association. "Canada has to legislate to show the average Canadian we are thinking of him, that we want to make Canada a safe place to invest and that we can have more confidence in the information companies give us," says Senator Leo Kolber, chairman of the Senate banking committee. In spite of all these bold words, there has not been an appreciable groundswell of interest from the public.

There can be little doubt that a narrow but important window of opportunity is upon us. The Canadian Security Administrators' Uniform Securities Legislation Project, a provincial ministerial committee and the federal government's "Wise Persons" committee and the OSC's Fair Dealing Model will all be coming together in late 2003. From there, a consensus will be forged and sweeping reforms can finally begin.

What Companies Can Do

Since individual stocks, bonds, royalty trusts and Exchange Traded Funds are all unbundled already, fund companies need to be prepared to compete on a level playing field where products are recommended solely based on appropriateness and merit. That means offering F Class versions of all funds immediately, but also creating low-load options if none exist so that FSPs (and clients) who will need a few years to make the transition can get on with it immediately.

Better and clearer prospectus disclosure will help too. An executive summary explaining the various elements of an MER will help many consumers to more clearly understand how these products work. Mutual funds remain suitable products for most people, but more could be done to illustrate just how they work, especially as it pertains to how FSPs get paid and how much of the MER goes toward the company, the FSP, costs and taxes.

Insurance companies could offer similar levels of transparency. Specifically, the ridiculous systems of bonuses and caveats that so often finds its way into Universal Life policies should be stripped out and the fees stripped down. Even the most experienced players in the insurance industry acknowledge that the terms and conditions associated with bonus features are impenetrably difficult for most consumers to understand. Stripping out these gratuitous bells and whistles would go a long way toward simplifying and enhancing the lives of people buying insurance products.

What Regulators Can Do

To begin, regulators can lighten up. Any FSP who does a 10% free redemption in order to place the proceeds into a no-load, low-load or F Class version of a fund should not be accused of churning. If the money goes back into a DSC version, then that's a different story. When assessing the conduct of any FSP who is proactively taking tangible steps to put clients first by moving away from the tyranny of embedded compensation, that FSP should be lauded for doing so. Don't punish early adopters just because they don't fit into narrow paradigms that are largely arbitrary in the first place.

Next, regulators can get tough. This is not inconsistent with the previous paragraph if it is applied thoughtfully. Too often in the past, white-collar crime and professional wrongdoing have been punished lightly. When a person steals from another, while wearing a conservative suit and using a line like "Trust me, I'm a professional," the victim is often just as badly harmed as if the thief were wearing a ski mask and saying "Your money or your life."

Most importantly, regulators can get on the same page and ensure that we have one single, simple repository for all regulatory limitations and obligations within the industry. There should be no excuse for not coming together and doing what is conspicuously right for the consumers whom they all purport to be protecting. Egos should be put aside so that the people who need protection can get it. *(Regulators protect own turf too!)*

What Bankers Can Do

Over time, FSPs will come to be accepted as true professionals. People see this as inevitable. One of the very genuine practical hurdles that will need to be faced is the financing of a professional practice. Our chartered banks will play a vital role in the delineation of salespeople from true professionals. Most banks will employ salaried salespeople at their branches, although many will also have qualified professionals on staff. These people will have a mandate either to offer advice directly or to do a quick set of diagnostic tests and then refer the client to someone in the bank's brokerage or planning arm for more specific advice. In either case, the clear delineation between bare-bones advice and true professionalism needs to be transparent.

This is especially true because there are many planning and advisory firms that will need banks to step in to facilitate an orderly transition from one FSP to another as the professional emerges and matures. Just as banks offer mortgages to allow people with modest equity to acquire suitable housing, they will increasingly be asked to step in and offer lending services to fledgling professional FSPs who have considerable skills, but a modest income.

Critics have said that the problem with the financial services industry today is that it favours size over competence. Those who have built up a big enough book of business/ practice will be financially viable as independent business owners under virtually any circumstances. On the other hand, newly minted graduates with the best and most current training in financial advice will be practically precluded from getting started because they won't have the financial resources to compete against established FSPs, who can always engage in predatory pricing to retain market share.

Again, it is instructive to examine what other professions do to get around this problem. There are thousands of doctors, many from modest socio-economic beginnings, who have massive student loans on the books when they graduate. They gain access to this money precisely because bankers understand that medical school students are excellent credit risks; they tend to pay off their loans promptly and often go on to become excellent clients. The same goes for dentists, lawyers, accountants, architects, engineers and other professionals.

Dentistry is a particularly useful example. There are plenty of young dentists who graduate dental school with zero clients and the need to spend $250,000 or more on office space, equipment and hiring receptionists, hygienists and the like. They often have massive student loans too. How do they get started? They go to their friendly neighbourhood banker and show them their DDS degree. That's about it. After a few questions and a couple of routine forms, the vault is opened and another fledgling dentistry practice is underwritten. Banks know that their young dentists will pay them back in no time.

This presents another example of why the financial services industry needs to unbundle its product offerings in order to become a true profession. As long as the industry survives on commissions, bankers will quite properly guard the vault with everything they've got. Salesmen are high-risk clients. Professionals are low-risk clients. Just ask any salesman what kind of experience he had going to a bank to "get the business started." No matter how sound the business plan, no matter how necessary the product, there's a very real chance that the clients might never come. The surest way to pass the torch from old school salespeople to young, bright, forward-looking professionals is to provide the seed money that will get the young turks started and send the salespeople packing.

The only way to gain certitude about cash flow, revenue, cost, net profit and all the other metrics that bankers quite properly look for is to have an established business model based on *recurring revenues*. Salespeople don't have it; professionals do. No reputable banker will lend to someone who will only pay him back if he makes a sale (and another, and another), but virtually any reputable banker will lend based on a predictable recurring cash flow based on an established clientele that pays regular, ongoing fees for professional services. The industry calls the conversion to fees "annuitizing your book of business." It is a vital precondition of being able to have banks facilitate the buying and selling of a practice. Otherwise, FSPs will come together to do transactions based on "best guess" estimates and highly uncertain assumptions.

Converting from commissions to fees is tantamount to converting a "book of business" into a bona fide "practice." Even as FSPs begin their final conversion from sales commissions to unbundled advisory fees, banks will need to develop profiles on the attributes of FSPs who might be deemed a "good credit risk." Factors might include age, geography, product mix, specialization and maturity of the practice. Most important, the practice will already have to be fee-based, otherwise the retiring FSP will not have an asset (client list) that can be reliably passed on to another FSP.

This is a wake-up call to all FSPs who are fifty-five or older and who have not yet attained a CFP designation. They will simply have to move up or move out. Within a few years, they will either be relegated to the lower status of salespeople or pushed out of the industry altogether if they are unwilling or unable to attain the CFP designation. These FSPs will cause the most sizable shift seen in financial services in some time and they should begin to assess their place in the industry right now.

Advocis is pushing the envelope of professionalism as we speak. In order to be a member in good standing in 2011, FSPs will need to have at least one suitable designation. To put this in perspective, there are over 100,000 FSPs in Canada today, but only about 16,000 are members of Advocis and only 26,000 are members of any professional organization at all. Of the 16,000 Advocis members, approximately 7,000 have no designation (there are about 2,500 CFPs and 4,000 CLUs).

Research done by CEG Worldwide shows that some traditional assumptions about offering financial advice are off the mark. First, the notion that all FSPs will be successful if they can just "stay in for the long run" may be erroneous. Of the FSPs surveyed, fully 29.6% are still earning less than $75,000 after more than ten years in the business. In contrast, there is a group of roughly equal proportion (25.9% of FSPs) who are earning over $150,000, in spite of being in the industry for fewer than five years.

If FSPs want any kind of residual value for a business they may have spent their entire life building up, they will have little choice but to convert to a fee-based model. Either that or they can continue to earn commissions until the last possible moment, but have no one to buy their practice from them when they want to ride into the sunset. On the positive side of the ledger, mature practices are generally the easiest to convert to fees, since DSC penalties ought to be the lowest and relationships ought to be the most entrenched.

No reputable professional retires from an industry without a practicable succession plan for his valued clients. Any FSP who wants to hang around for "just one or two more RRSP seasons" and then let his clients scatter is not a real professional. In fact, that person is acting in a manner so unprofessional as to be nearly reprehensible. Consumers need to confront older commission-based FSPs now to determine what the long-term plan is for the relationship. After all, long-term planning and meaningful relationships are what these FSPs are supposed to be all about.

Call To Action

In the end, change will come. If we (we being all the stakeholders in this discussion) sit back, it will come relatively slowly. If we take action, it will come more quickly. It seems only reasonable to choose the second path since the finality of the outcome seems so inevitable. Practically speaking, we're now at the point of determining whether change will be sweeping or piece-meal, reactive or purposeful.

What's different now is that a consensus is emerging. If everyone agrees on where we need to go, the next reasonable question is "How do we get there?" *This is a call to action. If you are involved in the financial services industry in any way—as a consumer, FSP, industry executive, legislator, regulator or journalist—do not simply put this book down and go on with your life. Instead, do something to effect meaningful change in an industry that desperately needs it.*

There is a popular saying that knowledge is power. I do not agree. I believe knowledge only becomes powerful when combined with deliberate, purposeful action. The time has come for everyone involved to put their knowledge into action and come to terms with the changes that will be necessary to move the rendering of financial advice forward and into the realm of a true profession.

There are recommended books listed at the end if you want to learn more. Listed below are important industry phone numbers and websites, if you want to get more involved. The time has come to create a new profession. If we're respectful of everyone's legitimate interests, we just might find a way to get this done to maximize the advantages for all concerned.

Provincial Regulators

Alberta Securities Commission 403-297-6454 www.albertasecurities.com
Alberta Insurance Council 780-421-4148 www.abcouncil.ab.ca
British Columbia Securities Commission 604-899-6500 www.bcsc.bc.ca
Insurance Council of B.C. 604-688-0321 www.fin.gov.bc.ca/inscounc.htm
Manitoba Securities Commission 204-945-2548 www.msc.gov.mb.ca
Manitoba Consumer and Corporate Affairs 204-945-2542
    www.gov.mb.ca/finance/cca/index.html
Insurance Council of Manitoba 204-988-6800 www.icm.mb.ca
NB Office of the Administrator 506-658-3060 www.gov.nb.ca
NB Superintendent of Insurance 506-453-2541

Nfld. and Labrador Securities Division 709-729-4189 www.gov.nf.ca
Nfld. and Labrador Insurance Division 709-729-2571
Nova Scotia Securities Commission 902-424-7768 www.gov.ns.ca/nssc
Nova Scotia Superintendent of Insurance 902-424-6331
 www.gov.ns.ca/enla/fin/super.htm
Ontario Securities Commission 416-593-8314 www.osc.gov.on.ca
Financial Services Commission of Ontario 416-590-7000 www.fsco.gov.on.ca
NWT Securities Registry 867-873-0243
NWT Superintendent of Insurance 403-873-7308
Nunavut Legal Registries 867-873-0586 www.gov.nu.ca/justice.htm
Quebec Securities Division 514-940-2150 www.gov.qc.ca
Quebec Insurance Division 418-528-9140
PEI Registrar of Securities 902-368-4551 www.gov.pe.ca/securities/
PEI Superintendent of Insurance 902-368-4550
Saskatchewan Securities Commission 306-787-5645
 www.ssc.gov.sk.ca/investors.html
Saskatchewan Superintendent of Insurance 306-787-5550
Yukon Registrar of Securities 867-393-6251 www.gov.yk.ca
Yukon Superintendent of Insurance 867-667-5940

Miscellaneous Financial Services Contacts
Advocis 416-444-5251, 1-800-563-5822 www.advocis.ca
Canadian Banking Ombudsman 416-287-2877, 888-451-4519
 www.bankingombudsman.com
Canadian Institute of Financial Planners 1-866-933-0233 www.cifps.ca
Canadian Securities Institute 416-681-2215, 1-866-866-2601 www.csi.ca
Canadian Venture Exchange/Toronto Stock Exchange 416-947-4670,
 1-888-873-8392 www.tsx.com
Certified General Accountants Assoc. of Canada www.cga-canada.org
Canada Life and Health Insurance Assoc. 800-268-8099 (English), 416-777-2221,
 800-361-8070 (French), 514-845-9004, 613-230-0031 www.clhia.ca
Canada Deposit Insurance Corp. 800-461-2342 www.cdic.ca
Chartered Accountants of Canada 416-977-3222 www.cica.ca
Credit Union Institute of Canada 800-267-CUIC (2842) www.cuic.com
Financial Planners' Standards Council of Canada (FPSCC) 416-593-8587,
 1-800-305-9886 www.cfp-ca.org
Institute of Canadian Bankers 800-361-7339 www.icb.org
Insurance Brokers Assoc. of Canada 416-367-1831, 613-232-7393 www.ibac.ca
Investment Counsel of Canada 416-504-1118 www.investmentcounsel.org
Investment Dealers Assoc. of Canada 416-364-6133, 1-877-442-4322
 www.ida.ca
Investment Funds Institute of Canada 888-865-4342, 416-363-2158
 www.ific.ca
Investor Learning Centre 888-452-5566 www.investorlearning.ca

Montreal Exchange 800-361-5353 www.me.org

Mutual Fund Dealers Assoc. 416-943-5827 www.mfda.ca

Office of the Superintendent of Financial Institutions 800-385-8647,
    416-973-6662 www.osfi-bsif.gc.ca

Quebec Deposit Insurance Board 418-643-3625, 1-888-291-4443
    www.igif.gouv.qc.ca

Society of Management Accountants of Canada 905-949-4200, 1-800-263-7622
    www.cma-canada.org

Of course, it also wouldn't hurt to contact your local MPP, MLA, or MNA to request immediate action on provincial regulatory matters or your local MP on federal matters. Contacting Premiers, Ministers of Finance and the Prime Minister's Office works even better. Why not consider doing all of the above by way of a letter sent with a carbon copy? If you're an FSP, why not copy your company's management. If you're a consumer, why not copy your FSP? Furthermore, anyone can write letters to the editor when they endure experiences (both internally and externally) that are less than "professional."

Consumers might also want to write letters to compliance departments and branch managers if they feel they've been hard done by. They should be sure it's a legitimate transgression they're writing about and not just a spurious grievance brought about by anger stemming from past practice. They should hold FSPs accountable for making disclosures about how and how much they get paid, but recognize that FSPs have every right to be paid for the services and perspective they provide.

For their part, FSPs should show some real initiative and start using letters of engagement and compensation disclosure *before* being asked to do so by their clients. Much needs to be done for rhetoric to catch up with reality. Bring peer transgressions to the attention of regulators; real professionals do not tolerate mediocrity. Perhaps most importantly, FSPs can set a good example for their peers and their industry, so the confidence that is currently waning can be re-established with honour and integrity.

The lead from within the industry will be taken by Advocis. According to Advocis, a recent Ipsos-Reid poll shows that only 37% of participants rate the financial planning industry as being extremely trustworthy or trustworthy. That puts the industry behind such corporate luminaries as beer companies, the liquor industry, newspapers and banks to name a few.

Advocis has vowed to fight "predatory regulation, industry fragmentation and consumer confusion," according to CEO Steve Howard. The organization aims to shift the current transaction-based regulatory model to an advice-based model by getting appropriate designations embedded as the requirement to work as an advice giver. In short, Advocis hopes to "embed professionalism" into the industry.

Bringing about constructive reform of the financial services industry and reinventing it as a genuine profession is everyone's business. Do your part.

Stop reading investment pornography. Focus more on those elements of your financial life in which you have direct control—things like taxes, planning and risk management.

Most importantly, do not think that "the powers that be" have the matter well in hand. That's what I thought when I entered the financial services industry more than ten years ago. After trying various avenues to bring about reform, the industry has shown itself to be more interested in talking about reform than in acting. Everyone's input matters. Do your part.

NOTES

1. The most current data from IFIC shows that there is $390.8 billion invested in mutual funds in Canada as of June 30, 2003. Since only about 95% of all mutual funds are members of IFIC, the calculation is $390.8 billion x 1.05 = $410.34 billion.

2. For the latest information on Costello's case before the OSC, go to www.cbc.ca/stories/2003/05/29/costello_030529.

3. Gary P. Brinson, L. Randolph Hood and Gilbert L. Beebower, "Determinants of Portfolio Performance," *Financial Analysts Journal*, July/ August, 1986. This research was later added to in Gary P. Brinson, Brian D. Singer and Gilbert L. Beebower, "Determinants of Portfolio Perfrmance II: An Update," *Financial Analysts Journal*, May-June, 1991.

4. This research was presented by Ibbotson Associates at a joint NCE/Optima Strategy presentation for Equion in 1995 in Toronto.

5. For details of the 2001 DALBAR study, go to www.ifa.tv/DalbarStudy2001.html.

6. The research report from CEG Worldwide is entitled "The Best of Times." It can be downloaded at www.cegworldwide.com/articles/Bowen_FP_Aug02.asp.

7. The data for this chart is from Morningstar Canada.

8. Matthew R. Morey, "Mutual Fund Age and Morningstar Ratings," *Financial Analyst's Journal*, Volume 58, Number 2, March/April 2002.

9. Fama's findings are conveniently summarized in Peter J. Tanous, *Investment Gurus*, New York: Prentice Hall Press, 1997.

10. "Investors Behaving Badly" was originally a research report done by CEG Worldwide for a private client that subsequently became part of the public domain.

11. This research is included in a recent AGF Harmony marketing paper. Research sources are Frank Russell Co., Standard and Poor's, RIMES Technologies Corp (12-31-01). All performance is historical and cannot guarantee future results. Indices are unmanaged and cannot accommodate direct investment. Reinvestment of capital gains and dividends assumed. Taxes, fees and other expenses are not assumed. Rebalancing every three years results in

a 16.67% allocation of each of the six indices (S&P 500, Russell 2000, Russell 1000 Value, Russell Mid-Cap, Russell 100 Growth, MSCI EAFE).

12. The Dalbar research is quoted in the above-mentioned AGF Harmony marketing paper.

13. Amin Mawani, Moshe Milevsky and Kampol Panyagometh, "The Impact of Personal Income Taxes on Returns and Rankings of Canadian Equity mutual Funds," *Canadian Tax Journal*, 2003.

FURTHER READING

For those of you who want to delve deeper, here are some additional resources that might be of interest:

The Lay of the Land
The Money Machine by Daniel Stoffman
Make the Most of What You've Got by Sandra E. Foster
The Wealth Management Index by Ross Levin
Ontario Securities Commission, Annual Report, 2002

Are FSPs True Professionals?
True Professionalism by David H. Maister
The Trusted Advisor by David H. Maister, Charles H. Green and Robert M. Galford
Creating Equity by John J. Bowen
Effort-Less Marketing for Financial Advisors by Steve Moeller
www.cegworldwide.com is John Bowen and Russ Alan Prince's site. It is perhaps the most influential site for getting FSPs to "walk the talk" of professionalism.
www.undiscoveredmanagers.com deals with industry trends and useful research
www.davidmaister.com is the site of the guy who "wrote the books" on professionalism

Back To School
There are no library books on the subject of FSP training, since there are no formal academic courses on the subject. Anyone interested in the licencing material that FSPs currently complete might want to consider taking one or more of the courses themselves through the following sites:
www.advisorimpact.com
www.dalbarcanada.com
www.foranfinancial.com
www.strategyinstitute.com deals

Behavioural Finance
Innumeracy by John Allen Paulos
Fooled By Randomness by Nassim Nicholas Taleb
Why Smart People Make Big Money Mistakes by Gary Belsky and Thomas Gilovich
The Ten Biggest Mistakes Canadians Make by Ted Cadsby

Parts and Labour Sold Separately
To the best of my knowledge, this is the first book about unbundling available in Canada. Related reports and discussion papers include:

Investment Funds in Canada and Consumer Protection, A Review by Glorianne
  Stromberg prepared for Office of Consumer and Corporate Affairs,
  Industry Canada, October, 1998
A Review of Medium and Long-term Retail Savings, A Consultation Document by
  Ron Sandler written for the U.K. Government and published in July, 2001
The Development of More Effective Product Disclosure, a report on market
  research commissioned by the Financial Services Authority (U.K.), March,
  2003
Rethinking Point of Sale Disclosure for Segregated Funds and Mutual Funds prepared
  by the Canadians Securities Administrators and the Canadian Council of
  Insurance Regulators, February 13, 2003
www.fundlibrary.com is Canada's leading website for the aggregation of mutual
  fund data. It is especially useful in researching actively managed funds
  where there is no index to purchase. I also offer my thoughts on fee based
  advice and capital markets in my "Professional Financial Advisor" column
  in theAdvisor's Alley section.
www.globefund.com is the *Globe and Mail*'s mutual fund resource site.
  Excellent information.
www.sedar.com is a great regulatory and reporting site.

The Ramifications of Unbundling
As above.

Most FSPs Add Value, Most Managers Don't
The Prudent Investor's Guide to Beating Wall Street at its Own Game by John J.
  Bowen with Dan Goldie
Stop Buying Mutual Funds by Mark J. Heinzl
Winning the Loser's Game by Charles D. Ellis
The Power of Index Funds by Ted Cadsby
The New Investment Frontier by Howard Atkinson with Donna Green
The Wealthy Boomer by Jonathan Chevreau, Michael Ellis and Kelly Rodgers
Common Sense on Mutual Funds by John Bogle
www.iunits.com is the site run by Barclay's Global Advisors.
www.tdassetmanagement.com is the site run by TD Bank.
www.streettracks.com is the site run by State Street Global Advisors.

Extending the Frontier
Pioneering Portfolio Management by David E. Swensen
Risk Is Still a Four Letter Word by George Hartman
Asset Allocation by Roger Gibson
The Intelligent Asset Allocator by William J. Bernstein
A Random Walk Down Wall Street by Burton Malkiel
Global Investing by Roger Ibbotson and Gary Brinson
CPP Investment Board, Annual Report, 2003

www.efficientfrontier.com is a site devoted entirely to modern portfolio theory and run by William J. Bernstein.

www.financialengines.com is Professor William F. Sharpe's we site. Next time someone tells you to buy into MPT, but not to use passive management, go to this site. They are two sides of the same coin.

www.ibbotson.com is the site of the highly regarded market research firm Ibbotson Associates.

Constructive Reform for Insurance

Insurance Logic by Moshe Milevsky

The Facts of Life by Paul Grimes

www.life-line.org.life/index.html offers good insurance information as well as a useful needs analysis tool.

www.quicken.ca/eng/life/rrsp/insurance/showcontent.jsp?cid=100357 offers a good summary of disability insurance issues.

www.insurance-canada.ca is the Federal Government site on insurance.

www.ccir-ccrra.org is the Canadian Council of Insurance Regulators' site.

Using an FSP or Going it Alone

Who's Minding Your Money? By Sandra E. Foster

www.globeinvestor.com and www.globeinvestorgold.com are two other sites run by the *Globe and Mail* that can be entirely useful if you like doing research and still buy into the notion that research on security prices or mutual fund performance is actually worth something.

www.horsesmouth.com is a site that supports retail FSPs and offers a list of reasons why it makes sense to work with one.

Winning With Ethics

Winning with Integrity by Leigh Steinberg

Leading Change by John P. Kotter

Business Ethics in Canada, edited by Deborah C. Poff and Wilfrid J. Waluchow

www.investorism.com is the site run by consumer advocate Joe Killoran.

www.osc.gov.on.ca is the site run by the Ontario Securities Commission and features good background regarding regulatory principles and procedures.

INDEX

MFDA

US.

org.

ACKNOWLEDGEMENTS

When I first told my colleagues Kish Kapoor and Al Steele of my desire to write a book about financial advisors becoming true professionals in early 2002, I wasn't certain where the project would take me. Nonetheless, I was delighted when Kish said "If you can prove it, you can print it." That's all a guy with high ideals, a reforming disposition and an inquiring mind needs to hear. Of course, it meant I would now have to demonstrate the inconsistencies I found in various aspects of the financial services industry.

I also knew I would ultimately be called upon to offer up something better. Pulling together a number of positions from disparate stakeholders and sprinkling those with a few ideas and examples of my own required some thought. *The Professional Financial Advisor* grew organically rather than sequentially, since ideas and opinions on different subjects sprang forward at different points in time. Often, I would write about whatever elements of the industry were making headlines at the time. Connections were made later, often in unexpected ways. By no means was this book written in a traditional, linear and sequential manner. It was more like getting all the dots on paper first and then connecting them. There were many people who contributed and generously spent time offering input and suggesting sources to refine the ideas discussed here.

Sincere thanks go out to Bruce Cumming, Matthew Younder, Rob Park and Ron Schreider, who helped with the chapter on insurance. I also owe my thanks to Steve Kangas for his technical expertise and careful research assistance. James Wanstall, Garnet Anderson, John Graham, David Swanson, Maureen Bird and Deborah Campbell were kind enough to point me to information that I would likely not have uncovered otherwise, while Brian Mc Ostrich, Sheila Wong, John (Jazz) Szabo, Andrew Mac Leod and Lino Magagna offered valuable input on how to make the text more coherent and readable. Richard Almonte, Marijke Friesen, Catherine Jenkins and Mike O'Connor at Insomniac have been enormously helpful in sprucing up my work. In spite of the efforts of these kind people, responsibility for any lack of clarity or attention to detail rests entirely with me.

I owe a debt of gratitude to the many excellent mentors I've had in my career. John Bowen, Michael Nairne, Andy Lank, Sandra Foster and Steve Moeller have been particularly excellent role models.

Thank you Jeff Cohen for keeping me on top of things in my day job.

My parents Neil and Mary De Goey have been instrumental in giving me my roots and wings, as Jonas Salk would say. The predisposition to get involved when things need to be changed comes from them. For that and so much more, I am grateful.

Most important, my daughter Sophie is a constant source of joy and my wife Marina continues to inspire me as my partner in the journey of life.

John J. De Goey, MPA, CIM, FCSI, CFP is a Senior Financial Advisor with Assante Capital Management Ltd., member CIPF. With over a decade of experience working with retail clients, John has gained a national reputation as an authority on professional, unbundled financial advice in Canada. A ubiquitous commentator on financial matters, he has written for a number of financial sources including *Advisor's Edge*, *Canadian MoneySaver* and *MoneySense* and has a regular column at www.fundlibrary.com. He has been quoted in a wide variety of publications including *Maclean's*, the *Globe and Mail* and the *National Post* and has made numerous appearances on a variety of personal finance television programs, including CBC's *The Money Show*, ROB TV and *Canada AM*. In 2001, John won the National Multi-Media Award conferred by the Canadian Association of Financial Planners (now Advocis).

A former employee at Consumer and Corporate Affairs Canada (CCAC) and a passionate voice for consumer interests, John believes in aligning the interests of financial advisors with the interests of their clients, fee transparency, consistent professional training and unbiased financial advice. He also believes that qualified financial advice is something most consumers should willingly pay for and that the payment should be through direct, transparent fees in keeping with the approach used by more established professions. His involvement in the financial services industry is wide-ranging:

- Past President, Toronto Chapter, Canadian Association of Financial Planners
- Chair, Program Action Committee, Sheridan College Financial Planning Program
- Chair, Professionalism and Education Subcommittee, Advocis
- Member, Canadian Advisory Committee on International Financial Planning Standards
- Member, Editorial Advisory Board, *Advisor's Edge* magazine
- Member, OSC Committee on Practice Transition (Fair Dealing)
- Contributing Editor, *Canadian MoneySaver* magazine

John lives in Toronto with his wife Marina and daughter Sophie.

Contact John

John J. De Goey is not only a prolific writer, he's also a financial advisor to a select number of Canadian families and a sought-after speaker and commentator on a wide range of national and international financial matters. Through his strategic alliance with The Knowledge Bureau, John conducts high-level industry training for his peers in the financial services industry. You can contact him at:

Toll Free: 1-866-884-0895
Direct: 1-416-216-6588
Work e-mail: jdegoey@assante.com
Home e-mail: jdegoey@rogers.com
Website: www.johndegoey.com

Through his publisher: Insomniac Press
                        192 Spadina Ave., Suite 403
                        Toronto, Ontario M5T 2C2
                        Canada
                        (416) 504-6270
                        www.insomniacpress.com

Through his agent: The Knowledge Bureau
(Intellectual Property Manager) (204) 953-4769
                               1-866-953-4769
                               reception@evelynjacksproductions.com